DATE DUE

GAYLORD			PRINTED IN U.S.A.

Messianic Hopes and Mystical Visions

Studies in Comparative Religion
Frederick M. Denny, Series Editor

Messianic Hopes and Mystical Visions

THE NŪRBAKHSHĪYA BETWEEN MEDIEVAL AND MODERN ISLAM

Shahzad Bashir

University of South Carolina Press

Published in Columbia, South Carolina, by the
University of South Carolina Press

Manufactured in the United States of America

07 06 05 04 03 5 4 3 2 1
Library of Congress Cataloging-in-Publication Data

Bashir, Shahzad, 1968–
Messianic hopes and mystical visions : the Nūrbakhshīya between medieval and modern Islam / Shahzad Bashir.
p. cm.
Includes bibliographical references and index.
ISBN 1-57003-495-8 (cloth : alk. paper)
1. Nūrbakhshīyah. I. Title.

BP189.7.N87B37 2003
297.8'3—dc21 2003050713

نانی امّاں مرحومہ اور نانا جان مرحوم کی یاد میں

یادِ وصلش نورِ جـــان چون رونقِ آئینہ آب
داغِ عشقش زیبِ دل چون زینتِ دستار گل

بیدل

Contents

Illustrations

FIGURES

CHARTS

MAPS

Series Editor's Preface

The world is currently experiencing some of the most emphatic and fateful expressions of religious activism in history. The series of which this book is a part has been privileged, since its inception nearly twenty years ago, to publish studies of important contemporary developments on such diverse subjects as Sufi singers in Egypt; Coptic nuns; Buddhist monks and political violence in Sri Lanka; Islamic ethics concerning abortion, war, and euthanasia; global Christian Pentecostalism; the study (and indeed the definition) of Hinduism(s) as a modern discourse; women rabbis in the United Kingdom; personal autonomy in American religious life; Confucianism in Japan; Neo-Pagan and Wiccan spirituality in the United States; Balkan socioreligious and political identities; and challenges to pluralism in Muslim majority Malaysia. A fair number of titles have treated premodern subjects as well, but with some interest in their contemporary significance for the academic study of religion.

Shahzad Bashir's *Messianic Hopes and Mystical Visions* is the first comprehensive study of the major Muslim messianic personality from Central Asia, Sayyid Muḥammad Nūrbakhsh (d. 1464), and the Sufi mystical order that he inspired in India and the Persian Shīʿite regions of Iran and Central Asia. Although this book focuses mostly on premodern history and developments relating to a specific personality and the movement he spawned, the author has a wider intent of providing a sophisticated and absorbing theoretical analysis and interpretation of the origins, meanings, types, and dynamics of messianic movements in Islamic history, generally, prior to the 15th century, as well as in the dwindling wake of Sayyid Nūrbakhsh and his movement over nearly half a millennium to the present, when a limited revival is taking place among certain factions in Pakistan and India.

The author persuasively argues that "activist messianism should be regarded as a significant paradigm for understanding the development of Islamic religious history in general. . . . [However, in Twelver Shīʿism] a person from this tradition who proclaims himself the messiah is a grave transgressor against the right of the hidden imam [that subtradition's expected messiah], even though he intends to actualize the religion's greatest hope. . . . My effort in this book to see the world from Nūrbakhsh's eyes seeks to enhance our understanding of both the consciousness of an individual messiah and the specifically Islamic reasons for the salience of messianism as a religious perspective. The emphasis on eliminating disunity among Muslims which runs through the whole history of the Nūrbakhshīya responds to a critical dysfunction that has been a part of Islamic religious history from the very beginning. Although the united Muslim community is a ubiquitous ideal in Islamic rhetoric, it has eluded Muslims from virtually the moment of Muhammad's death."

There is much in this study of a specific messianic and mystical movement within Shīʿite Islam that sheds light on current events and concerns of Muslims worldwide, helping us to discern and understand the roots of some of their contemporary fears, frustrations, disagreements, ideals, and hopes. Among the most persistent and persuasive notions that the author authenticates in his painstaking historical and textual analyses and interpretations is that the main thrust is not politics—as important as that has been in the history of the Nūrbakhshīya—but a vision of religious commitment and unity, whether considered as orthodox, subversive, heretical, or as a paradoxical, not unprecedented Islamic combination of all three qualities.

Frederick M. Denny
Series Editor

Preface

This book tells the story of the Nūrbakhshīya, an Islamic movement born of a messianic mission first disclosed in a remote Central Asian Sufi hospice in the year 1423. Muḥammad Nūrbakhsh (d. 1464), the movement's eponymous founder, felt himself called to a reformation of Islam whose primary purposes were to eliminate Islamic sectarian boundaries and to promulgate a religious viewpoint rooted in Sufi terminology and practice. This reformist stand itself matured into a new sectarian identity under Nūrbakhsh and his successors in Iran during the late Tīmūrid and early Ṣafavid periods (fifteenth and sixteenth centuries C.E.). Although the sect lost its ideological uniqueness in Iran under the force of Ṣafavid religious policies, Nūrbakhsh himself is still remembered as a crucial link in a chain of transmission of mystical authority originating in Muḥammad and currently represented by Iranian Sufis active around the world. Moreover, a missionary of the sect was able to get a firm foothold in Kashmir, Baltistan, and Ladakh in South Asia during the sixteenth century, and the Nurbakhshıya survives in its distinctive sectarian form today in Pakistan and India.

The temporal and spatial markers mentioned in this skeletal summary of the Nūrbakhshīya allow us to situate the movement in the narrative of Islamic history. My aim in this book is not only to flesh out the details of this story through historical contextualization but to retrieve the religious worldviews maintained by Nūrbakhshīs in various times and places over the course of more than half a millennium. Following other recent historical studies, I take the view that understanding a messianic or millenarian movement comprehensively requires a careful study of the religious discourse that lies at its base.[1] Although messianism is a political phenomenon almost by definition, historical and structural analyses of genuine messianic figures or movements must regard the politics as a function of the religion, instead of the other way around.[2]

From the perspective of the history of religions, messianic movements are governed by two seemingly contradictory facts: first, by objective measure, the vast majority of such movements attain very limited (if any) success in realizing their stated goals; and second, the lack of worldly success has little immediate impact on the commitment of the movements' followers, although in the long run it may lead to a movement's extinction.[3] The lack of correlation between proof of

1. Representative examples of such recent historical studies focused on individual movements include Abbas Amanat, *Resurrection and Renewal: The Making of the Babi Movement in Iran, 1844–1850* (Ithaca, N.Y.: Cornell University Press, 1988); Yohanan Friedmann, *Prophecy Continuous: Aspects of Aḥmadī Religious Thought and Its Medieval Background* (Berkeley: University of California Press, 1989); Paul Vanderwood, *The Power of God against the Guns of Government* (Stanford, Calif.: Stanford University Press, 1998); and Jonathan Spence, *God's Chinese Son: The Taiping Heavenly Kingdom of Hong Xiuquan* (New York: W. W. Norton, 1996). For a recent general consideration of these issues, see also Abbas Amanat, "Introduction: Apocalyptic Anxieties and Millennial Hopes in the Salvation Religions of the Middle East," in *Imagining the End: Visions of Apocalypse from the Ancient Middle East to Modern America*, ed. Abbas Amanat and Magnus Bernhardsson (London: I. B. Tauris, 2002), 1–19.

2. The word *genuine* here intends simply to exclude movements that may utilize messianic rhetoric and ideology to enhance their appeal without basing themselves in an explicit messianic claim. A good example is the religious side of the movement leading up to the Iranian revolution of 1979, which relied heavily on Twelver Shīʿī messianic symbolism but was not propelled by the message of a messiah. Ayatollah Khomeini, the movement's leader, did not declare himself the mahdī but relied on messianic symbols in his pronouncements and assigned many of the functions reserved for the mahdī to jurists. For the use of messianic rhetoric during the Iranian Revolution, see Sabine Schmidtke, "Modern Modifications in the Shiʿi Doctrine of the Expectation of the Mahdī (Intiẓar al-Mahdi): The Case of Khumaini," *Orient* 28, no. 3 (1987): 389–406; Michael M. J. Fischer and Mehdi Abedi, *Debating Muslims: Cultural Dialogues in Postmodernity and Tradition* (Madison: University of Wisconsin Press, 1990), 335–82; and Annabelle Sreberny-Mohammadi and Ali Mohammadi, *Small Media, Big Revolution: Communication, Culture, and the Iranian Revolution* (Minneapolis: University of Minnesota Press, 1994).

3. The classical social scientific work to highlight this issue is Leon Festinger, Henry W. Riecken, and Stanley Schachter, *When Prophecy Fails: A Social and Psychological*

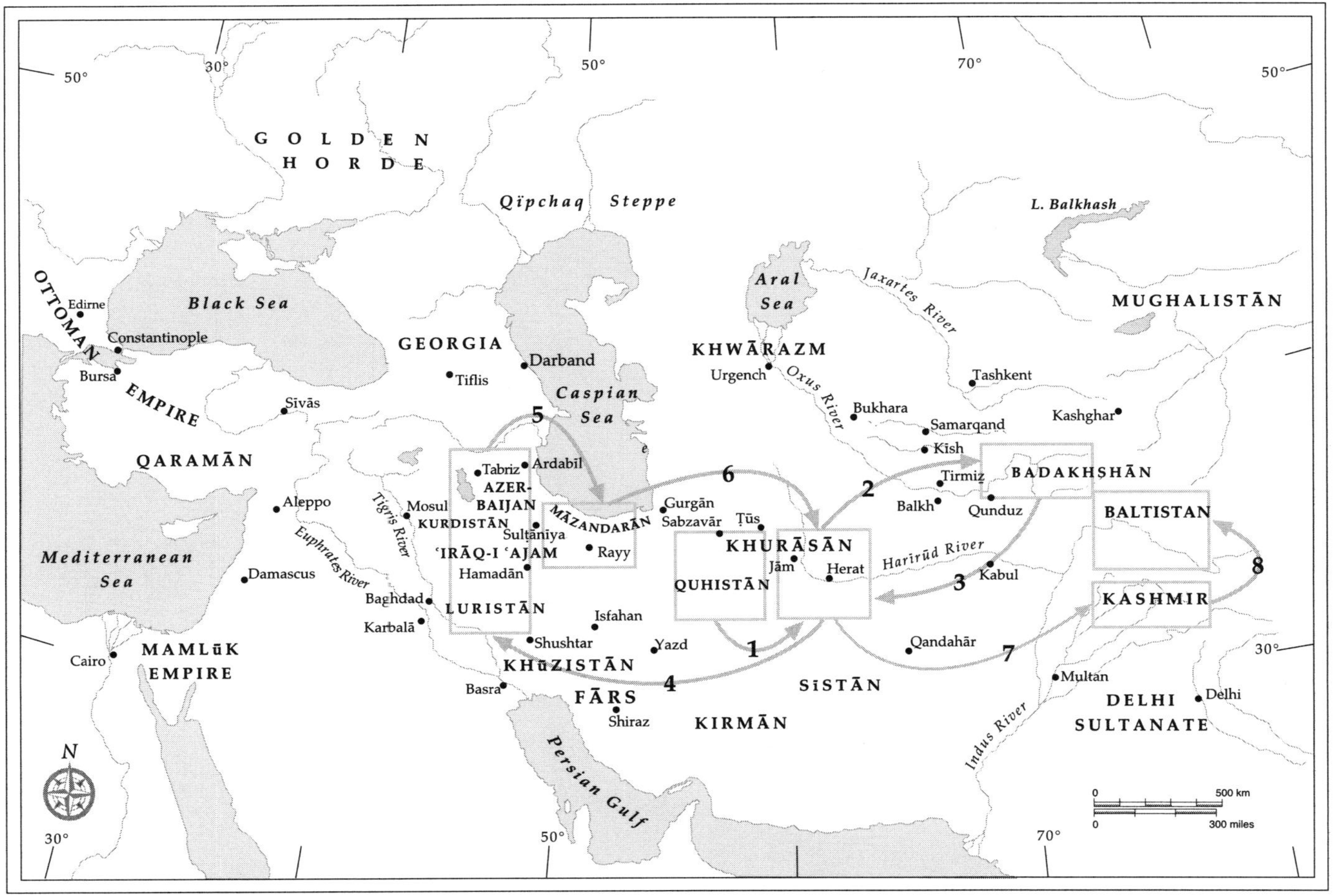

MAP 1: Zones of Nūrbakhshī Activity in the Islamic East

success and personal commitment implies that, in assessing messianic ideologies, we are concerned first and foremost with expressions of religious consciousness. Followers of a messianic figure may indeed attempt to subvert existing worldly reality, but their primary investment lies outside the purely material sphere. Messianic activity cannot, therefore, be explained away solely in socioeconomic or political terms, though the historical circumstances surrounding a messianic movement must certainly be appreciated for a proper understanding of its origins and destiny.

In a way similar to historical reductionism, the "relative deprivation" theory often used to explain messianic or millenarian movements in the social sciences provides, in my view, only a partial exposition of the phenomenon. This theory stems from the observation that unorthodox religiosity is most often observed under conditions of social disorganization and relative material deprivation. The explanation contends that human societies are based on social norms that provide security for the orderly conduct of daily life. In times when the social milieu fails to provide norms or when existing structures come under threat, new normative systems emerge to take their place. Messianic movements constitute one type of answer to such unstable and insecure sociocultural environments. Although sometimes useful in explaining the general rise of messianic activity in a given historical setting, this theory falls short of providing comprehensive analyses of particular movements by minimizing the role of their religious perspectives as significant factors.[4] Furthermore, the functionalist emphasis of the sociological

---

Study of a Modern Group that Predicted the Destruction of the World (New York: Harper & Row, 1964). For critiques of this work and refinements to the theory, see J. F. Zygmunt, "When Prophecies Fail," *American Behavioral Scientist* 16 (1972): 245–67; J. G. Melton, "Spiritualization and Reaffirmation: What Really Happens When Prophecy Fails," *American Studies* 26 (1985): 17–29; Mathew Schmalz, "When Festinger Fails: Prophecy and the Watch Tower," *Religion* 24, no. 4 (1994): 293–309; and Diana Tumminia, "How Prophecy Never Fails: Interpretive Reason in a Flying-Saucer Group," *Sociology of Religion* 59, no. 2 (1998): 157–71.

4. For cogent expositions of the relative deprivation theory, see Kenelm Burridge, *New Heaven, New Earth: A Study of Millenarian Activities* (Oxford: Basil Blackwell,

perspective often leads to downplaying the strong emotional and interpersonal aspects of a community bound together by a single overarching concern.

As with the history of other messianic movements, that of the Nūrbakhshīya encapsulates the generation, unfolding, and preservation of hope in a resplendent future stemming from faith in a person seen as the bearer of an extraordinary universal mission. In the Islamic context, the eventual root of such a faith is the idea that the divine being designates living persons to call humanity to his true will. The Muslim messiah demands to be accepted as the spokesman of God's wishes in the manner of earlier divinely appointed prophets. Nūrbakhsh clearly saw himself as a part of the elect group of humanity chosen by God to represent him, and his followers have continued to believe in this idea in more or less attenuated forms to the present day.

My rendition of Nūrbakhshī history in this book contends that activist messianism should be regarded as a significant paradigm for understanding the development of Islamic religious history in general. Movements such as the Nūrbakhshīya are important indicators of the ideological diversity that has been a part of the Islamic tradition in all periods. The criterion for being a good Muslim has been a matter of considerable debate in Islamic history, and studying the evolution of a movement that self-consciously wishes to portray itself as a rejuvenator allows us a condensed view into this aspect of the Islamic tradition. Moreover, the specifics of the Nūrbakhshī case enable us to see the interplay between a majority center of Islamic societies and the periphery of minority traditions whose attraction stems from powerful aspects of central Islamic principles.[5]

1969), and Stephen Sharot, *Messianism, Mysticism, and Magic: A Sociological Analysis of Jewish Religious Movements* (Chapel Hill: University of North Carolina Press, 1982). Whatever its general usefulness, this theory clearly does not apply to all societies showing a consistent presence of messianic activity over the course of history. For a critique based on the case of Iranian history, see Juan R. I. Cole, "Millennialism in Modern Iranian History," in *Imagining the End: Visions of Apocalypse from the Ancient Middle East to Modern America,* ed. Amanat and Bernhardsson, 282–311.

5. I prefer the terms *majority* and *minority* to *orthodox* and *heterodox* in the Islamic context since Sunnism and Shīʿism, the principle internal factions, developed their

This idea can be illustrated by imagining the overall community of Muslims to be divided into a set of concentric circles expanding outward from a center constituted by the majority Sunnism. To begin with the primary bifurcation, Shīʿism's claim of being the champion of the Prophet's house plays upon the loyalty to Muḥammad and his progeny that is readily accepted as a source of socioreligious legitimacy by the majority Sunnīs. Shīʿī dedication to the descendants of Muḥammad's daughter Fāṭima and her husband ʿAlī is, therefore, the radicalization of an idea acceptable to Muslims at large, which places Shīʿism in a circle larger than the Sunnī center.

Within Shīʿism, the imām descended from Muḥammad is at the core of religion since he inherits the Prophet's charisma and special knowledge and is expected to correct the tragedy of early Islamic history. However, the precise identity of the imām at a given moment in history has been a matter of dispute among Shīʿīs, leading to the development of various subsects. In Twelver Shīʿism, the subsect in which Muḥammad Nūrbakhsh was raised, the imām has been in occultation since the year 874 C.E. and is expected to become visible as the messiah (entitled mahdī, or the "rightly-guided") just prior to the final apocalyptic end of the universe. The Twelver Shīʿī religious system matured after the occultation of the imām and is consequently built on the imām's hidden, rather than apparent, presence. Therefore, a person from this tradition who proclaims himself the messiah is a grave transgressor against the right of the hidden imām, even though he intends to actualize the religion's greatest hope. A mahdī with a Twelver Shīʿī background stands opposed to both Twelver dogma and the majority Sunnism, though he appeals to Muslims through beliefs held in common with the whole community or its subsets. The articulation of the messianic claim in this context expands the religion in a new direction (forming a circle larger than Twelver Shīʿism itself) even though the messiah's stated aim is to restore the tradition to its pristine perfection. The unfolding of this whole process in historical time makes the messianic

---

perspectives concurrently with each other rather than one splitting off from the other. The orthodox/heterodox dichotomy is more appropriate for talking about the subsects that developed from within the various solidified sectarian traditions.

impulse in Islam a substantial factor in propelling the course of religious development. The career and thought of Muḥammad Nūrbakhsh constitute a case study for the workings of Islamic messianic claims, and the long-term fate of his movement illustrates the dynamics of Islamic sectarianism by highlighting the interaction between new religious groups and established sects.

Besides discussing theoretical issues in Islamic studies, this book intends also to address a lacuna in our understanding of Islamic intellectual life during the Mongol and Tīmūrid periods. Analyzing Nūrbakhsh's thought in detail brings to light the mechanics of the confluence of Sufism and Shīʿism characteristic of the period's religious history. Although recent work on the origins of the Ṣafavid dynasty has contributed considerably to this field, the root concern there leads eventually to issues of politics and empire. None of the movements from the period whose primary focus was religion rather than political power have until now received extensive scholarly attention. The topic is significant not only for the period itself but also for later history since major rulers such as the Ṣafavids Ismāʿīl and ʿAbbās, the Ottoman Süleyman the Magnificent, and the Mughal Akbar, considered messianic charisma a part of their imperial legitimacy. Studying the formation and eventual demise of the Nūrbakhshīya in the fifteenth and sixteenth centuries provides important clues for understanding the relationship between religion and political life during the age of the great empires starting in the sixteenth century.

Based upon this theoretical and historical prospectus, the book is divided into two parts: "A Messianic Claim in Its Historical Context" (chapters 1 through 4), and "The Nūrbakhshīya after the Messiah" (chapters 5 through 7). Chapter 1 elucidates the bases for Nūrbakhsh's messianic claim by reviewing aspects of the messianic tradition in Islam prior to the fifteenth century. My discussion emphasizes the sectarian nature of Islamic messianic doctrines and develops a comparative grid across the major sects. The greater role given to the messiah in Shīʿī subsects is explained through the fact that Shīʿīs regard early Islamic history as a tragedy in need of redress before the world ends. While the Sunnī mahdī is a vague eschatological figure who may herald either a religious renewal or the apocalypse, persons accepted as mahdīs by the major Shīʿī sects are revealers of new dispensations in which the balance between good and evil is finally set right. The overall context of the messianic doctrine gives the Shīʿī mahdī a far more powerful role than any imagined in Sunnism and, consequently, a Shīʿī mahdī such as Nūrbakhsh is seen by his following to have a tremendous divine mandate to propel the world toward the truth through his teachings and actions.

The book's treatment of Muḥammad Nūrbakhsh's life and thought is divided into chapters concentrating on history, messianic ideology, and Sufi worldview (chapters 2 through 4). Chapter 2 presents the story of Nūrbakhsh's life as a part of the general rise in messianic activity in the Islamic East during the late medieval period. Most of the chapter is devoted to the circumstances of Nūrbakhsh's life, including the announcement of the messianic claim in Central Asia, his struggle with the Tīmūrid ruler Shāhrukh (d. 1447), and his role as a Sufi teacher in various parts of Iran.

Punctuated by alternating moments of triumph and tribulation, Nūrbakhsh's life represents the typical fate of a mahdī. His articulation of the messianic claim, discussed in chapter 3, was a sustained attempt to rationalize an audacious assertion. For Nūrbakhsh, the mahdī's knowledge lifted the veils from esoteric secrets of the cosmos that had hitherto been a preserve of the spiritual elect such as prophets and great saints (*awliyāʾ*). As the mahdī, Nūrbakhsh hoped to convince all Muslims to transcend their differences and form a single community dedicated to a mystical religion. His Sufi worldview, treated in detail in chapter 4, was a unique synthesis incorporating themes particular to his Kubravī spiritual lineage, such as the appearance of colored lights during mystical experience, and Persianate versions of mystical philosophy originating in the work of Ibn al-ʿArabī (d. 1240). While Nūrbakhsh's theoretical discussions attempt a rationalized pairing of Sufism with messianism, his purely mystical works represent the Sufi intellectual and social environment of the fifteenth century.

The second part of the book divides the fate of the Nūrbakhshīya after the mahdī's death into three parts based on geography and chronology. Chapter 5 deals with attempts by Nūrbakhsh's immediate successors to rationalize his death and the circumstances under which the movement's fortune took a negative turn with the rise of the Ṣafavid dynasty in Iran. The material covered in chapter 5 illustrates the process through which the Nūrbakhshīya gradually disappeared as an independent religious viewpoint in Iran and Anatolia during the seventeenth century.

A distinctive Nūrbakhshī movement managed to survive only through transplantation in Kashmir, Baltistan, and Ladakh in the sixteenth century. Chapter 6 reviews the life of Shams ad-Dīn ʿIrāqī (d. 1526), a disciple of Nūrbakhsh's son and chief successor Qāsim Fayżbakhsh (d. 1513–14), who took the movement to South Asia. ʿIrāqī's labors eventually came to naught, however, when a new political order descended upon Kashmir and subjected the Nūrbakhshī community to severe repression. The movement never recovered. The incorporation of Kashmir into the Mughal Empire at the end of the sixteenth century eventually, over the course of the seventeenth century, facilitated the conversion of Kashmiri Nūrbakhshīs to either Twelver Shīʿism or Sunnism.

The Nūrbakhshīya was able to preserve itself into the modern period only in the relatively isolated regions of Baltistan and Ladakh, where Nūrbakhshīs are now present on both sides of the strategic line of control dividing the territory of the former princely state of Kashmir between Pakistan and India. Chapter 7 examines the situation of these Nūrbakhshīs, with a particular emphasis on their recent greater self-consciousness about their religious heritage in the face of intense proselytization by Sunnī and Twelver Shīʿī Muslims. The Nūrbakhshīs of Baltistan, in particular, have of late undertaken a significant publishing program, allowing outsiders a window into their current perspective on Nūrbakhsh's mission. Although they deny or downplay Nūrbakhsh's identity as the mahdī, one faction of the modern Nūrbakhshīya still places immense emphasis on Nūrbakhsh's message of unity of all Muslims, now proffering it as a panacea for the Sunnī-Shīʿī violence that has dominated the religiopolitical environment in Pakistan in recent years. The messianic idea proclaimed in a medieval social context thus appears as a worthwhile solution to the ills of an age of nation-states and technology.

As the first comprehensive study of the Nūrbakhshīya, this book is based on original sources pertaining to various phases in the movement's history. These include, first of all, the "internal" Nūrbakhshī tradition, composed of Nūrbakhsh's own treatises, works by his immediate and later followers, and the modern literary output of the Nūrbakhshīs of Baltistan. Nūrbakhsh's extant works, written in Arabic and Persian, represent one of the largest surviving funds of direct discourse by any late medieval mahdī.[6] Among these, his messianic confession entitled *Risālat al-hudā* is of particular significance since it not only gives a detailed explanation for the messianic claim but also includes a list containing the names and religious qualities of 212 of his followers (only one of them a woman).[7]

In addition to Nūrbakhsh's own writings, works by his disciples Shams ad-Dīn Lāhījī (d. 1506–7) and ʿAlī Kiyā (d. before 1454) provide

6. For a list of Nūrbakhsh's extant works, including details of manuscripts and published versions, see Shahzad Bashir, "Between Mysticism and Messianism: The Life and Thought of Muḥammad Nūrbakš (d. 1464)," Ph.D. diss., Yale University, 1997, 260–73. In the present book, Nūrbakhsh's works are cited according to the following scheme: *Risālat al-hudā* is referred to with parts (*RH,* I and II) and passage numbers of the edition included in my dissertation (Bashir, "Between Mysticism and Messianism," 275–304 [part I], 305–23 [part II]); works published in Jaʿfar Ṣadaqiyānlū's *Taḥqīq dar aḥvāl va āṡār-i Sayyid Muḥammad Nūrbakhsh Uvaysī Qūhistānī* (Tehran: n.p., 1972) are cited with page numbers after the notation *AA;* Nūrbakhsh's poetry, edited by Muḥammad Shafīʿ (*Oriental College Magazine* 1, no. 1 [1925], 1–28 [appendix]), is cited as *Dīvān; ar-Risāla al-iʿtiqādīya* is cited from Marijan Molé's edition in "Professions de foi de deux Kubrawīs: ʿAlī-i Hamadānī et Muḥammad Nurbaḫš," *Bulletin d'études orientales* 17 (1961–62): 133–203; and full citations are provided for works still in manuscript. An updated version of my edition of the text of Nūrbakhsh's *Risālat al-hudā* is now available in Shahzad Bashir, "The *Risālat al-hudā* of Muḥammad Nūrbakš (d. 869/1464): Critical Edition with Introduction," *RSO* 75, nos. 1–4 (2001): 87–137.

7. My edition of the *Risālat al-hudā* (hereafter, *RH*) mentioned above is based on two manuscripts in the Süleymaniye Library, Istanbul: MS. Esad Efendi 3702, fols. 85b–108a, and MS. Fatih 5367, fols. 101a–139a. Nūrbakhsh's comment on the daughter of ʿAlāʾ ad-Dīn Kiyā, the only woman included in the list, is that although she was a woman from the apparent aspect (*ẓāhir*), in her esoteric reality (*bāṭin*) she was among the men who have reached the station of the greatest of saints (*RH,* II:78). Based upon the gender ideology inherent in this statement and because virtually all the historical information available to us is limited to Nūrbakhsh's male followers, I use male pronouns for the Sufis discussed in this book.

important details about Nūrbakhshī practices and ideology. Of even greater significance than these, however, are hagiographical works by Muḥammad ʿAlī Kashmīrī (d. after 1550) and Qāẓī Nūr Allāh Shushtarī (d. 1610), both of whom identified themselves as Nūrbakhshīs but lived long after the mahdī's death. Kashmīrī's *Tuḥfat al-aḥbāb* is an extensive work devoted to Shams ad-Dīn ʿIrāqī, the Nūrbakhshī proselytizer who brought the movement to Kashmir. It is not only a major source for the Kashmiri phase of the movement but also preserves extensive information concerning the lives of Nūrbakhsh and his descendants in the Iranian setting.[8] Similarly, Shushtarī was inducted into the Nūrbakhshī order through the tradition of Nūrbakhsh's disciple Shams ad-Dīn Lāhījī, though by his time the movement had merged into normative Twelver Shīʿism in Iran. Shushtarī's account of the movement's beginnings in his expansive *Majālis al-muʾminīn* is derived from the *Tazkira-yi mazīd* of Nūrbakhsh's close companion Muḥammad Samarqandī, which is no longer extant.

Since relatively little is known about the premodern history of Baltistan, the materials covered in chapter 7 have their origins mostly in the twentieth century. Various factions among the Nūrbakhshīs of Baltistan have published works against proponents of other sects as well as against each other, and the overall controversy surrounding the community is observable in the journal *Navā-yi ṣūfiya,* published from Islamabad irregularly since 1986. These are my chief sources for presenting the modern Nūrbakhshīs, and I would like to emphasize that this chapter is not an in-depth study based on extensive fieldwork. Instead, my aim is to give a general impression of how the Nūrbakhshīs became established in Baltistan and Ladakh, how they position themselves with respect to the premodern tradition, and what particular issues modernity has brought to the fore in the movement's continuing historical evolution.

8. The *Tuḥfat al-aḥbāb* is a rare work with known copies only in Baltistan and Kashmir. I am deeply grateful to Ghulām Ḥasan Nūrbakhshī of Khaplū, Baltistan, for providing me a copy of his own photocopy of a manuscript belonging to the late Nūrbakhshī hereditary guide (*pīr*) ʿAwn ʿAlī Shāh of Kirīs. References to the *Tuḥfat al-aḥbāb* in modern studies on Kashmir suggest that the Kashmiri copies of the work do not include a substantial middle portion. The Baltistan manuscript utilized here is, therefore, the only known complete copy of the work.

In addition to the Nūrbakhshī tradition itself, a reconstruction of Nūrbakhshī history requires collation of information from a wide variety of original sources in the major languages of Islamic culture. This material can be divided into four groups of historical, hagiographic, and religiocultural works corresponding to the major contexts in which the Nūrbakhshīya has been a significant presence. The first group pertains to the life of Muḥammad Nūrbakhsh and includes sources commenting on the religious and sociopolitical environment in Iran and Central Asia in the fifteenth century. In political terms, this implies works concerned with the era of Tīmūr's successors (the Tīmūrids and the Qaraqoyunlu and Aqqoyunlu Turkoman federations) from the time of the conqueror's death in 1405 to Nūrbakhsh's death in 1464.[9]

The second set of external sources to comment on the Nūrbakhshīya consists of works on the end of the Tīmūrid era in Khurāsān under the rule of Sulṭān Ḥusayn Bāyqarā (d. 1506) and the rise of the Ṣafavid dynasty in central Iranian lands.[10] The histories, hagiographies, dictionaries of poets, and polemical works included in this category provide information about both Nūrbakhsh's life and the fate of his successors and descendants throughout Iran and Central Asia.

The two other sets of original sources relevant to the Nūrbakhshīya take us from Iran to South Asia. The first of these includes histories of Kashmir and Mughal India, reporting on the period from the late fifteenth to the end of the sixteenth century. These works, as well as

9. For a review of the major sources in this category, see Michel Mazzoui, *Origins of the Ṣafawids: Šīʿism, Ṣūfism and the Ġulāt* (Wiesbaden: F. Steiner, 1972), 15–21. Details of historical works pertaining to particular dynasties are discussed in John Woods, "The Rise of Tīmūrid Historiography," *JNES* 46, no. 2 (1987): 81–108; idem, *The Aqquyunlu* (Minneapolis: Bibliotheca Islamica, 1976), 16–37; Faruk Sümer, *Kara Koyunlular* (Ankara: Türk Tarih Kurumu Basımevi, 1967), 1:145–51; Cemal Kafadar, *Between Two Worlds* (Berkeley: University of California Press, 1995), 50–117; C. A. Storey, *Persian Literature* (London: Luzac, 1970), 1:348–66; and ʿAbbās al-ʿAzzāwī, *Taʿrīf bi l-muʾarrikhīn fī ʿahd al-Mughūl wa-t-Turkumān* (Baghdad: Shirkat at-Tijāra wa-ṭ-Ṭibāʿa, 1957).

10. For Ṣafavid historiography, which covers the later Tīmūrid period as well, see A. J. Newman, "Ṣafawids," *Encyclopaedia of Islam,* 2d ed. (hereafter, *EI*²), 8:786–87, and Sholeh Quinn, *Historical Writing during the Reign of Shah Abbas: Ideology, Imitation, and Legitimacy in Safavid Chronicles* (Salt Lake City: University of Utah Press, 2000).

some polemical treatises directed against the Nūrbakhshīs, shed light on the careers of Shams ad-Dīn ʿIrāqī and his political patrons.[11] And lastly, works on the religious situation in modern India and Pakistan provide the context for understanding the activities of the Nūrbakhshīs of Baltistan. This category is particularly rich in polemical works generated by modernizing Islamic groups connected to different sects. Starting only in the second half of the twentieth century, the Nūrbakhshīs are latecomers to this genre and have consequently tried to emulate the techniques and styles of their predecessors.

Given the controversial nature of Nūrbakhsh's messianic claim, all primary materials available for this study can be said to be "opinionated" in one way or another. Internal Nūrbakhshī works strongly affirm Nūrbakhsh's status as either the mahdī or a great Sufi teacher who may, as a minor error, have overstated his personal significance. Most external sources, on the other hand, criticize Nūrbakhshīs for their exaggerated claims in varying degrees of severity. The historical information provided by all sources is, consequently, colored by their authors' perspective on the messianic mission. In using this material in the present study, I have attempted to remain consistently cognizant of the contexts in which the sources were composed. The information provided by a source is thus evaluated based on the positive, negative, or—rarely—neutral motivations of its author. In cases of contradictory accounts, I present information from all sources along with my judgment regarding the matter. Retaining the multiplicity of the information as a part of the narrative is important since it conveys the disputed nature of the movement's legacy that is a prominent aspect of Nūrbakhshī history in general.

In addition to these various categories of primary sources, the Nūrbakhshīya as a significant fifteenth-century movement is mentioned in almost all secondary introductory works on Sufism, Shīʿism, and

11. For Kashmiri historiography relating to this period, see Mohibbul Hasan, *Kashmīr under the Sulṭāns* (Calcutta: Iran Society, 1959), 1–16; Abdul Qaiyum Rafiqi, *Ṣūfism in Kashmīr from the Fourteenth to the Sixteenth Centuries* (Varanasi: Bharatiya Publishing House, 1972), xv–xxxv; and Muḥammad Ṣiddīq Niyāzmand, "Kashmīr mēñ fārsī tārīkh-navīsī: Ibtidāʾ va irtiqāʾ," in *Sarmāya-yi ḥayāt: Taḥqīqī awr tanqīdī maqālāt kā majmūʿa* (Srinagar: Uvays Vaqqāṣ Publishing House, 1996), 94–125.

religious life during the Tīmūrid and Ṣafavid periods.[12] The most significant treatments in European languages include articles by Marijan Molé and Devin DeWeese that represent the only relatively recent critical assessments of aspects of the topic.[13] Among works in Islamic languages, Jaʿfar Ṣadaqiyānlū's introduction and notes to his editions of Nūrbakhsh's works represent a significant contribution,[14] and Muḥammad Shafīʿ's articles in Urdu, written seventy-five years ago, still constitute one of the best summaries of the movement's whole history.[15] A general summary of information is also given in Hamid Algar's recent encyclopedia article.[16] The issue of ideological bias applies to secondary works published by modern Muslim scholars as well, and some surveys have a tendency to downplay the movement's historical significance in order to uphold views currently held by Muslims in areas where intersectarian antagonism remains a significant social issue.[17]

Coming in the wake of this considerable primary and secondary literature, this book treats the Nūrbakhshīya as a religious and social

12. See for example Heinz Halm, *Shiism* (Edinburgh: Edinburgh University Press, 1991), 78; Julian Baldick, *Mystical Islam: An Introduction to Sufism* (New York: New York University Press, 1989), 109; Moojan Momen, *An Introduction to Shiʿi Islam* (New Haven: Yale University Press, 1986), 208–13; Biancamaria Scarcia Amoretti, "Religion during the Tīmūrid and Ṣafavid Periods," in *Cambridge History of Iran: The Timurid and Safavid Periods* (hereafter, *CHIr*), eds. Peter Jackson and Laurence Lockhart (Cambridge: Cambridge University Press, 1986), 6:610–97; Said Amir Arjomand, *The Shadow of God and the Hidden Imam* (Chicago: University of Chicago Press, 1984), 74–76; Amanat, *Resurrection and Renewal,* 70–83.

13. Marijan Molé, "Les Kubrawiya entre sunnisme et shiisme au huitième et neuvième siècles de l'hégire," *REI* 29 (1961): 61–142; Devin DeWeese, "Sayyid ʿAlī Hamadānī and Kubrawī Hagiographical Traditions," in *The Legacy of Medieval Persian Sufism,* ed. Leonard Lewisohn (London: Khanqahi Nimatullahi Publications, 1992); idem, "The Eclipse of the Kubraviyah in Central Asia," *Iranian Studies* 21, nos. 1–2 (1988): 59–83.

14. Ṣadaqiyānlū, *Taḥqīq dar aḥvāl va ās̱ār.*

15. Muḥammad Shafīʿ, "Firqa-yi Nūrbakhshīya," parts I, II, and III, *Oriental College Magazine* 1, no. 1 (1925): 3–15; 1, no. 2 (1925): 49–69; 5, no. 4 (1929): 1–15.

16. Hamid Algar, "Nūrbakhshiyya," *EI²*, 8:134–36. D. S. Margoliouth's article on the Nūrbakhshīya in *Encyclopaedia of Islam,* 1st ed. (7:961–62), is a summary of the report from Nūr Allāh Shushtarī's *Majālis al-muʾminīn.*

17. An example of such distortion in a major survey is S. A. A. Rizvi, *A History of Sufism in India,* 2 vols. (New Delhi: Munshiram Manoharlal, 1978),

movement propelled by the momentum of Nūrbakhsh's messianic claim. Although "autonomous" in this sense, the movement's specific historical trajectory has been fashioned by the circumstances of the various contexts it has inhabited over nearly six centuries. The story begins with Nūrbakhsh's feeling that his spiritual encounters indicated a special divine designation for him. It progresses with the faith of his companions in him as the awaited messiah, predicted in numerous traditions and ratified through the occurrences of the times, leading eventually to a community of believers who dedicate themselves to the cause. The faith is modified, but not forsaken, when the prophetic life comes to an end with Nūrbakhsh's death, and it undergoes transformations with changes of cultural venue and historical time. Like other religious groups, throughout these changes the community of Nūrbakhshī faithful has carried within itself an internal debate about the content of faith and what it asks of the believer in terms of spiritual as well as worldly action. The Nūrbakhshī texts that form the basis of this study are our primary witnesses for the ideas of individuals who have belonged to the movement over the centuries. In attempting to describe the movement from within, I hope to bring to the fore some of the vitality of messianic faith in my retelling of Nūrbakhshī lives.

My effort in this book to see the world from Nūrbakhsh's eyes seeks to enhance our understanding of both the consciousness of an individual messiah and the specifically Islamic reasons for the salience of messianism as a religious perspective. The emphasis on eliminating disunity among Muslims, which runs through the whole history of the Nūrbakhshīya, responds to a critical dysfunction that has been a part of Islamic religious history from the very beginning. Although the united Muslim community is a ubiquitous ideal in Islamic rhetoric, it has eluded Muslims from virtually the moment of Muḥammad's death. Nūrbakhsh's messianic claim was an attempt to synthesize a solution to this contradiction, and examining the formation and fate of his thought provides a window into this facet of Islamic religious history.

1:298–99. Despite citing original sources that identify Shams ad-Dīn ʿIrāqī as a Nūrbakhshī and not a Twelver Shīʿī, Rizvi states that he used the Nūrbakhshīya only as a disguise for spreading Shīʿism. Muslim intersectarian conflict in South Asia that forms the basis for such judgments is treated in chapters 6 and 7.

Acknowledgments

It is my pleasure to acknowledge here the personal and institutional support I have received leading to the completion of this book. My work on understanding the life and thought of Muḥammad Nūrbakhsh began as a dissertation at Yale University under the guidance of Gerhard Böwering. I am grateful to him for taking me on as a student and then giving generously of his time and erudition through the completion of the dissertation. Also at Yale, I would like to thank Abbas Amanat for sharing his knowledge of Iranian intellectual and social history. Without his advice and encouragement, I may not have pursued the Nūrbakhshīya as a major research topic.

The chapters of this book dealing with Kashmir and Baltistan could not have been written without the materials provided by friends in Pakistan. I am particularly indebted to Ghulām Ḥasan "Ḥasanū" Nūrbakhshī of Khaplū for generously sharing his copies of Nūrbakhshī manuscripts preserved in Baltistan. Similarly, Dr. Ghāzī Naʿīm was very kind in providing back issues of the journal *Navā-yi ṣūfīya* published from Islamabad. While my presentation of the Nūrbakhshīya may differ from the views of most contemporary Nūrbakhshīs, I hope that the movement's followers will find this book a respectful and honest treatment of their tradition.

Numerous friends and colleagues in the field of Islamic studies have helped me think about the Nūrbakhshīya and put the research into words. I am deeply grateful to Devin DeWeese for reading the manuscript with great care and for bringing the meticulous erudition so evident in his own work to bear on this project. Ahmet Karamustafa and Frederick Denny also read the manuscript, and their words of affirmation were a source of considerable gratification. Other colleagues who have aided or encouraged in various ways include Kathryn Babayan, Sima Fahid, Cornell Fleischer, Farooq Hamid, Adnan Husain, Roger Jackson, Adeeb Khalid, Vickie Langohr, Sholeh Quinn, Kishwar Rizvi, Linda Rossi, Omid Safi, Walid Saleh, Mathew Schmalz, and Sara Wolper.

The Yale Center for International and Area Studies funded my first trip to Iran and Turkey in 1994 to examine many of the manuscript sources used in this study. In fall 1998, the Council on Middle East Studies at the center hosted me as a Mellon/Sawyer postdoctoral fellow in millennialism studies. A John F. Enders fellowship from Yale Graduate School allowed me to work in libraries in the United Kingdom in 1995. A National Endowment for the Humanities fellowship from the American Research Institute in Turkey facilitated my utilizing libraries in Istanbul for this and other research projects in spring 1999. The president and dean of Carleton College very graciously provided funds during the final processes leading to the book's publication. The Foundation for Iranian Studies awarded my dissertation on Muḥammad Nūrbakhsh its annual prize in 1998 and I am grateful for that recognition. I am thankful also to libraries in Turkey, Iran, Pakistan, France, the United Kingdom, and the United States for allowing me access to their collections. Paul Mirocha turned my rough drawings into the maps and figures that appear in this book. Rachel Benedict worked very patiently to harmonize the notes and the bibliography. Barry Blose and other editors at the University of South Carolina Press were a pleasure to work with, and I thank them for so smoothly taking care of all the details of publication.

On a personal level, I am thankful to my family members in Pakistan and the United States for their love and support. My leaving Pakistan has not been easy for my parents, and I would like to especially acknowledge their part in enabling me to pursue a nontraditional vocation of my own choice. My visits to Pakistan have been all too infrequent, and I regret the loss of intimate contact with my parents, grandparents, and siblings that has been an inevitable result of my settling in the United States. The example of my granduncle Sheikh Zafar Iqbal first introduced me to the idea of a life devoted to reading and writing. My circumstances have provided a considerably easier path to such a life, but his perseverance, despite numerous adversities, will always remain an inspiration to me. I am thankful also to my parents-in-law, June and Chester Hill, for the love, respect, and encouragement they have extended to me ever since I have known them.

It is not an exaggeration to say that I owe my vocation of being an Islamicist to Jamal Elias. His knowledge and perspective first motivated me to explore the possibility of graduate study in the field, and I am gratified and honored that, over the last decade, we have become close friends. His many contributions to my work on the Nūrbakhshīya include a thorough critical reading of the original dissertation, the trip to Baltistan that resulted in the photographs of Nūrbakhshī monuments included in this book, and numerous discussions concerned with appraising the Nūrbakhshīs of Kashmir and Baltistan. I am deeply thankful to him for giving so generously of himself despite a very busy life and for his tremendous sense of humor under all circumstances.

The love and support of my wife, Nancy Hill, have been invaluable resources for me in this project and everything else in life. I am profoundly grateful to her for all her generosity of heart and the encouragement provided by her optimism in my work. The sounds and steps of the first three years of the life of our son, Zakriya, are woven throughout my memories of finishing this book. Even though he does not yet know this himself, Zakriya's presence has brought tremendous joy to all aspects of our lives. The sad news of the death of my beloved grandparents reached me during the process of finishing the manuscript. I dedicate this book to their memory, recalling, with great fondness, the beauty and tranquility of early mornings spent in their company in Bahawalpur.

Note on Transliteration

Names and terms in Arabic, Persian, and Urdu used in this book are transliterated according to the scheme given in the table below. In general, words and names are transliterated according to the language of the work in which they occur, rather than the original language (e.g., Arabic, Turkish, and Indian words in Persian are transliterated as Persian). The Arabic definite article is assimilated in words beginning with sun letters (e.g., *ash-shams*), and it is omitted from proper names (e.g., ʿIrāqī and not al-ʿIrāqī). The ending *t* in the Arabic *iḍāfa* is vocalized (e.g., *Risālat al-hudā*), and, for Persian, the ending *h* is given only as *a*. The Persian *iżāfa* is indicated as *-i* (*-yi* for words ending in vowels) in textual references, but it is omitted in personal names (e.g., ʿAlī Balkhī and not ʿAlī-yi Balkhī). In keeping with the general historical context of the narrative, Sufi technical terms are indicated in Persian. Conventional English spellings are used for words and place-names that have become part of common English usage. Premodern Turkish is transliterated according to modern Turkish orthography.

	Ar	Per	Ur
ء	ʼ		
ب	b		
پ		p	
ت	t		
ٹ			t̄
ث	th	s̱	
ج	j		
چ	ch		
ح	ḥ		
خ	kh		
د	d		
ڈ			d̄
ذ	dh	ẕ	
ر	r		
ڑ			r̄
ز	z		
ژ		zh	
س	s		
ش	sh		
ص	ṣ		
ض	ḍ	ż	
ط	ṭ		
ظ	ẓ		
ع	ʿ		

	Ar	Per	Ur
غ	gh		
ف	f		
ق	q		
ك	k		
گ		g	
ل	l		
م	m		
ن	n		
ں			ñ
و	w	v	v/w
ه	h		
ي	y		
ے			ē
ا	ā		
ى	ā		
و	ū		ū/ō
ـَ	a		
ـُ	u		
ـِ	i		
ة	a		
أو	aw		
أي	ay		

Abbreviations

Primary Sources

AA Jaʿfar Ṣadaqiyānlū, *Aḥvāl va āṡār-i Sayyid Muḥammad Nūrbakhsh*

BS Anonymous, *Bahāristān-i shāhī*

HI Amīn Aḥmad Rāzī, *Taẕkira-yi Haft iqlīm*

ḤS Ghiyāṡ ad-Dīn Khwāndamīr, *Ḥabīb as-siyar*

MA ʿAlī al-Kūrānī, *ed.*, *Muʿjam aḥādīth al-Imām al-Mahdī*

MJ ʿAbd al-Vāsiʿ Niẓāmī Bākharzī, *Maqāmāt-i Jāmī*

MM Qāżī Nūr Allāh Shushtarī, *Majālis al-muʾminīn*

NS *Nava-yi ṣūfiya*

RH Muḥammad Nūrbakhsh, *Risālat al-hudā*

RJJJ Ibn al-Karbalāʾī, *Rawżāt al-jinān va jannāt al-janān*

TA Muḥammad ʿAlī Kashmīrī, *Tuḥfat al-aḥbāb*

TB Ghulām Ḥasan Suhravardī Nūrbakhshī, *Tārīkh-i Baltistān*

ṬḤ Maʿṣūm ʿAlī Shāh Shīrāzī, *Ṭarāʾiq al-ḥaqāʾiq*

TS Sām Mīrzā Ṣafavī, *Taẕkira-yi tuḥfa-yi Sāmī*

Secondary Sources and Journals

BSOAS	*Bulletin of the School of Oriental and African Studies*
CHIr	*Cambridge History of Iran*
EI²	*Encyclopaedia of Islam, Second Edition*
EIr	*Encyclopaedia Iranica*
IJMES	*International Journal of Middle East Studies*
JA	*Journal Asiatique*
JAOS	*Journal of the American Oriental Society*
JRAS	*Journal of the Royal Asiatic Society*
JNES	*Journal of Near Eastern Studies*
MW	*Muslim World*
REI	*Revue des Études Islamiques*
RHR	*Revue de l'Histoire des Religions*
RMM	*Revue du Monde Musulman*
RSO	*Rivista degli Studi Orientali*
SI	*Studia Islamica*
SIr	*Studia Iranica*
WZKM	*Wiener Zeitschrift für die Kunde des Morganlandes*
ZDMG	*Zeitschrift der Deutschen Morgenländischen Gesellschaft*

PART ONE

A Messianic Claim in Its Historical Context

Chapter One

Messianism in Islamic Religious History

Muslim tradition relates that during the farewell pilgrimage in Mecca in the year A.H. 10 (632 C.E.), Muḥammad prepared his followers for his approaching death by indicating that he had very nearly accomplished all the objectives of his prophetic mission. Affirming the Prophet's sentiments, Qurʾanic verses revealed at the occasion stated: "Today I have perfected your religion for you, and I have completed my blessing upon you, and I have approved Islam for your religion."[1] For early Muslims, the vindication of Islam's status as the perfect religion came in the form of victories of Arab armies that swept away centuries-old empires within a few decades. As evident in the framework of classical Islamic historiography, Muslims living in the first Islamic century espoused a triumphalist view of their historical destiny. The divine messenger sent to them had completed previous scriptures, and his followers had been successful on a nearly unimaginable scale. Muḥammad's fulfillment of earlier messianic prophecies meant that faithful Muslims could now justifiably expect history to be a catalog of the success and spread of their perfect religion.

It is a conspicuous fact of Islamic history that, despite its status as a golden age in the eyes of most later Sunnī Muslims, the first century

1. Qurʾan 5:3. For the earliest accounts of Muḥammad's farewell pilgrimage, see Ibn Isḥāq, *The Life of Muḥammad,* trans. Alfred Guillaume (Oxford: Oxford University Press, 1955), 649–52, and Martin Lings, *Muḥammad: His Life Based on the Earliest Sources* (Rochester, Vt.: Inner Traditions International, 1983), 332–36.

after Muḥammad's death was a period of intense sociopolitical as well as religious turmoil in the Muslim community.[2] The question of succession to Muḥammad became a source of tension among Muslims immediately following the Prophet's death, leading eventually to the Sunnī-Shīʿī differentiation that remains salient to the present.[3] The idea of an Islamic messianic deliverer was, in its origins, a product of this disquieting age, and the degree to which it was regarded as a central doctrine depended on a given group's reading of the fortunes of early Islamic society and polity. Once raised, the question of the messiah elicited various responses from the community, ranging from complete denial of the possibility to a general expectation of a renewer who would bring back the certainty of Muḥammad's days. Some also ascribed the role to Jesus in his Second Coming, while others believed in the return of a deceased Muslim protagonist. With the maturation of Islamic religious doctrines over subsequent centuries, these various perspectives on the messiah were absorbed into dogmas of the sects that evolved out of early Islamic groups. As the end result of this process, Islamic messianism became a fundamentally sectarian doctrine, espoused or shunned in keeping with the overall ideological position of various sects within the Islamic spectrum.

This chapter provides the general context of Muḥammad Nūrbakhsh's messianic claim by laying out the overall map of Islamic messianic doctrines. My treatment of the issue is loosely chronological, following the development of the idea over Islamic history with markers for the

2. The significance of this theme for early Muslims is evident from the fact that, in addition to suppression of apostasy (*ridda*) and conquests (*futūḥ*), internal dissension (*fitna*) is one of the most prevalent themes in early Islamic historiography. For surveys of sources on this issue, see Tarif Khalidi, *Arabic Historical Thought in the Classical Period* (Cambridge: Cambridge University Press, 1994), 13–16; and Albrecht Noth, *The Early Arabic Historical Tradition: A Source Critical Study,* trans. Michael Bonner, 2d ed. in collaboration with Lawrence I. Conrad (Princeton, N.J.: Darwin Press, 1994), 26–35.

3. For the most comprehensive treatment of the dispute over succession to Muḥammad, see Wilferd Madelung, *The Succession to Muḥammad* (Cambridge: Cambridge University Press, 1996).

points at which the major sects adopted their standard positions. The discussion begins with the early caliphal and Umayyad period (632–750), during which the idea initially became a part of Islamic religious imaginations. This is followed by a review of the use of messianic rhetoric during the ʿAbbāsid Revolution in 750 and the evolution of the concept in early Shīʿī communities until the death of the sixth imām, Jaʿfar aṣ-Ṣādiq (d. 765). All themes later to become parts of the tradition had been proposed by the end of this period and were utilized in various permutations by Ismāʿīlī Shīʿīs in the course of their history until the twelfth century. Twelver Shīʿism was chronologically the last sect to adopt the idea fully, though its heavy eventual investment in identifying the Twelfth Imām as the messiah in occultation until the end times makes it the most messianic of all major Islamic sects. This sect is of particular concern to us also because Nūrbakhsh was born into a Twelver family and his messianic ideology was assembled in response to Twelver ideas about the messiah.

Messianic Ideas in the Early Caliphal and Umayyad Periods, 632–750

As already pointed out, the expectation of a religious savior entered the fund of Islamic thought during the clarification of religious ideas in the early Islamic period.[4] The Qurʾan does not contain the term *mahdī* or

4. For previous general overviews of Islamic messianism, see Wilferd Madelung, "al-Mahdī," *EI*^{2}, 5:1230–38; I. K. Poonawala, "Apocalyptic in Muslim Iran," *Encyclopaedia Iranica* (hereafter, *EIr*), 2:157–60; Said Amir Arjomand, "Messianism, Millennialism and Revolution in Early Islamic History," in *Imagining the End: Visions of Apocalypse from the Ancient Middle East to Modern America,* ed. Abbas Amanat and Magnus Bernhardsson (London: I. B. Tauris, 2002), 106–25; Abdulaziz A. Sachedina, *Islamic Messianism: The Idea of Mahdī in Twelver Shīʿism* (Albany: State University of New York Press, 1982), 1–38; Amanat, *Resurrection and Renewal,* 1–18; E. Sarkisyanz, *Russland und der Messianismus des Orients* (Tübingen: J. C. B. Mohr, 1955), 223–51; D. S. Margoliouth, "On Mahdis and Mahdism," *Proceedings of the British Academy* 7 (1915), 213–33; Snouk Hurgronje, "Der Mahdi," in *Versprede Geschriften* (Bonn: K. Schroeder, 1923), 1:145–81; James Darmsteter, *Le Mahdi depuis les origines de l'Islam jusqu'à nos jour* (Paris: Ernest Leroux, 1885); G. van Vloten, *Recherches sur la domination des Arabes, le Chiitisme et les croyances messianiques sous le Khilafat des Omayades* (Amsterdam: J. Müller, 1894). A useful collection of

the prediction of a Muslim savior to rise in the future, though derivatives of the root *h-d-y,* signifying divine guidance in human affairs, are quite common in the scripture.[5] This conforms well with the overall perspective of the Qurʾan, where moral exhortation occupies a far more significant place than historical specificity. As Tarif Khalidi states in his recent overview of the development of the early Islamic historiographic tradition, the scripture contains "no glad tidings of a new man about to be born nor yet the awful tidings of a catastrophe about to engulf the earth but an ever-presentness which infuses past and future at once, obliterating historical signposts. True, the early Meccan verses of the Qurʾan are densely apocalyptic, but even these verses are less pronouncements about what is to come soon and more like moral images of the end of the world. If history is the science of particulars, there are hardly any particulars in the Qurʾan."[6]

While the Qurʾan itself stands apart from or above history in this way, its bearers in the early Islamic period soon saw the text to contain messages about the sociopolitical chaos that surrounded their lives despite Islamic successes. The intellectual milieu of the period combined this personalized version of the Qurʾan's categorical morality (usually expressed in apocalyptic terms) with preexisting Judeo-Christian and

---

articles on mahdīs and messianic doctrines in various social contexts can be found in Mercedes García-Arenal, ed., *Mahdisme et millénarisme en Islam, Revue des Mondes musulmanes et de la Méditerranée,* 91–94 (Aix-en-Provence: Éditions Édisud, 2000). An extensive descriptive bibliography of works on mahdism published primarily in the Islamic world is contained in ʿAlī Akbar Mahdīpūr, *Kitābnāma-yi Ḥażrat-i Mahdī,* 2 vols. (Qum: ʿAlī Akbar Mahdīpūr, 1996). The most comprehensive index of Islamic traditions about the mahdī is ʿAlī Kūrānī, ed., *Muʿjam aḥādīth al-Imām al-Mahdī,* 4 vols. (Qum: Muʾassasat al-Maʿārif al-Islāmīya, 1990).

5. Muḥammad Fuʾād ʿAbd al-Bāqī, *Muʿjam al-mufahras li-alfāẓ al-Qurʾān al-karīm* (Beirut: Dār al-Ḥadīth, 1988), 731–36. For a subject index of *guidance* (*hidāya*), see also Muḥammad Fāris Barakāt, *Jāmiʿ li-mawāḍīʿ āyāt al-Qurʾān al-karīm* (Beirut: Dār Qutayba, 1985), 184–86. Dictionaries of classical Arabic define the term *mahdī* in both its literal meaning ("one whom God has guided to the truth") and as the messianic figure to appear in the end-times (Ibn Manẓūr, *Lisān al-ʿarab,* 6 vols. [Cairo: Dār al-maʿārif, 1981], 6:4639; Muḥammad Murtaḍā Zabīdī, *Tāj al-ʿarūs,* 10 vols. [Benghazi: Dār al-Lībīyā li-n-Nashr wa-t-Tawzīʿ, 1966], 10:406–9).

6. Khalidi, *Arabic Historical Thought,* 13.

Zoroastrian messianic and apocalyptic ideas to give birth to a specifically Islamic messianic tradition. The concept existed as a part of the general cultural mood in the first decades after Muḥammad's death, but it became transformed into a concrete tradition with specific markers and expectations following the careers of early religiopolitical figures.

A survey of early Islamic history shows that the appellation *mahdī,* later to become the standard term for the Muslim messianic deliverer, and the belief in a religious redeemer originated separately during the caliphal and Umayyad periods. The title mahdī signifying a "rightly-guided" person in a nontechnical sense is attested for religiopolitical leaders such as Muḥammad,[7] ʿAlī[8] and rulers from the Umayyad house.[9] The bearer of the title in this instance was one who received *hudā* (guidance) from God and conveyed it to the rest of the world through his actions. During this period, *khilāfa* (vicegerency, or caliphate) and *hudā* were more or less synonymous terms; so a caliph was automatically also a mahdī, in the literal sense.[10] Although the way the title was used for Umayyad caliphs did suggest a kind of charismatic quality,[11] this reflected the theory of rulership itself and not the bearer's messianic function.

The nontechnical application of the title mahdī was reserved either for actual rulers or those who led agitations to gain political power. Mahdīhood in this sense was a device legitimating a ruler whose subject population recognized divine guidance (*hudā*) as a substantial source for

7. Ḥassān b. Thābit, *Dīwān,* ed. Walīd ʿArafāt, 2 vols. (London: Luzac, 1971), 1:269; Anthony A. Bevan, ed., *The Naḳāʾiḍ of Jarīr and al-Farazdaḳ,* 3 vols. (Leiden: E. J. Brill, 1905–7), 1:349.

8. Ibn al-Athīr, *Usd al-ghāba fī maʿrifat aṣ-ṣaḥāba,* 4 vols. (Tehran: al-Maktaba al-Islāmīya, 1958), 4:31.

9. Bevan, *Naḳāʾiḍ,* 1:374; Jarīr b. ʿAṭīya, *Dīwān Jarīr bi-sharḥ Muḥammad b. Ḥabīb,* ed. Nuʿmān Muḥammad Amīn Ṭāhā, 2 vols. (Cairo: Dār al-Maʿārif, 1969), 1: 225, 288; 2:717.

10. Patricia Crone and Martin Hinds, *God's Caliph: Religious Authority in the First Centuries of Islam* (Cambridge: Cambridge University Press, 1986), 34–42.

11. Ibid., 37. To illustrate this point, Crone and Hinds cite the following verse by Farazdaq in reference to Sulaymān b. ʿAbd al-Malik (d. 717): "He answered our prayer and saved us from evil through the caliphate of the *mahdī*" (Bevan, *Naḳāʾiḍ,* 1:374).

political legitimacy. This type of mahdī was quite different from the redeemer figure whose bid to gain power was in itself a function of his exceptional religious status.

Among Islamic sects surviving past the Umayyad period, nontechnical use of the title *mahdī* for a leader became the standard in Zaydī Shīʿism. The Zaydīya began with Zayd b. ʿAlī, a grandson of Ḥusayn, who was killed after leading an unsuccessful revolt against the Umayyads in 740. In contradistinction with other branches of Shīʿism, the Zaydīs believe that, after Ḥusayn, any member of the ʿAlid house willing to struggle for the community's rights can be the imām. This view of the imāmate essentially equates the imām/mahdī with any activist political leader among the ʿAlids.[12] Consequently, the Zaydīya does not have the idea of a single redeemer to rise in the future, and the honorific title of mahdī has been applied to a number of Yemeni Zaydī imāms over the course of history.[13]

The historical personality whose career established the general parameters for the Islamic redeemer belongs also to the first Islamic century. Although not addressed as mahdī, ʿAbdallāh b. az-Zubayr (d. 692), who led a significant revolt against the Umayyads between 681 and 692, set the pattern for what was to be expected of future messiahs.[14] As Wilferd Madelung has shown, a ḥadīth report that became the defining criterion for the Muslim redeemer can be traced back to Ibn az-Zubayr based upon both its contents and its chain of transmitters. In the text of this report, Muḥammad predicts:

12. Halm, *Shiism,* 206–7; B. Abrahamov, "Al-Ḳāsim ibn Ibrāhīm's Theory of the Imamate," *Arabica* 34 (1987): 80–105.

13. Cf. articles on various imāms by R. Strothmann, G. R. Smith, and J. R. Blackburn in *EI*², 5:1240–42. A subsect found in western Yemen called the Ḥusaynīs is an exception from the general Zayḍī attitude since it expected the return of the imām al-Ḥusayn al-Mahdī li-Dīn Allāh (cf. W. Madelung, *Der Imam al-Qāsim b. Ibrāhīm und die Glaubenslehre der Zaiditen* [Berlin: Walter de Gruyter, 1965], 198–201).

14. Wilferd Madelung, "ʿAbdallāh b. al-Zubayr and the Mahdī," *JNES* 11 (1981): 291–305. For a discussion of the significance of this ḥadīth and other issues concerned with early messianic tradition, see also Sandra Campbell, "Millennial Messiah or Religious Restorer: Reflections on the Early Islamic Understanding of the Term *Mahdī*," *Jusūr* 11 (1995): 1–11.

> There will arise a difference after the death of a caliph, and a man of the people of Medina will go forth fleeing to Mecca. Then some of the people of Mecca will come to him and will make him rise in revolt against his will. They will pledge allegiance to him between the Rukn and the Maqām. An expedition will be sent against him from Syria but will be swallowed up in the desert between Mecca and Medina. When the people see this, the righteous men of Syria and the troops of the people of Iraq will come to him and pledge allegiance to him. Thereafter a man of the Quraysh will arise whose maternal uncles are of Kalb. He will send an expedition against them, but they will defeat them. This will be the expedition of Kalb, and the disappointment will be for those who did not witness the spoils of the Kalb. He will then divide the wealth and act among them according to the Sunna of their Prophet. Islam will settle down firmly on the ground. He will stay seven years and then die, and the Muslims will pray over him.[15]

The first part of this report parallels exactly the career of Ibn az-Zubayr, and the text changes from history to prediction after "the righteous men from Syria." The original context of this ḥadīth was forgotten in later times when it was included, quite prominently and unproblematically, in chapters on the mahdī in various collections. The career and ambition of an individual were thus transformed into a paradigm for the future by being put into the mouth of the Prophet.

To develop a typology of the messianic figure in Islam, this report can be divided into five parts with corresponding elements in the redeemer paradigm:

(i) The need for a savior arises in an unstable political environment such as after the death of a caliph.

15. Madelung, "ʿAbdallāh b. al-Zubayr and the Mahdī," 291; Kūrānī, *Muʿjam aḥādīth,* vol. 1, no. 303 (hereafter, *MA*). Through analysis of the chains of transmitters (*isnād*) of various versions of this ḥadīth, Madelung shows that it can be traced back to ʿAbdallāh b. al-Ḥarīth b. Nawfal (d. 83/702 or 84/703), a Hāshimite aristocrat related through his mother to the house of Umayya, who played a brief but important role in the history of Basra during the second civil war (*fitna*). Much of Madelung's article is devoted to establishing the career of this man.

(ii) In the ensuing vacuum of power, a man becomes noticeable as a potential leader and is given allegiance by a number of his contemporaries.
(iii) He reluctantly accepts the leadership role thrust upon him and sways all the righteous people to his cause.
(iv) His career reaches its apogee in a battle with an arch enemy, representative of evil forces, who is defeated and killed.[16]
(v) Finally, he fulfills his mission by redistributing wealth and strengthening the influence of religion on society. He dies after a short reign.

This analysis of the report lays out the skeleton of the awaited mahdī's career, which was fleshed out further in later Islamic history.

The redeemer figure predicated on Ibn az-Zubayr's career became synonymous with the title mahdī through proclamations surrounding a Shīʿī contender. The first person to be called mahdī in a messianic sense was ʿAlī's son Muḥammad b. al-Ḥanafīya (d. 81/700–701).[17] More than Ibn al-Ḥanafīya himself, the figure of interest in the episode bringing him to prominence was Mukhtār b. Abī ʿUbayd ath-Thaqafī (d. 67/687),[18] who called himself the agent (*wazīr* and *amīn*) of Ibn al-Ḥanafīya and carried out propaganda under his name in Kūfa. Resident in Mecca at the time, Ibn al-Ḥanafīya was less than enthusiastic about this activity on his behalf. Nonetheless, Mukhtār proclaimed him the awaited mahdī, conducting "his propaganda in a type of rhyming prose which is grandiloquent and obscure at the same time and is, presumably, intended to convey a claim to some sort of inspiration."[19] Mukhtār's demeanor thus began the aura of mystery that became standard for the

16. For the mahdī's traditional enemies, see the discussion of Nūrbakhsh's mahdism in chapter 3.

17. For a brief biography, see F. Buhl, "Muḥammad Ibn al-Ḥanafiyya," *EI*², 7:402–3.

18. G. R. Hawting, "Mukhtār b. Abī ʿUbayd al-Thaqafī," *EI*², 7:521. For extended discussions of the factions that backed Mukhtār, see G. R. Hawting, *The First Dynasty of Islam* (London: Croom Helm, 1986), 51–53; Jan-Olaf Blichfeldt, *Early Mahdism: Politics and Religion in the Formative Period of Islam* (Leiden: E. J. Brill, 1985), 105–17; and W. M. Watt, "Shiʿism under the Umayyads," *JRAS* (1960): 158–72.

19. Hawting, "Mukhtār," *EI*², 7:522.

discussion of the mahdī in later times. The mahdī now became the repository of special knowledge, and his expected political function became tied permanently to a religious inspiration.

Ibn al-Ḥanafīya's followers were also the first significant group to adopt the view that the imām had gone into occultation (*ghayba*) and was expected to stage a return (*rajʿa*). The first movement to suggest this idea was the Sabaʾīya, followers of ʿAbdallāh b. Sabaʾ, an ʿAlid sympathizer who was banished by ʿAlī to Madāʾin for his heretical beliefs.[20] After the assassination of ʿAlī, Ibn Sabaʾ believed that ʿAlī had not died at all, was alive in the clouds, and would return one day to fill the world with justice.

A segment of the Sabaʾīya surviving in Kūfa at the time of Mukhtār's agitation joined his movement.[21] After Mukhtār was killed by Ibn az-Zubayr's forces (67/686–87) and Ibn al-Ḥanafīya publicly acknowledged ʿAbd al-Malik b. Marwān as the caliph (73/692), Mukhtār's Kūfan followers (the Mukhtārīya) developed the "hope for a state that would be established in the future before the Day of Judgement in a general resurrection."[22] Ibn al-Ḥanafīya died in 81/700, but this group (now called the Kaysānīya, after Mukhtār's lieutenant Abū ʿAmr Kaysān) combined its postponement of worldly ambitions with Ibn Sabaʾ's ideas to claim that Ibn al-Ḥanafīya was still alive. They believed that he was in concealment (*ghayba*) in the mountains of Raḍwa, near

20. M. G. S. Hodgson, "ʿAbdallāh b. Sabaʾ," *EI²*, 1:51; Heinz Halm, *Die Islamische Gnosis: Die Extreme Schia und die ʿAlawiten* (Zurich: Artemis Verlag, 1982), 33–42; Ḥasan b. Mūsā Nawbakhtī and Saʿd b. ʿAbdallāh al-Qummī (combined ed.), *Kitāb firaq ash-shīʿa,* ed. ʿAbd al-Munʿim (Cairo: Dār ar-Rashād, 1992), 32–33; Israel Friedlaender, "ʿAbdallāh b. Sabā, der Begründer der Shīʿa und sein jüdischer Ursprung," *Zeitschrift für Assyrologie* 23 (1909): 296–327, and 24 (1910): 1–46. Secondary sources other than Friedlaender doubt that ʿAbdallāh b. Sabāʾ was in fact of Jewish origin.

21. Wadād Qāḍī, "The Development of the Term Ghulāt in Muslim Literature with Special Reference to the Kaysāniyya," in *Akten des VII Kongresses für Arabistik und Islamwissenschaft, Göttingen, 15 bis 22 August 1974,* ed. Albert Dietrich (Göttingen: Vandenhoeck & Rupricht, 1976), 300; Halm, *Islamische Gnosis,* 43–83. For a detailed discussion of the intellectual development of the Kaysānīya, see Wadād Qāḍī, *Kaysānīya fī t-tārīkh wa-l-adab* (Beirut: Dār ath-Thaqāfa, 1974).

22. Qāḍī, "Development of the Term Ghulāt," 301.

Mecca, and would soon return to assume political power. This formulation brought forth "for the first time in the history of Shīʿī thought, the idea of the living mahdī who will come from concealment before the end of time to fill the earth with justice, as it had been filled formerly with injustice and despotism."[23] The idea of occultation acquired much greater significance in later times when a majority of Shīʿīs accepted the occultation of the Twelfth Imām in a specific line of ʿAlid descent.

The general outlook of the Kaysānīya and its related groups in Kūfa became the basis for Shīʿī groups collectively known as the Ghulāt (the exaggerators). These sects eventually discontinued their belief in Ibn al-Ḥanafīya's mahdīhood, but they retained some idea of an inspired religious leader (called qāʾim, or riser) to arrive in the future. Together with Muḥammad, ʿAlī, Ḥasan, Ḥusayn, and Muḥammad b. al-Ḥanafīya, this person was considered to possess a special substance for his soul. His manifestation was to begin a new dispensation of righteousness on earth, but this expectation was not the central focus for these sects.[24]

Besides the messianic inclinations of various factions, early Islamic history is also notable for the production of eschatological literature often featuring a redeemer. The traditions forming this literature (generally termed *malāḥim*) contained auguries about the circumstances of the end-times and were a continuation of pre-Islamic Semitic divinatory practices. In Islamic usage, the descriptions melded together aspects of ḥadīth literature, early Islamic history, and beliefs of past peoples, to generate an extensive tradition in which the eschatological savior often had a prominent role.[25] Works in the genre lost their focus

23. Ibid.

24. This tradition is visible in references to the savior figure in the earliest Ghulāt texts. Cf. V. Ivanow, "Umm'l-kitāb," *Der Islam* 23 (1936): 16, 21, 45–46; al-Mufaḍḍal b. ʿUmar al-Juʿfī, *Kitāb al-haft wa-l-aẓilla,* ed. Aref Tamer and Ign.-A Khalifé (Beirut: Dār al-Mashriq, 1970), 161; Halm, *Islamische Gnosis,* 161.

25. For reviews of this literature, see T. Fahd, *La divination arabe: Études religieuses, sociologiques et folkloriques sur le milieu natif de l'Islam,* 2d ed. (Paris: Sindbad, 1987), 224–28; idem, "Malḥama," *EI²*, 6:247; Suliman Bashear, "Muslim Apocalypses and the Hour: A Case Study in Traditional Interpretation," *Israel Oriental Studies* 13 (1993): 75–99; David Cook, "Moral Apocalyptic in Islam," *SI* 86, no. 2

on eschatological matters in later centuries and became limited to historical prognostications about the rise and fall of dynasties.

To summarize the discussion so far, the mahdī became designated as the Islamic savior through the confluence of a number of different traditions and events in early Islamic history. First, the title mahdī designated religiopolitical figures without a messianic function until the end of the Umayyad period; second, the expected career of a Muslim messianic savior was standardized when the circumstances of ʿAbdallāh b. az-Zubayr's attempt at the caliphate became a ḥadīth report; third, the early Kūfan Ghulāt combined the title mahdī and the expected savior by designating ʿAlī's son Muḥammad b. al-Ḥanafīya as the mahdī; and last, a slightly later group of Ghulāt believed that the mahdī had already existed on the earth, was now in hiding, and would return in the future to lead his partisans to worldly dominion. These four components of the pre-ʿAbbāsid view of the savior were then combined in different permutations to form the perspectives of Islamic sects in later history.

Shīʿī Imāms until Jaʿfar aṣ-Ṣādiq and the ʿAbbāsid Revolution

After Ibn al-Ḥanafīya, the title mahdī in its messianic sense was applied to other ʿAlids such as Ibn al-Ḥanafīya's son Abū Hāshim (d. 98/716),[26] ʿAbdallāh b. Muʿāwīya (d. ca. 130/748), Muḥammad b. ʿAbdallāh an-Nafs az-Zakīya (d. 145/762), and Jaʿfar aṣ-Ṣādiq (d. 148/765).[27] As Shīʿism defined itself more as a religious rather than political movement during the imāmate of Jaʿfar aṣ-Ṣādiq, the concept of the redeemer came to be discussed in theoretical terms.[28] The name of choice for the figure in this period was, however, al-Qāʾim (the riser), rather than mahdı.

(1997): 37–69; Maḥmūd Dihsurkhī, *Muʿjam al-malāḥim wa-l-fitan,* 4 vols. (Qum: Muḥammad al-Dihsurkhī, 1999).

26. Abū Hāshim is a significant historical figure since the ʿAbbāsids later claimed that they had acquired ʿAlid support for their rule through him (cf. Marshall Hodgson, *The Venture of Islam,* 3 vols. [Chicago: University of Chicago Press, 1974], 1:273).

27. Madelung, "al-Mahdī," *EI*², 5:1235.

28. This crucial period in Shīʿī history is analyzed in Marshall Hodgson, "How Did the Early Shiʿa Become Sectarian?" *JAOS* 75 (1955): 1–13.

Reports about the qāʾim generated during the incubatory period of Shīʿism vary considerably among themselves, though they are agreed that he will rise (sometimes explicitly militarily) to avenge the injustice done to the ʿAlids.[29] The title qāʾim was applied to all imāms in a general sense due to the special hereditary knowledge imputed to them.[30] However, as indicated in a report from the fifth imām, Muḥammad al-Bāqir (d. 113/731–32), the last qāʾim was set apart as the messianic deliverer who would reverse the fortunes of the house of the Prophet: "When al-Qāʾim from the family of the Prophet will rise he will distribute equally among the people and will establish justice among his subjects. Thus, those who obey him will obey God and those who defy him will defy God; but he will be called al-Mahdī, the one who will guide, since he will guide to the secret matters (*amr al-khafī*) and will bring out the Torah and other books of God from a cave in Antioch and will rule the people of the Torah according to the Torah, and the people of the Gospel according to the Gospel, and the people of the Qurʾan according to the Qurʾan."[31]

The term *mahdī* in this instance was an additional attribute appended to the person of the qāʾim, and other traditions in Shīʿī sources from the period reflect the same attitude.[32] Although his role in world history was predicted quite clearly, the exact identity of the qāʾim was privileged information that could not be divulged for the sake of his safety. Signs enabling one to identify the qāʾim were, in fact, one of the earliest matters of belief to come under the Shīʿī duty of pious dissimulation (*taqīya*).[33]

Messianic doctrine among mainstream Shīʿīs became more complicated when the old Kaysānīya idea of the savior's occultation was incorporated into the speculation. Groups now began to regard dead imāms as qāʾims who would rise again in the future. The most significant

29. Wilferd Madelung, "Ḳāʾim Āl Muḥammad," *EI*[2], 4:456–57.

30. Sachedina, *Islamic Messianism,* 15.

31. Muḥammad b. Ibrāhīm b. Jaʿfar an-Nuʿmānī, *Kitāb al-ghayba* (Tabriz: Maktabat aṣ-Ṣābirī, 1383/1963), 124; trans. Sachedina, *Islamic Messianism,* 61.

32. Shīʿī expectation of the deliverer during this period is analyzed in detail in Mohammad Ali Amir-Moezzi, *The Divine Guide in Early Shiʿism,* trans. David Streight (Albany: State University of New York Press, 1994), 99–123.

33. Ibid., 103.

example of such a group were the Wāqifa (the 'stoppers'), who considered the seventh imām Mūsā al-Kāẓim (d. 183/799) the qāʾim after his death.[34] The exact nature of his removal from, and return to, the world were disputed issues since "most of them believed that he had not died and was alive hiding, [but] others held that he had died and would rise from death."[35] Ambiguity about the qāʾim's identity until the death of Jaʿfar aṣ-Ṣādiq was the principal breeding ground for the development of Shīʿī subsects.

The concept of a savior and the term *mahdī* were used also during the ʿAbbāsid Revolution. The founder of the dynasty, Abū l-ʿAbbās (d. 754), gave himself the title as-Saffāḥ (spiller of blood), which had originally been used for the messianic deliverer in Kūfa.[36] Furthermore, ḥadīth reports generated during the revolution later became a part of the corpus foretelling the mahdī's career.[37] When ʿAbbāsid messianic pretensions were challenged by the ʿAlids, the caliph Abū Jaʿfar al-Manṣūr (d. 775) gave his heir apparent Muḥammad the title al-Mahdī (d. 785) to revive the tradition.[38] A few decades later, ʿAbdallāh al-Maʾmūn (d. 833) attempted to have himself recognized as the *imām al-hudā,* or "rightly guiding leader," whose judgments in religious matters were supposed to have the same legitimacy among his Muslim subjects as his political power. It is precisely this contention that set in motion the famous Inquisition (*miḥna*) that caused the ʿAbbāsid persecution of religious scholars such as Aḥmad Ibn Ḥanbal (d. 855).[39]

34. The term *wāqifa* was used in both general and particular senses. For the former, a *wāqifīya* movement announced itself following the death of every imām after al-Bāqir. In the particular sense, however, Wāqifa refers to the followers of Mūsā al-Kāẓim, who were especially active in discussing this view with reference to their own imām. For a summary description of the various *wāqifī* sects, see Momen, *Introduction to Shiʿi Islam,* 45–60.

35. Madelung, "al-Mahdī," *EI*^{2}, 5:1236.

36. H. F. Amedroz, "On the Meaning of the Laqab 'al-Saffāḥ' as applied to the First ʿAbbāsid Caliph," *JRAS* (1907): 660–63.

37. See *MA,* vol. 1, nos. 250–57.

38. Jere L. Bacharach, "Laqab for a Future Caliph: The Case of the Abbasi al-Mahdī," *JAOS* 113 (1993): 271–74.

39. Cf. Michael Cooperson, *Classical Arabic Biography: The Heirs of the Prophets in the Age of al-Maʾmūn* (Cambridge: Cambridge University Press, 2000), 33–35, 109–12.

ʿAbbāsid caliphs thus continued their predecessors' tradition of calling rulers by the title mahdī, but by now the term had also acquired a distinct messianic flavor. The accumulated mainstream literature on the mahdī was canonized during the heyday of ʿAbbāsid rule through inclusion in four of the six Sunnī collections of ḥadīth.[40] From here on, the mahdī became accepted widely by the Sunnīs as an eschatological savior, though the belief was never standardized in Sunnī creeds and many authors continued to doubt the possibility of the mahdī's appearance in later centuries.

Along with the ʿAbbāsid dynasty itself, the revolution of 750 also brought to prominence the figure of Abū Muslim Khurāsānī (d. 755), whose legend developed into a separate messianic paradigm. Although little is known with certainty about Abū Muslim's background, his fame derives from his activities as the principal agent of the ʿAbbāsids in the city of Merv, in Khurāsān, that turned out to be the very springboard of the revolution.[41] Abū Muslim himself was assassinated by the caliph al-Manṣūr in the process of consolidating the power of the ruling house, though the charisma associated with him as the champion of the downtrodden acquired a life of its own in the form of works devoted to his heroic qualities.[42] As Kathryn Babayan has shown, Abū Muslim was adopted as a hero by the early Ghulāt, and a continuous tradition can be traced between the remnants of the Kaysānīya active in southern Iraq in the eighth century and the propaganda of the militarized Ṣafavid order in Iran and Anatolia in the fifteenth.[43] Although not a mahdī in the strict sense, Abū Muslim, as a legendary "helping" figure, is significant for the Islamic messianic tradition since he could be

40. The collections by Bukhārī and Muslim do not contain chapters on the mahdī.

41. Cf. Ḡ. Ḥ. Yūsofī, "Abū Moslem," *EIr,* 1:341–44. For detailed information about Abū Muslim, see Ghūlām Ḥusayn Yūsufī, *Abū Muslim sardār-i Khurāsān* (Tehran: Ibn Sīnā, 1966).

42. Cf. Irene Melikoff, *Abu Muslim: Le "Porte-Hache" du Khorassan dans la tradition epique turco-iranienne* (Paris: A. Maisonneuve, 1962).

43. Kathryn Babayan, "Sufis, Dervishes, and Mullas: The Controversy over Spiritual and Temporal Domain in Seventeenth-Century Iran," in *Safavid Persia,* ed. Charles Melville (London, I. B. Tauris, 1996), 121–25; idem, "The Waning of the Qizilbash: The Temporal and the Spiritual in Seventeenth Century Iran," Ph.D. diss., Princeton University, 1993, 195–227.

adopted into revolutionary causes associated with "heterodox" Shīʿī movements such as the Qizilbāsh Turkoman tribesman who brought the Ṣafavid dynasty to power in Iran in the sixteenth century.

Ismāʿīlī Doctrines regarding the Savior

The Shīʿīs suffered a major split after the death of the sixth imām, Jaʿfar aṣ-Ṣādiq, when two different factions chose his sons Ismāʿīl (who predeceased his father) and Mūsā al-Kāẓim respectively as next in the line of imāms.[44] As in other doctrinal matters, these two factions differed as they further developed the figure of the qāʾim. The followers of Ismāʿīl initially considered the rise of the qāʾim to be imminent, while in the second group, al-Kāẓim's descendants succeeded one after another until the Twelfth Imām. Although some Shīʿīs did consider Ismāʿīl b. Jaʿfar himself the qāʾim, due to lack of evidence it is difficult to judge the strength of this faction. Ismāʿīl's son Muḥammad contested al-Kāẓim for Shīʿī leadership, but, having met little success, he eventually moved away from Medina, the original site for the dispute, to Iraq or Khūzistān.[45]

Our concrete knowledge about the doctrines of this sect begins with a man named ʿAbdallāh, who began preaching in the city of ʿAskar Mukram in southwestern Iran around the middle of the ninth century.[46]

44. Although al-Kāẓim eventually became the seventh imām for the majority, the non-Ismāʿīlī faction of the Shīʿīs initially considered Jaʿfar's son ʿAbdallāh to be the imām. However, this imām died shortly (one to four months) after the death of his father and his followers (called the Afṭaḥiyya) gradually switched their allegiance to al Kāẓim. ʿAbdallāh's name was excised from the list of the imāms in later years, when he was forgotten due to the brevity of his imāmate (cf. W. M. Watt, "Sidelights on Early Imamate Doctrine 2: The Fuṭ'ḥiyya or Afṭaḥiyya," *SI* 31 [1970], 293–300).

45. Cf. Farhad Daftary, *The Ismāʿīlīs: Their History and Their Doctrines* (Cambridge: Cambridge University Press, 1991), 91–102, where all available information about the dispute over the imāmate is reviewed.

46. Heinz Halm, *The Empire of the Mahdī: The Rise of the Fatimids,* trans. Michael Bonner (Leiden: E. J. Brill, 1996), 6–14. Halm's account for the events discussed here is based largely upon sources edited and translated in W. Ivanow, *Ismaili Tradition Concerning the Rise of the Fatimids* (Calcutta: Oxford University Press, 1942). For a critique of Halm's reconstruction of the history, see Michael Brett, "The Mīm, the ʿAyn, and the Making of Ismāʿīlism," *BSOAS* 57, no. 1 (1994): 25–39.

He may have been connected to the circle of Muḥammad b. Ismāʿīl and his descendants since later sources record his belief in the latter's designation as the qāʾim or mahdī. Calling themselves the followers of the true religion (*dīn al-ḥaqq*), ʿAbdallāh and the subsequent two generations of his family eventually settled in Iraq and Syria and developed a distinctive religious doctrine with Manichaean overtones.[47] They believed that Muḥammad b. Ismāʿīl was alive and would announce himself imminently as the redeemer, and that in his temporary absence, ʿAbdallāh and his successors (now resident in Salamīya in Syria) were the imām's deputies or proofs (*ḥujja*). Along with the functions of the redeemer discussed so far, these early Ismāʿīlīs also believed that he would abrogate exoteric divine law (*sharīʿa*) to reveal the true religion.[48]

Secret Ismāʿīlī propaganda in the name of this mahdī was particularly successful in the regions near Rayy and Kūfa. The Iraqi side of the movement eventually acquired the name Qarāmiṭa after the conversion of an energetic future leader named Ḥamdān b. al-Ashʿath, known as Qarmaṭ (short-legged), in 875 or 878.[49] The propaganda later spread to other regions such as Bahrain and other localities in the Persian Gulf, Daylam, Yemen, Sind, and North Africa.

By the year 287/900, the Ismāʿīlīs had gathered a considerable number of followers throughout the Islamic world who were in perpetual readiness for the battle expected to ensue once Muḥammad b. Ismāʿīl revealed himself as the mahdī. This was not to be, however, since the central directorate of the secret movement now decided to change the identity of the mahdī. The movement underwent a split as a result of this change of policy because the Iraqi followers, who were later joined by members from some other locations, continued to regard Muḥammad b. Ismāʿīl as the mahdī.

47. Halm, *Empire of the Mahdī,* 18.

48. Ibid., 21.

49. Ibid., 29–32; W. Madelung, "Fatimiden und Baḥrainqarmaṭen," *Der Islam* 34 (1959): 34–88, translated as "The Fatimids and the Qarmaṭīs of Baḥrayn," in *Mediaeval Ismaʿili History and Thought,* ed. Farhad Daftary (Cambridge: Cambridge University Press, 1996), 21–74. For other interpretations of the name Qarmaṭ, see Ivanow, *Ismaili Tradition,* 69; W. Madelung, "Ḳarmaṭī," *EI*², 5:660.

The center at Salamīya, in contrast, now maintained that three separate individuals were to be seen as imām, mahdī, and qāʾim. Abū sh-Shalaghlagh, the "proof" of the movement at the time, declared that he himself was the imām descended from Muḥammad b. Ismāʿīl. Even more significantly, he further stated that his nephew Saʿīd b. al-Ḥusayn (d. 934), who was his designated successor, was the mahdī, and that the mahdī's son ʿAbd ar-Raḥmān (d. 946) was the qāʾim.[50] The declaration assigned separate identities to the mahdī and the qāʾim, which thus far had been represented by synonymous terms in Ismāʿīlī thought. Although the division of functions between the two is not completely clear, it seems that the mahdī was supposed to usher in a new dispensation, while the qāʾim was responsible for its firm establishment in the world.

Islamic history during the early ninth century eventually came to fashion the Ismāʿīlī view of the savior. After a series of events with complicated details, mahdī Saʿīd b. al-Ḥusayn (later called ʿAbdallāh or ʿUbayd Allāh al-Mahdī) was eventually proclaimed a ruler and caliph in Ifriqīya (Tunisia) in 296/909.[51] This occurrence inaugurated the Fāṭimid countercaliphate, which was passed on from the mahdī to his son al-Qāʾim bi-Amr Allāh in 934. The identity of the mahdī and the qāʾim in Ismāʿīlism stabilized once the Fāṭimids were accepted as the imāms by most Ismāʿīlīs. However, the scholars of the community were now faced with the task of rationalizing these identities with pre-Fāṭimid traditions about the savior.

To this end, Fāṭimid scholars such as the famous Qāḍī Nuʿmān (d. 363/974) produced theories that explained how al-Mahdī the caliph had fulfilled all the traditional requirements for the savior. In considerable contrast with the initial Ismāʿīlī outlook, the mahdī was

50. Halm, *Empire of the Mahdī,* 59.

51. Ibid., 139. For the details of the mahdī's rise to power, see also, James E. Lindsay, "Prophetic Parallels in Abū ʿAbd Allah al-Shiʿi's Mission among the Kutama Berbers, 893–910," *IJMES* 24, no. 1 (1992): 39–56. The mahdī explained after his ascension that Saʿīd b. al-Ḥusayn had only been his pseudonym until the time of the declaration of his status. Fāṭimid theory also posited such pseudonyms for other supposed imāms between Muḥammad b. Ismāʿīl and al-Mahdī (cf. Daftary, *Ismāʿīlīs,* 112).

now portrayed most prominently as the protector of law and order and the caliph who would unite the Muslim community.[52] These two aspects of the savior's function coincided best with the Fāṭimids' objectives as temporal rulers, while the figure's eschatological function, commonly accepted by this time, was deemphasized. Similarly, for all supernatural acts expected of the mahdī, the title was now seen to indicate the whole Fāṭimid dynasty and not just the founder.[53] The mahdī was stripped of most of his extraordinary qualities, and the central focus came to be the mundane affairs of government expected of him.

Ismāʿīlī understanding of the savior (mahdī or qāʾim) underwent another transformation following the movement's split into Mustaʿlī and Nizārī branches in 487/1094. The bifurcation of the community was caused by a Fāṭimid dynastic dispute between the brothers Nizār (d. 488/1095) and al-Mustaʿlī bi-llāh (d. 495/1101). The Mustaʿlī faction remained in control in Egypt until the end of the Fāṭimid caliphate in 567/1171 and followed the doctrines developed under the earlier caliphs. The only faction of this subsect to survive past the end of the caliphate eventually came to believe that aṭ-Ṭayyib, a son of al-Āmir, the tenth caliph (d. 524/1130), had been born a few months before his death and had succeeded him. The Mustaʿlī followers of Ṭayyib reverted to an older Ismāʿīlī theory that the institution of the imāmate works in alternating cycle of visible and hidden imāms. Ṭayyib had inaugurated a new hidden cycle so that he himself and his descendants were not visible to his followers, and the next visible cycle would start with another qāʾim. Mustaʿlī communities surviving past the twelfth century believe in a hidden Ṭayyibī imām, and a qāʾim among his descendants who will rise some time in the future.[54]

The Nizārī Ismāʿīlīs, who proved to be more adventuresome in their doctrinal speculations, evolved a new idea of the mahdī within the next century. Nizār himself died in 488/1095 without acquiring the allegiance

52. Qāḍī Nuʿmān, *Sharḥ al-akhbār fī faḍāʾil al-aʾimma al-aẓhār,* ed. Sayyid Muḥammad al-Ḥusaynī al-Jalālī, 3 vols. (Qum: Muʾassasat an-Nashr al-Islāmī, 1988), 3: 353–431; Ivanow, *Ismāʿīlī Tradition,* 99, 113.

53. Ivanow, *Ismāʿīlī Tradition,* 122.

54. Daftary, *Ismāʿīlīs,* 256–59; Zāhid ʿAlī, *Hamārē Ismāʿīlī maẕhab kī ḥaqīqat awr us kā niẓām* (Hyderabad: Academy of Islamic Studies, 1954), 351–53.

of the bureaucracy in Cairo, but his followers gradually gathered a state for themselves consisting of a chain of small fortresses running from Syria to northeastern Iran. The Nizārīs initially believed that the imām (Nizār's descendant) was in hiding, and until his appearance the community was to follow the directives of his deputy (the *ḥujja*). The first person to occupy this office was Ḥasan aṣ-Ṣabbāḥ (d. 518/1124), the first lord of Alamūt, and the title was later passed on to other rulers of the same fortress.[55] After a contentious existence surrounded by an overwhelming Sunnī majority, the Nizārīs eventually came to believe that Ḥasan II (d. 1166), the fourth lord of Alamūt, was the imām. His proclamation as such was made in the dramatic ceremony of the resurrection *(qiyāma)*, where he declared himself the imām and caliph, a ruler with direct divine guidance, and abrogated divine law *(sharīʿa)* by claiming that the end of the world had finally come.[56] Ḥasan's claims were given elaborate explanations by later Nizārī scholars, and it was thought that he had fulfilled all Ismāʿīlī expectations for the eschatological savior.[57] Other imāms followed in his genealogical line, leading up to the Aga Khans of the modern period.

The surviving factions of the Mustaʿlī and Nizārī sects represent two poles of the Ismāʿīlī doctrine of the savior. The former believe in a hidden imām who, however, is sometimes considered to be accessible through his agents in this world. A descendant from the genealogical line going back to the twelfth century will appear at some point in the future to begin a new cycle of visible imāms. Until then, the absence of the imāms is seen as a part of natural cosmic processes, and on the whole the Mustaʿlī religious system is not focused on the expectation. Conversely, the Nizārīs do not expect the advent of a savior in the future

55. Marshall Hodgson, *The Order of the Assassins The Struggle of the Early Nizārī Ismāʿīlīs Against the Islamic World* (The Hague: Mouton, 1955), 66–69.

56. Ibid., 150–51.

57. This is evident from the fact that in the anonymous *Haft bāb,* his followers are called *qāʾimīyūn.* The unknown author was most likely present at the resurrection (W. Ivanow, *Two Early Ismaili Treatises: Haft-babi Baba Sayyid-na and Matlubu'l-muʾiminin by Tusi* [Bombay: Islamic Research Association, 1933], 2–5, 12 [Persian text]). The Nizārīs were made subject to the *sharīʿa* again under other imāms, but the details of their later history are not relevant for the present topic.

at all because the imām, who is a descendant of the qāʾim, Ḥasan II, is already present on earth. Consequently, Nizārī Ismāʿīlī doctrine from the twelfth century onward does not contain an imminent expectation of the eschatological savior called mahdī or qāʾim.

It should be noted that despite the lack of doctrinal necessity, Nizārī Ismāʿīlī history since the twelfth century does contain episodes of messianic propaganda carried out particularly in areas such as Daylam, Quhistān, and Gīlān, which had been centers of Nizārī power prior to the Mongol invasion. This activity, however, was motivated not by the future expectation of a messiah but on behalf of the living imām, who was in hiding. The available sources do not provide adequate information to reconstruct Nizārī history between the thirteenth and fifteenth centuries satisfactorily. All that can be said is that the Nizārīs overwhelmingly practiced pious dissimulation (*taqīya*) for the sake of their safety and that the meager literature available from the period shows pronounced signs of infusion of Sufi ideas.[58] For the purposes of the present book, it is relevant that Muḥammad Nūrbakhsh was born and raised in Quhistān, a region with substantial Ismāʿīlī connections, and it is possible that some diffused messianic propaganda by the Nizārīs may have affected his own or his ancestors' ideas in this regard.[59]

Twelver Doctrine of the Imām's Occultation

Against the Ismāʿīlīs, the Shīʿī group that accepted Mūsā al-Kāẓim as the imām after Jaʿfar aṣ-Ṣādiq's death has continued to expect the qāʾim, or mahdī, until the present. Its speculation about the figure was standardized after the death of the eleventh imām, al-Ḥasan b. ʿAlī al-ʿAskarī, in 260/874. In this view (later known as the main distinguishing doctrine of the Twelvers), the chain of imāms continued after al-Kāẓim in succession from a father to son until al-ʿAskarī. He

58. Cf. Daftary, *Ismāʿīlīs,* 443–56; idem, "Ismāʿīlī-Sufi Relations in Early Post-Alamūt and Safavid Persia," in *The Heritage of Sufism,* vol. 3, ed. Leonard Lewisohn and David Morgan (Oxford: One World, 1999), 275–89.

59. As discussed in chapter 3, there is no evidence of direct Ismāʿīlī influence in Nūrbakhsh's thought. However, it is impossible to preclude indirect connections in light, particularly, of the considerable crossover between Ismāʿīlism and Sufism in the thirteenth and fourteenth centuries.

was succeeded by his infant son Muḥammad, who has, for the time being, gone into occultation. The Twelfth Imām was initially expected to return within a normal human life span; he communicated with his followers through an agent (*ṣafīr*) during the period known as the "lesser occultation."[60] When this return suffered an extended delay, Twelver Shīʿī leaders were obliged to devise a new version of the doctrine to explain the situation to their followers. The result was the theory of the "greater occultation," where now the Twelfth Imām became an eschatological/messianic figure who would return to restore justice to the world before its final dissolution.[61]

In essence, the final Twelver belief first identified the Twelfth Imām as the qāʾim figure who had been a part of Shīʿī speculation from the time of the first six imāms. Subsequently, Twelver scholars combined this specifically Shīʿī deliverer with the eschatological mahdī who had become accepted by Muslims at large by this time.[62] The imām's occultation thus both explained his mysterious disappearance and provided the Shīʿīs with a venue to tap into the messianic hope that had become

60. For a review of the activities of the four agents who occupied this position one after another, see Jassam Hussain, *Occultation of the Twelfth Imam* (London: Muhammadi Trust, 1982), 79–98.

61. Twelver adoption of this tenet is reviewed in Etan Kohlberg, "From Imāmiyya to Ithnā-ʿAshariyya," *BSOAS* 39 (1976): 521–43. The formulation of the doctrine of occultation has received considerable scholarly attention; see, for example, Hussain, *Occultation of the Twelfth Imam;* Hossein Modarressi, *Crisis and Consolidation in the Formative Period of Shiʿite Islam* (Princeton, N.J.: Darwin Press, 1994), 78–105; Sachedina, *Islamic Messianism,* 78–108; Amir-Moezzi, *Divine Guide,* 108–15. Among original sources from the formative period, the doctrine is defended extensively in Muḥammad b. Ibrāhīm an-Nuʿmānī (Ibn Abī Zaynab), *Kitāb al-ghayba* (Tehran: n.p., 1900); ʿAlī b. Muḥammad al-Khazzāz, *Kifāyat al-athar fī n-nuṣūṣ ʿalā l-aʾimma l-ithnay ʿashar* (Qum: Intishārāt-i Baydār, 1980); Muḥammad b. ʿAlī Ibn Bābawayh, *Kamāl ad-dīn wa-tamām an-niʿma* (Tehran: Kitābfurūshī-yi Islāmīya, 1959); and Muḥammad b. al-Ḥasan aṭ-Ṭūsī, *Kitāb al-ghayba* (Najaf: Maktabat aṣ-Ṣādiq, 1965). The general intellectual environment of the period during which Twelver doctrines became consolidated is discussed in Andrew Newman, *The Formative Period of Twelver Shīʿism: Ḥadīth as Discourse between Qum and Baghdad* (Richmond, U.K.: Curzon, 2000).

62. The term *mahdī* appears very rarely in mainstream Shīʿī literature before the occultation. As reviewed above, the standard name for the deliverer during this

a part of popular Islamic belief. By the end of the tenth century, the identity between the Twelfth Imām and the mahdī was firmly established in Twelver Shīʿī thought and, by the thirteenth century, several Sunnī scholars had also accepted this view.[63]

The Mahdī between Islamic Sects

The survey above can now be summarized by specifying major Islamic sects' views regarding the messiah by the thirteenth century (chart 1). The first instance of a Muslim savior who would rise to quell evil and unite the Muslim community is traceable to ʿAbdallāh b. az-Zubayr's revolt against the Umayyads in 681. The origins of Islamic messianism lie, therefore, in a non-ʿAlid faction from early Islamic history. Although the mahdī became a part of popular Sunnī outlook from early times, theoretical discussion about him never acquired a central position in Sunnī thought.[64] Numerous Sunnī authors continued to cast doubt on the possibility of a savior,[65] and the potential for a personal mahdist claim was also obviated by emphasizing the prophetic report that the title mahdī was a name for Jesus in his eschatological Second Coming.[66]

---

period was Qāʾim (cf. Modarressi, *Crisis and Consolidation,* 89; Sachedina, *Islamic Messianism,* 69).

63. Madelung, "al-Mahdī," 5:1236. Madelung cites the *Kitāb al-bayān fī akhbār ṣāḥib az-zamān* of the Syrian Shāfiʿī traditionist Muḥammad b. Yūsuf al-Ganjī al-Qurashī (d. 658/1260), as well as works by Kamāl ad-Dīn Muḥammad b. Ṭalḥa al-ʿAdawī an-Niṣībīnī (writing in 650/1252) and the Sibṭ Ibn al-Jawzī (d. 654/1256) as examples of this trend.

64. Ibid. For a summary of the Sunnī view of the mahdī, see Ibn Ḥajar al-Haythamī, *Qawl al-mukhtaṣar fī ʿalāmāt al-mahdī al-muntaẓar,* ed. ʿAbd ar-Raḥmān b. ʿAbdallāh at-Turkī (Cairo: az-Zahrāʾ li l-iʿlām al-ʿArabī, 1994). Sunnī ideas about charismatic religious authority after Muḥammad in general are reviewed in Friedmann, *Prophecy Continuous,* 83–101.

65. The most prominent basis for Sunnī skepticism about the mahdī is that the ḥadīth collections of Bukhārī and Muslim do not include reports on him. The remaining four canonical collections, however, contain sections on the mahdī. The possibility of a mahdī's rise is doubted also by Ibn Khaldūn after his extensive description of traditions relevant to the topic (Ibn Khaldûn, *The Muqaddimah: An Introduction to History,* trans. Franz Rosenthal, 3 vols. [New York: Pantheon Books, 1958], 2:156–200).

66. *MA,* vol. 1, no. 381.

CHART 1. Messianism in Islamic Religious History

Muḥammad (ca. 570–632)	• Mahdī or savior not mentioned in the Qurʾan; • Muḥammad becomes a predictor of the savior in ḥadīth literature;	
Early Caliphate (632–661)	• ʿAbdallāh b. Sabaʾ and the Sabaʾīya: speculation that ʿAlī will return after death; • Mahdī as a title equivalent to caliph;	
Umayyads (658–750)	• Career of Ibn az-Zubayr (d. 692) turned into a messianic prophecy in his lifetime; • Ibn al-Ḥanafīya (d. 700–701) declared a messianic mahdī; • Popularization of literature describing the end of the world; • Kaysānīya: belief that Ibn al-Ḥanafīya would return after death;	
	• Messianic expectations incorporated in the ʿAbbāsid Revolution; • The activity of Abū Muslim Khurāsānī (d. 755) and the formation of his myth; • Continuation of mahdī as a caliphal title; • Various Shīʿī imāms to return after death;	
ʿAbbāsids (750–1258)	***Standardization of sectarian views regarding the savior***	
	Sunnīs:	nonuniversal belief in an eschatological savior (mahdī), who may be Jesus or, in later thought, the Shīʿī Twelfth Imām;
Fāṭimids (909–1171)	*Ghulāt:*	expectation of a qāʾim or mahdī without uniform theoretical elaboration;
	Zaydīs:	any ʿAlid who fights for the cause—every imām is a qāʾim;
	Ismāʿīlīs:	
	Qarmaṭīs:	Muḥammad b. Ismāʿīl will return as qāʾim;
	Fāṭimids:	ʿAbdallāh (d. 934), the first caliph, was the mahdī;
	Mustaʿlīs:	imām is hidden since 1130 and will return as qāʾim;
	Nizārīs:	Ḥasan II (d. 1166) was qāʾim;
	Twelvers:	Twelfth Imām, Muḥammad b. al-Ḥasan, is in occultation since 874 and will return as the qāʾim/mahdī;
Mongols and Tīmūrids (1258–ca.1500)	*Mahdīs with Sufi backgrounds:* • Fażlallāh Astarābādī (d. 1394) • Muḥammad b. Falāḥ Mushaʿshaʿ (d. 1462) • Muḥammad Nūrbakhsh (d. 1464)	

Despite this ambivalence, a number of Sunnī individuals have declared themselves mahdīs over the years. Examples of the most successful among these include Ibn Tūmart (d. 524/1130) in North Africa;[67] the mahdī of Jawnpūr (d. 910/1505) in India;[68] Muḥammad Aḥmad (d. 1885), the mahdī of the Sudan;[69] Mīrzā Ghulām Aḥmad (d. 1908) in India;[70] and Shehu Usuman dan Fodio (d. 1817) and a number of other influential religious figures in Muslim West Africa.[71] These mahdīs are distinguishable from their Shīʿī counterparts by their central focus being most often a reinvigorated application of Islamic law (*sharīʿa*), rather than the beginning of a new religious dispensation.[72]

67. Cf. J. F. P. Hopkins, "Ibn Tūmart," *EI*², 3:958–60. Ibn Tūmart's proclamations were principally responsible for the production of traditions that suggested that the mahdī would appear in the West (Madelung, "al-Mahdī," *EI*², 5:1236). However, it has also been argued that these traditions resulted from the popularization of beliefs held by Maghribī Sufis such as Ibn Qasī (d. 536/1141) and Ibn al-ʿArabī (d. 638/1240) (cf. Gerald Elmore, *Islamic Sainthood in the Fullness of Time: Ibn al-ʿArabī's Book of the Fabulous Gryphon* [Leiden: E. J. Brill, 1999], 178). For various North African mahdīs, see articles by Michael Brett, Maribel Fierro, Tilman Nagel, Houari Touati, Mercedes García-Arenal, and Julia Clancy-Smith in *Mahdisme et millénarisme en Islam,* ed. García-Arenal.

68. Cf. T. W. Arnold and B. Lawrence, "Mahdawīs," *EI*², 5:1230; Derryl MacLean, "Le sociologique et l'engagement politique: Le Mahdawîya indien et l'État," in *Mahdisme et millénarisme en Islam,* ed. García-Arenal, 239–56; Dr. Qamaruddin, *The Mahdawi Movement in India* (Delhi: Idarah-i Asabiyat-i Delhi, 1985); Stephen Fuchs, *Rebellious Prophets: A Study of Messianic Movements in Indian Religions* (Bombay: Asia Publishing House, 1965), 167–71; Sayyid Nuṣrat Mahdī Yaddallāhī, *Urdū adab meñ mahdavīyōñ kā ḥiṣṣa, 1496–1800* (Hyderabad: Iʿjāz Printing Press, 1984).

69. Cf. P. M. Holt, *Mahdist State in the Sudan, 1881–1889* (Oxford: Oxford University Press, 1970), and, most recently, Aharon Layish, "The Mahdi's Legal Methodology as a Mechanism for Adapting the Sharîʿa in the Sudan to Political and Social Purposes," in *Mahdisme et millénarisme en Islam,* ed. García-Arenal, 221–38.

70. Cf. Friedmann, *Prophecy Continuous.*

71. Cf. Mervyn Hiskett, *The Sword of Truth: The Life and Times of the Shehu Usuman dan Fodio,* 2d ed. (Evanston, Ill.: Northwestern University Press, 1994); Peter B. Clarke, *Mahdism in West Africa: The Ijebu Mahdiyya Movement* (London: Luzac Oriental, 1995).

72. In saying this, I follow the observation made by Abbas Amanat (*Resurrection and Renewal,* 5–6). However, the implications of this difference in tenor between Sunnī and Shīʿī mahdīs remain to be evaluated in full.

The earliest ʿAlid faction to believe in a messianic deliverer was the Kaysānīya, who considered ʿAlī's son Muḥammad b. al-Ḥanafīya the mahdī during his lifetime. They continued their belief after his death, now expecting his imminent return in the role of the savior. This idea was generalized in later Ghulāt sects who maintained belief in the qāʾim or mahdī leading them to both worldly dominion and a new spiritual dispensation. Among Shīʿī sects, the Zaydīya equated the mahdī with any of their imāms since both offices had to be occupied by an ʿAlid who would actively struggle for the ʿAlid cause.

The Ismāʿīlīs and Twelver Shīʿīs began with speculations about a revolutionary imām, the qāʾim, who would rise in the future to redress the wrongs suffered by the ʿAlids. This viewpoint underwent numerous turns in Ismāʿīlī history, finally resulting in two views: for the Mustaʿlīs, the current imām is a descendant of the Fāṭimid caliph al-Āmir and he or one of his descendants will become manifest some time in the future; and for the Nizārīs, the imām is present in the community and there is no need for a future savior.

The Twelvers eventually canonized the Twelfth Imām as the eschatological mahdī. He was born around 260/874 and is in occultation until just before the end of the world. He is expected to become visible at that time and vindicate the truth of Twelver beliefs. Twelver Shīʿism is, therefore, the only Shīʿī sect to be focused wholly on the expectation of a mahdī with a determined identity. Given the qualities attributed to all imāms in Twelver theory, the mahdī occupies an extremely high status among human beings in general. He possesses the charisma of the house of Muḥammad and deserves unconditional obedience by his followers in both religious and worldly affairs.

While the mahdī as a concept and invisible presence is ubiquitous in Twelver Shīʿī learning,[73] actual claimants to mahdīhood have always encountered vehement opposition from the community's scholars. This antipathy is understandable, given both that the mahdī's identity is already determined and that the scholars are religious guardians of the community only until the imām reappears. Accepting a claimant as the

73. For Twelver literary production on this issue over the ages, see the bibliography in Madelung, "Ḳāʾim Āl Muḥammad," *EI²*, 4:457.

mahdī would render the work of scholars unnecessary, leading to a breakdown of the existing system of religious authority. Being a mahdī in a Shīʿī context necessarily requires going beyond traditional belief since the claimant has to argue against the very basis of the idea of "twelve" uniquely guided imāms who, according to the sect's orthodoxy, have already existed in history. Conversely, however, it is crucial for a mahdī to access the charisma inscribed in traditions regarding the Twelfth Imām in order to acquire spiritual and political power through the claim. This tension, endemic to the situation of a mahdī rising from a Twelver milieu, marks the claimant as one who is the gravest transgressor against accepted dogma while simultaneously being an embodiment of Shīʿism's greatest hope. Resolving this tension to his own benefit was the principal task of a Twelver Shīʿī mahdī such as Muḥammad Nūrbakhsh.

Chapter Two

A Messiah's Life

Muḥammad Nūrbakhsh, 1392–1464

One night during the year 826 of the Islamic calendar (1423 C.E.), the elderly mystical guide of a Central Asian Sufi hospice interrupted his spiritual exercises and called his most prized disciple to his seclusionary chamber. In the interview that followed, the master gave the student the following extraordinary news: "It has been unveiled to me that you are the mahdī promised for the end of time. . . . I bear witness that you are the promised imām. . . . God will protect you from your adversaries, though there is profound wisdom in the hardship put upon prophets and saints."[1] The young mystic took the remarkable announcement to heart and spent the rest of his life attempting to live up to its responsibilities while awaiting what was due him from the world.

This, in synopsis, is how Muḥammad Nūrbakhsh would have liked us to see his life. His messianic confession, written more than thirty years after the interview with his master Khwāja Isḥāq Khuttalānī (d. 1423), uses the revelatory moment as a fulcrum balancing two different parts of his life. The announcement was preceded by thirty-one years filled with auspicious omens pointing to Nūrbakhsh's special mission, and after it came four decades of alternating persecution and partial success in establishing his mission. By the end of his life, Nūrbakhsh headed a dedicated community of followers and still hoped to be

1. *RH*, I:21.

vindicated as the mahdī. He therefore never lost faith in Khuttalānī's vision, and the circumstances of his life in general seemed to him to be a confirmation of the special mission for which God had chosen him.

Distancing ourselves from the messiah's own perspective, we realize that the story has, of course, many more complications and twists. The purpose of this chapter is to reconstruct Nūrbakhsh's life to the best detail allowed by the sources, keeping in mind the messianic consciousness that permeates his works. A biography of the messiah is a necessary precursor to the subsequent chapters of the book that elaborate Nūrbakhsh's justification for the messianic claim and his overall religious worldview.

To begin, Nūrbakhsh's life needs to be seen as a part of the upsurge in messianic activity in the Islamic East during the fourteenth and fifteenth centuries. Consequently, the first part of this chapter lays out, in broad strokes, the overall characteristics of the religious environment crucial as the context for Nūrbakhsh's activities. Nūrbakhsh's life itself can be divided into three periods based upon his intellectual development and the geographical foci of his activity. He spent the first phase of his life (1392–1423) in Quhistān, Khurāsān, and Transoxiana and there acquired both his initial training and his sectarian and mystical affiliations. This is the period of preparation for mahdīhood, when the messianic idea came to permeate his thought as a result of his personal experiences and the impact of the religious scene that surrounded him.

The second period (1424–ca. 1442–43) was the most troubled part of Nūrbakhsh's life since he endured numerous punishments at the hands of the Tīmūrid ruler Shāhrukh (d. 1447) and was obliged to travel extensively through various parts of Central Asia and Iran. This period reflects the resilience of Nūrbakhsh's faith in his own designation despite overwhelmingly negative odds. In contrast, in the last period of his life (ca. 1443–64), he settled down as a Sufi teacher, first in Gīlān and later in a permanent Nūrbakhshī community in the village of Suliqān, near Rayy. His major concerns during this period were writing and the training of disciples who would later continue to propagate his ideas beyond his death. Nūrbakhsh died under peaceful circumstances in Suliqān, but in centuries to come his legacy continued to be a controversial matter.

The Making of a Messianic Age in Tīmūrid Iran and Central Asia

Muḥammad Nūrbakhsh advanced his messianic claim in an age particularly well known in Islamic history for the rise of activist messiahs. Bounded by the end of unified Īlkhānid rule and the establishment of the Ṣafavid, Ottoman, Uzbek, and Mughal states in the Islamic East (1335–ca. 1500 C.E.), the period in question saw the rise of Tīmūr (d. 807/1405) and the fragmentation of his vast empire in the hands of his successors.[2] A comprehensive explanation for the rise of messianic activity, which contextualizes the phenomenon in the period's social history, can be offered only once a number of movements such as the Nūrbakhshīya have been studied in detail. It is possible here, however, to highlight certain aspects of political, social, and intellectual history that constitute the general background for Nūrbakhsh's life.

From a history of religions perspective, a period rich in politically charged messianic movements suggests the presence of two complementary factors. On the social level, the increase in such messianic activity indicates society's greater receptivity toward new syntheses of religion and politics, an element implying, in turn, a weakening of existing models of political legitimacy. This diversification of political paradigms may, however, lead to messianic movements only if the society's religious discourse already includes a messianic model that can be appropriated for articulating religious and sociopolitical visions. An explanation for the upsurge in messianic activity must then relate to both the social and the intellectual history of a given context.

On one level, the rise in messianic religion during the Tīmūrid period can be seen to represent the search for alternative structures of legitimation undergirding the relationship between the rulers and the ruled in societies of the Islamic East. Before the fifteenth century,

2. For general reviews of the religious history of this period, see Bashir, "Between Mysticism and Messianism," 8–78; Amoretti, "Religion under the Tīmūrids and the Ṣafavids," *CHIr,* 6:610–23; Mazzaoui, *Origins of the Ṣafavids,* 1–6, 83–85; Arjomand, *Shadow of God and the Hidden Imam,* 66–84; and Annemarie Schimmel, "The Ornament of the Saints: The Religious Situation in Pre-Ṣafavid Times," *Iranian Studies* 7 (1974): 88–111.

political legitimacy in this cultural zone rested predominantly on ideologies vesting universal rulership in royal genealogical lines. Between 750 and 1258, the ʿAbbāsid caliphs (themselves heirs to the pre-Islamic Persian model of kingship) claimed sovereignty over the whole of central Islamic lands, although their actual power became severely circumscribed from the tenth century. The Mongol destruction of Baghdad in 1258 ended the ʿAbbāsid dynasty, and in the arena of political legitimacy ʿAbbāsid ideology was supplanted by the equally universalistic royal tradition of the house of Chingīz Khān (d. 1227). As the holder of Chingīzid patrimony, the Īlkhānid ruling house maintained this tradition between 1258 and 1335, with the Chingīzid political tradition becoming Islamized after the conversion of the Īlkhān Ghāzān in 1295.[3]

The death of Abū Saʿīd, the last effective Īlkhān, in 1335 resulted in the breakup of the Mongol empire into a number of smaller states. Most important among these for our purposes was the Sarbadār polity centered in Sabzavār, whose historical trajectory was greatly influenced by the activities of a number of Sufi leaders tracing themselves to the inspiration of a certain Shaykh Khalīfa (d. 1335).[4] Instead of dynastic rule, political power in the Sarbadār state was distributed among factions ranging between military commanders, heads of local tradesmen's guilds, and the religiously defined group led by Shaykh Khalīfa's successors Shaykh Ḥasan Jūrī (d. 1342), Darvīsh ʿAzīz (d. 1362–63), and Darvīsh Rukn ad-Dīn (d. 1380–81). The fickle politics of the Sarbadār state reflected the complex interaction between the various factions throughout its existence (1335–80), though the fact that such a state survived for forty-five years indicates in itself the fluidity of political

3. Cf. Charles Melville, "Pādshāh-i Islām: The Conversion of Sultan Maḥmūd Ghāzān Khān," *Pembroke Papers,* ed. Charles Melville (Cambridge: University of Cambridge Center of Middle Eastern Studies, 1990), 159–77; Reuven Amitai-Preiss, "Ghazan, Islam and the Mongol Tradition: A View from the Mamluk Sultanate," *BSOAS* 59, no. 1 (1996): 1–10.

4. For the role played by Shaykh Khalīfa's followers in the Sarbadār state, see Bashir, "Between Mysticism and Messianism," 12–34. The Sarbadār government itself is treated most recently in Yukako Goto, "Der Aufstieg zweier Sayyid-Familien am Kaspischen Meer: "Volksislamische" Strömungen in Iran des 8/14. und 9/15. Jahrhunderts," *WZKM* 89 (1999): 51–63.

paradigms in the wake of the end of the Īlkhānid Empire. Furthermore, the political viability of the Shaykhīya, a group based solely on a radicalized religious ideology, reflects the increasing significance of religion in political matters.

Although not the sole predominant reality after 1335, the universalistic political ideal of the Chingīzid house continued to exercise considerable influence on the region's political culture. This fact is evident most strongly in Tīmūr's articulation of his own status as only an "amīr," who maintained a Chingīzid puppet ruler in Samarqand as an official figurehead despite founding a massive empire based on his own spectacular military successes.[5] The fiction of universal kingship under a ruler legitimized by his bloodline came under considerable stress after Tīmūr's death in 1405, when his numerous sons and grandsons began to pose their own royal claims and counterclaims now stemming from the Tīmūrid tradition.[6] Taken together with other factors discussed below, the lack of a single conclusive heir to Tīmūr and the resulting dilution of the tradition under the impact of rival claims allowed alternatives like messianic legitimacy to gain social significance.

In conjunction with the declining potential of the universal rulership model, the Mongol and Tīmūrid period also witnessed an appreciable erosion of urban high culture in the eastern Islamic world due to military campaigns, unstable political regimes, and predatory state policies. This trend was exacerbated during Tīmūr's own time due to his unceasing campaigns throughout the vast reaches of his empire between 1370 and 1405. The sack of major cities led to a weakening of the traditional elites who had customarily mediated between the rulers and the ruled. After Tīmūr's death, the military amīrs, who had by now replaced the earlier established classes in society, became divided among the various claimants to Tīmūr's legacy.[7] Their frequent switches in allegiance further weakened social hierarchies and led to an uncertain socioeconomic environment. In this situation, too, a messianic

5. Beatrice Forbes Manz, *The Rise and Rule of Tamerlane* (Cambridge: Cambridge University Press, 1989), 14–15.

6. Cf. ibid., 128–47; Roger M. Savory, "The Struggle for Supremacy in Persia after the Death of Tīmūr," *Der Islam* 40 (1964): 35–65.

7. For the organizational structure of Tīmūr's empire, see Manz, *Rise and Rule,* 107–27.

deliverer, who invoked direct divine commission and legitimized his quest through the possibility of an era of peace and justice, appealed to peoples seeking greater security in the orderly conduct of societal functions. The messiah's purported divine appointment paralleled the universalism of the ʿAbbāsid and Chingīzid paradigms, and the promise of worldly as well as eternal salvation catalyzed social cohesion in groups that came to form particular movements. The weakening of established sociopolitical paradigms thus made room for the messianic idea to emerge and take hold among substantial segments of the population (particularly those at a distance from the main cities) as a political option in the Tīmūrid period.

Despite its functionalist appeal, a focus on political legitimacy alone is not by itself a wholly satisfactory explanation for the increase in messianic activity during the Tīmūrid era. It may be objected, for example, that along with the decline of some urban centers, the period also saw the creation of new great capitals like Samarqand and Herat, and that Tīmūr as well as many of his successors supported a lavish court culture that was a worthy successor to the earlier universalistic imperial traditions.[8] Historical sources from the period do not reflect an unequivocal sense of a crisis of political legitimacy, casting doubt on the validity of the historical projection part of the hypothesis above. Even accepting the argument regarding political legitimacy, moreover, such a situation would not automatically lead to an increase in messianic activity. Indeed, it could be said that the question of political legitimacy explains only the substantial success of messianic movements, rather than their origins. We must, therefore, deepen the analysis by identifying some of the elements held in common between the messianic claimants from the period themselves.

Although the ideal of dynastic universal rule may have become less effective, its basis, the charisma of a genealogical line, seems ironically

8. For glimpses into aspects of Tīmūrid court life, see Lisa Golombek and Maria Subtelny, eds., *Timurid Art and Culture: Iran and Central Asia in the Fifteenth Century* (Leiden: E. J. Brill, 1992), and Wheeler M. Thackston, *A Century of Princes: Sources on Timurid History and Art* (Cambridge, Mass.: Aga Khan Program for Islamic Architecture, 1989).

to have gained wider social significance in the Tīmūrid period. Reflecting a kind of democratization of the dynastic principle, the period's history saw an increase in the social prestige of genealogical classes such as sayyids (Muḥammad's descendants) and hereditary heirs of prominent Sufi shaykhs, the latter often being also the custodians of major shrine complexes in various parts of the eastern Islamic world.[9] The increasing significance of sayyid status is partly reflected in the rise of local sayyid dynasties as rulers in places such as Gīlān and Māzandarān.[10] Furthermore, it is noteworthy that three major messianic movements from the period were led by individuals claiming sayyid status based upon descent from the seventh Shīʿī imām, Mūsā al-Kāẓim (d. 799). Fażlallāh Astarābādī (d. 1394), the founder of the Ḥurūfīya, Muḥammad b. Falāḥ Mushaʿshaʿ (d. 1462), and Muḥammad Nūrbakhsh all based at least a part of their messianic claim in their genealogical distinction.[11] This commonality between the three messiahs may be explained in part by recalling that there was a traditional belief that the mahdī was a descendant of Muḥammad: anyone claiming the office was likely to come from a sayyid family. However, the prominence of sayyid

9. A substantial secondary literature discussing Sufi communities between the thirteenth and the sixteenth centuries is now available. For three examples that contextualize the issue in the regional history of Central Asia, Iran, and India, respectively, see Devin DeWeese, "Yasavī *Šayḫs* in the Timurid Era: Notes on the Social and Political Role of Communal Sufi Affiliations in the 14th and 15th Centuries," in *La civilità timuride come fenomeno internazionale, Oriente Moderno,* ed. Michele Bernardini, n.s. 15 (1996): 172–88; Monika Gronke, "La religion populaire en Iran Mongol," in *L'Iran face à la domination Mongole,* ed. Denise Aigle (Tehran: Institut Français de Recherche en Iran, 1997), 205–30; Richard Eaton, "The Political and Religious Authority of the Shrine of Bābā Farīd," in *Moral Conduct and Authority: The Place of* Adab *in South Asian Islam,* ed. Barbara Metcalf (Berkeley: University of California Press, 1982), 333–56.

10. Cf. Goto, "Der Aufstieg zweier Sayyid-Familien am Kaspischen Meer."

11. For primary and secondary literature pertaining to Astarābādī and Mushaʿshaʿ, see Shahzad Bashir, "Deciphering the Cosmos from Creation to Apocalypse: The Hurufiyya Movement and Medieval Islamic Esotericism," in *Imagining the End,* ed. Amanat and Bernhardsson, 168–84; idem, "The Imam's Return: Messianic Leadership in Late Medieval Shiʿism," in *The Most Learned of the Shiʿa,* ed. Linda Walbridge (New York: Oxford University Press, 2001), 21–33.

status as a means of political legitimacy more broadly was a new element particular to the period.

The genealogical commonality between the three mahdīs continued into the overall pattern of their religious discourses as well. The central feature of all three ideologies was a self-consciously new religious discourse that nevertheless drew its appeal from existing intellectual paradigms. Fażlallāh Astarābādī proclaimed himself the revealer of esoteric secrets (and hence the mahdī) based on a complex religious worldview incorporating symbolic interpretations of various "systems" such as the letters of the Arabo-Persian alphabet, the human body, and geography. His vision gave birth to the Ḥurūfī sect, which had an appreciable following in Iran and Anatolia until at least the sixteenth century.[12] Individual elements of his religious worldview can be traced to earlier Sufi and Shīʿī precedents, but his genius lay in synthesizing this material into a new outlook that appealed to his audience.

Against Astarābādī's primarily religious focus, the Mushaʿshaʿ put his personal claim of being the mahdī's direct representative to political and military use in southern Iraq and Khūzistān during the fifteenth century.[13] Basing himself on Sufi and Ghulāt Shīʿī concepts from earlier periods, Mushaʿshaʿ claimed that his body was a veil (*ḥijāb*) that contained the spiritual essence of the Twelfth Imām. This quality gave him all the rights and privileges of the mahdī himself, and his various wars and puritanical application of law on the population under his control were in fact the will of the mahdī. The Mushaʿshaʿ's followers were successful in maintaining political control in the region of his activity after his death, and his descendants remained important local overlords in southern Iraq until modern times. The fact that Fażlallāh, the Mushaʿshaʿ, and Nūrbakhsh were able to garner appreciable movements indicates

12. For the most recent evaluation of Fażlallāh Astarābādī and his movement, see Bashir, "Deciphering the Cosmos," and idem, "Enshrining Divinity: The Death and Memorialization of Fażlallāh Astarābādī in Early Ḥurūfī Thought," *MW* 90, nos. 3 and 4 (2000): 289–308.

13. For Mushaʿshaʿ and his movement, see P. Luft, "Mushaʿshaʿ," *EI*², 7:672–75; ʿAlī Riżā Ẕakāvatī Qarāguzlū, "Nahżat-i mushaʿshaʿī va guzārī bar *Kalām al-mahdī*," *Maʿārif* 13, no. 1 (1996): 59–67.

a relative opening up of the religious field in conjunction with the changeover in the bases of political legitimacy.

Paralleling their religious discourses, the three mahdīs' sociopolitical ideals also contained direct appeals to norms of Sufi and Shīʿī religious authority. On the Sufi side, their tremendous sense of self-significance underscored the transformation of the figure of the Sufi shaykh during the fourteenth and the fifteenth centuries from a religious guide to an influential member of the social elite. Under the influence of Ibn al-ʿArabī and his followers, Persianate Sufism during this period was permeated by ideas such as the Seal of Sainthood (*khātam-i valāyat*) and the perfect man (*insān-i kāmil*), which posited the existence of spiritual hierarchies presided over by supreme guides.[14] The growing ideological centrality of the master to Sufi discourse became fused with Sufi networks' role as primary agents of social cohesion, leading to recognized Sufi masters and heirs acquiring highly elevated positions in local social hierarchies throughout the region. Because of their social status, the major Sufi families formed marriage alliances with ruling houses such as the Tīmūrids and the Aqqoyunlu and Qaraqoyunlu Turkoman federations, resulting in the interpenetration of religious and political genealogical claims.[15] The growing similarity and connections between religious and political elites eventually led to an actual overlap of the two domains, and it is precisely this interpenetration that became

14. The influence of these ideas in Nūrbakhsh's context is discussed in detail in chapter 4. It should be noted that the "perfect man" for many Sufi theorists was not an actual person; the term denoted the macrocosm that paralleled an individual human being at the microcosmic level. For an extended example of such a formulation, see ʿAzīz Nasafī, *Kitāb al-insān al-kāmil,* ed. Marijan Molé (Tehran: Departement d'Iranologie de l'Institut Franco-Iranien, 1962).

15. Sufi orders (*ṭuruq*) and masters indulged in or shunned the practice of associating with rulers in varying degrees according to group practice or personal preference. For some prominent examples of the phenomenon, see Lawrence Potter, "Sufis and Sultans in Post-Mongol Iran," *Iranian Studies* 27, nos. 1–4 (1994): 77–102; Aziz Ahmad, "The Sufi and the Sultan in Pre-Mughal Muslim India," *Der Islam* 38 (1963): 142–53; and Jo-Ann Gross, "Khoja Ahrar: A Study of the Perceptions of Religious Power and Prestige in the Late Timurid Period," Ph.D. diss., New York University, 1982.

explicit through the rise of mahdīs using Sufi language to make grandiose religiopolitical claims.

In addition to the enhancement of Sufis' societal functions, the Tīmūrid period is known also for a kind of rapprochement between Sufism and Shīʿism leading to messianic doctrines and other "syncretistic" ideological formations.[16] With his religious prestige and political pretensions, the new type of Sufi shaykh now becoming common approximated more and more closely the status given to the religiopolitical figure of the imām in Shīʿism. As discussed in the preceding chapter, the major Shīʿī sects had settled on particular lines of imāms by the thirteenth century. Under the impact of the sociointellectual environment of the post-ʿAbbāsid Islamic East, some Shīʿī individuals and communities during the period began to revisit their established sectarian certainties. Twelver Shīʿism underwent a kind of resurgence in the Mongol period, when the sect's adherents were no longer subject to outright suppression and some Mongol rulers even toyed with the idea of adopting the Twelver creed.[17] Until this period, persecution had been a significant part of Twelver Shīʿī self-definition, and release from its pressure led to a liberalization in the sect's dogmatic principles.

Opposite to the Twelver situation in the Mongol period, Nizārī Ismāʿīlī Shīʿism lost much of the intellectual vigor and social appeal that had been one of its characteristic features within the religious spectrum of central Iranian lands prior to the Mongol destruction of Alamūt in 1256. Bereft of a political arm and an effective central organization, the Nizārī tradition became assimilated into the population at large, now also adopting the language of Sufism in its intellectual discourse.[18] The Nizārī imām in particular survived only through concealing his true

16. The case for such a rapprochement is articulated most forcefully for the Kubravīya in Molé, "Les Kubrawiya entre sunnisme et shiisme." While Molé's general argument has been criticized rightly in recent years for overemphasizing the Shīʿī proclivities of all Kubravī shaykhs, his conclusions do fit the individual case of Muḥammad Nūrbakhsh (cf. DeWeese, "Sayyid ʿAlī Hamadānī and Kubravī Hagiographical Traditions").

17. For a summary of Twelver Shīʿī history during the Mongol period, see Jean Calmard, "Le chiisme imamite sous les Ilkhans," in *L'Iran face à la domination Mongole,* ed. Denise Aigle (Tehran: Institut Français de Recherche en Iran, 1997), 261–92.

18. Daftary, *Ismāʿīlīs,* 452–54.

identity, and his genealogical line reappeared on the social scene under the imām Mustanṣir billāh II around 868/1463–64, in the area near Anjudān, central Iran, in a form parallel to the functions of a Sufi order headed by a powerful and prosperous hereditary shaykh.[19] During the period, at the same time as Nizārī Ismāʿīlism became colored heavily by Sufi intellectual and social norms, some Nizārī ideas about the significance of the imām/shaykh bled into the fabric of Sufism.

The generally more open marketplace of religions in the post-ʿAbbāsid period led also to the greater visibility of smaller Shīʿī currents such as the group designated by the term *Ghulāt* (the exaggerators). The Ahl-i Ḥaqq sect, which survives in Iran, Iraq, and Turkey to the present, represents a continuation of Ghulāt ideas given particular form and mythology during the fifteenth century.[20] The Mushaʿshaʿ's ideas also show a clear connection to Ghulāt doctrines, and similar notions can be traced to the religious outlooks of the Turkoman Qizilbāsh tribesmen who eventually became the mainstay of the Ṣafavid Sufi order, leading to the ascension of Ismāʿīl I to the throne of Iran in 1501.

The various major changes brought to Shīʿism during the Mongol and Tīmūrid period eventually led to both the blurring of boundaries between Twelver, Ismāʿīlī, and Ghulāt sects and the concurrent widespread adoption of Sufi ideas. This situation stimulated the generation of a new Shīʿism that retained its connection to the claims of the family of ʿAlī, but strained against particular sectarian doctrines. Messiahs such as Fażlallāh Astarābādī, the Mushaʿshaʿ, and Nūrbakhsh gave voice to these new formations through discourses connecting to both Shīʿī and Sufi ideas, though without complete allegiance to any existing system. Working in the opposite direction, the period also saw ʿAlid loyalism become a major tenet of Sufism in general, although that did not imply connection to any particular Shīʿī dogma.[21]

Through their appeals to Sufi and Shīʿī notions, messiahs such as Fażlallāh Astarābādī, the Mushaʿshaʿ, and Nūrbakhsh attempted to put

19. Ibid., 458–60.

20. Primary and secondary literature pertaining to the Ahl-i Ḥaqq sect is reviewed in Bashir, "Between Mysticism and Messianism," 60–73.

21. Hodgson, *Venture of Islam,* 2:495–500.

themselves on a par with the heirs of ruling houses and Sufi families, thereby making messianic legitimacy a part of the period's sociopolitical landscape. While the mahdīs did not succeed to the degree they would have liked, their descendants used their own recognized messianic charisma to establish themselves as hereditary religiopolitical leaders commanding considerable spiritual as well as material capital.[22] The legacies of the three messiahs thus led to the establishment of new *silsilas* (chains of authority), becoming a part of the spectrum of Sufi "orders" undergoing gradual solidification during the late medieval period. Moreover, sociointellectual trends coming to prominence in the sixteenth century indicate that the messianic rhetoric at the base of movements such as the Ḥurūfīya, the Mushaʿshaʿīya, and the Nūrbakhshīya was a significant part of the legacy of Tīmūrid religious history bequeathed to the new states that now came to dominate the region. This is evident most clearly in the case of Ismāʿīl I, who founded the Ṣafavid dynasty after coming to power as the leader of a chiliastic movement.[23] Messianic rhetoric can, moreover, be detected in the discourses of the Ottoman, Mughal, and Uzbek dynasties as well.[24] The mahdīs of the fifteenth century thus constitute the middle point

22. Nūrbakhsh's descendants are discussed later in this book; for the Mushaʿshaʿ and the Ḥurūfīya, see P. Luft, "Mushaʿshaʿ," *EI²*, 7:672–75, and Bashir, "Deciphering the Cosmos," 179–83.

23. The rise of the Ṣafavids is discussed in detail in Mazzaoui, *Origins of the Ṣafavids,* and Arjomand, *Shadow of God and the Hidden Imam.* The messianic elements of Ismāʿīl's self-understanding are particularly evident in his poetry (cf. Vladimir Minorsky, "The Poetry of Shāh Ismāʿīl I," *BSOAS* 10 [1942]: 1006–53; İbrahim Arslanoğlu, *Şah İsmail Hatayî ve Anadolu Hatayîleri* [Istanbul: Der Yayınevi, 1992]).

24. Cf. Cornell Fleischer, "The Lawgiver as Messiah: The Making of the Imperial Image in the Reign of Süleymân," in *Süleymân the Magnificent and his Time: Acts of the Parisian Conference Galeries Nationales du Grand Palais, 7–10 March, 1990,* ed. Gilles Veinstein (Paris: École des Hautes Études en Sciences Sociales, 1990), 163–67; Abū l-Fażl ʿAllāmī, *Akbarnāma of Abu-l-Fazl,* trans. H. Beveridge (Delhi: Ess Ess Publications, 1977), 3:364; Douglas E. Streusand, *The Formation of the Mughal Empire* (Delhi: Oxford University Press, 1989), 132; Nurten Kılıç, "Change in Political Culture: The Rise of Sheybani Khan," *Cahiers d'Asie Centrale* 3–4 (1997): 57–68; András J. E. Bodrogligeti, "Muḥammad Shaybānī Khān's Apology to the Muslim Clergy," *Archivum Ottomanicum* 8 (1993–94): 85–100.

between the demise of the ʿAbbāsid/Chingīzid paradigm and the emergence of new political ideologies articulated in the sixteenth century.

This brief review of Mongol and Tīmūrid history identifies five factors stimulating the messianic impulse prior to Muḥammad Nūrbakhsh's activity. On the sociopolitical level, the greater social viability of messianic ideologies stemmed from a weakening of the paradigm of universal rule, the deterioration of social order in the wake of Mongol and Tīmūrid conquests, and the rise of genealogical groups such as sayyids and Sufi shaykhs and their hereditary heirs as prominent social actors throughout the Islamic East. Concurrently, in the intellectual sphere, messianism was nurtured by the increasing theoretical significance of the shaykh in Sufi cosmologies, and the reformulation of Shīʿism under the influence of Sufi ideas in the post-ʿAbbāsid world. Interaction between these factors produced a new religious sensibility that partook of both Sufi and Shīʿī ideas in responding to contemporary social conditions. At the head of this new religiosity stood the various mahdīs, who as messianic deliverers both reflected the religious environment of the time and embodied the hope for a better future. With this background, we now turn to a detailed consideration of Muḥammad Nūrbakhsh's legacy.

Muḥammad Nūrbakhsh's Childhood and Early Training

Muḥammad, son of Muḥammad, son of ʿAbdallāh,[25] later given the title Nūrbakhsh (light giver) by his master, places his own birth on

25. Whether Nūrbakhsh's father's name was "Muḥammad" or "ʿAbdallāh" has sometimes been a matter of dispute. The source of the problem is Nūrbakhsh's citation of the well-known ḥadīth that the mahdī will have the same name and *kunya* as the Prophet (*RH,* I:6). One manuscript of *Risālat al-hudā* gives his own name as "Muḥammad b. ʿAbdallāh" (Fatih 5367, 101a), while the other reads: "Muḥammad b. Muḥammad b. Abdallāh" (Esad Efendi 3702, 85b). The matter is resolved within the same work since both manuscripts give his brother's name as "Aḥmad b. Muḥammad b. ʿAbdallāh" (*RH,* II:83). The form of Nūrbakhsh's own name in MS. Fatih 5367 is, therefore, a scribal error. ʿAbd al-Vāsiʿ Niẓāmī Bākharzī, an author hostile to Nūrbakhsh, wrongly accuses Nūrbakhsh of dissimulating that his father's name was ʿAbdallāh (*Maqāmāt-i Jāmī,* ed. Najīb Māʾil-i Hiravī [Tehran: Nashr-i Nay, 1992], 191 [hereafter, *MJ*]).

Friday, 27 Muḥarram, 795 (December 13, 1392), in the village of Sāwijān, near the city of Qāʾin in Quhistān Province (map 2).[26] His father claimed descent from the Twelver imām Mūsā al-Kāẓim and had traveled from the Shīʿī region of Qaṭīf, in Bahrain, to Khurāsān to visit the grave of the ninth Shīʿī imām ʿAlī ar-Riḍā (d. 818) in Mashhad.[27] He settled in Qāʾin after the pilgrimage and, according to Nūr Allāh Shushtarī, played some role in the conversion of Nizārī Ismāʿīlīs of the city of Tūn to Twelver Shīʿism.[28] In the *Risālat al-hudā,* Nūrbakhsh claims that his father knew that his son would be the mahdī even before his birth: "[My father] once experienced a severe attack of jaundice during which his friends feared the end of his life. Discerning their apprehension, he said to them, 'do not be sorrowful, because God will keep me (here) until Muḥammad is born to me and reaches seven years of age.' God kept His promise since this is when he went to the lasting abode."[29] Nūrbakhsh's father, Muḥammad b. ʿAbdallāh, thus died around the year 802/1399–1400, when Nūrbakhsh was approximately eight years of age.

It is likely that Nūrbakhsh's father married after arriving in Qāʾin and that his mother was of Turkish origin. Nūrbakhsh cites a tradition from Ibn ʿAbbās in defense of his mahdism stating that the mahdī's mother was to be descended from Turkish kings. He also relates from Ibn al-ʿArabī that one of the mahdī's parents was to be an Arab and the other an "ʿAjamī," which Nūrbakhsh's defines as a Persian or a Turk.[30] Since Nūrbakhsh's father was of Arab descent, his use of these traditions implies that his mother came from Turks settled in Quhistān.

The little information we have about Nūrbakhsh's natal environment reveals that his father left a significant impression on him despite his early death. He is invoked in the *Risālat al-hudā* to ratify Nūrbakhsh's

26. *RH,* I:18–19. Muḥammad Ḥusayn Āyatī calls the village Sīwajān and states that it is in the district of Sanjābrūd, near Qāʾin (*Bahāristān dar tārīkh va tarājim-i rijāl-i Qāyināt va Quhistān* [Mashhad: Intishārāt-i Dānishgāh-i Firdūsī, 1992], 17).

27. Qāżī Nūr Allāh Shushtarī, *Majālis al-muʾminīn,* ed. Ḥājj Sayyid Aḥmad, 2 vols. (Tehran: Kitābfurūshī-yi Islāmīya, 1975), 2:143 (hereafter, *MM*).

28. Ibid., 1:113.

29. *RH,* I:17.

30. Ibid., I:11.

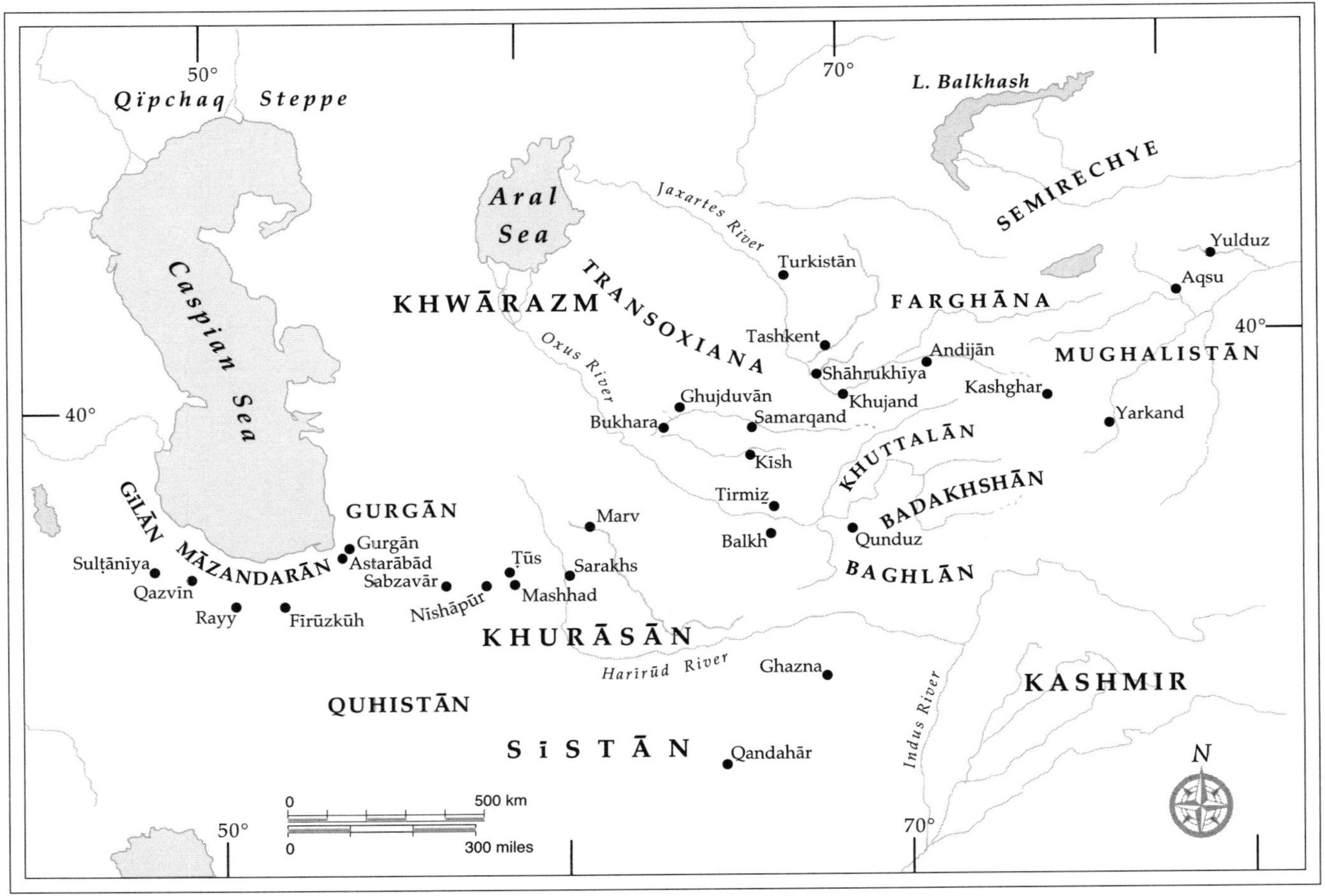

MAP 2: Iran and Central Asia in the Fifteenth Century

mahdism and to affirm the spiritual station of Nūrbakhsh's brother Aḥmad.[31] These references imply that, whether in reality or in Nūrbakhsh's wishful projection backward in time, the germ of his later proclamation was planted by his father. Quhistān, the region of Nūrbakhsh's birth, was a Nizārī Ismāʿīlī stronghold until the thirteenth century.[32] Nizārī communities of the area continued to flourish long after the destruction of Alamūt in 1256, and it may be that Nūrbakhsh and his father were influenced by the general oppositional stance of this sect. Although theoretically attractive, this line of thought is highly speculative since there is no mention of Ismāʿīlism in any of Nūrbakhsh's works, and nothing in his thought links him to the sect. Any possible influence, then, could only be of a general kind, absorbed through the overall religiocultural environment in the area.

Little definitive information is available on Nūrbakhsh's life between the age of seven and when he was twenty-four (802/1400–819/1416), though this must have been the period of his initial schooling. It is reported that he memorized the Qurʾan at the age of seven and also became adept in other religious sciences early in life.[33] His studies took him at some point to Herat, where he first contemplated joining the Kubravī Sufi path at an unspecified date. This was proposed to him by Ibrāhīm Khuttalānī, a vicegerent (*khalīfa*) of the master Khwāja Isḥāq Khuttalānī, who, impressed by his intelligence, invited him to the Kubravī khānqāh in Khuttalān.[34] Nūrbakhsh accepted the offer and moved to Khuttalān to become a disciple of Khwāja Isḥāq. Here he participated vigorously in spiritual exercises and excelled to the point that he was soon put in charge of training junior disciples.

31. Ibid., II:83.

32. For Nizārī activity in Quhistān, see Āyatī, *Bahāristān,* 76–92; Hodgson, *Order of the Assassins,* 244–46, 275–78; Daftary, *Ismāʿīlīs,* 412–14, 444.

33. *MM,* 2:143.

34. Ḥāfiẓ Ḥusayn Ibn al-Karbalāʾī, *Rawżāt al-jinān va jannāt al-janān,* ed. Jaʿfar Sulṭān al-Qurrāʾī, 2 vols. (Tehran: Bungāh-i Tarjuma va Nashr-i Kitāb, 1970), 2:248–49 (hereafter, *RJJJ*). Ibrāhīm Mubārakkhānī Khuttalānī was a major disciple of Isḥāq Khuttalānī and, before him, ʿAlī Hamadānī (Ḥaydar Badakhshī, *Manqabat al-javāhir,* MS. 1850, India Office Collection, British Library, London, 376a, 392a). He is not listed by Nūrbakhsh among his companions, which means that he either died before the proclamation of mahdīhood or chose not to back the mahdī claim.

Nūrbakhsh's report of a dream seen repeatedly during Ẕū l-Qaʿda 819 (December 21, 1416–January 19, 1417) in Khuttalān places him in Khuttalānī's company by the age of twenty-four at the latest.[35] He considered this dream a sign that he was the seal of sainthood (*khātam-i valāyat*), indicating that, by this time, he had started to entertain thoughts about his spiritual preeminence in (at least) Sufi terms. This feeling was reinforced when, some time before 826/1423, one of his associates, named Khalīl, had a dream in which light descended upon Nūrbakhsh from the sky and was dispersed to others on earth through him. When Khuttalānī heard of the dream, he gave him the title Nūrbakhsh (light giver), which became his sobriquet from that time onward.[36] Although Nūrbakhsh was prominent in Khuttalānī's circle, none of the sources portray him as the sole leading deputy to Khuttalānī at this point. His association with the Kubravīya nonetheless became permanent during this period, and he retained this as one of his primary affiliations through the rest of his life (chart 2).[37]

The Messianic Proclamation in Central Asia

The internal political environment of the khānqāh in Khuttalān had become more charged by 1423, the year Nūrbakhsh was proclaimed the mahdī. The circumstances of the proclamation led to a split within the Kubravīya, and the incident is preserved differently in literature stemming from the two opposed factions. Nūrbakhsh's rival in claiming the mantle of Isḥāq Khuttalānī was Sayyid ʿAbdallāh Barzishābādī (1387–1468), who arrived in Khuttalān on 12 Ẕū l-Ḥijja, 822 (December 30, 1419), at least three years later than Nūrbakhsh.[38] Ibn

35. *RH,* I:35. The place of this dream in Nūrbakhsh's mahdist doctrine is discussed in chapter 3.

36. *RJJJ,* 2:249. The associate Khalīl is probably Khalīl Allāh b. Rukn ad-Dīn Baghlānī, who is mentioned twice in *Risālat al-hudā* (*RH,* I:24, II:1). He also narrates traditions about ʿAlī Hamadānī in Ḥaydar Badakhshī's *Manqabat al-javāhir* (441b). In Shushtarī's account, Khuttalānī gave Nūrbakhsh the title based upon a dream seen by the master himself (*MM,* 2:144).

37. Nūrbakhsh's spiritual lineage is given in his *Risāla-yi kashf al-ḥaqāʾiq* (MS. Persan 39, Bibliothèque Nationale, Paris, 63b–64a).

38. *RJJJ,* 2:233.

CHART 2: Muḥammad Nūrbakhsh's Chain of Mystical Authority

Muḥammad Nūrbakhsh
↑
Khwāja Isḥāq Khuttalānī
↑
Sayyid ʿAlī Hamadānī
↑
Maḥmūd Mazdaqānī
↑
ʿAlāʾ ad-Dawla Simnānī
↑
Nūr ad-Dīn ʿAbd ar-Raḥmān Isfarāʾinī
↑
Aḥmad Jūrfānī
↑
Rażī ad-Dīn Lālā
↑
Najm ad-Dīn Kubrā
↑
ʿAmmār Yāsir
↑
Abū n-Najīb Suhravardī
↑
Aḥmad Ghazzālī
↑
Abū Bakr Nassāj
↑
Abū l-Qāsim Gurragānī
↑
Abū ʿUs̱mān Maghribī
↑
Abū ʿAlī Kātib
↑
ʿAlī Rūdbārī
↑
Junayd Baghdādī
↑
Sarī Saqaṭī
↑
Maʿrūf Karkhī
↑
ʿAlī b. Mūsā ar-Riżā
↑
Line of Twelver imāms from ʿAlī b. Abī Ṭālib
↑
Muḥammad

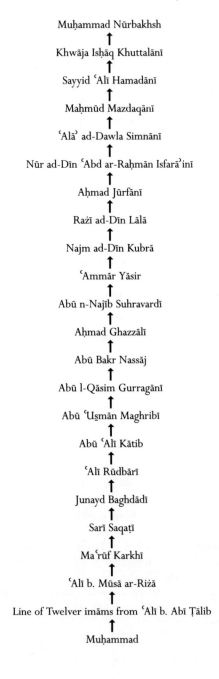

al-Karbalāʾī cites the date of Khuttalānī's license for teaching (*ijāza*) for Barzishābādī as 19 Rabīʿ II, 825 (April 12, 1422) and states that the master put Barzishābādī in charge of all students in the khānqāh soon after the latter's arrival in Khuttalān.[39]

Ibn al-Karbalāʾī's version of events leading to the Kubravī split relates that some time after Khuttalānī appointed Barzishābādī his successor, Nūrbakhsh had a dream suggesting that he was the mahdī.[40] He described this dream to Barzishābādī, who, however, rejected Nūrbakhsh's interpretation. Subsequently, Nūrbakhsh and a number of his followers approached Khuttalānī directly, and the shaykh approved Nūrbakhsh's interpretation since he could no longer himself judge such matters due to his age. When Barzishābādī got wind of this development, he went to Khuttalānī and convinced him to rescind his acquiescence. But by this time Nūrbakhsh could not be dissuaded from thinking of himself as the mahdī, and a little later, when Khuttalānī sent Barzishābādī on business to the nearby town of Munk,[41] Nūrbakhsh and his followers started an agitation in Khuttalān and Badakhshān in the name of his mahdist claim.

The Tīmūrid ruler Shāhrukh was informed in Herat that Khuttalānī had proclaimed a sayyid as mahdī, and a force was dispatched to contend with the trouble. The army defeated the insurgents after killing approximately eighty Sufis (including two sons of Khuttalānī). Both Khuttalānī and Nūrbakhsh were captured alive.[42] Some of Shāhrukh's

39. Ibid., 2:236–40, 249.

40. DeWeese states that, according to Ibn al-Karbalāʾī, Nūrbakhsh thought himself to be the mahdī based upon the same dream of Khalīl that garnered him the title Nūrbakhsh ("Eclipse of the Kubravīyah," 59). However, in the original text, Nūrbakhsh's mahdist claim resulted from a dream he himself saw (*RJJJ,* 2:249).

41. Munk had been one of the largest cities in Khuttalān since the fourth/tenth century (Guy Le Strange, *Lands of the Eastern Caliphate* [Cambridge: Cambridge University Press, 1905], 438). Beatrice Manz calls the city "Shahr-i Mung" and describes it, based upon Sharaf ad-Dīn Yazdī's *Ẓafarnāma,* as both a summer capital of local Khuttalānī amīrs and a center for the Apardï tribe during Tīmūr's time (*Rise and Rule of Tamerlane,* 159).

42. Shāhrukh's suppression of the rebellion was probably a minor matter since none of the standard political histories of the period mention this incident. Consequently, the information presented here is derived solely from authors reporting on Nūrbakhsh's life. For Shāhrukh's life and the history of his reign, see Beatrice Forbes

courtiers bore a grudge against Khuttalānī because he belonged to the family of amīrs of Khuttalān, who had resisted Tīmūr (Shāhrukh's father) in the early part of the conqueror's career. Upon their recommendation, Khuttalānī was put to death in Ramaẓān 827 (August 1424) in Balkh. Nūrbakhsh was left unharmed since he was seen as a mere pawn in the hands of his shaykh.[43] Ibn al-Karbalāʾī thus holds Nūrbakhsh responsible for the whole affair (including Khuttalānī's death) since he had insisted on his mahdist claim.

Against Ibn al-Karbalāʾī, the pro-Nūrbakhsh account of the mahdist proclamation identifies Khuttalānī as the initiator of the whole affair. Nūrbakhsh himself relates the affair through the story of his interview with Khuttalānī with which I began this chapter. After informing Nūrbakhsh of the extraordinary designation, he himself pledged formal allegiance to his student: "One night during a forty-day retreat (*arbaʿīnāt*) he beckoned the companions of the seclusion (*khalwa*) to him. They obeyed and I went with them. He then pointed to me and said to those present: 'even though this Muḥammad appears to be my disciple, in reality he is my shaykh.' That night he dressed me in the mantle (*khirqa*) of his shaykh, this being the garment in which I will travel from the transient to the everlasting world."[44] This report is corroborated by Shushtarī, who states, based on the *Tazkira-yi mazīd* of Nūrbakhsh's disciple Muḥammad Samarqandī, that Khuttalānī expressly designated Nūrbakhsh his successor. He adds that twelve companions pledged allegiance (*baʿya*) to Nūrbakhsh in the retreat mentioned above, though the number may reflect a surfacing of Shushtarī's Twelver Shīʿī bias.[45] Khuttalānī then asked all his disciples to

Manz, "Shāh Rukh b. Tīmūr," *EI²*, 9:197–98; İsmail Aka, *Mirza Şahruh ve zamanı (1405–1447)* (Ankara: Türk Tarih Kurumu Basımevi, 1994).

43. Ibn al-Karbalāʾī's date for Khuttalānī's death is almost certainly askew by a year since the agitation in Khuttalān happened in Rajab 826/June 1423 and all the evidence indicates that Khuttalānī was captured shortly thereafter. We can assume that he was executed within a year since Nūrbakhsh states that the length of his own imprisonment was only six months. Khuttalānī was most likely executed two months after the insurgency, at the end of Ramaẓān 826/Sept. 1423 (and not Ramaẓān 827/Aug. 1424).

44. *RH*, I:21.

45. *MM*, 2:143–45.

recognize Nūrbakhsh as their leader, and everyone agreed except Barzishābādī who was not present in the khānqāh at the time. He urged Nūrbakhsh to start a rebellion against unjust rulers, as expected of the mahdī, but Nūrbakhsh resisted the idea and argued that his following was not capable of confronting the armies of Shāhrukh. Khuttalānī's insistence eventually convinced Nūrbakhsh, however, and he and a small band of his followers gathered in the fort at Kūh-i Tīrī in Khuttalān on Friday, 14 Rajab, 826 (June 23, 1423) publicly to call people to his cause.[46]

When Barzishābādī heard that Khuttalānī had pledged allegiance to Nūrbakhsh, he decided to sever all ties with the master. The latter, in return, disowned Barzishābādī, proclaiming that he had left the circle (*dhahaba ʿAbdallāh*), and his statement caused Barzishābādī's faction of the Kubravīya to be named Dhahabīya/Ẕahabīya.[47] Some enemies of Khuttalānī in the company of the local Tīmūrid governor, Sulṭān Bāyazīd, informed him of the rebellion, and the governor sent a force to the fort to contend with the agitators.[48] The army captured all the rebels and sent them to Herat, preceded by a messenger bearing a report of the events for Shāhrukh.

When the Tīmūrid ruler first read the account, he ordered the execution of all culprits; however, he was seized by a severe stomachache as soon as he issued the command, and his physician, who was also a close associate, told him that his ailment was caused by his intention to execute a talented and spiritually adept sayyid. He then decided to modify his command and asked that Nūrbakhsh be brought to Herat while the remaining prisoners be put to death. The second message

46. The printed edition of *Majālis al-muʾminīn* reads only "Friday 14, 826" (*MM,* 2:145), but we know that the omitted month was Rajab since Nūrbakhsh has Naṣīr ad-Dīn Ṭūsī predict in the *Risālat al-hudā* that the mahdī would proclaim himself in the middle of Rajab, 826/1423 (*RH,* I:15).

47. The Ẕahabī tradition itself sees its name to have been derived from gold (*dhahab,* in Arabic), rather than from an act of Barzishābādī's.

48. Sulṭān Bāyazīd held the hereditary government of Khuttalān under Shāhrukh. He was given the title amīr-i tūmān (in charge of an area supposed to provide 10,000 men) and contributed troops to Shāhrukh's campaigns during 1414, 1435, and 1446 (Shiro Ando, *Timuridische Emire nach dem Muʿizz al-ansāb* [Berlin: K. Schwarz, 1992], 132).

reached the party of prisoners in Balkh, and Khuttalānī and his brother were put to death in this city, while Nūrbakhsh continued on to Herat. Here, Nūrbakhsh was first put in a well in the fort of Ikhtiyār ad-Dīn for eighteen days and then imprisoned in the city.[49] He was then taken to Shīrāz and from there to Bihbahān on the outskirts of Khūzistān,[50] where he was released on the orders of Shāhrukh's son Ibrāhīm Sulṭān (d. 828/1435).[51] As Nūrbakhsh recalled twenty years later in a letter to Shāhrukh, the total period of his captivity during this incident was six months.[52] Upon his release some time between Muḥarram and Rabīʿ I, 827 (December 1423 to March 1424),[53] Nūrbakhsh became the leader of one faction of the Kubravīya. His activity after this release represents the beginning of the Nūrbakhshīya as a suborder of the Kubravīya. His first incarceration initiated the struggle between Nūrbakhsh and Shāhrukh—a struggle that remained the dominant feature of Nūrbakhsh's life for the next twenty-five years.

The two separate accounts of the circumstances of Nūrbakhsh's mahdist proclamation present a number of historical problems that need separate consideration before proceeding further with the narrative of Nūrbakhsh's life. The main question regarding events around the mahdist proclamation is: who was responsible for the uprising—Nūrbakhsh or Khuttalānī? A majority of discussions have followed Shushtarī to state that Khuttalānī had virtually forced his young disciple into rebellion. In contrast, in a more recent study that attempts to

49. The fort (*qalʿa*) of Ikhtiyār ad-Dīn was located in the center of the city in Herat (cf. Terry Allen, *Timurid Herat* [Wiesbaden: Reichert, 1983], 12–13).

50. Bihbahān was a Tīmūrid stronghold in the area and is first mentioned in the sources in the context of Tīmūr's campaigns. It may have been first settled by Kūhgilū nomads on Tīmūr's orders (cf. Ahmed Eqtedārī, "Behbahān," *EIr,* 2:94–96; Le Strange, *Lands of the Eastern Caliphate,* 269).

51. Ibrāhīm Sulṭān was the governor of Fārs for more than twenty years, between 1414 and 1435 (cf. R. M. Savory, "Ibrāhīm b. Shāhrukh," *EI²*, 3:989, Priscilla Soucek, "Ibrāhīm Sulṭān's Military Career," in *Iran and Iranian Studies: Essays in Honor of Iraj Afshar,* ed. Kambiz Eslami [Princeton, N.J.: Zagros Press, 1998], 24–41).

52. Nūrbakhsh, *Maktūb beh Mīrzā Shāhrukh, AA:*74.

53. The earlier date is directly six months after the proclamation; the later one is six months from the death of Khuttalānī in Ramażān 826/Sept. 1423.

explain the decline of the Kubravīya in Central Asia, Devin DeWeese suggests that Ibn al-Karbalāʾī's account is more plausible.

DeWeese argues that both Kubravī hagiographical tradition and historical information about Central Asia in the second half of the fourteenth century indicate that Khuttalānī was a member of the ruling family of Khuttalān that had resisted Tīmūr's attempt to bring the area under his control.[54] Some in the court of Tīmūr's son Shāhrukh had retained the memory of this insubordination and had prompted the ruler to seek Khuttalānī's death upon learning of his involvement in an insurrection. Consequently, Khuttalānī's execution resulted from his background and not from the part he played in a minor rebellion—a rebellion whose main culprit was himself set free. DeWeese finds Ibn al-Karbalāʾī's account more believable also because it acknowledges Khuttalānī's formal complicity in the affair since he ratified (at least initially) Nūrbakhsh's claim. The author could have dispensed with this fact if his sole purpose was to discredit Nūrbakhsh. Ibn al-Karbalāʾī's alternative, Shushtarī, on the other hand, puts the responsibility of the affair on Khuttalānī, designates Barzishābādī as the schismatic, and exonerates Nūrbakhsh from all faults. The latter account is, therefore, the more tendentious of the two.

Previous scholarship has not evaluated evidence from Nūrbakhsh's own works to clarify this matter. Nūrbakhsh's articulation of his mahdist claim shows that the mahdī idea was in his mind since earlier than the events that transpired in Khuttalān during 826/1423. Nūrbakhsh thought that his father knew about his designation as mahdī before his birth. Similarly, the dream in which he saw himself as the seal of sainthood occurred in 819/1416–17, indicating that he harbored visions of grandeur in his heart at quite an early date. Even retaining some of our skepticism regarding Nūrbakhsh's veracity in reporting these events, his unflinching commitment to the messianic identity through most of his life makes it likely that he thought of himself as an

54. DeWeese, "Eclipse of the Kubravīyah," 54–60; idem, "The *Kashf al-Hudā* of Kamāl ad-Dīn Ḥusayn Khorezmī: A Fifteenth Century Sufi Commentary on the *Qaṣīdat al-Burdah* in Khorezmian Turkic" (text ed., trans., and historical intro.), Ph.D. diss., Indiana University, 1985, 61–62.

extraordinary person in at least a general sense before the mahdist proclamation.

Against this evidence, none of Nūrbakhsh's works give any indication of a militaristic attitude toward the vindication of his claim. This may in part be due to the fact that most of these works were written after the debacle in Khuttalān, which may have cured Nūrbakhsh of any desire for military adventurism. However, given the overall "academic" bent of Nūrbakhsh's personality observable in his works, it is likely that his primary attitude toward the messianic idea was that he was *destined* to be the mahdī irrespective of an active struggle.[55] He cites the thirteenth-century Sufi master Saʿd ad-Dīn Ḥamuvayī (d. 649/1252) in *Risālat al-hudā* to affirm that the mahdī "will repel his enemies by spiritual power and not through bodily armaments."[56] Although Nūrbakhsh did expect to gain temporal rule, the fulfillment of the expectation was cast into the future even as late as 859/1454–55, when the *Risālat al-hudā* was composed: "Philosophers and astrologers . . . have determined that (my) lifetime is eighty-eight solar years—meaning ninety-one lunar years. . . . Thus, if God pleases, I will acquire temporal rule when I am eighty solar years of age since, according to the Messenger of God's truthful statement, 'the length of his rule is seven, eight, or nine years.' Even if I do become a ruler earlier than this, the full extent (of my political power) will be realized after the passing of eighty solar years of my life."[57] The fatalism evident in this statement suggests that Nūrbakhsh was not the main instigator behind the actual rebellion in Khuttalān.

The assessment of the affair is complicated further by the variant reports on its magnitude. Ibn al-Karbalāʾī states that the altercation caused the death of eighty Sufis, but Shushtarī implies that Nūrbakhsh's supporters were suppressed before they could form an effective force.[58] Shushtarī's version is supported by the *Risālat al-hudā* since none of the twenty-four disciples Nūrbakhsh inherited from Khuttalānī listed here

55. Nūrbakhsh's mahdist argument is treated in detail in chapter 3.

56. *RH,* I:12.

57. Ibid., I:32.

58. *RJJJ,* 2:250; *MM,* 2:145.

are called martyrs.[59] Given Nūrbakhsh's praise for his followers and his extolling Khuttalānī for sacrificing himself for his cause, it is impossible that Nūrbakhsh would not mention even one among the supposedly eighty Sufis killed trying to support his mahdist claim. Furthermore, the relatively mild punishment Nūrbakhsh received for the rebellion indicates that the affair was militarily insignificant and that, as Ibn al-Karbalāʾī reports, Khuttalānī's death was arranged by his enemies among Tīmūrid courtiers.

To summarize, DeWeese's assessment combined with evidence from Nūrbakhsh's own works show that the Kubravīya became divided into the Nūrbakhshīya and the Ẕahabīya in 826/1423 as a result of both Nūrbakhsh's mahdist claim and the fact that Khuttalānī's leadership of the community was approaching its end due to his advanced age. Nūrbakhsh had arrived in Khuttalān by 819/1416–17 at the latest and had shortly become one of Khuttalānī's prominent deputies. Subsequently, some time after Barzishābādī joined the circle in 822/1419, the Sufis became divided into two camps with an eye toward selecting the khānqāh's next leader. This split eventually became formalized through the bifurcation of the order upon Khuttalānī's death.

It was crucial for later generations of the two factions to portray themselves as rightful heirs to Kubravī tradition. This is apparent in the sources' similarity in showing the transmission of authority from Khuttalānī. Ibn al-Karbalāʾī maintains that Khuttalānī had appointed Barzishābādī the chief administrator of the khānqāh and had said that he was like his shaykh, ʿAlī Hamadānī, to him.[60] In an exact parallel, Shushtarī states that Khuttalānī had handed over the control of the khānqāh to Nūrbakhsh, and Nūrbakhsh insists that Khuttalānī saw him in place of ʿAlī Hamadānī.[61] Moreover, both versions justify their perspective through the idea of projection, or *burūz* (discussed in detail in chapter 3), according to which the spirit of a deceased master can

59. In fact, only one (ʿAlī Ḥuwayzavī) of the eighty-two deceased companions mentioned in this work is described as a martyr (*RH*, II:6).

60. *RJJJ*, 2:236–38, 263. He also relates a dream seen by ʿAlī Balkhī in which ʿAlī Hamadānī stated that Barzishābādī's words are the same as his own. ʿAlī Balkhī is counted by Nūrbakhsh among his companions in *Risālat al-hudā* (II:27).

61. *MM*, 2:144; *RH*, I:21–22; Nūrbakhsh, *Vāridāt*, *AA*:139.

return to dwell in the body of an heir.[62] It is impossible to determine whether both factions inherited this concept of transmission of authority from Khuttalānī or one borrowed it from the other. Its use by both nevertheless underscores their common quest for legitimacy in spiritual succession.

The competition between Nūrbakhsh and Barzishābādī was brought to a head by Nūrbakhsh's suggestion that he was the mahdī.[63] Khuttalānī agreed with this claim, as stated in both sources, though he was subject to manipulation by the factions. Sulṭān Bāyazīd, the local governor who (in Shushtarī's version) quelled the rebellion, patronized Barzishābādī for four months after Isḥāq Khuttalānī's execution.[64] This association makes it probable that the governor moved against Nūrbakhsh and Khuttalānī upon Barzishābādī's instigation, and the latter resorted to this after losing to Nūrbakhsh in the struggle within the khānqāh. Barzishābādī's status as a member of a family of amīrs would have also helped him garner support from the local ruling establishment due to the connections between such families and the superstructure of Tīmūrid government.[65] The breakup of the Kubravīya thus resulted from both the rivalry between Nūrbakhsh and Barzishābādī and Khuttalānī's ineffectiveness due to his advanced age. Nūrbakhsh's mahdist claim brought the situation to a climax and provided Khuttalānī's enemies with a pretext to exact their revenge.

Nūrbakhsh's Persecution and Travel in Iranian Provinces

The Kubravī khānqāh in Khuttalān disappears from our sources after 826/1423.[66] The order's activity shifts toward other areas of Central Asia, Khurāsān, and India. Barzishābādī left for Khurāsān four months

62. The concept is explained in strikingly similar terms in Nūrbakhsh's *Risālat al-hudā* (*RH,* I:11) and Ibn al-Karbalā'ī's *Rawżāt al-jinān* (*RJJJ,* 2:263).

63. Ibn al-Karbalā'ī states literally that the rivalry between Nūrbakhsh and Barzishābādī was a competition between two adept and unique sayyids (*RJJJ,* 2:247).

64. Ibid., 2:240.

65. For Barzishābādī's family, see ibid., 2:207–13.

66. The khānqāh may have been close to the mausoleum of Sayyid ʿAlī Hamadānī in Tajikistan—a mausoleum that is still intact (cf. V. L. Voronina, "The Tomb of the Amir of Hamadan: Preliminary Report," trans. M. Raziullah Azmi, in *Shah-e-Hamadan Commemorative Volume,* ed. Agha Hussain Hamadani and Muhammad Riaz [Muzaffarabad: Institute of Kashmir Studies, 1988], 88–91).

after Khuttalānī's death and died in his ancestral village of Barzishābād, near Mashhad, in 872/1467–68.[67] His branch of the order (called, in Central Asia and Kashmir, Hamadānīya-Kubravīya, and in Iran, Ẕahabīya) continued in later centuries.[68]

For his part, Nūrbakhsh traveled westward after his release in Bihbahān, visiting Shushtar, Baṣra, and Baghdad.[69] One report states that he also went to Ḥilla to study with Ibn Fahd al-Ḥillī (d. 840/1437), a prominent Twelver Shīʿī scholar of the period.[70] Nūrbakhsh himself makes no mention of Ḥillī in his works, and the contact is reported only by Shushtarī and later sources using his work. Shushtarī's account is suspicious, given both Nūrbakhsh's habit of citing prominent scholars in support of his mahdist claim and Shushtarī's bias in favor of normative Twelver Shīʿism. Shushtarī was himself affiliated with the Nūrbakhshī order, and he may have inserted the reference to Ibn Fahd in Nūrbakhsh's biography to improve the latter's credentials among the Twelver scholarly establishment.

After a period of freedom, Nūrbakhsh was once again captured on Shāhrukh's orders during his campaign in Azerbaijan. Of Shāhrukh's three expeditions to the region, this must have occurred in 838–40/1434–36[71] since Nūrbakhsh was released a second time in 840/1436.[72]

67. *RJJJ,* 2:243.

68. For Central Asian successors of Barzishābādī, see DeWeese, "Eclipse of the Kubravīyah," 65–78. The Iranian side of Barzishābādī's spiritual descendants is traced to modern times in Richard Gramlich, *Die schiitschen Derwischorden Persiens,* 3 vols. (Wiesbaden: Franz Steiner, 1965–81), 1:4–18, and Leonard Lewisohn, "An Introduction to the History of Modern Persian Sufism, part II: A Socio-cultural Profile of Sufism, from the Dhahabī Revival to the Present Day," *BSOAS* 62, no. 1 (1999): 36–59.

69. *MM,* 2:145–46.

70. Ibid., 2:579. For Ḥillī, see Muṣṭafā Kāmil ash-Shaybī, *aṣ-Ṣila bayn at-taṣawwuf wa-t-tashayyuʿ,* 2 vols., 3d ed. (Beirut: Dār al-Andalus, 1982), 2:257–69. Āyatī cites Shushtarī to say that Nūrbakhsh had studied with Ibn Fahd before his induction into the Kubravīya (*Bahāristān,* 187). This is certainly a mistake since Shushtarī's original report in *Majālis al-muʾminīn* places his contact with Ibn Fahd at a much later date.

71. According to *Maṭlaʿ-i saʿdayn,* Shāhrukh set out from Herat on 2 Rabīʿ II, 838/5 Nov. 1434, and, after wintering at Rayy, marched on Tabriz on 1 Muḥarram 839/27 July 1435. He left Tabriz for Herat after the campaign on 2 Rabīʿ II, 840/14 Oct. 1436 (cf. R. Savory, "The Struggle for Supremacy in Persia after the death of Tīmūr," *Der Islam* 40 [1964]: 41).

72. *MM,* 2:146.

Nūrbakhsh spent the interval between the two imprisonments (827/1424–ca. 840/1436) traveling first in Iraq and then in Kurdistān, Luristān (Bakhtiyārī territory), and Gīlān. Although it is impossible to determine the length of his stay in each region, he relates a dream in *Risālat al-hudā* experienced by his companion Muḥammad b. ʿAlī b. Bahrām Qāʾinī in Irbil (Kurdistān) as early as 827/1424.[73] Assuming Nūrbakhsh's presence in Irbil at this time, he must have made his way to Kurdistān after a very brief period in Iraq.

According to Shushtarī, Nūrbakhsh experienced the greatest success of his career as a mahdī during his stay in "Kurdistān-i Faylī va Bakhtiyārī," implying lands of the Lur tribes. This area was divided into Great Lur (Lur-i Buzurg) and Little Lur (Lur-i Kūchik) during the Mongol period, but under the Ṣafavids the two parts were respectively renamed Kūh-Gīlū and Bakhtiyārī, and Luristān-i Faylī, or simply Luristān.[74] Bakhtiyārī and Faylī are subcategories within the designation Lur so that Shushtarī's inclusion of Kurdistān in his report is either a scribal error or a loss of distinction between the Kurds and the Lur.

Nūrbakhsh was accepted as the mahdī by a significant part of the local population, and Shushtarī reports that they struck coins and read the Friday sermon (*khuṭba*) in his name for a while. A majority of this region's population today belongs to the Ahl-i Ḥaqq sect, which considers Nūrbakhsh an important figure in its mythical early history. Ahl-i Ḥaqq sources do not preserve historical details about Nūrbakhsh, but in the oral tradition he is seen as an incarnation of either Bābā Yādigār, a late-sixteenth-century pīr buried in Ban Zarda near Zuhāb,[75] or Shāh Ibrāhīm, a close companion of Sulṭān Ṣaḥāk, the sect's alleged founder.[76]

73. *RH,* I:51.

74. For the area and its inhabitants, see E. Ehlers, "Bakhtiārī Mountains," *EIr,* 1:551–53, and the following *Encyclopaedia of Islam* articles by Vladimir Minorsky, "Kurds, Kurdistān," "Lur," "Lur-i Buzurg," "Lur-i Kūchik," "Luristān" (*EI²*, 5:449–64, 822–32).

75. Vladimir Minorsky, "Notes sur la secte des Ahlé Haqq," *RMM* 40–41 (1920): 35–36.

76. Ḥājj Niʿmat Allāh Mujrim Mokri, *Shāh-nama-ye ḥaqīqat: Le Livre des rois de vérité,* ed. Mohammad Mokri (Tehran: Departement d'Iranologie de l'Institut Franco-Iranien, 1966) 1:521–23, 2:533. For general descriptions of the Ahl-i Ḥaqq

Nūrbakhsh probably played some role in the religious history of this area during the fifteenth century, though his personality did not have a long-lasting impact. His presence in Luristān can be inferred also from the fact that a number of his companions were from places in this region.[77] However, neither Nūrbakhsh's own works nor any other external source can corroborate Shushtarī's statement that he enjoyed privileges of rulership at any point in his career.

Shushtarī relates that, while in Azerbaijan, Shāhrukh heard of Nūrbakhsh's presence in Kurdistān and wrote to local rulers to capture him and his followers and to send them to the imperial camp. The manhunt was successful, and Nūrbakhsh received a severe admonition from Shāhrukh when he appeared in the ruler's court. Interpreting this show of anger as a precursor to execution, Nūrbakhsh escaped from the camp, alone, and spent three nights in snow-covered mountains without any provisions. He was eventually captured again, by the governor of Khalkhāl, who sent him back to Shāhrukh. He now received the punishment of fifty-three days in a well and, at the end of this period, he was taken to Herat and was ordered to climb the pulpit (*minbar*) of the main mosque during Friday prayer and disavow his caliphal claim. He ascended the pulpit in fetters and pronounced an ambiguous disclaimer: "They relate certain things from this wretch, which, whether we have said them or not, 'O lord, we have wronged ourselves; if You do not forgive us and have mercy upon us, we will certainly be among the losers' (Qurʾan 7:23)."[78] He said the Fātiḥa after this statement, descended the *minbar,* and was set free with instructions to teach only the conventional sciences (*ʿulūm-i rasmī*) and not to aggrandize himself or wear a black turban.

---

sect, see V. Minorsky, "Ahl-i Ḥaḳḳ," *EI*², 1:262; H. Halm, "Ahl-e Ḥaqq," *EIr,* 1:635–36; Bashir, "Between Mysticism and Messianism," 60–73; Ziba Mir-Hosseini, "Faith, Ritual and Culture Among the Ahl-e Haqq," in *Kurdish Culture and Identity,* ed. Philip Kreyenbroek and Christine Allison (London: Zed Books, 1996); and C. J. Edmonds, "The Beliefs and Practices of Ahl-i Ḥaqq of Iraq," *Iran* 7 (1969): 89–106.

77. The regional composition of Nūrbakhsh's following is discussed later in this chapter.

78. *MM,* 2:146.

The black turban (or black attire generally) is connected historically to revolutionary activity as far back as the ʿAbbāsid Revolution. While Nūrbakhsh's own works do not mention the issue, the significance of wearing black is discussed by both his predecessors and followers in the Kubravī line. A small treatise attributed to ʿAlī Hamadānī states that darkness as the precursor of light is unavoidable. He contends that while the color white is better for common people, the spiritually adept prefer black since it signifies the ineffable and unknowable quality of God's essence. Muḥammad wore black at the battle of Uḥud and often during prayers because of this connection, and Sufis do the same in his emulation.[79] Following his shaykh, Hamadānī's disciple Isḥāq Khuttalānī also wore a black turban, which in a recorded incident offended Tīmūr.[80]

Nūrbakhsh relates a dream in *Risālat al-hudā* in which Muḥammad Aẕkānī, a disciple of the prominent Kubravī shaykh ʿAlāʾ ad-Dawla Simnānī, saw the mahdī approaching from the east dressed completely in black.[81] Closest to Nūrbakhsh himself, his disciple ʿAlī Kiyā explains that the color black is appropriate for Sufis based on prophetic traditions and the fact that it indicates that the person has seen black light, the penultimate station of mystical perfection.[82] Nūrbakhsh combined the Sufi significance of wearing black with the Shīʿī convention that a black turban signified descent from Muḥammad. Although Shāhrukh's order was intended to neutralize its political potential, the prohibition on the black turban stripped Nūrbakhsh of both his genealogical distinction as a sayyid and the outward sign of his status in the Kubravī order.[83]

79. The work is entitled *Risāla fī sawād al-layl wa-libs al-aswad* and is described in the catalog of the Institute of Oriental Studies in Tashkent (cf. A. A. Semenov, *Sobranie vostochnykh rukopisei Akademii nauk Uzbekskoi SSR,* vol. 3 [Tashkent: Izd-vo Akademii nauk UzSSR, 1955], 244). I am grateful to Amy Adams for translating the description from Russian.

80. *RJJJ,* 2:244.

81. *RH,* I:20. Aẕkānī (or Adkānī) died at the age of eighty in 778/1376 (cf. ʿAbd ar-Raḥmān Jāmī, *Nafaḥāt al-uns,* ed. Maḥmūd ʿĀbidī [Tehran: Intishārāt-i Iṭṭilāʿāt, 1997], 446).

82. ʿAlī Kiyā, *Risāla-yi nūrīya, AA:*18–20. For this companion, see below. The place of black light in Nūrbakhsh's mystical worldview is discussed in chapter 4.

83. Shushtarī also relates a conversation between Ismāʿīl I and Nūrbakhsh's student Shams ad-Dīn Lāhījī, where the latter states that he wore black to signify

Nūrbakhsh's reception in Herat at the time of his public disavowal is described also in the hostile account of ʿAbd al-Vāsiʿ Niẓāmī Bākharzī (d. 903/1497–8). He states that Nūrbakhsh was presented to the prominent scholar Shaykh Bahāʾ ad-Dīn ʿUmar (d. 857/1453), who censured him for choosing the way of error and greed despite both knowledge (*ʿilm*) and ancestry (*siyādat*).[84] Nūrbakhsh then repented of his acts and addressed the public from the *minbar:* "When we earlier called ourselves the promised mahdī based upon certain methods of dream interpretation (*taʿbīr*), we intended only that we can provide guidance (*hidāya*) on the path of acquiring high desires and stations (*maṭālib-i ʿalīya va marātib-i sunnīya*). Guidance and support are from God, indeed he is the praiseworthy and the glorious." Nūrbakhsh was released after this disavowal, but he had scarcely reached the environs of Simnān when he reverted to this "meaningless claim."[85]

Both Bākharzī and Shushtarī purport to relay the account of Nūrbakhsh's activities in Herat from first-hand sources. Bākharzī represents the viewpoint of the prestigious scholars (*ʿulamāʾ*) of Herat, while Shushtarī's narrative of Nūrbakhsh's life until this point comes from the *Tazkira-yi mazīd* of Muḥammad Samarqandī. The disavowal in both cases is somewhat ambiguous, though it is certainly more definite in Bākharzī's version. Since Nūrbakhsh was released after the visit to the mosque, Bākharzī's report on his statement from the *minbar* is probably closer to the truth. However, given Bākharzī's glorification of the scholars (his work is a laudatory account of the life of ʿAbd ar-Raḥmān Jāmī), it is likely that he or his sources manipulated the facts by inserting Bahāʾ ad-Dīn ʿUmar into the story as the intermediary who made Nūrbakhsh see reason. The choice of Bahāʾ ad-Dīn is in itself significant since he also claimed Kubravī spiritual lineage going back to ʿAlāʾ ad-Dawla Simnānī, which was meant to be juxtaposed against Nūrbakhsh's claims to the Kubravī mantle.[86] On the other side,

---

perpetual mourning for Ḥusayn's death (*MM,* 2:152). Lāhījī's works do not show him as a devoted Shīʿī. This report reflects Shushtarī's excessive Twelver Shīʿī zeal.

84. *MJ,* 192.

85. Ibid.

86. Ibid., 194.

Nūrbakhsh probably had to make a stronger statement than given by Shushtarī to attain freedom.

Whatever the exact nature of the disavowal, it is certain that Nūrbakhsh was set free in Herat after an imprisonment that lasted a total of four months.[87] He reverted to the claim very soon thereafter, however, since, according to Shushtarī, Shāhrukh had him captured once again on 15 Ramażān, 840 (23 March, 1437). He was taken to Tabriz and the area's governor was ordered to expel him into Anatolia (Rūm). The period of freedom was, then, only about four months, but he claimed in a letter to Herat that he had encountered a hundred thousand devotees desirous of meeting him during this time. He was released a third time after two months,[88] and contrary to instructions he now first went to Shirvān and then traveled eastward to Gīlān.[89] The decade-long stay in Gīlān (1437–47) was the first period of tranquility in his life since the declaration of the messianic mission.

Nūrbakhsh's continuing contact with the religious circle of Herat after his two imprisonments in the city is discernible also from a story about a meeting between the influential Naqshbandī shaykh Khwāja Aḥrār (d. 1490) and a disciple of Isḥāq Khuttalānī named Sayyid Zayn

87. The duration of the imprisonment is cited in Nūrbakhsh's letter to Shāhrukh (Nūrbakhsh, *Maktūb beh Mīrzā Shāhrukh, AA*:75).

88. Ibid.

89. None of Nūrbakhsh's authentic works mention a stay in Shirvān. A work entitled *ash-Shajara al-wafīya fī dhikr al-mashāyikh aṣ-ṣūfīya* usually attributed to Nūrbakhsh contains a number of "Shirvānīs," some of whom the author claims to have met personally in Shamākhī (Muḥammad Taqī Dānishpazhūh, "*Silsilat al-awliyā'*-yi Nūrbakhsh-i Quhistānī," in *Mélanges offerts à Henry Corbin,* ed. Seyyed Hossein Nasr [Tehran: McGill University Institute of Islamic Studies, Tehran Branch, 1977], 53, 58). Although this work is stylistically very similar to *Risālat al-hudā,* it is unlikely that the whole of it was composed by Nūrbakhsh on chronological grounds. The author mentions Sayyid Yaḥyā Bākū'ī, who is described as dead at the time of writing (58). This Khalvatī shaykh died in 869/1464, the year Nūrbakhsh himself passed away, which necessitates the very unlikely possibility that Nūrbakhsh composed the work just before his own death. The stylistic similarity may imply that the work was begun under Nūrbakhsh's guidance but was completed after his death. For Yaḥyā Bākū'ī, see Nathalie Clayer, *Mystiques, état, et société: Les Halvetis dans l'aire balkanique de la fin du XVe siècle à nos jours* (Leiden: E. J. Brill, 1994), 5–7.

al-ʿĀbidīn. ʿAbd al-Avval Nīshāpūrī, Aḥrār's hagiographer and son-in-law, states that Aḥrār asked Sayyid Zayn al-ʿĀbidīn whether Sayyid Muḥammad Qāʾinī was truly the mahdī. He replied that this was a disputed matter in Khuttalānī's circle and that Nūrbakhsh had written him a letter after conquering a village near Rayy in which he had called himself a guide toward God (*al-hādī ilā'llāh*) and modified his name to Muḥammad b. ʿAbdallāh to accord with the messianic tradition. Based on this encounter, Khwāja Aḥrār later told his disciples that Nūrbakhsh had been imprisoned four times during the reign of Shāhrukh, but had consistently reverted to his false claims.[90] Whatever the full truth of Nūrbakhsh's letter, these statements by the hagiographer and Khwāja Aḥrār reflect the presence of a continuing discussion about Nūrbakhsh at the Tīmūrid capital throughout the fifteenth century.

Nūrbakhsh's last contact with Shāhrukh came in the form of a letter written around 846/1442–43 in which Nūrbakhsh claimed that the ruler had persecuted him for nearly twenty years.[91] Now he invited Shāhrukh to repent from his past behavior and refrain from the sin of harming Muḥammad's progeny, among whom he himself claimed a particularly high station as the mahdī.[92] He stated that the end of Shāhrukh's reign and the time of the rule of sayyids, were both imminent. The ruler was accused of thinking to arrest Nūrbakhsh yet again, but he considered this impossible since a dream seen by Shihāb ad-Dīn

90. ʿAbd al-Avval Nīshāpūrī, *Majālis-i ʿUbayd Allāh Aḥrār,* MS India Office DP 8090, British Library, 181b; MS 7, Asiatic Society of Bengal, Calcutta, 158b–159a. For the general contents of this work (known also as *Masmūʿāt*), see Jo-Ann Gross, "Authority and Miraculous Behavior: Reflections on Karāmāt Stories of Khwāja ʿUbaydullāh Aḥrār," in *The Heritage of Sufism,* vol. 2, ed. Leonard Lewisohn (Oxford, U.K.: One World, 1999), 159–71. An uncritical edition of this work has been published with incorrect attribution: Qāżī Muḥammad Zāhid, *Masmūʿāt* (Istanbul: İhlâs Vakfı Yayındır, 1996), 142–43.

91. Nūrbakhsh, *Maktūb beh Mīrzā Shāhrukh, AA:*74.

92. Based on one of the three manuscripts used to prepare his edition, Ṣadaqiyānlū suggests that Nūrbakhsh referred to himself as the "deputy of the Mahdī (*nāʾib-i imām-i ākhir-i zamān va mahdī-yi mawʿūd*)," rather than the mahdī (*AA:*75). This is clearly an adjustment of the truth given overwhelming evidence to the contrary.

ʿUmar in Herat had indicated that the mahdī would be imprisoned only three times.[93]

The confident tone of Nūrbakhsh's letter to Shāhrukh indicates that he felt quite safe in Gīlān. However, as Nūrbakhsh himself indicates, the letter may have been written upon receiving the news of a new effort by Shāhrukh to capture and silence the mahdī. It is significant that the letter begins by reminding the ruler of his duty to protect sayyids, not harm them; it is precisely this distinction that likely saved Nūrbakhsh from execution during his three previous captures by Tīmūrid forces. Nūrbakhsh's intuition that Shāhrukh would not make a serious effort to hunt him down was proven correct in this instance, and there is no evidence of contact between Nūrbakhsh and Tīmūrid forces between the time the letter was written and Shāhrukh's death in 850/1447. Nūrbakhsh was in a relatively remote area during the period, and Shāhrukh was busy quelling rebellions by other Tīmūrid pretenders to the throne. Shāhrukh also suffered a severe illness during 849/1445–46, which may have prompted Nūrbakhsh to write such a bold admonition.[94]

Nūrbakhsh's personal sense that Shāhrukh was his archenemy, the Dajjāl (Islamic antichrist)[95] to his mahdī, is evident from a report about the manner in which the news of Shāhrukh's death was received in his circle. Muḥammad ʿAlī Kashmīrī's *Tuḥfat al-aḥbāb* relates that Muḥammad Ghaybī, a principal disciple of Nūrbakhsh during the last phase of the mahdī's life, initially ingratiated himself to the master by being the first person to bring him the news of Shāhrukh's death.[96] Ghaybī was originally from the region of Rayy, but he decided to travel to Gīlān to meet Nūrbakhsh after hearing about his spiritual qualities. When he

93. Shihāb ad-Dīn ʿUmar is probably Shihāb ad-Dīn Jūrānī, who is listed as one of the principal deceased companions in *Risālat al-hudā* (*RH,* II:79). He is mentioned again in a poem (*Dīvān,* 20), and the *Risāla-yi nūrīya* was written as a response to his questions (*AA:*148).

94. Savory, "Struggle for Supremacy in Persia," 43.

95. For summary information about this figure, see A. Abel, "Dadjdjāl," *EI²*, 2:76–77.

96. Kashmīrī, *Tuḥfat al-aḥbāb,* 78–85 [hereafter, *TA*]. The author of this crucial source for Nūrbakhshī history is discussed in detail in chapter 6.

reached the village of Kūra,[97] Nūrbakhsh's residence at the time, he grew despondent of the possibility of receiving direct instruction from the master because of the throngs that surrounded him every day. One of his acquaintances also present there at the time then told him that Nūrbakhsh had a standing offer that whoever brought him the news of Shāhrukh's death would immediately receive free and unlimited access to him.

Ghaybī then decided that it would be best to travel to Balkh, where Shāhrukh was camped at the time, and shadow the ruler's movements until his death, when he could quickly return to Nūrbakhsh and be the first to bring the news. Present in Shāhrukh's garrison when the messenger bringing Nūrbakhsh's letter to Shāhrukh arrived at the court, he was greatly pleased to see Nūrbakhsh's prediction that Shāhrukh was about to die since that would fulfill his plan. Shāhrukh died within a year of receiving the letter, and Ghaybī immediately departed for Shaft, in Gīlān, where Nūrbakhsh was now stationed.[98] As Ghaybī approached Shaft, Nūrbakhsh, who already knew the news through mystical apprehension, was informed of the arrival of a rider. He smiled, knowing the news, but said that it was best to see what Ghaybī had to say since he had gone to extraordinary trouble for it. Ghaybī arrived, told the news, and then went into a trance because of the effect of Nūrbakhsh's gaze on him. He and others then started dancing, in a state combining mystical experience with euphoria over the news of the ruler's death. Nūrbakhsh kept his promise, making Ghaybī his disciple and giving him immediate authority to teach on his behalf. Shāhrukh's death ended the second period of Nūrbakhsh's life; its dominant features had been persecution at the hands of the Tīmūrid ruler and travel through Khurāsān, Luristān, Kurdistān, Azerbaijan, Shirvān, and Gīlān.

97. Ibid., 78.

98. Ibid., 83–85. For the location of Shaft (a part of the modern Fuman *shahristān*), see Marcel Bazin, et. al., *Gilan et Azarbayjan oriental: cartes et documents ethnographiques* (Paris: Editions Recherche sur les civilisations, 1982), carte 2.

Nūrbakhsh's Life as a Sufi Shaykh in Gīlān and Suliqān

Nūrbakhsh spent the last period of his life in apparent tranquility, free from persecution. This phase began with a decade in Gīlān, followed by the establishment of a permanent Nūrbakhshī community in the village of Suliqān, near Rayy.[99] He left Gīlān soon after Shāhrukh's death, and once established in Suliqān he busied himself with training deputies and had some (now amicable) interaction with political authorities.

After Shāhrukh, Nūrbakhsh came into contact, via writing, with two Tīmūrid rulers. His letter to Shāhrukh's grandson ʿAlāʾ ad-Dawla is extant, and since it is addressed with royal titles, it was probably written during his brief accession to the throne at Herat between Ẕū l-Ḥijja 850/March 1447 and early 852/spring 1448.[100] For the second contact, his communication with Mīrzā Abū l-Qāsim Bābur (r. 852–61/1449–57) can be inferred from the ruler's reply bearing the imperial seal.[101] The letter to ʿAlāʾ ad-Dawla is quite different from the earlier missive to Shāhrukh: in it, without mentioning his personal claims, Nūrbakhsh encourages ʿAlāʾ ad-Dawla to seek the company of the spiritually adept.[102] Nūrbakhsh's tone shows that he desired associations with temporal authorities in a manner typical for the relationship between a ruler and a Sufi shaykh. Abū l-Qāsim Bābur's reply similarly does not mention the mahdist claim; it praises Nūrbakhsh for his spiritual attainments among sayyids and hopes for a meeting between the two.

Besides the Tīmūrids, Nūrbakhsh's extant correspondence with ruling circles includes a reply to the letter of a vizier and two letters to

99. *MM,* 2:147. This information is related by Shushtarī as heard from (unnamed) sources other than Muḥammad Samarqandī. The village is sometimes called Sulighān as well. It is described as a fertile inhabitation sixteen kilometers north on the road between Tehran and Qazvīn (*Farhang-i jughrāfiyā-yi Īrān,* 10 vols. [Tehran: Intishārāt-i Dāyira-yi Jughrāfiyā, 1949], 1:118).

100. J. Woods, "ʿAlāʾ al-Dawla, Rokn-al-Dīn Mīrzā b. Bāysonqor b. Shāhrokh," *EIr,* 1:771.

101. ʿAbd al-Ḥusayn Navāʾī, ed., *Asnād va makātibāt-i tārīkhī-yi Īrān* (Tehran: Bungāh-i Tarjuma va Nashr-i Kitāb, 1962), 297–98. Bābur's reply forms a part of the collection of Ḥaydar Īvāghlī (Evoğlu) described in Navāʾī's introduction (23).

102. Nūrbakhsh, *Maktūb beh ʿAlāʾ ad-Dawla, AA:*78–82. Although this letter is not confrontational in the same way as the one to Shāhrukh, it does predict an upcoming age of the rule of the spiritually adept.

Amīr ʿAlāʾ ad-Dīn ʿAlī Kiyā-yi Gīlānī. The vizier cannot be identified from the letter's contents, and the second Amīr could be one of a number of individuals named "ʿAlī Kiyā" from the sayyid family of Gīlān.[103] The contrast between his relationship with Shāhrukh and the other rulers implies that the former's hostility toward Nūrbakhsh did not mean that the ruling establishment uniformly saw Nūrbakhsh as a political threat throughout the mahdī's life. Since Nūrbakhsh was only punished, not executed, Shāhrukh's persecution of Nūrbakhsh may have been a part of his effort to bolster the specifically "Islamic" aspects of his political legitimacy. The reestablishment of a "true Islam" after Mongol rule over Islamic populations was a dominant religiopolitical theme during the fourteenth and fifteenth centuries. Shāhrukh consciously tried to disassociate himself from Tīmūr's legacy by discontinuing the use of Mongol royal titles and eliminating the practice of maintaining a Chingīzid puppet as the nominal monarch of the empire.[104] He therefore saw himself as a patron of true religion, which made religious pretenders such as Nūrbakhsh ideologically intolerable.[105]

103. ʿAlāʾ ad-Dīn and his daughter are mentioned in the *Risālat al-hudā* (*RH,* II:77–78). His connection to the ruling family is evident only through the appellation "Kiyā," which was the customary title for rulers in Gīlān. Nūrbakhsh is not mentioned in any of the local histories of Gīlān of the period, suggesting that either the relationship was informal or this ʿAlī Kiyā was a minor relation to the rulers (cf. Sayyid Ẓahīr ad-Dīn Marʿashī, *Tārīkh-i Ṭabaristān va Rūyān va Māzandarān,* ed. ʿAbbās Shāyān [Tehran: Chāpkhāna-yi Firdūsī, 1955], and *Tārīkh-i Gīlān va Daylamistān,* ed. Minūchihr Sutūda [Tehran: Muʾassasa-yi Iṭṭilāʿāt, 1985]; Goto, "Aufstieg zweier Sayyid-Familien am Kaspischen Meer," 63–65).

104. H. R. Roemer, "The Successors of Tīmur," in *CHIr,* 6:104–5. For Tīmūr's attitude to political legitimacy, see Manz, *Rise and Rule of Tamerlane,* 14–18. This comment on Shāhrukh's possible motivations is not to suggest that he disassociated himself completely from his father's ideology; however, there does seem to be a shift in emphasis in dynastic legitimacy, motivated in part by the pressure of the religious classes on state practices as can be observed in the career and work of the scholar Jalāl ad-Dīn Muḥammad Qā'inī (cf. Maria Eva Subtelny and Anas B. Khalidov, "The Curriculum of Islamic Higher Learning in Timurid Iran in the Light of the Sunni Revival under Shāh-Rukh," *JAOS* 115, no. 2 [1995]: 210–36; Shiro Ando, "The *Shaykh al-Islām* as a Tīmūrid Office: A Preliminary Study," *Islamic Studies* 33, nos. 2–3 [1994]: 266–70).

105. It is also possible that Shāhrukh's reaction to the rebellion in Khuttalān was based upon the area's Central Asian location. The Tīmūrid ruling establishment had

The last period of Nūrbakhsh's life presents valuable information about his role as a teacher. Shams ad-Dīn Muḥammad b. Yaḥyā Lāhījī (d. 1506–7), later recognized as Nūrbakhsh's most talented disciple, recalls meeting the master for the first time in Gīlān in Rajab 849/ October 1445. In his *masnavī* entitled *Asrār ash-shuhūd,* Lāhījī relates that he decided to seek Nūrbakhsh's company after hearing from someone that he was in the area.[106] He left Lāhījān one morning without telling family and friends about his plans lest they try to dissuade him. After traveling alone for one or two days, he was joined by two others also journeying to Nūrbakhsh's camp. Nūrbakhsh met them the day after they reached their destination and told them very kindly of the hardships of their prospective path. Lāhījī then agreed to renounce all worldly concerns, and he served Nūrbakhsh as a disciple for the next sixteen years.[107]

Against Lāhījī's straightforward report, two other sources provide us with more mythical accounts of Nūrbakhsh's activities during his stay in Gīlān. The first is the story of the conversion of Muḥammad Samarqandī to the cause; the second represents the viewpoint of Nūrbakhsh's opponents. The *Tuḥfat al-aḥbāb* relates that Muḥammad Samarqandī was an important religious scholar in Samarqand when he heard of a Sayyid Muḥammad Qāʾinī, who had declared himself the mahdī and had become famous in Khurāsān and Iraq.[108] He and one of his companions decided to unmask the pretensions of this wayward

---

been apprehensive about the proliferation of radical Sufi ideas among the recently Islamized Turks from the time of the conqueror himself. The most notable case for this was the expulsion of Shāh Niʿmat Allāh Valī Kirmānī (d. 834/1431) from Central Asia on Tīmūr's orders (cf. introduction to Jean Aubin, ed., *Matériaux pour la biographie de Shah Niʿmatullah Wali Kermani* [Tehran: Département d'Iranologie de l'Institut Franco-Iranien, 1956], 13–14).

106. Shams ad-Dīn Muḥammad Asīrī Lāhījī, *Asrār ash-shuhūd,* ed. ʿAlī Āl-i Dāvūd (Tehran: Mūʾassasa-yi Muṭaliʿāt va Taḥqīqāt-i Farhangī, 1989), 85–87. The year 849/1445 is mentioned also in Lāhījī's *Mafātīḥ al-iʿjāz fī sharḥ Gulshan-i rāz,* ed. Muḥammad Rižā Bārzgar Khalīqī and ʿIffat Karbāsī (Tehran: Zavvār, 1992), 67.

107. Lāhījī, *Mafātīḥ al-iʿjāz,* 586. He quotes the last of his three *ijāzas* from Nūrbakhsh here.

108. *TA,* 12–14.

man and traveled to Gīlān, where they asked the local people whether Nūrbakhsh was averse to any particular religious group. They told them that he is friendly to everyone except Qalandars and Ḥaydarīs, whom he considers hopeless.[109] They then put the special hat of the Ḥaydarīs on their heads and dressed themselves as Qalandars to go to Nūrbakhsh's abode. Nūrbakhsh received them well at his place and began talking to them normally since he was aware that they were not really Qalandars. His true powers then revealed themselves when he asked Samarqandī, instead of the usual prayer leader, to lead the prayer and made their hearts open up during the prayer. They then completely abandoned their former lives to become his devotees and remained so to the end of their days, despite the criticism of their former associates.

Against the positive accounts by both Lāhījī and Kashmīrī, Bākharzī, in his *Maqāmāt-i Jāmī,* portrays Nūrbakhsh as a charlatan who tried to swindle the people of Gīlān into believing in his mahdist claim. He relates that Nūrbakhsh once attempted to impress people by claiming that he could make the sun (*kawkab-i munīr*) rise from the west.[110] He and his companions devised a round contraption made of glass or crystal (*ābgīna*), with a lamp inside. They first attached a rope to it and covered it and then slowly took off the cover while raising it behind the branches of a tree. The overall effect of the trick was to make the contraption look like the moon rising in the sky. The deception ended in failure because the headman (*dārūgha*) of the area unmasked them and caused Nūrbakhsh great humiliation.[111]

This story is a satirical fabrication: it confuses the sun and the moon, and it is difficult to believe that Nūrbakhsh would stoop to such petty falsification. However, Nūrbakhsh's alleged actions here are similar in

109. Qalandars and Ḥaydarīs were antinomian Sufi groups who deliberately defied social conventions such as wearing clothing and performing religious obligations as a sign of their total commitment to being religious (cf. Ahmet Karamustafa, *God's Unruly Friends* [Salt Lake City: University of Utah Press, 1994]). For more details about Samarqandī's possible connection to antinomian Sufi groups, see below.

110. The sun rising in the west was a popularly accepted omen for the advent of the mahdī.

111. *MJ,* 193.

spirit to his literary efforts to prove his mahdīhood. In the *Risālat al-hudā,* for example, he is keen to demonstrate that events traditionally expected to occur during the mahdī's career have happened in his life. Bākharzī's mockery indicates that Nūrbakhsh's arguments were known to the scholarly circles in Herat by the time the story was produced.

Nūrbakhsh moved to Suliqān, a village near Rayy, soon after Shāh-rukh's death, and there he spent the last nineteen years of his life (850/1447–869/1464). The first permanent Nūrbakhshī community was established at this time, when Nūrbakhsh busied himself with oral and written instruction of his disciples. We can surmise that, among other works, the *Risālat al-hudā,* which articulates his mahdist claim, was written during this period since the last year mentioned in it is 859/1454–55, when his son Qāsim Fayżbakhsh began instructing students.[112]

The Regional Composition of Nūrbakhsh's Following

It is instructive at this point to assess the general character of Nūrbakhsh's following during his lifetime. Nūrbakhsh's *mas̱navī* entitled *Ṣaḥīfat al-awliyāʾ* and the second part of *Risālat al-hudā* provide valuable information about his companions. Other sources for the Nūrbakhshīya give no details about the cross-section of the group, and very few names listed by Nūrbakhsh can be traced outside of his own description. Nūrbakhsh's own works are, therefore, our only sources for the character of the movement during the mahdī's lifetime.

Nūrbakhsh's followers with names indicating geographical locations (*nisba*) can be divided into five groups from particular regions in Central Asia and Iran (see map 1). His works mention twenty-two companions from Transoxiana, thirteen of whom were deceased at the time of writing the *Risālat al-hudā.*[113] Most of these followers joined the Kubravī path in the khānqāh at Khuttalān, and, as Nūrbakhsh indicates in some of his entries, they accepted Nūrbakhsh as their guide after the death of Isḥāq Khuttalānī. Nūrbakhsh never returned to that area after

112. *RH,* II:91.

113. The particular place-names in Transoxiana are Badakhshān, Khuttalān, Ürgench, Tirmiz̤, Farghāna, Samarqand, Kishm, and Rustābāzār.

his first arrest in 1423, so the Transoxianan group can be presumed to have formed Nūrbakhsh's entourage during the first phase of his life.

In parallel with his Central Asian "spiritual" heritage, Nūrbakhsh's lifelong connection to his familial roots in Quhistān is reflected in a group of thirteen names from that area. These include a number of Nūrbakhsh's relatives going back particularly to the cities of Qāʾin and Tūn. The third group reflects Nūrbakhsh's activity in Luristān and Kurdistān; it includes seventeen names linked to the provinces of Jibāl and Azerbaijan,[114] three Kurds, and four Jūrānīs.[115] Similarly, his extended stay in Gīlān is reflected in the fourth group (thirty-five names) related to localities along the southern and southwestern shores of the Caspian Sea.[116] The last group, smaller than the rest, includes five disciples from Rayy, two from Qazvīn, and a solitary "Suliqānī." Aside from these groups, Nūrbakhsh's company included individuals from most other regions in present-day Iran (Khurāsān, Fārs, Khūzistān), Baghdad, Bahrain, Anatolia, Ghazna, Delhi, and Multan.

Nūrbakhsh's description of his following also shows some connections to antinomian Sufi groups active in the fifteenth-century Islamic East. Nūrbakhsh's own description of Muḥammad Samarqandī, mentioned above in the context of Nūrbakhsh's role as a shaykh in Gīlān, states that he was an author and poet who had traveled in Syria, Egypt, and Arabia and had eventually gone to Anatolia because he was one of the Abdāls.[117] The story, given by Kahsmīrī in *Tuḥfat al-aḥbāb,* that Samarqandī had only *pretended* to be an antinomian Sufi to test

114. Abhar, Bidlīs, Khalkhāl, ʿIrāq-i ʿAjam, Karahrūd, Kalūr, Khurramābād, Sulṭānīya, Burūjird, Irbil, and Tabriz.

115. Gūrān (Arabicized to Jūrān) is one of the major Kurdish tribes (cf. Vladimir Minorsky, "Kurds" in *EI²*, 6:456). For the definition of Gūrān as a distinct cultural entity, see D. N. MacKenzie, "Gūrān," *EI²*, 2:1139–40, and Vladimir Minorsky, "The Gūrān," *BSOAS* 11 (1943): 75–103.

116. The places of origin are Jīlān, Āmul, Rustamdār, Daylam, Rasht, Rūdbār, Shirvān, Ṭālish, Fūmin, Lāhijān, and Māzandarān.

117. Nūrbakhsh, *Maṡnavī ṣaḥīfat al-awliyāʾ*, *AA*:53–54; *RH,* II:85. The text in the latter source states: "*Muḥammad as-Samarqandī wa-lahu fī l-ḥaqāʾiq wa-l-maʿārif muṣannafāt wa-ashʿār, wa-hūwa min al-abdāl wa-li-dhālik māla ar-Rūm wa-sakana bihā.*" For the Abdāls, see H. J. Kissling, "Abdāl," *EI²*, 1:95; Karamustafa, *God's Unruly Friends,* 70–78.

Nūrbakhsh is thus likely to be a later gloss on the truth.[118] Nūrbakhsh himself also mentions a Qalandar named Bābā Ḥasan, described as an inebriated Turk (*Turk-i mast*), whose unkempt appearance hid his spiritual excellence.[119] Nūrbakhsh's ideological viewpoint indicates that although he did not encourage antinomianism, he believed that such Sufis could actually have a high spiritual status.[120]

The geographical survey shows that Nūrbakhsh was successful in attracting students in every area where he spent an extended period of time. The composition of his following changed, therefore, during the course of his life as he moved from Central Asia to various provinces in Iran. Quite significantly, the majority of followers came from remote towns, rather than urban centers, and the areas to yield the greatest number of students had a reputation for supporting "extremist" Shīʿī trends (Luristān, Kurdistān and the southern Caspian basin). The institutional base of his movement was thus anchored in populations not under the strict administration of scholarly (particularly juridical) Islam. It is precisely in such areas that messianic claims had the best potential for supplanting existing political doctrines of universal rule. Among companions mentioned by Nūrbakhsh, only one is described as a judge (*qāżī*),[121] while all the rest are praised for their competence in the esoteric (*bāṭinī*) sciences.

Prominent Companions Who Predeceased Nūrbakhsh

Among the 212 companions Nūrbakhsh mentions in the *Risālat al-hudā*, eighty-two had already died by the time the work was written. A number of these played prominent roles in Nūrbakhsh's life: they figure in both his other works and external sources. Besides Isḥāq Khuttalānī, Nūrbakhsh remembers Maḥmūd al-Kāmil as his teacher in Sufism (*taṣavvuf*) and ḥadīth; Maḥmūd is also listed by Ibn al-Karbalāʾī as a

118. *TA,* 12–14.

119. Nūrbakhsh, *Maṣnavī ṣaḥīfat al-awliyāʾ*, *AA*:55.

120. Nūrbakhsh, *Maʿāsh as-sālikīn,* MS. 3702, Esad Efendi, Süleymaniye Library, Istanbul, 60a–60b; idem, *Insān-nāma,* MS. Persan 39, Bibliothèque Nationale, Paris, 87a.

121. Ghiyāṣ ad-Dīn Muḥammad b. ʿAbdallāh as-Sayyid al-Ḥusaynī was a judge in Sulṭānīya and Qazvīn (*RH,* II:138).

prominent companion of Khuttalānī.[122] Others who were teachers with their own circles and had chosen Nūrbakhsh as their guide after Khuttalānī included Khalīl Allāh b. Rukn ad-Dīn Baghlānī, Isḥāq b. Yūsuf Ṭāliqānī, Muḥammad b. ʿAlī b. Bahrām Qāʾinī, ʿAlāʾ ad-Dīn Nawandākī, and Ḥusayn Badakhshī.[123]

A number of disciples acquired by Nūrbakhsh in his own right are also reported to have died within his lifetime. Prominent among these were ʿAlāʾ ad-Dīn Kiyā (mentioned above) and Shihāb ad-Dīn Jūrānī (or Gūrānī), who spent thirty years in Nūrbakhsh's service.[124] At least a small external network of the Nūrbakhshīya existed during Nūrbakhsh's lifetime since he writes that his disciples Khāmūsh Balkhī and Aḥmad Shīrāzī (originally from Farghāna) instructed students in Burūjird and Shīrāz, respectively.[125] Nūrbakhsh's fond remembrance of his deceased companions, which includes poetic tributes, suggests that the early Nūrbakhshīya formed a close-knit community.[126] However, Nūrbakhsh describes them all in purely religious terms, and there is no indication that any of them were politically or militarily adventurous.

The Mahdī's Death

Nūrbakhsh retained his belief in his messianic claim to the end of his life. We know this because a group of his successors (discussed later in this book) continued to project that idea as the order's defining doctrine after his death. His passing away in Suliqān on 14 Rabīʿ I, 869 (November 14, 1464) was a moment of great sorrow for his followers, as exemplified in Muḥammad Ghaybī's elegy comparing him to the prophets and great Sufis of the past.[127] He is praised as the Imām Mahdī and the ultimate guide of the time, whose arrival in the world fulfilled Muḥammad's prediction about Jesus' Second Coming. As "Nūrbakhsh" (light giver) he attempted to illuminate the world through his mystical

122. *RH,* I:23; *RJJJ,* 2:248.
123. *RH,* II:1, 2, 3, 8, 19.
124. Ibid., II:79.
125. Ibid., II:38, 67.
126. Cf. *Dīvān,* 19–20, where he mourns the death of ʿAlāʾ ad-Dīn Kiyā.
127. *TA,* 72–77, 86. Shushtarī gives the date as 15 Rabīʿ I, 869 (*MM,* 2:147).

teachings, and the loss of his guidance caused the eyes of all true saints throughout the world to gush with tears. He was buried in Suliqān where his grave has remained a pilgrimage place for Nūrbakhshīs from the fifteenth century to the present.[128]

An Evaluation of Nūrbakhsh's Messianic Mission

Nūrbakhsh's career as a mahdī has been interpreted variously by scholars concerned with the late medieval Islamic East. His life is most often seen as either an appendix to the history of the Kubravī Sufi lineage or a precursor to the revolutionary Shīʿism of the Ṣafavids. For the former, Marijan Molé saw Nūrbakhsh's open Shīʿism as the culminating point for the Shīʿitization of the Kubravīya.[129] Recent authors on the Kubravīya have criticized this interpretation of the order's history and have emphasized its Sunnī (Shāfiʿī) character.[130] Nūrbakhsh for them is an exception, rather than the logical fulfillment of a historical pattern.

The present comprehensive survey of Nūrbakhsh's life supports the latter viewpoint since his Shīʿī inclinations decidedly came from his family background. Furthermore, as discussed in chapter 3, Nūrbakhsh's Shīʿism is rather quixotic and deviates substantially from the doctrines of established Shīʿī sects. Quite significantly, in one of his works Nūrbakhsh even praises the caliphs Abū Bakr, ʿUmar, and ʿUthmān,[131] and a closer look at him disproves Molé's assertion that he culminated a trend inherent in Kubravī thought with his mahdist claim.

The discussion in this chapter shows that Nūrbakhsh spent most of his public life in the middle of two roles whose demands were sometimes at odds with each other. Although it is impossible to disentangle his status as a Sufi shaykh from the messianic claim, it is helpful, for the purposes of analysis, to see them as separate parts of his personality. He was successful as a mystical guide due to his genealogical legitimacy as a sayyid and his position in the prestigious, influential, and widespread Kubravī Sufi lineage. In addition, the presence of a substantial following

128. See chapters 5–7, below.

129. Molé, "Les Kubrawiya entre sunnisme et shiisme," 136–38.

130. DeWeese, "Sayyid ʿAlī Hamadānī and Kubravī Hagiographical Traditions," 121.

131. Nūrbakhsh, *Insān-nāma,* 86a.

during his lifetime attests to his personal charisma. These characteristics by themselves would have made him a person sought after by rulers and commoners alike in the context of his religious environment. However, the more radical implications of the messianic claim reduced his followers to only those who were willing to see him as a pivotal figure, not just in their own times but in cosmic history. As discussed in chapter 5, it may even be the case that many of his followers did not subscribe to the messianic claim and attached themselves to him solely for his Sufi competence. Without the messianic claim, Nūrbakhsh would have been an ideal candidate for the widespread "Sufi and Sultan" phenomenon, but the messianic designation precluded this by the fact that, in the end, it is necessary for the messiah to gain direct political power.

Nūrbakhsh's failure in realizing the political side of the messianic mission indicates that even though his contemporary context made room for the emergence of messianism, durable political legitimacy in the end hearkened back to royal genealogies and support from large preexisting social groups. This point is best illustrated by comparing him to Ismāʿīl I, founder of the Ṣafavid dynasty, who also espoused an extreme religious claim and did in fact succeed in gaining political power in Iran less than fifty years after Nūrbakhsh's death.[132] The disparity of outcome between the two pertains both to aspects of Nūrbakhsh's personality and the societal situation in Iran during the fifteenth century.

Nūrbakhsh's idea of the mahdī's role was passive, at least after the failure of the military exercise at the very outset of his career. In contrast, the militarized Ṣafavid order pursued an activist messianic agenda under Ismāʿīl and his father Ḥaydar. As discussed in detail in chapter 3, Nūrbakhsh waited throughout his life for a righteous group to accept him as the mahdī and sweep him to universal prominence. A study of his thought reveals fatalism as a central theme in his view of the mahdī through most of his life, while the Ṣafavids' military adventurism was a far more important element of their outlook compared with their "intellectual" radicalism.

132. Mazzaoui, *Origins of the Ṣafavids,* 71–84.

Nūrbakhsh's inability to gain political power resulted also from his not garnering the loyalty of groups of people whose ties to each other went beyond religious conviction alone. Aside from his inconsequential association with Lur and Kurdish tribesmen, he never formed ties with social groups that could have carried him to power. Ismāʿīl's success, on the other hand, would have been impossible without the allegiance of the Qizilbāsh tribesman to the Ṣafavid order.[133] Furthermore, Nūrbakhsh was only a disputed heir to the Kubravī tradition and had no specifically political ancestral charisma to command loyalty. Both Ḥaydar and Ismāʿīl were, in comparison, sole heirs to the important Ṣafavid order that, moreover, shared matrimonial alliances with the Aqqoyunlu ruling house.[134] Nūrbakhsh was not born in a politically privileged situation, and he never pursued connections to such circles diligently to gain derivative legitimacy.

Adventurers such as Ḥaydar and Ismāʿīl sought to collapse the influential "Sufi and Sultan" paradigm into a single individual who was both the religious guide and the temporal ruler. Nūrbakhsh, in contrast, for at least pragmatic reasons was willing to portray himself as only a Sufi, and he never acquired any other means of political legitimacy besides the religious claim. His idea of his station was entirely spiritualistic, and he devoted his energy to justifying his claim and showing its intellectual foundations, rather than attempting to implement the mahdī's privileges. He proclaimed himself the revealer of secrets in the "age of unveiling"[135] and produced a complex religious system to rationalize his messianism. While the emphasis on proper knowledge and spiritual excellence made him a good teacher as attested to by his disciples, his personality lacked the worldly dynamism and perhaps even the ruthlessness required of a politically successful messiah.

In contrast with the political impasse, Nūrbakhsh did in fact assemble a coherent messianic discourse based on Islamic messianic traditions,

133. James J. Reid, *Tribalism and Society in Islamic Iran, 1500–1629* (Malibu, Calif.: Undena Publications, 1983), 25–31; Masashi Haneda, *Le Châh et les Qizilbāsh: Le systeme militaire safavide* (Berlin: K. Schwarz, 1987), 62–66.

134. For the Ṣafavids' relationship with the Aqqoyunlu, see Woods, *Aqquyunlu,* 179–84.

135. Nūrbakhsh, *Maktūb beh ʿAlāʾ ad-Dawla, AA:*79.

personal experiences, and the mystical ideas that pervaded the world surrounding him. He should, then, be seen as a "successful" messiah in the religious sense, whose mind gestated a new tradition from the period's intellectual environment. A religious vision no matter how brilliant or representative did not, however, translate directly into terrestrial dominion in his times. On this score, just as in many other features of his career, Nūrbakhsh shared a fate common to most messiahs —across both religious traditions and time periods.

Chapter Three

Articulating the Messianic Message

In justifying his messianic claim to his audience, Muḥammad Nūrbakhsh's task was to prove both that the time for the mahdī's appearance had come and that he himself should be accepted as the awaited figure. To his mind, the sociohistorical situation of the day contained all that had been suggested in Islamic tradition for the time of the mahdī, and his personal circumstances, ranging from his physical appearance to the events of his life, clearly pointed to the fact that he was the promised savior. Even more significantly, however, both he himself and people associated with him at different times in his life had received direct affirmation of his status in the form of dreams and mystical visions. Reading Nūrbakhsh's writings leads one to step into a worldview permeated by the direct presence of both divine intuition and spirits of deceased religious heroes. The most crucial component of his articulation of the messianic message stated that his physical body had become the repository of the souls of numerous deceased prophets and spiritual masters. It was, in fact, their presence both with him and within him that compelled him to pursue his messianic mission despite his personal desire to retire to a life of travel and spiritual pursuits. Since the career of the mahdī was a crucial element in divinely ordained cosmic history, these luminaries themselves had been commanded directly by God to promote the mission.

In structural terms, Nūrbakhsh's messianic doctrine was a response to Twelver Shīʿī tradition about the mahdī. As discussed in chapter 1, Twelver Shīʿism among all major Islamic sects is the one most singularly focused on the arrival of the mahdī as the ultimate form of worldly salvation. However, in normative Twelver Shīʿism, the role of the mahdī is reserved exclusively for the Twelfth Imam. A mahdī rising from a Twelver Shīʿī milieu, therefore, has to negate sectarian dogma and argue against the very basis of the idea of "twelve" unique imāms who, according to the religion's orthodoxy, have already existed in history. Conversely, however, it is crucial for such a mahdī to portray himself as the fulfillment of traditions regarding the Twelfth Imam in order to claim charismatic authority. The tension necessitated by this paradox is evident throughout Nūrbrakhsh's messianic discourse since his overall effort was to reinterpret the tradition in such a way that it retained its legitimizing potential while allowing for alternative readings of the mahdī's identification. The result was obviously unacceptable to those faithful to the literal word of the tradition. It must be remembered, however, that Nūrbakhsh's audience was not the class of learned Shīʿī scholars but a group with mixed sectarian affiliation whose primary religious loyalty was to Sufism, rather than the dogma of any established sect.

Nūrbakhsh's intensive focus on visions and dreams as the arena for the fulfillment of messianic traditions was consistent with the worldview of Persianate Sufism in the later medieval period. His works reflect a thorough acquaintance with the canon of Sufi literature, while his Shīʿī affiliation remained at the level of ancestral attachment, rather than as a scholar of the tradition. Examined from a Sufi viewpoint, Nūrbakhsh's justification for his messianic claim was, in fact, a defensible argument, although most other Sufis would have balked at the way he turned theoretical ideas into his personal prerogatives.

In a general sense, Nūrbakhsh's messianic discourse was a system that grafted Shīʿī traditions onto Sufi cosmology. My purpose in this chapter is to lay out Nūrbakhsh's major arguments for the messianic claim, while chapter 4 will deal in depth with his Sufi worldview. We are fortunate that Nūrbakhsh's extant works include a detailed messianic confession, a relatively rare document for the whole course of the history of Islamic messianism. My treatment of his defense of the claim divides his discourse into sections on the traditional and experiential proofs for the claim and his metaphysical argument about the mahdī's status. The discourse is then compared with the normative messianic tradition to see the divergences Nūrbakhsh employed to turn the messianic idea from theory into a personal commission. In the process of actualizing the tradition, Nūrbakhsh articulated a new theory of sainthood that amalgamated Islamic sectarian and mystical ideas in a creative way.

Nūrbakhsh's Treatise on Guidance (*Risālat al-hudā*)

Our main source for Nūrbakhsh's messianic doctrine is his work *Risālat al-hudā,* which I have already used extensively in presenting Nūrbakhsh's life.[1] This work stands out in Islamic literature as a relatively rare first-person account of a mahdī presenting an extended justification for his claim. After stating that it is necessary for an accomplished saint (*valī*) to make his knowledge available to others, Nūrbakhsh writes: "I am obliged to commit to writing the signs, characteristics, qualities, and distinctions from the sayings of my predecessors and the discoveries of my contemporaries about this poor man [i.e., myself]. With these, everyone who has not already done so can recognize me and be rescued from the ignorance mentioned in (Muḥammad's) statement, 'he who dies without knowing the imām of his age dies the death of ignorance (*jāhilīya*).'[2] In addition, through these (descriptions) those who already know me may increase their knowledge."[3]

Nūrbakhsh's express purpose in writing the text was, therefore, to make known his status as the mahdī. As reviewed in chapter 1, the mahdī has usually had an "activist" function in Islamic thought and individuals who have claimed the title for themselves have generally concentrated on "rising" against perceived injustice and implementing their vision of a just society.[4] It is rare to find mahdīs ruminating extensively on their status in writing, and even in cases where a mahdī's

1. The only previous discussion to appraise this work in the original is Molé, "Les Kubrawiya entre Sunnisme et Shiisme," 131–37.

2. *MA,* vol. 2, nos. 551–55.

3. *RH,* I:6. This goal is restated in passage I:40.

4. The activism of various mahdīs is compared in Margoliouth, "On Mahdis and Mahdism," 226–33.

original discourse is extant, it is not an apology for the claim but a blueprint for what needs to be done.[5] The *Risālat al-hudā* is, therefore, an exceptional text for a history of Islamic messianic thought.

In terms of its sources, the *Risālat al-hudā* relies most heavily on the Qurʾān and the ḥadīth and has very few references to later literature. Nūrbakhsh cites the Qurʾān fourteen times[6] and mentions thirty-three ḥadīth reports (including two *ḥadīth qudsī* or divine sayings spoken through Muḥammad and not the Qurʾan), most of them containing predictions about the mahdī. Surprisingly for one raised as a Twelver Shīʿī, Nūrbakhsh invokes ʿAlī only four times in this text,[7] and the other imāms are mentioned twice in an incidental fashion with no references to their traditions.[8]

Among past authorities, the largest group of Nūrbakhsh's references in the *Risālat al-hudā* are those to his Sufi forebears. These include a number of masters associated with the Kubravī silsila, or chain, Nūrbakhsh's personal affiliation, and Ibn al-ʿArabī.[9] The Sufi shaykhs invoked are, in chronological order: Saʿd ad-Dīn Ḥamuvayī (d. 650/1252–53), including one reference to his *Kitāb al-maḥbūb,*[10] the only

5. For other writings by mahdīs, see Muḥammad b. Falāḥ Mushaʿshaʿ, *Kalām al-mahdī,* MS. 10222, Parliament Library, Tehran; Ibn Tūmart, *Aʿazzu mā-yuṭlab,* ed. ʿAmmār Ṭālibī (Algiers: al-Muʾassasa al-Waṭanīya li l-Kitāb, 1985); and Muḥammad Aḥmad al-Mahdī, *Āthar al-kāmila li l-Imām al-Mahdī,* ed. Muḥammad Ibrāhīm Abū Salīm, 5 vols. (Khartoum: Dār Jāmiʿat al-Kharṭūm li n-Nashr, 1990). The Bāb's *Dālā'il-i sabʿa* is comparable to the *Risālat al-hudā* as a mahdī's apologia in defense of his claim (cf. Amanat, *Resurrection and Renewal,* 375; Denis McEoin, *The Sources for Early Bābī Doctrine and History: A Survey* [Leiden: E. J. Brill, 1992], 85–88).

6. These citations, in the order of appearance in the text, are 51:56, 48:1, 3:159, 3:103, 35:28, 42:23, 9:119, 4:82, 42:13, 6:153, 6:116, 10:36, 52:23, 53:28.

7. *RH,* I:9, 10, 33, 44.

8. Ibid., I:49, II:91. The first reference is a small section in verse that mentions all the Twelver imāms, while the second refers only to the sixth imām Jaʿfar aṣ-Ṣādiq. It is interesting to note that the writings of another mahdī, the Bāb, also refer to "Muḥammad, ʿAlī, Ḥusayn and occasionally Jaʿfar Ṣādiq, but seldom others" (Amanat, *Resurrection and Renewal,* 143).

9. *RH,* I:11, 35.

10. This extensive work, extant in numerous manuscripts, is referred to by Nūrbakhsh in one of his letters as well; there he gives the name as *Maḥbūb al-muḥibbīn*

other work mentioned by name besides the Qurʾan;[11] Najm ad-Dīn Dāya Rāzī (d. 654/1256);[12] ʿAlāʾ ad-Dawla Simnānī (d. 736/1336);[13] Maḥmūd Mazdaqānī (d. 766/1364–65);[14] ʿAlī Hamadānī (d. 786/1385);[15] and Khwāja Isḥāq Khuttalānī.[16]

Besides religious figures, Nūrbakhsh also mentions philosophers' predictions about the time of the appearance of the mahdī. He refers twice to ancient sages (*ḥukamāʾ*) in general, once to Ptolemy, and once to the famous Shīʿī polymath Naṣīr ad-Dīn Ṭūsī (d. 672/1274), who relates a tradition from the pre-Islamic Persian astrologer Jāmāsp.[17] Nūrbakhsh contends that Ṭūsī predicted that the mahdī would begin his mission in the middle of Rajab, 826 (June–July 1423), but an actual

---

(cf. Nūrbakhsh, *Maktūb beh Mawlānā Ḥasan Kurd, AA:*97; Jamal Elias, "The Sufi Lords of Bahrabad: Saʿd al-Din and Sadr al-Din Hamuwayi," *Iranian Studies* 27, nos. 1–4 [1994]: 62–63). I was unable to trace the exact section cited by Nūrbakhsh while looking through one manuscript, although the work does contain extensive discussions regarding the mahdī and the seal of saints (cf. Saʿd ad-Dīn Ḥamuvayī, *Kitāb al-maḥbūb fī t-taṣawwuf,* MS. Ayasofya 2058, Süleymaniye Library, Istanbul, fols. 1b–205b).

11. *RH,* I:12.

12. Ibid., I:14.

13. Ibid., I:16, 46.

14. Ibid., I:17.

15. Ibid., I:22, 56.

16. Ibid., I:21–22, and numerous times in part II.

17. *RH,* I:15. Jāmāsp, who is mentioned also in Nūrbakhsh's *Insān-nāma* (83b), was particularly well known in the Islamic philosophical tradition for his predictions based upon astrological conjunctions. For works attributed to Jāmāsp, see Fuat Sezgin, *Geschichte des arabischen Schrifttums,* 4:59–60, 7:86–88; and E. Blochet, "Études sur le Gnosticisme musulman," *RSO* 4 (1911–12): 278–91. Jāmāsp's association with apocalypticism in pre-Islamic Persian literature is described in Tord Olsson, "The Apocalyptic Activity: The Case of Jāmāsp Nāmag," in *Apocalypticism in the Mediterranean World and the Near East,* ed. David Hellholm, 2d enlarged ed. (Tübingen: J. C. B. Mohr [Paul Siebeck], 1989), 21–49. The role of astral conjunctions in Islamic messianism has not yet received extensive scholarly attention. However, it has been suggested that the appearance of comets may have triggered messianic fervor at various points in Islamic history (cf. David Cook, "Messianism and Astronomical Events during the First Four Centuries of Islam," in *Mahdisme et millénarisme en Islam,* ed. García-Arenal, 29–51).

excerpt from Ṭūsī's poem *Jāmāsp-nāma* states the time as only sometime after A.H. 800.[18] These references indicate that Nūrbakhsh was familiar with aspects of Islamic philosophy and astrology, though he was liable to modify the original pronouncements to make them fit his own agenda.

This summary of the authorities behind the *Risālat al-hudā* reveals that Nūrbakhsh based the legitimacy of his claim primarily on the Qur'an, Muḥammad, ʿAlī, and Sufi ideas originating from Ibn al-ʿArabī and shaykhs part of the Kubravī silsila. His many references to prophetic ḥadīth reflect his familiarity with Shīʿī literature on the mahdī's functions and his occultation. The absence of references to the imāms after ʿAlī places Nūrbakhsh quite outside the scholarly paradigms of his ancestral Twelver Shīʿism. By concentrating on Muḥammad and ʿAlī, Nūrbakhsh's mahdism appropriated Shīʿism's charisma as the ideological system representing the Prophet's family. However, the postprophetic and postimāmate intellectual orientation used by Nūrbakhsh was Sufism, rather than any strain of mature Shīʿī thought. The "past" Nūrbakhsh considered crucial was the Shīʿī claim to religiopolitical leadership and the sociointellectual complex represented by medieval Sufism.

Proofs and Prerogatives of the Messianic Claim

Nūrbakhsh's messianic doctrine begins with the belief that the time for the savior to rise has come. He uses commonly accepted ḥadīth reports to describe the physical and social conditions to prevail before the figure's purported arrival. Matching aspects of the traditional picture with his own situation, he relates the report that "the mahdī will arrive from the direction of the east," and, along similar lines, he reiterates Muḥammad's supposed statement "if you see that the black banners have arrived from Khurāsān, go to them even if you have to crawl over the snow, for with them is God's vicegerent, the mahdī."[19] Furthermore, he reports

18. Molé, "Les Kubrawiya entre Sunnisme et Shiisme," 131, based upon *Jāmāsp-nāma az guftār-i Khwāja Naṣīr Ṭūsī* (MS. Aya Sofya 4795, Süleymaniye Library, Istanbul, 824b–26a). I was unable to see this manuscript personally since it was under repair in Spring 1999.

19. *RH,* I:8; *MA,* vol. 1, nos. 253, 251.

from ʿAlī that these incidents are to occur during a time of upheaval resulting from the reign of tyrannical rulers and wars led by Turks.[20]

Nūrbakhsh supplements these circumstantial clues about the mahdī's appearance with proofs from astrology and numerology. He cites three observations by Ptolemy describing the horoscope of individuals destined to achieve rulership and contends that they are present in his own horoscope.[21] When these signs are combined with his spiritual superiority over all others at the time, it becomes obvious that he is the mahdī.

Moving to even greater certainty about the issue, Nūrbakhsh states that the year of the mahdī's appearance can be calculated by subjecting a verse by Saʿd ad-Dīn Ḥamuvayī to numerological analysis. The verse states that "the mahdī will rise following fasting (*ʿaqīb ṣawm*) plus *basmala*."[22] The predicted year is deduced by adding the values of the *basmala* formula (786) and *mīm* (40), the last letter in the word *ṣawm*. The verse, therefore, predicts A.H. 826, the year Nūrbakhsh was proclaimed the mahdī in Khuttalān.

Nūrbakhsh relates in the *Risālat al-hudā* that the mahdī's exact date of birth was revealed to the Egyptian Sufi master Nūr ad-Dīn ʿAbd ar-Raḥmān Qurayshī. Qurayshī, who is attested as an influential shaykh,[23]

20. *RH,* I:10. The verses that comprise these predictions are not from *Nahj al-balāgha* or ʿAlī's sayings about the mahdī collected in *MA.*

21. Ibid., I:34. The use of horoscopes to predict political events was a common feature in medieval times in both the Islamic world and Europe (cf. Nicholas Campion, *The Great Year: Astrology, Millenarianism, and History in the Western Tradition* [London: Arkana, 1994], 523–26).

22. *RH,* I:12. This verse forms a part of Ḥamuvayī's general speculation on the *basmala* formula (cf. *Kitāb sharḥ-i bismillāh,* MS. Çorlulu Ali Paşa 445, Süleymaniye Library, Istanbul, fols. 1b–7b). It is discussed by Ibn al-Karbalāʾī (*RJJJ,* 2:392) and appears also as a justification for messianic expectation in an excerpt from a Ḥurūfī work (Ḥasan b. Ḥaydar Astarābādī, *Az Hidāyatnāma,* MS. Farsça 139, Istanbul University Library, fols. 57b–58a).

23. Jāmī mentions Qurayshī both in his own right and as the teacher for Zayn ad-Dīn Khwāfī (d. 838/1435), the eponym of the Zaynīya order, which later gained prominence in Ottoman lands (*Nafaḥāt al-uns,* 492–95). Qurayshī's name also occurs in the *Shajara al-wafīya fī dhikr al-mashāyikh aṣ-ṣūfīya* or *Silsilat al-awliyāʾ* attributed to Nūrbakhsh (Dānishpazhūh, "*Silsilat al-awliyāʾ*-yi Nūrbakhsh Quhis-

saw that the mahdī would be born on the morning of Friday, 27 Muḥarram, 795 (December 13, 1392), which, Nūrbakhsh informs us, was the date and time of his own birth.[24] Astrological data, numerological signs, and a Sufi master's intuition thus indicated both that the time for the mahdī to rise had come and that Nūrbakhsh was the expected savior.

Prophetic Ḥadīth and Sufi Forebears as Predictors of the Mahdī's Advent

Just as the mahdī was to appear under well-defined social and material conditions, he was also ascribed definite genealogical and physical traits based on the sayings of Muḥammad and various Sufi masters. Nūrbakhsh established the mahdī's genealogy, first of all, through the following ḥadīth: "If the world were to continue for only one more day, God would lengthen that day until a man from my progeny, whose name will be my name and whose *kunya* will be my *kunya,* would (rise to) fill the earth with equity and justice, just as it was filled with darkness and injustice."[25] This designation was made more exact through another report stating that the mahdī would be a descendant of Muḥammad's grandson Ḥusayn[26] and that he was included in an auspicious seven-person group from the clan of ʿAbd al-Muṭṭalib (Muḥammad's grandfather), all of whom would eventually reign as leaders of the people of paradise.[27]

After prophetic ḥadīth, Nūrbakhsh predicted the mahdī's parentage through citing a statement from Ibn al-ʿAbbās, the famous early Qurʾan commentator, that his mother would be a Turkish princess. This idea was affirmed also through a saying ascribed to Ibn al-ʿArabī that "the final seal of sainthood will be both an Arab as well as a non-Arab."[28]

---

tānī," 48). Qurayshī's appearance in Nūrbakhsh's defense of his claim may reflect his connection to a local lineage stemming from the Egyptian master. However, I have not found any other sources to elaborate on this connection.

24. *RH,* I:19.

25. Ibid., I:6; *MA,* vol. 1, nos. 64, 69, 70, 75, 85, 93.

26. *RH,* I:7; *MA,* vol. 1, nos. 74, 76, 81.

27. *RH,* I:8; *MA,* vol. 1, no. 110. The seven from the clan of ʿAbd al-Muṭṭalib are Muḥammad, ʿAlī, Ḥamza, Jaʿfar, Ḥasan, Ḥusayn, and the mahdī.

28. *RH,* I:11. For Nūrbakhsh, the mahdī is also the final seal of sainthood (discussed below).

Nūrbakhsh's citation of these reports suggests that Nūrbakhsh's father, who was an Arab, had married a local woman of Turkish origin in Quhistān, where he had settled after his visit to Mashhad.

In parallel with his physical genealogy, the mahdī was said to have his spiritual home in the traditions and practices of the Kubravī Sufi silsila, as ratified in the following statement attributed to ʿAlāʾ ad-Dawla Simnānī: "The Mahdī will be the fifth pole (*quṭb*) after me in my chain. He will be a descendant of the Messenger of God in three ways: through physical lineage because of being a sayyid; by the heart because of his virtue; and in truth (*ḥaqqīya*) because of his sainthood. He will be a Ḥusaynī from the paternal side and a Ḥasanī from some of the mothers of his forefathers."[29] This prediction of the mahdī's Kubravī affiliation is corroborated further from the report of Maḥmūd Mazdaqānī, another prominent member of the line.[30]

Nūrbakhsh sees the mahdī's physical appearance also predicted in ḥadīth. He would have "an aquiline nose, clear (hairless) brow, thin hair, sensitive nose, his complexion that of an Arab, his body that of a Jew (Isrāʾilī), and a mole on his right cheek."[31] The mole is seen as a particularly significant mark, and Nūrbakhsh explains that it has to be a black square and not an oval or rectangle. Also from ḥadīth, Nūrbakhsh states that the mahdī would be forty years of age at the time of his proclamation.[32] Since this tradition was contrary to Nūrbakhsh's own situation (he was thirty or thirty-one years old in 1423), he states without explanation that this implies that his age would be between thirty and forty years.[33]

29. *RH,* I:16.

30. Ibid., I:17. Both Simnānī and Mazdaqānī are cited without reference to particular written sources.

31. Ibid., I:7; *MA,* vol. 1, nos. 71, 72, 88, 222, 235.

32. *RH,* I:8; *MA,* vol. 1, no. 91. The most obvious significance of forty is, of course, that according to the traditional account Muḥammad received revelation for the first time at this age. For numerous other connotations attached to the number forty in Islam as well as other religions, see Annemarie Schimmel, *The Mystery of Numbers* (New York: Oxford University Press, 1993), 245–53.

33. One variation of the tradition given in Kūrānī's compendium states that he would be between thirty and forty at the time of proclamation (*MA,* 1:164, based

Nūrbakhsh contends that both ḥadīth literature and the predictions of prominent Sufis point to his mahdīhood. His discourse shows that although he was quite familiar with prophetic ḥadīth, he did not feel the need to invoke statements by Shīʿī imāms after ʿAlī to justify his claim. This omission reflects the facts that his education took place among Sufis, rather than Twelver Shīʿī traditionists, and an appeal to the normative Shīʿī paradigm was not significant for his audience. In both cases, it is evident that he was neither working from nor projecting toward a social reality segregated along traditional sectarian lines.

The Testimony of the Elders

The largest number of reports related by Nūrbakhsh in *Risālat al-hudā* in support of his messianic claim derive from personal experience. These include the observations of his contemporaries as well as his own mystical experiences. He relates statements from his father and two teachers and from numerous companions of his own generation as well as his students. These experiences contain dialogues with God, Muḥammad, ʿAlī, and Sufi luminaries of the past, who are all shown to have sanctioned Nūrbakhsh's claim. In addition, these experiences also attest to the spiritual station of his companions.

Nūrbakhsh portrays his father in the *Risālat al-hudā* as a spiritual adept who was aware of the honor to be bestowed upon his family even before Nūrbakhsh's birth. He states from family tradition that "(once) my father put his hand on his loins during a public meeting and said: 'Muḥammad the Mahdī is in my loins.' And he also said: 'By the time my son Muḥammad reaches the age of forty, no one anywhere in the world would be able to rival his knowledge.'"[34] His intuition regarding the destiny of his son had continued after this incident. This can be seen in the report about the time of Nūrbakhsh's birth: "While I was still in my mother's womb, he would often point to her and say, 'this is my son

upon Aḥmad b. Ḥajar al-Haythamī [d. 974/1566–67], *Qawl al-mukhtaṣar fī ʿalāmāt al-mahdī al-muntaẓar,* fol. 18 of MS. in Maktaba al-Imām Amīr al-Muʾminīn al-ʿĀmma, Najaf, Iraq). Perhaps Nūrbakhsh meant to refer to this tradition, but the text of *Risālat al-hudā* does not make this clear. The variant tradition is not included in the published edition of Haythamī's work.

34. *RH,* I:17.

Muḥammad, such and such.' Given his hyperbole about me, Fāṭima, the daughter of Sayyid Quṭb ad-Dīn, teased him by telling him of the birth of a daughter when I was born in Sāwijān. He became angry and, taking hold of his beard, exclaimed: 'if my child is not a son, I am not a descendant of ʿAlī b. Abī Ṭālib.' Then she recanted and told him that it was a son with blue eyes.[35] He said, 'No! by God it is not so,' and it was ascertained that he was correct."[36] Nūrbakhsh's stories about his father suggest that the germ of the messianic proclamation had been planted in his mind long before the proclamation in 1423. There is, however, no way to verify his statements about his father, and it may be that he "recalled" these incidents only when he was compelled to defend his claim.

Nūrbakhsh contended also that his shaykh Khwāja Isḥāq Khuttalānī had declared him the mahdī after a spiritual revelation.[37] The shaykh's estimation of his status is evident from a vision in which he saw Nūrbakhsh's merit akin to that of the prophet Joseph. This was affirmed further when he told Nūrbakhsh, "I saw that your feet were made of light and they illuminated every place they approached . . . so that the whole world became lit by them."[38] Since light was a metaphor for the flowing of God's knowledge to the world in Nūrbakhsh's thought, Khuttalānī's dream made Nūrbakhsh the mediator between God and his creation.

Nūrbakhsh claimed that Khuttalānī had not only recognized him as the mahdī but had instructed all his followers to do the same. He once gathered all his disciples together and told them that although Nūrbakhsh appeared to be his student, in reality he was his shaykh. He then dressed Nūrbakhsh in his Sufi robe (*khirqa*) to symbolize the transferal of the khānqāh's leadership.[39]

35. Nūrbakhsh's understanding of physiognomy explains why the mahdī could not have blue eyes. He writes that blue-gray eyes are a sign of immodesty or shamelessness (*bīsharmī*), whereas eyes between dark and light blue indicate fear (*tars*) and cowardliness (*jubn*) (Nūrbakhsh, *Insān-nāma,* 84b).

36. *RH,* I:18.

37. Ibid., I:21.

38. Ibid. The significance of light in Nūrbakhsh's thought is discussed in chapter 4.

39. Ibid.

Nūrbakhsh's higher status in comparison with his own teachers is affirmed also by Maḥmūd al-Kāmil, who is elsewhere attested as one of Khuttalānī's lieutenants.[40] He once said to Nūrbakhsh: "During a spiritual observation, I saw you sitting on a bed. You had hair [fur?] on your head according to the custom of the ʿAlids, and there were six pearls in your hand, some of them not completely clear. People were coming to you to promise their allegiance and we were all sure that you were the Promised Imām."[41] The seriousness of Maḥmūd's commitment to Nūrbakhsh is evident from the fact that the teacher sacrificed himself for his pupil's cause.[42] Between his father and his teachers, Nūrbakhsh felt that he had been ratified in his messianic claim by the adept of the generation immediately preceding him.

The Spiritual Experiences of Nūrbakhsh's Companions and Students

Nūrbakhsh's companions, whether inherited from Khuttalānī or acquired on his own, provided the greatest fund of spiritual experiences to legitimize his messianism. Their significance as a group is reflected in the extended list of companions interposed in the middle of *Risālat al-hudā* (part II). His attention to them underscores Nūrbakhsh's basic worldview in which Sufis can apprehend higher truths, including knowledge of the past and future, due to their spiritual station. The numerous reports in this category highlight different facets of the special knowledge that becomes available by following the mystical path.

Nūrbakhsh's status was affirmed in visions seen by his companions Muḥammad b. Saʿd Hamadānī and Muḥammad b. ʿAlī b. Bahrām Qāʾinī in which both were informed directly by God that he would cause the death of a number of Nurbakhsh's adversaries.[43] Nūrbakhsh reports in the *Risālat al-hudā* that these predictions had either come true already or were expected to be fulfilled in the near future. God also cast out the doubt in Qāʾinī's mind in the following incident:

40. Ḥaydar Badakhshī, *Manqabat al-javāhir,* 378a.

41. *RH,* I:23.

42. Nūrbakhsh, *Vāridāt, AA:*139.

43. *RH,* I:29, 25. These individuals are listed among Nūrbakhsh's companions (*RH,* II:84, 3). Another companion, Aḥmad al-Qurayshī (*RH,* II:98), was also able to predict the future through a vision of Saʿd ad-Dīn Ḥamuvayi (*RH,* I:13).

> Once when we were traveling toward the Alburz mountains to escape persecution, we decided to observe a forty-day retreat. At the end of this period, [Qāʾinī] became saddened because of all our tribulations and the persistence of our enemies. He then asked me, "Will we ever get anything else besides hardships from the call to the Imāmate?" I replied, "Turn toward the Invisible World (*ʿālam al-ghayb*), and I will abandon the [quest for the] Imāmate if a sign comes telling us to do so." When he did this he saw himself in a place where he heard that the mahdī was coming and that he and the public at large were preparing to welcome him. When the mahdī came close and his face became visible, [Qāʾinī] saw that the rider was none other than me. He thus regained his certainty that I was the Promised Imām.[44]

The companion was thus convinced that the faithful would one day be rewarded by God for all their troubles.

As an accomplished Sufi shaykh, Nūrbakhsh saw himself in the same position of spiritual leadership as God's prophets until Muḥammad. The very beginning of the *Risālat al-hudā* explicitly equates the functions of the prophets and God's friends (*awliyāʾ*),[45] and the mahdī's status as a near-prophet is made clear also through the report of a vision experienced by Shihāb ad-Dīn Jūrānī. He saw the angel Gabriel in the form of a bird above Nūrbakhsh's head, with his wings hanging down toward the earth. When questioned about his behavior, Gabriel stated: "I am doing this so that the blow of any weapon such as a sword, spear, or arrow, aimed at him falls upon my wings and not on him."[46] Jūrānī's vision convinced him that God would protect Nūrbakhsh from any harm in the same way that he had protected the prophets.

Nūrbakhsh's companions also reported seeing important religious figures such as Muḥammad, ʿAlī, and famous Sufis attesting to his status. Muḥammad appeared to Khalīl Allāh b. Rukn ad-Dīn Baghlānī in a vision and told him and others to pledge allegiance to Nūrbakhsh, his

44. Ibid., I:25. A similar experience is reported also from Isḥāq b. Yūsuf Ṭāliqānī (*RH,* II:2), who saw Nūrbakhsh ride into Mecca as the mahdī (*RH,* I:26).

45. Ibid., I:2.

46. Ibid., I:27.

descendant, since he was the promised imām.[47] Similarly, Qāʾinī saw another vision where Muḥammad pointed toward Nūrbakhsh and indicated that, as the mahdī, he was the only person to posses the truth regarding all matters.[48]

ʿAlī also confirmed Nūrbakhsh's status in a vision seen by Muḥammad b. Saʿd Hamadānī:

> I saw ʿAlī b. Abī Ṭālib and asked him how many times could God make himself manifest to a man in a single night? He replied that only eleven men during the time of the Messenger of God had experienced divine epiphany (*tajallī*). One of them once told the Messenger that he had received forty epiphanies, and that pleased the Messenger. Then I said, "Prince of Believers, at present there are many in Nūrbakhsh's company who are rewarded with more than 300,000 epiphanies, annihilations (*fanāʾ*) and subsistences (*baqāʾ*) in him in a single night." He replied that this was so because although he is my son in appearance (*ẓāhir*), esoterically (*bāṭin*) he is my father; I am a body for which he is the soul.[49]

The remarkable aspect of this vision is that in it Nūrbakhsh is exalted above even Muḥammad and ʿAlī. The indication here that Nūrbakhsh thought himself to be a virtual reembodiment of early figures such as ʿAlī is a crucial element of his claim and will be discussed in detail later in this chapter.

Nūrbakhsh hints that all spiritual adepts alive during his lifetime were aware of his station irrespective of whether they had actually come into contact with him or not. Muḥammad b. Saʿd Hamadānī related: "Once during a journey I came upon one of the *abdāl,* named Maḥmūd al-Anjawānī, in the village of Wasma in the Farāhān region of Persian Iraq (ʿIrāq-i ʿAjam). He first correctly related the circumstances of my journey and then said to those present, 'respect this man because he is a son of the Imām Muḥammad al-Mahdī.'"[50] This incident

47. *RH,* I:24, and (for Baghlānī), II:1.
48. Ibid., I:27.
49. Ibid., I:28.
50. Ibid., I:29.

occurred, Nūrbakhsh states, two years before Hamadānī joined his circle. In addition to affirming Nūrbakhsh's status, this account also stresses the universal significance of becoming one of his associates.

The Direct Claim to Spiritual Eminence

In reading Nūrbakhsh's works, it is impossible not to notice the self-aggrandizement that permeates his whole discourse.[51] Although quite striking at first, this arrogance is natural for a mahdī, an individual expected to have both direct divine guidance and worldly dominion. The personal experiences that undergirded Nūrbakhsh's self-praise are a critical part of his worldview, and the justifications for his exaggerations on this score represent some of the most innovative ideas in his messianic doctrine.

Nūrbakhsh relates a visionary interaction with ʿAlī to illustrate the supernatural help he had received from the hidden world: "I saw that the Prince of Believers ʿAlī came to me during a period when persecution had greatly saddened and troubled me. I stood up and welcomed him, and he sat down close by my side after embracing me. . . . He said, 'your affair will definitely proceed forward.' I asked him, weeping, 'how and when will that happen?' Then, in unspoken, metaphoric speech (*kalām maʿnawī*), he promised me that (it would happen) sometime in the unspecified future. I am now waiting for this moment since it is impossible that the promise of a believer, indeed of the Prince of Believers, would not come true!"[52] Nūrbakhsh's intimacy with ʿAlī, the first imām, is crucial for legitimizing his claim in Shīʿī terms.

Nūrbakhsh considered himself spiritually the highest-ranked person of his age by virtue of his messianic designation. This was a necessary condition for the imām, who is, by definition, the highest authority in

51. For particulary noteworthy examples in this regard, see *RH,* I:6, 25, 28, 30–31, 36–37, 39, 41–44, 56; Nūrbakhsh, *Masnavī ṣaḥīfat al-awliyā, AA:*49; idem, *Maktūb beh Mīrzā Shāhrukh, AA:*73, 76; idem, *Maktūb dar naṣīḥat-i murīdān, AA:*99–100; idem, *Vāridāt, AA:*137–40; idem, *Risāla-yi nūrīya, AA:*172–73; and numerous parts of the *Dīvān.*

52. *RH,* I:33.

all religious matters, as well as the mundane.[53] Nūrbakhsh's thought reflects the Shīʿī view of imāmate on this point, and he believed also that the mahdī was ranked above all the other imāms. Visions seen by two of his companions affirm this perspective:

> Abū Yazīd Khalkhālī said, "I saw that your station in the worlds of essences (*ʿawālim al-maʿnawīya*) was above that of the perfect. In fact, it was more perfect than the perfected by a hundred degrees, with each degree separated from the next by a thousand years." And Muḥammad Ṭūsī said, "I saw the highest abode inhabited by the perfected people among both our predecessors and our contemporaries. You were not there so I asked them about you, and they replied that his place is knowledge (*ʿilm*) reachable by knowledge alone, stripped of both body and soul. I separated from [my body and soul] so that nothing remained of me except knowledge and then traveled for a thousand years to reach your abode."[54]

Nūrbakhsh's transcendence above all other sages that have appeared in the world is confirmed in these reports.

The Future according to the Mahdī: Triumph and Resurrection

Nūrbakhsh's expectation of the future, given in the *Risālat al-hudā* and other works, is simultaneously triumphalist and apocalyptic. He often felt that he received premonitions through his own visions and those of his companions. Quite remarkably, he had worked out the exact year of his death, which he then used to make other predictions. His life expectancy was revealed to his disciple Muḥammad Hamadānī, who was told by God in a vision that Nūrbakhsh would live "a hundred minus twelve years." This prediction confirmed astrological calculations estimating that his age at death would be eighty-eight solar (ninety-one lunar) years.[55] Nūrbakhsh combined this prediction with the ḥadīth that the mahdī would rule for seven, eight, or nine years,[56]

53. Ibid., I:42.
54. Ibid., I:30–31.
55. Ibid., I:32.
56. *MA,* nos. 44, 53.

to declare that he would gain temporal rule around his eightieth (solar) birthday. He thought that even if he did acquire temporal rule before this age, it would be partial, and true world dominion would be realized only at the appointed time.

Once the mahdī accomplished his mission of bringing peace to the world, he was expected to rule magnanimously and justly. Nūrbakhsh relates the ḥadīth that the mahdī "will open up treasures, conquer cities of polytheism (*shirk*), and inundate (the world) with goods so that if a beggar comes to him and says, 'O mahdī give me,' he will give him gold to the extent he can carry."[57] The mahdī was also described as a virtuous man who would act according to Muḥammad's sunna[58] and subdue tyrannical kings dominant at the time of his proclamation.[59]

Some ḥadīth reports cited by Nūrbakhsh portray the mahdī as a militaristic figure fulfilling the activist function many Muslims expected of the messianic savior. However, this aspect of the mahdī was attenuated in Nūrbakhsh's outlook through Sufi ideas such as the following statement attributed to Saʿd ad-Dīn Ḥamuvayī: "The Mahdī will repel enemies through spiritual force and not by bodily armaments."[60] Ḥamuvayī is credited with a number of other opinions about the mahdī as well, including that the savior will be aided by the souls of martyrs during his (presumably spiritual) combat. This made him comparable to Moses, who had received help from the souls of the children killed by Pharaoh's armies. The tradition cited from Ḥamuvayī echoes the popular Shīʿī notion that martyrs would come back alive at the time of the mahdī and would be instrumental in his success.[61]

57. *RH,* I:8; *MA,* nos. 139, 144.

58. *RH,* I:9; *MA,* no. 73.

59. *RH,* I:9; *MA,* no. 2.

60. *RH,* I:12. A short work by Ḥamūvayī on the appearance of the seal of saints, whom the author equates with the mahdī, contains his belief that the savior's "conquests" would be spiritual rather than military (cf. Saʿd ad-Dīn Ḥamuvayī, *ar-Risāla fī ẓuhūr khātam al-walāya,* MS. Ayasofya 2058, Süleymaniye Library, Istanbul, 206a–207b).

61. Madelung, "Ḳāʾim Āl Muḥammad," *EI*^{2}, 4:457. It should be emphasized that, despite this parallel, Ḥamuvayī was not a Shīʿī and followed the Shāfiʿī Sunnī school. This is clearly evident in his treatise dealing with the properties of letters

Nūrbakhsh's use of ḥadīth reports predicting the end of the world after the mahdī's reign marks his viewpoint as apocalyptic. He mentions the conquest of Constantinople and Daylam that is to be accomplished by the mahdī close to the Hour, though he makes no comment on the fact that Constantinople had indeed been captured by a Muslim ruler, the Ottoman Mehmed Fātiḥ, in 1453, before the completion of the *Risālat al-hudā* (1454–55).[62] In a Shīʿī vein, he also reports ʿAlī's statement that "all peoples have a reign, and our reign will be at the end of time."[63]

Nūrbakhsh's general understanding of resurrection is, however, comparable to the Sufi outlook of ʿAlāʾ ad-Dawla Simnānī, a prominent shaykh in the Kubravī silsila.[64] He explains that resurrections (*qiyāma*) are of two types—internal (*anfusīya*) and external (*āfāqīya*)—and each of these has separate associated punishments and rewards.[65] These two resurrections each have four aspects: small (*ṣughrā),* middle (*wusṭā*), great (*kubrā*), and the supreme (*ʿuẓmā*). The four aspects of internal resurrection correspond to the voluntary death indicated in the ḥadīth favored by the Sufis, "Die before you die." The full internal resurrection thus occurs when the mystic becomes completely dead in his base nature and is resurrected at a higher plane of existence. The four levels of this process are: (1) death of the "soul inciting to evil"; (2) progressing from the abode of Mulk (kingdom) to that of Malakūt (God's sovereignty); (3) traveling further to the abode of Jabarūt (God's unity); and (4) finally reaching the world of Lāhūt (God's singularity). The internal resurrection is a metaphor for the mystic's journey up the cosmic ladder while being alive in the lower world.[66] The four external

---

where the four Sunnī legal schools are lauded with the Shāfiʿī path exalted above the others (cf. Saʿd ad-Dīn Ḥamuvayī, *Risāla dar ḥurūf,* MS. Pertev Paşa 606, Süleymaniye Library, Istanbul, 13b–18a).

62. *RH,* I:9; *MA,* no. 230.

63. *RH,* I:10. This statement is not included in *Nahj al-balāgha.*

64. Jamal Elias, *The Throne Carrier of God: The Life and Thought of ʿAlāʾ ad-dawla as-Simnānī* (Albany: State University of New York Press, 1995), 143.

65. Nūrbakhsh, *Risāla al-iʿtiqādīya,* 196–201; idem, *Risāla-yi nūrīya, AA:*179–80.

66. For details of Nūrbakhsh's cosmology, see chapter 4.

resurrections refer, in contrast, to the physical death experienced by human beings. The four aspects of these are: (1) an individual's physical death; (2) the death of a large number of people, such as in a plague; (3) catastrophic death all over the earth as reported during Noah's flood; and (4) the destruction of everything save God. Nūrbakhsh explains that the supreme external resurrection (*al-qiyāma al-ʿuẓmā al-āfāqīya*) is, in God's words, "the Hour regarding which there is no doubt" (18:21). The final resurrection, the ultimate apocalyptic moment in world history, is to occur soon after the mahdī's appearance.

Nūrbakhsh's eschatological references are motivated largely by his desire to be accepted as the mahdī. By correlating the recommended religious path in this life with events to occur after death, Nūrbakhsh emphasizes the connection between righteousness and recognizing the mahdī as a sign of the Hour. His eschatology is, therefore, tied to his soteriology and the imperatives of his personal messianic claim. As a Sufi mahdī, Nūrbakhsh claims ultimate status as instructor in both the esoteric and exoteric spheres; he is, therefore, the ultimate reference point for both internal and external resurrections.

Metaphysical Arguments about the Mahdī's Status

The review of Nūrbakhsh's works shows that his messianic doctrine was based, first of all, on his perception that ḥadīth predictions about the figure had come true in his experience. Beyond Muḥammad, to justify his claim he invoked ʿAlī, his predecessors and companions among the Sufis, and philosophers and astronomers. He supplemented these "traditional" affirmations by assigning a metaphysical significance to the mahdī's person based upon Ibn al-ʿArabī's theory of the seal of sainthood. To understand Nūrbakhsh's particular interpretations of this idea, I will begin with a brief summary of the general concept.

Ibn al-ʿArabī on the Seal of Sainthood and the Mahdī

Patterned on Muḥammad's status as the seal of prophecy (*khātam-i nubūvat*) and first suggested in the work of al-Ḥakīm at-Tirmidhī (d. ca. 295/905),[67] the seal of sainthood (*khātam-i valāyat*) is a major theme in

67. Cf. al-Ḥakīm at-Tirmidhī, *Khatm al-awliyā,'* ed. Othman Yahia (Beirut: Al-Maṭbaʿa al-Kathulikīya, 1965); Bernd Radtke and John O'Kane, trans., *The Concept*

the work of Ibn al-ʿArabī. In simplified form, his general theory about the concept distinguishes between different types of sainthood whose spiritual progenitors are twenty-seven prophets from Adam to Muḥammad.[68] All these prophets derive their status from their relationship with the Muḥammadan Reality (*ḥaqīqa muḥammadīya*), the first substance created by God.[69] The only complete physical or elemental manifestation of this primordial substance was Muḥammad's earthly body, but all other prophets are also partial refractions of this single metaphysical entity.

All prophets are simultaneously saints or friends (*awliyāʾ*) of God, and people can still attain to the station of a saint after the death of the last prophet. Every saint in the postprophetic period either possesses complete sainthood (if he is heir to Muḥammadan sainthood), or he has partial sainthood, if he inherits his status from one of the other twenty-six prophets.[70] The most accomplished saint in each class at a given moment in time is called the pole (*quṭb*), and the pole of Muḥammadan sainthood is naturally the highest in status among them all. He sits atop an elaborate hierarchy of saints in the world, and it is through his presence that God sustains the universe. In summary, all saints—the prophets as well as those born after Muḥammad—are related in some way to the Muḥammadan Reality, and the status of an individual saint depends on how close he is to this entity.

Based upon this theory, Ibn al-ʿArabī predicted the existence of two different seals who are to bring finality to sainthood. He identified Jesus as the seal of universal sainthood since he is the only prophet who, in his Second Coming, will exist on earth in a physical form after the end of prophecy. He will literally be the last saint in the world since no one else born between the time of his appearance and the world's final

of Sainthood in Early Islamic Mysticism: Two Works by al-Ḥakīm al-Tirmidhī (Richmond, U.K.: Curzon Press, 1996).

68. Michel Chodkiewicz, *The Seal of the Saints* (Cambridge, U.K.: Islamic Texts Society, 1993), 48–52. Ibn al-ʿArabī's work *Fuṣūṣ al-ḥikam* is devoted specifically to this issue (ed. A. A. Affifi, 2 vols. [Beirut: Dār al-Kitāb al-ʿArabī, 1966]). For an English translation of this work, see *The Bezels of Wisdom,* trans. R. W. J. Austin (London: Missionary Society of St. Paul, 1980).

69. Chodkiewicz, *Seal of the Saints,* 68–69.

70. Ibid., 74–88.

destruction can be called a saint. The second seal will be the seal of Muḥammadan sainthood, an Arab who will bring to perfection the sainthood derived from Muḥammad's heritage. Unlike Jesus, this seal is not expected at a given time, and his appearance does not imply that there will be no other saints after him. His role is to bring sainthood to perfection (and not closure), whereas Jesus as the seal will literally be the last person to possess sainthood.[71]

Ibn al-ʿArabī's works reveal that he considered himself the seal of Muḥammadan sainthood. He hinted at this possibility in his interpretation of a ḥadīth in which Muḥammad states: "My place among the prophets is as when a man builds a wall and completes it except for one brick. I am that brick, and after me there is neither Messenger nor Prophet." Ibn al-ʿArabī writes in his *al-Futūḥāt al-makkīya:*

> While I was in Mecca in 599 [1202–3], I had a dream in which I saw the Kaʿba built of alternate gold and silver bricks The building was complete; nothing remained to be done. I looked at it and admired its beauty. But then I turned to face the side between the Yemeni corner, and I saw, nearer the Syrian corner, a gap where two bricks, one gold and one silver, had not been laid in two of the rows of the wall. In the top row a gold brick was missing, and in the row below a silver one. Then I saw myself placed in the gap made by these two missing bricks. I myself was these two bricks, by means of which the wall was completed and the Kaʿba made perfect. . . . When I was interpreting this vision, I said to myself: my place among the "followers," in my category [i.e., the category of the *awliyāʾ*] is like that of the Messenger of God among the prophets, and perhaps it is through me that God has sealed sainthood.[72]

In addition to this report, other insinuations in Ibn al-ʿArabī's work also suggest that he hoped or believed that he was the seal of Muḥammadan sainthood.

71. Ibid., 117–27.

72. Chodkiewicz, *Seal of the Saints,* 128–29; Ibn al-ʿArabī, *Futūḥāt al-makkīya,* 4 vols. (Beirut: Dār Ṣādir, 1968), 1:318–19.

Before moving to Nūrbakhsh's interpretation of the seal, mention needs to be made of Ibn al-ʿArabī's view of the mahdī. He discusses the figure in the *Futūḥāt,* highlighting his eschatological function and the fact that he would be aided by Jesus in his mission.[73] At least on the surface, therefore, he distinguishes quite clearly between the identity and functions of the mahdī and the two seals of sainthood discussed above.[74] His views were interpreted differently in later times when some of his commentators considered the mahdī to be the same person as the seal of Muḥammadan sainthood.[75] Of particular interest in this regard is Sayyid Ḥaydar Āmulī (d. after 787/1385), a Shīʿī admirer of Ibn al-ʿArabī, who claimed that the eminent master had been mistaken in his identification of the seals. He suggested, instead, that the seal of universal sainthood was ʿAlī, not Jesus, and the seal of Muḥammadan sainthood was not Ibn al-ʿArabī himself, but the mahdī.[76] This view seems to be a necessary condition for synchronizing Sufi and Twelver Shīʿī views of spiritual authority.

Nūrbakhsh as Mahdī and Seal of Sainthood

Like Āmulī, Nūrbakhsh also considered the mahdī (i.e., himself) to be the seal. In the *Risālat al-hudā,* he mentions that all indications about the mahdī had come true for him during his youth except the dream with the two bricks seen by Ibn al-ʿArabī. He therefore explicitly equates the seal of sainthood with the mahdī, and goes on to say:

> I had a dream resembling [Ibn al-ʿArabī's] but not exactly the same. I saw one wall with "there is no God but God, Muḥammad is the Messenger of God" written on it in gold, and another with "our God,

73. Ibn al-ʿArabī, *Futūḥāt,* 3:327–40.

74. Chodkiewicz prefers this interpretation (*Seal of the Saints,* 137), but it has been suggested that, in his work *ʿAnqāʾ mughrib,* Ibn al-ʿArabī projects himself as both the mahdī and the seal (Elmore, *Islamic Sainthood,* 55–60).

75. Cf. Ibn Khaldūn, *Muqaddimah,* 2:189; ʿAbd al-Razzāq Qāshānī, *A Glossary of Sufi Technical Terms,* trans. Nabil Safwat (London: Octagon Press, 1991), 158 (orig.), 110 (trans.); R. A. Nicholson, *Studies in Islamic Mysticism* (Cambridge: Cambridge University Press, 1921; reprint 1989), 135.

76. Ḥaydar Āmulī, *Muqaddimāt min Kitāb naṣṣ an-nuṣūṣ fī sharḥ al-fuṣūṣ,* ed.

> prayers be upon Muḥammad and upon Muḥammad's descendants" written in silver. Then I saw that I alternately became these lines and was embodied as a human being. This occurred repeatedly, and I was pleased that I could transform myself into becoming script or human. I could make this happen at will during a forty-day seclusion in the companionship of my shaykh in Khuttalān, in Dhū l-Qaʿda of the year 819 [December 21, 1416–January 19, 1417].[77]

Nūrbakhsh's admission that he had not seen the same dream as Ibn al-ʿArabī may seem, at first, to be the only insecure moment in the defense of his messianic claim. However, he changed the occurrences of the dream in order to reflect Ibn al-ʿArabī's mistake of thinking himself the seal. The dreams are, nonetheless, close enough that Nūrbakhsh's "truer" experience does not negate Ibn al-ʿArabī's spiritual station in its totality.

Nūrbakhsh's appeal to Ibn al-ʿArabī's doctrine of sainthood goes deeper than just the dream of the bricks. He remarks that the fact that Muḥammad and the mahdī/seal both have the dream about the brick signifies that they are both complete earthly forms of the Muḥammadan Reality. He thus assumes Ibn al-ʿArabī's metaphysical explanation about Muḥammad and sainthood but uses an innovative concept to explain how the Muḥammadan Reality comes to reside in the seal. He envisions the transference in a far more physical way than Ibn al-ʿArabī and states that the Muḥammadan Reality appears in the human body through the process of "projection (*barazāt*), which is not transmigration (*tanāsukh*). The difference between the two is that transmigration occurs when a soul departs one body and enters an embryo ready for a soul—meaning the fourth month from the time the sperm settled in the womb—and this removal from one body and arrival at the other occurs instantaneously, without a time interval. However, projection occurs when a complete soul pours into a perfect being *(kāmil)* in the same way that epiphanies pour into him and he becomes their locus of manifestation

Osman Yahia (Tehran: Departement d'Iranologie de l'Institut Franco-Iranien de Recherche, 1975), 175.

77. *RH,* I:35.

(*maẓhar*)."[78] Nūrbakhsh thus imagines the seal/mahdī to be a physical reembodiment of Muḥammad's spiritual essence. He distinguishes projection (*barazāt* or *burūz*) from transmigration through the way the soul is transferred, but the actual event that takes place is essentially the same in the two processes.

The idea of "projection" is Nūrbakhsh's most innovative concept in linking himself as mahdī to Muḥammad, the prototype for Islamic religiopolitical leadership.[79] While the Arabic term *burūz* itself is attested in Sufi literature before Nūrbakhsh, the connotation attached to it in *Risālat al-hudā* was Nūrbakhsh's innovation. For Ibn al-ʿArabī, *burūz* signifies the unfolding of God's essence during the creation of the cosmos,[80] and among later authors ʿAlī Hamadānī also uses the term in the same meaning.[81] In this interpretation, the term signifies a transference that takes place between God and the created world, not between two created entities.

The term *burūz* is employed in a meaning closer to Nūrbakhsh's sense in Jaʿfar Badakhshī's biography of ʿAlī Hamadānī. Badakhshī was a close companion of Hamadānī, and this usage may be the source for Nūrbakhsh's explanation. Badakhshī considers *burūz* the miraculous ability of accomplished saints to transport themselves to distant places without any effort. He explains that they deposit a nonmaterial lookalike of themselves in one place while they travel great distances so that they "appear" to be present in more than one place at a time.[82]

78. Ibid., I:11.

79. Molé translates the term *burūz* into French as *apparition* ("Les Kubrawiya entre Sunnisme et Shiisme," 136).

80. William Chittick, The *Sufi Path of Knowledge: Ibn al-ʿArabi's Metaphysics of Imagination* (Albany: State University of New York Press, 1989), 134.

81. See ʿAlī Hamadānī, *Risāla-yi iṣṭilāḥāt,* MS. Şehid Ali Paşa 2794, Süleymaniye Library, Istanbul, 479a. For the connection between the thought of Hamadānī and Nūrbakhsh, see chapter 4.

82. Nūr ad-Dīn Jaʿfar Badakhshī, *Khulāṣat al-manāqib,* ed. Sayyida Ashraf Ẓafar (Islamabad: Markaz-i Taḥqīqāt-i Fārsī-yi Īrān va Pākistān, 1995), 224; Teufel, *Lebensbeschreibung,* 108. Teufel translates the term *burūz* into German as *exteriorisation.* The supernatural ability described here is one of the minor miracles (*karāmāt*) Sufis attribute to themselves (cf. R. Gramlich, *Die Wunder der Freunde Gottes* [Wiesbaden: Steiner, 1987], 287–91).

Nūrbakhsh's use of *burūz* is significantly different from his predecessors although he probably encountered the term first in the discourse of his Kubravī teachers. Besides using it to connect himself to Muḥammad, he also connects himself to Jesus and the Shīʿī Twelfth Imām in order to controvert obvious objections to his claims. The tradition that the mahdī was none other than Jesus is fulfilled in a vision seen by a companion: "Muḥammad b. ʿAlī b. Bahrām Qāʾinī saw in Irbil in the year 827 [1423–24] that one day people gathered together to wait for Jesus to descend from the sky. He saw that he descended in the form of light rather than body, and flowed toward me and held me. The same night I saw that I was present in the sky and in a human body on earth in the same instant."[83] Nūrbakhsh's explanation satisfies a popular tradition about the mahdī, but here again he deviates from Ibn al-ʿArabī's theory of sainthood. While it is true that, as a prophet, Jesus derived his essence from the Muḥammadan Reality, Ibn al-ʿArabī makes a distinction between Jesus as the seal of universal sainthood and he himself as the seal of Muḥammadan sainthood. In Nūrbakhsh's conception, the three individuals—the two seals and the mahdī—all become conflated into his own person.

Nūrbakhsh also connects himself to the Shīʿī imāms through the concept of spiritual projection. He first contends that the Twelver Shīʿī belief that there could be no more than twelve imāms is misleading since the numerical limitation was one of the myths created by the ʿAbbāsids to demean the ʿAlids and deprive them of capable leaders.[84] He claims that the truth of the matter is that "the appearance of Muḥammad b. al-Ḥasan [the Twelfth Imām] is impossible except through a projection; his physical body is now like the bodies of his noble fathers and his great ancestors."[85] Although not stated outright, the implication here is that, through projection, Nūrbakhsh himself had become a receptacle for the soul of the Twelfth Imām.

83. *RH,* I:51.

84. Ibid., I:45–46. He claims also that the ʿAbbāsids had invented the myth of Ḥamza's bravery to downplay ʿAlī's capabilities in this field.

85. Ibid., I:51.

Going further down the spiritual hierarchy, Nūrbakhsh also suggests that he was a reembodiment of the Kubravī master ʿAlī Hamadānī. He relates a number of stories in which his own teacher, Isḥāq Khuttalānī, saw him as indistinguishable from Hamadānī:

> During a seclusion my shaykh saw his shaykh Sayyid ʿAlī Hamadānī order sweetmeats (*ḥalwāʾ*) for the Sufis' meal. He forgot what he saw, but that night, the tenth, I ordered the servant Yūsuf to cook sweetmeats. When the servant put them in front of him, he remembered his vision and called me and asked me who had ordered the servant to cook them. I said it was me, upon which he related what he had seen and wondered over me. Once more during this seclusionary period, I forbade some young boys from entering the quarters where the seclusion was taking place due to their beardlessness. I did not, however, stop them from duties in the kitchen. My shaykh was unaware of my orders but he saw that his shaykh had ousted some boys from the khānqāh. . . . He related his vision one night upon which some of the attendants started smiling. He asked them the reason and they pointed me out as the man who had ousted the boys.[86]

The identity between Nūrbakhsh and Hamadānī exemplified here was interpreted by Nūrbakhsh by reference to projection. The procedure is thus open to saints other than the prophets and the imāms, as pointed out also in an obituarial poem wherein Nūrbakhsh suggests that one of his companions (ʿAlī Kiyā) may return to earth as a projection into another saint's body.[87] The main condition for the process was that both persons involved in the transaction had to have exceptional religious credentials.

Between Jesus, Muḥammad, the Twelfth Imām, and the Sufi shaykh, Nūrbakhsh presented himself as the projection of a central figure in the traditional Islamic understanding of both prophecy and sainthood. He saw himself not merely as the possessor of the knowledge of the prophets, the imāms, and the Sufis, but as an actual re-presentation of the original individuals themselves. The doctrine of projection later

86. Ibid., I:22.
87. *Dīvān,* 19–20 (no. 45).

became the hallmark of Nūrbakhsh's mystical school since it occurs in Persian translations of Nūrbakhsh's explanation in *Risālat al-hudā* in two different sources. Ibn al-Karbalāʾī repeats Nūrbakhsh's definition of *burūz* in his *Rawżāt al-jinān* without attributing it to the mahdī. He illustrates the point by referring to an incident when, upon looking into a mirror, Jaʿfar Badakhshī saw himself as ʿAlī Hamadānī.[88] In comparison, the author of *Dabistān-i maẕāhib* (written between 1063/1653 and 1069/1658–59) repeats the text from *Risālat al-hudā,* but states that he had seen the explanation in Nūrbakhsh's *Silsilat al-awliyāʾ*.[89] Nūrbakhsh's use of the concept resolved the problem of traditions that identified specific individuals such as Jesus or the Twelfth Imām as the mahdī. Even more significantly, however, the concept allowed him to posit an ontological identity between himself and Muḥammad, the ultimate model for the Islamic savior.

Nūrbakhsh and the Paradigmatic Mahdī

The survey of Nūrbakhsh's messianic doctrine in this chapter shows it to be a coherent system with distinctive features. Nūrbakhsh justified many of his assertions about the mahdī by referring to predictions about the mahdī from the traditional Islamic (particularly Twelver Shīʿī) paradigm. However, a number of important features of that paradigm are completely missing from his discussion.

Nūrbakhsh's mahdism reflects a clear belief that the mahdī is to appear at a special time in world history. Apart from the eschatological

88. *RJJJ,* 2:263. As discussed in chapter 2, Ibn al-Karbalāʾī belonged to a Kubravī faction rival to the Nūrbakhshīya. His belief in projection may mean that it was a Kubravī doctrine going to the period before the order split into the Nūrbakhshīya and the Ẕahabīya. However, this is unlikely since no pre-Nūrbakhsh Kubravī source contains the explanation and the text in *Rawżāt al-jinān* is close enough to *Risālat al-hudā* to be a translation. Ibn al-Karbalāʾī's work contains other citations from the *Risālat al-hudā* as well (cf. *RJJJ,* 1:396–97; *RH,* II:94).

89. Kaykhusraw Isfandiyār, *Dabistān-i maẕāhib,* ed. Raḥīm Rižā-zāda Malik, 2 vols. (Tehran: Kitābkhāna-yi Ṭahūrī, 1983), 1:357. The author of this work also cites Nūrbakhsh's *Ṣaḥīfat al-awliyāʾ* and *Risāla-yi miʿrāj* (1:44, 349). For the problem of attribution of this work and the date of composition, see the editor's introduction and notes (2:16–20, 46–76) and Fath Allah Mojtaba'i, "Dabestān-e Maẕaheb," *EIr,* 6:532–34.

references discussed above, he states also that the enlightened know that spiritual truths hidden so far are to become apparent during the present age.[90] His definition of the mahdī's function maintains that he himself is the agent of this final complete unveiling of the truths. The mahdī's primary function is thus spiritual, and numerous references in Nūrbakhsh's works make clear that although he did expect to gain temporal rule, his paramount concern was spiritual knowledge and not a military struggle.

Nūrbakhsh's messianic doctrine contains a particular focus on the mahdī's function as the mediator between different Islamic sects. The savior figure first became a part of Islamic theoretical speculation in the face of discord within the community. In his theological discussions, Nūrbakhsh points out that the views held by the various Islamic sects and groups on subjects such as resurrection, paradise and hell, and so forth are only different ways of explaining the same issue.[91] Nūrbakhsh transcends the differences between these factions by contending that knowledge regarding these matters has to be understood contextually: all opinions are correct (or incorrect) depending on whether one sees them from the inside or outside of the system from which they are articulated. As discussed in later chapters of this book, this aspect of Nūrbakhsh's ideology has remained a significant feature of Nūrbakhshī thought throughout the movement's history.

Nūrbakhsh states that the greatest evils plaguing the Muslim community in his day are disunity (*ikhtilāf*), doubt (*ẓann*), and groups of tyrants and corrupt scholars (*ʿulamāʾ as-sūʾ*).[92] He proposes to dissolve the disputes between different factions through the doctrine of relativism

90. Nūrbakhsh, *Maktūb beh ʿAlāʾ ad-Dawla, AA:*81.

91. These discussions deal with the following questions: will the gathering promised at resurrection be in the body or in the spirit? (Nūrbakhsh, *Javāb-i maktūb-i ḥakīm,* AA:95); are paradise and hell physical entities or metaphors? (Nūrbakhsh, *Javāb-i maktūb-i ḥakīm,* AA:95); will the meeting with God promised for the End occur physically or in spirit? (Nūrbakhsh, *Dar bayān-i āya-ī, AA:*141); are entities other than God primordial or accidental? (Nūrbakhsh, *Javāb-i suʾāl-i Amīr Kiyā, AA:*88); and did Muḥammad go on the celestial journey (*miʿrāj*) in his body or just in his soul? (Nūrbakhsh, *Risāla-yi miʿrājīya, AA:*115–16).

92. *RH,* I:53–55.

described above, and the certain knowledge he brings as the mahdī is poised to replace the doubt that has weakened Muslims' belief. He condemns corrupt scholars who reign along with the tyrants by legitimizing their rule and warns both groups with the punishment of the Fire. His eventual hope is that the full realization of the mahdī's mission would rid the world of these corrupting influences.

Nūrbakhsh's messianism differs from the traditional paradigm in that he makes no mention of an archenemy who is supposed to die at the hands of the mahdī. The tradition contains such figures under the names Dajjāl, Sufyānī, and the beast (*dābba*) that is one of the signs of world coming to an end.[93] The only person to be persistently inimical to him during his life was the Tīmūrid ruler Shāhrukh, who, however, died a natural death within Nūrbakhsh's lifetime. Nūrbakhsh's letter to him asks him to stop maltreating him, but does not contain a summary condemnation.[94] Similarly, Nūrbakhsh's works make no mention of the mahdī's expected military campaigns in the Arabian peninsula (Ḥijāz and Yemen), Syria, Egypt, and the Maghrib, which were a major part of the tradition.[95] Some of the visionary experiences discussed above show that he thought that such traditions could be realized in the metaphysical realm rather than in actuality (e.g., his arrival in Mecca on a horse in a vision seen by Isḥāq b. Yūsuf Ṭāliqānī).

Nūrbakhsh's mainstay for his religious speculation was Sufism, particularly the doctrines originating in the masters of the Kubravī silsila and the school of Ibn al-ʿArabī. He had been trained as a Sufi from an early age, and Sufism was the most pervasive intellectual orientation in the area where he spent his life. As he stated in his work *Risāla-yi nūrīya,* the period in which he lived was special precisely *because* Sufism had

93. *MA,* vol. 1, nos. 281–93, 343–53 (Sufyānī); vol. 1, nos. 372–77, vol. 2, nos. 382–482 (Dajjāl); vol. 2, nos. 500–534 (*dābba*); see also: Wilferd Madelung, "The Sufyānī between Tradition and History," *SI* 63 (1984): 5–48; A. Abel, "Dadjdjāl," *EI*², 2:76–77.

94. Nūrbakhsh, *Maktūb beh Mīrzā Shāhrukh, AA:*73–77. As discussed in chapter 2, some Nūrbakhshīs did regard Shāhrukh as the antichrist; however, the movement in general was not invested greatly in seeing the struggle between Nūrbakhsh and the ruler in cosmic terms.

95. *MA,* 2:509–13 (topical index).

become accepted by the population at large.[96] The ascendancy of Sufism in society thus played a formative role in the construction of his messianic claim.

Although Nūrbakhsh clearly had a very high opinion of his own status, he felt that he had no choice but to accept the travails as well as privileges reserved for the mahdī. He wrote at the end of his defense of the claim in *Risālat al-hudā:*

> Some ignoramuses among the tyrants allege that my claim of imāmate stems from my desire for worldly status or for acquiring wealth. This is what the unbelievers used to insinuate about the seal of the prophets. [Their accusation] is false since I did not proclaim the imāmate by myself; the Pole and other great saints have ordered, or rather forced, me to it. They have pledged allegiance to me and have promised to fulfill their vows in the path of God. I cannot oppose their command since they have received it from God through unveiling and inspiration, and have not issued it by themselves. I doubly swear by God that my personal inclination was toward hiding and obscurity and wandering around the world in emulation of the Second ʿAlī, ʿAlī Hamadānī. However, the tranquility of such a situation is not available to me except in my heart. I cannot oppose what God, His messenger, and many among His saints, have commanded me. I place my trust in God, delegate my affairs to Him, and await what He has promised me—He is the "best of the victorious" (3:150).[97]

Nūrbakhsh's conviction about his claim is evident in this statement, and the circumstances of his life also bear witness to his tenacity in pursuing the cause. The proofs from tradition, logic, and inspiration found in the articulation of his claim reveal that his mahdism was backed by a coherent theoretical structure in his mind.

The Intricacies of Saintly Designation

Nūrbakhsh's mahdism is an amalgamation of Shīʿī and Sufi doctrines combined to fit the needs of his personal situation. His main concern

96. Nūrbakhsh, *Risāla-yi nūrīya, AA:*167.
97. *RH,* I:56.

in appropriating from both these systems was the question of spiritual authority. As the self-proclaimed mahdī/imām and the seal of sainthood, he had to convince his audience that he occupied the highest spiritual station among humans whereby he should be accorded all privileges reserved for such a person.

Spiritual authority is discussed in both Shīʿism and Sufism most often under the term *valāyat* (Arabic: *walāya/wilāya*), rendered as sainthood in the present discussion. In its basic application, the Shīʿī concept of *valāyat* exalts the status of the imāms above all others living during their lifetimes. By accepting the imāms as *awliyāʾ* (bearers of *valāyat*), the Shīʿīs contend that the imāms possessed special spiritual knowledge conveyed from one generation to the next through an imām's designation of one of his sons as his successor. The Twelfth Imām is particularly significant in this regard since he has been a constant invisible presence in the community since his occultation and is expected to bring closure to the world in his eschatological role.[98]

The Shīʿī view of *valāyat* is univocal since only the imāms possess such authority. Shīʿī discussions on the topic are, therefore, concerned largely with the functions possessed by the imāms/saints due to their status. In comparison, Sufi ideas about *valāyat* are quite diffused and have changed considerably over time.[99] The identity of the saints is in itself a substantive concern for Sufi authors, and in one classification

> there are 355 or 356 such figures, upon whom life and death of all nations depends: 300 "whose heart is after the heart" of Adam; 40 who are in the same relationship to Moses (or Noah); 7 to Abraham; 5 (or 4) to the angel Gabriel; 3 to Michael; and one to Seraphiel (Isrāfīl, the angel of resurrection). If one of them dies, God substitutes for him one of the next lower class. The substitutes of the lowest class (the 300) are taken from the common people (*al-ʿāmmah*). The single one is

98. Hermann Landolt, "Walāya" in *The Encyclopedia of Religion,* 15:319–20; Amir-Moezzi, *Divine Guide,* 125–31. I am concerned here only with Twelver Shīʿī notions of *valāyat* since other branches of Shīʿism have little relevance for a discussion of Nūrbakhsh's ideas.

99. For an extensive discussion of *valāyat* in Sufi history and theory, see Chodkiewicz, *Seal of the Saints,* 21–46.

> commonly called the "pole" (*quṭb*) or the "rescue" (*ghawth*), while terms such as *abdāl* . . . and *ṣiddīqūn* . . . refer either to a class, or to saints generally, like *awliyā*ʾ. *Wilāyah,* then, is the special charismatic quality of a sufi, that which enables him to be the subject of miracles or, more precisely, charismata (*karāmāt*).[100]

The function of saints is, thus, predetermined in Sufism as they are possessors of miracles and parts of the system that sustains the world. In the postprophetic period, they carry out the guiding functions of the prophets without announcing a new revelation or exoteric law. The main difference of emphasis between the Shīʿī and Sufi discussions of *valāyat* is that the former is concerned more with the functions of saints and the latter with their identity.

Nūrbakhsh's greatest underlying endeavor in his messianic doctrine was to produce a definition for sainthood that would identify him as the saint par excellence in both Shīʿī and Sufi terms. On the issue of identity, he posited himself to be the mahdī *and* the seal (the ultimate pole), relying on Shīʿī traditions and Sufi theory, respectively, to prove his claim. On the level of the saint's functions, he sought the attainment of all privileges (including temporal rule) reserved for the mahdī as the last imām. And as the seal of sainthood, he gave the names of all the Sufis who had trained under him and had affirmed his status as the greatest spiritual teacher of the time.[101] Nūrbakhsh argued that the first and the last imāms, ʿAlī and mahdī, were the only two to receive the privilege of complete sainthood: "According to perceptive saints, the Imāmate is constructed on four pillars: knowledge, sainthood, descent from the Prophet, and temporal rule. The Imāmate of all holders of the office from the People of the House after ʿAlī encompassed only three of these—namely, knowledge, sainthood, and descent from the Prophet—since none of the twelve Imāms besides ʿAlī possessed temporal rule. Even these three pillars (raised them) above all remaining saints and scholars, but the promised imām (surpasses them) since, like ʿAlī, he will possess all the pillars (of Imāmate)."[102] Nūrbakhsh

100. Landolt, "Walāya," 321.
101. *RH,* I:36–37.
102. Ibid., I:48.

departs from the usual Twelver doctrine by claiming that he himself, and not the Twelfth Imām, is the mahdī who is entitled to the four pillars of imāmate.

Nūrbakhsh's messianic claim made him stand apart from the norm in both Twelver Shīʿism and Sufism. While his thought derived its major concepts from these two Islamic persuasions, his outlook represented a new perspective that may be termed Sufi Shīʿism. His messianic thought was an effort to articulate a new definition of sainthood congruent with his times. As discussed in chapter 2, the interpenetration of Sufism and Shīʿism in the Islamic East during the fourteenth and fifteenth centuries gave birth to new intellectual paradigms. Nūrbakhsh's thought exteriorized this historical circumstance in the field of religious discourse so that he was an interlocutor for the socioreligious currents permeating the context in which he lived.

Chapter Four

Nūrbakhsh's Sufi Worldview

Muḥammad Nūrbakhsh's messianic claim discussed in the preceding chapter was part of a comprehensive religious outlook grounded in his Sufi worldview. His discourses emphasize those ideas that underscore the significance of his own status on the Sufi path. This status is upheld through a complex religious system reflecting Nūrbakhsh's position as intellectual heir to two significant Sufi traditions. Constitutive elements of his worldview demonstrate his dependence on various shaykhs part of the Kubravī silsila and Persian Sufism based in the teachings of Ibn al-ʿArabī. Although he was influenced by the intermingling of these two traditions in the work of ʿAlī Hamadānī (d. 786/1385), a prolific Kubravī predecessor, Nūrbakhsh's Sufi system is a distinct synthesis encompassing both previous ideas and innovative interpretations.

Nūrbakhsh's Sufi thought is principally grounded in concepts denoted by three terms: oneness of being, the perfect man, and the seal of sainthood (*vaḥdat-i vujūd, insān-i kāmil,* and *khātam-i valāyat*). His perspective varies from most other authors on these themes in that he explicitly personalizes the designations to correlate them to his messianic claim. He calls himself the perfect man as well as the seal of sainthood and narrates visions of mystical union with God. This experiential verification of oneness of being leads Nūrbakhsh to posit a total identity of form and function between himself and God in the moment of union. He sees this as the station of the perfect man, the comprehensive locus of manifestation (*maẓhar*) of God's essence. In his messianic doctrine, Nūrbakhsh portrays himself as a reembodiment of Muḥammad, the archetype of Islamic religious leadership. This effort places him in Islamic (and cosmic) history, while in his Sufi thought, his definition for the perfect man exalts him to a near-divine status above the rest of creation. He thus sees himself as the consummation of both human history and the ontological hierarchy culminating in God's essence.

This chapter elicits the general parameters of Nūrbakhsh's mystical thought and situates his worldview relative to the work of his Sufi forebears. Besides explaining Nūrbakhsh's outlook, this description adds to the reconstruction of Kubravī intellectual history that has been under way in recent years.[1] By specifying a Kubravī "tradition," I do not wish to imply that individuals who identified themselves as such all self-consciously belonged to a single social or intellectual confraternity traceable from Najm ad-Dīn Kubrā to the later centuries. I concur with Devin DeWeese that Sufi "orders" such as the Kubravīya or Naqshabandīya cannot be substantiated as historical entities prior to the fifteenth century at the earliest, and even after that individual cases have to be adjudicated separately since affiliation with a silsila does not make a person part of an order automatically.[2] For Nūrbakhsh's case, it is significant that his thought is consciously derived from shaykhs who occur in the particular Kubravī lineage in which he placed himself. The Kubravī "order" for him then represents the conglomeration of distinctive ideas that he identified with his own Sufi lineage and to which he felt himself to be an heir. To show the continuity of doctrine between generations of Kubravīs in this sense, I compare Nūrbakhsh's formulations to the thought of earlier masters wherever appropriate. Highlighting Nūrbakhsh's use of Ibn al-ʿArabī's ideas also sheds light on this school's impact on the Islamic East by the fifteenth century.

1. Major figures who occur in Kubravī spiritual lineages and have received attention so far are Najm ad-Dīn Kubrā, Najm ad-Dīn Dāya Rāzī, Saʿd ad-Dīn Ḥamuvayī, ʿAzīz-i Nasafī, Nūr ad-Dīn Isfarāʾinī, ʿAlāʾ ad-Dawla Simnānī, ʿAlī Hamadānī, and Kamāl ad-Dīn Ḥusayn Khwārazmī. For studies on these shaykhs, see the bibliography for works by Fritz Meier, Hamid Algar, Jamal Elias, Marijan Molé, Hermann Landolt, Gerhard Böwering, Devin DeWeese, and Johann Teufel.

2. Cf. Devin DeWeese, *Islamization and Native Religion in the Golden Horde: Baba Tükles and Conversion to Islam in Historical and Epic Tradition* (University Park: Pennsylvania State University Press, 1994), 138–39.

My summary of Nūrbakhsh's Sufi thought aims to reconstruct his perception of both the world surrounding him and his own position within the cosmos. The presentation divides Nūrbakhsh's worldview into four categories: cosmology, epistemology, methodology, and the psychology of mystical experience. The description of Nūrbakhsh's cosmological thinking consists of the hierarchy of the different worlds (*ʿavālim*) and ontological connections between categories of beings. The forms of knowledge that bring the cosmos into human comprehension are treated in the second section. Nūrbakhsh's classification of knowledge is intrinsically linked to the structure of the cosmos since the connections between visible reality and the unseen world are comprehended only after understanding the cosmos.

The third section of the chapter discusses the practical concerns of mystical life described in Nūrbakhsh's work. These include the Sufi ethical code and the routine of spiritual exercises needed to progress on the Sufi path. The last section summarizes Nūrbakhsh's description of psychological states experienced during the mystical journey. This aspect of his thought includes a typology of mystical experience, the seven parts of the human being and their respective recollections (*ẕikr*), and God's self-disclosure to the Sufi resulting from his endeavors. Nūrbakhsh's psychology includes colored lights seen during mystical experience, a feature he shares in common with some predecessors in his spiritual lineage.

Nūrbakhsh's effort to consistently relate the theoretical discussions of mystical experiences and properties to his mahdism makes him stand apart from other Sufis. The ever-present need to justify the messianic claim obliges him to place himself at the pinnacle of the ontological, epistemological, and experiential hierarchies embedded in his outlook. Conversely, he also believes that his preeminence as a Sufi is the primary justification for the messianic designation. His mystical thought, therefore, represents an innovative case within the overall intellectual environment of the fifteenth-century Islamic East.

The Cosmos and Its Inhabitants

Nūrbakhsh's cosmology presupposes oneness of being—the idea that God is the only truly existent Being and the apparent diversity of the cosmos is caused by emanations from his essence flowing to ontologically lower realms.[3] The concept necessitates at least a partial identity between God and the created world since all existent entities derive from the one Being. The ramifications of this perspective generated intense debate in Sufi circles from the thirteenth century onward, and it became common to define the overall mystical outlook of a Sufi by reference to his position on this matter.[4] Although Nūrbakhsh's extant works do not discuss Ibn al-ʿArabī or any other proponent of oneness of being directly,[5] his cosmology clearly reflects his familiarity with such authors.[6] For Nūrbakhsh, "Being (*vujūd*) is only God (*ḥaqq*),"[7] while he himself is "a single drop from the ocean of Being."[8] The explanation for this relationship envisions the cosmos as a multitiered structure containing realms that are host to specific aspects of divine Being.

3. The term *vaḥdat-i vujūd* (Arabic: *waḥdat al-wujūd*) was coined by Ibn al-ʿArabī's disciple Ṣadr ad-Dīn Qūnavī to denote his teacher's complex metaphysical theories. For more detailed discussions of the history of the term, see W. Chittick, "Ṣadr al-Dīn Qūnawī on Oneness of Being," *International Philosophical Quarterly* 2 (1981): 171–84; Claude Addas, *Quest for the Red Sulphur: The Life of Ibn ʿArabī* (Cambridge, U.K.: Islamic Texts Society, 1993), 278–80; A. E. Affifi, *The Mystical Philosophy of Muhyid-din Ibnul Arabi* (Cambridge: Cambridge University Press, 1964; reprint, Lahore: Sh. Muhammad Ashraf, 1979), 54–65; Toshihiko Izutsu, *Creation and the Timeless Order of Things: Essays in Islamic Mystical Philosophy* (Ashland, Ore.: White Cloud Press, 1994), 66–97.

4. Details of some medieval controversies regarding oneness of being are reviewed in Michel Chodkiewicz, *An Ocean Without Shore: Ibn Arabi, the Book and the Law* (Albany: State University of New York Press, 1993), 1–18, and Alexander Knysh, *Ibn ʿArabi in the Later Islamic Tradition* (Albany: State University of New York Press, 1999).

5. He refers to Ibn al-ʿArabī as the leader of the perfected men (*raʾīs-i kummal*) in his versified *Vāridāt (AA:*138), but the only context in which he comments on his theories is the dream of the seal of sainthood (*khātam-i valāyat*), discussed in chapter 3.

6. Nūrbakhsh's emphasis on systemization suggests that he assimilated this perspective from summary discussions.

7. Nūrbakhsh, *ʿAvālim al-ḥiss, AA:*188.

8. Nūrbakhsh, *Masnavī ṣaḥīfat al-awliyāʾ*, *AA*:49. A drop of water losing its identity in the ocean is probably the most common poetic metaphor for oneness of being (cf. Schimmel, *Mystical Dimensions,* 284–86).

The Five Abodes

Every perceptible entity in the cosmos is, in Nūrbakhsh's thought, a realm, or world, unto itself. Its connection to other beings (particularly God's essence) determines its particular state of existence. Although the cosmos has an infinite number of realms, the individual entities are categorized into a five-tier hierarchy of abodes (*ʿavālim*) consisting of: Lāhūt (divinity), Jabarūt (God's omnipotence), Malakūt (God's sovereignty), Mulk (sense perception), and Nāsūt (perfect man).[9] The names of these abodes were in common use among Sufis by the fifteenth century, but Nūrbakhsh's arrangement is distinct in its specifics. Each of these realms contains a different aspect of divine emanation or manifestation and has particular entities as its residents.

Nūrbakhsh's scheme begins with God as the only independently existent Being in the cosmos. This level is described as God's essence (*ẕāt*), resident in the abode of Lāhūt, or divinity (chart 3).[10] Lāhūt does not allow any multiplicity, and its inhabitant, the completely unrestricted and noncontingent being (*vujūd muṭlaq*), prefigures all existent things (*mawjūdāt*) in a general sense.[11] Although it is the ultimate reality behind all realities (*ḥaqīqat-i ḥaqāʾiq*), the essence is a singularity (*aḥadīyat*) completely beyond physiological descriptions obtained by asking the questions "how" (*kayf*), "how much" (*kam*), and "where" (*ayna*).[12] This realm is also called the completely invisible unknown (*ghayb majhūl*) due to its radical isolation; knowing something requires the duality of the knower and the known, which would violate its singularity. Lāhūt is also the most primordial aspect of the cosmos since it is identified as the cloud (*ʿamāʾ*) that was, according to a ḥadīth, God's dwelling place before he created the world.[13]

9. For the historical background of Sufi use of these terms, see Elias, *Throne Carrier of God,* 154–57, and A. J. Wensinck, *On the Relationship between Ghazālī's Cosmology and His Mysticism* (Amsterdam: N. V. Noord-Hollandische Uitgevers-Maatschappij, 1933), 1–25.

10. Nūrbakhsh, *ʿAvālim al-ḥiss, AA:*188; *Dīvān,* 21 (no. 49).

11. Nūrbakhsh, *Maktūb beh Mawlāna Ḥasan Kurd, AA:*96.

12. *Dīvān,* 16 (no. 32).

13. Nūrbakhsh, *Taʾvīl-i ḥadīs̱-i nabavī, AA:*144–45. The primordial cloud, or

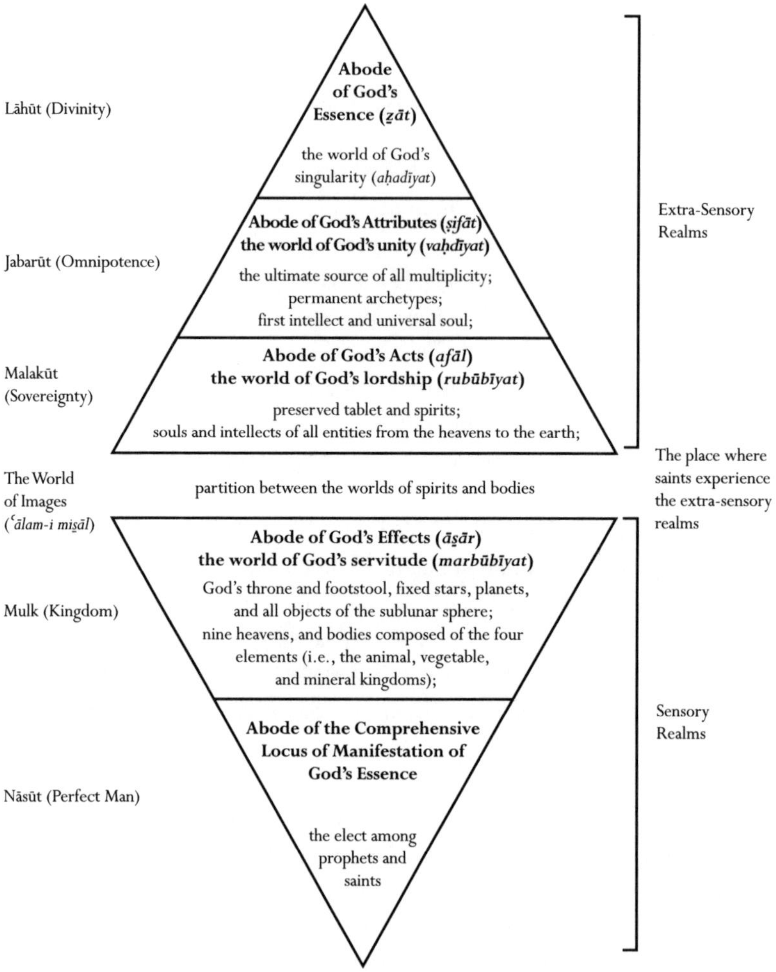
Abode of God's Essence (*ẕāt*)
the world of God's singularity (*aḥadīyat*)
Lāhūt (Divinity)
Abode of God's Attributes (*ṣifāt*)
the world of God's unity (*vaḥdīyat*)
the ultimate source of all multiplicity; permanent archetypes; first intellect and universal soul;
Jabarūt (Omnipotence)
Abode of God's Acts (*afʿāl*)
the world of God's lordship (*rubūbīyat*)
preserved tablet and spirits; souls and intellects of all entities from the heavens to the earth;
Malakūt (Sovereignty)
Extra-Sensory Realms
The World of Images (*ʿālam-i miṡāl*)
partition between the worlds of spirits and bodies
The place where saints experience the extra-sensory realms
Abode of God's Effects (*āṡār*)
the world of God's servitude (*marbūbīyat*)
God's throne and footstool, fixed stars, planets, and all objects of the sublunar sphere; nine heavens, and bodies composed of the four elements (i.e., the animal, vegetable, and mineral kingdoms);
Mulk (Kingdom)
Abode of the Comprehensive Locus of Manifestation of God's Essence
the elect among prophets and saints
Nāsūt (Perfect Man)
Sensory Realms

CHART 3: Structure of the Cosmos

The second abode, Jabarūt, is the highest element of the created world. It contains God's emanation in the form of his essential attributes (*ṣifāt*), the first entities to evolve from his essence during his self-manifestation.[14] Jabarūt is the world of unity (*vaḥdīyat* or *vāḥidīyat*), constituting also the first concretely determinable entity (*taʿayyun avval*) that is the source proper of all cosmic diversity. This world is also seen as the receptacle of all of God's knowledge as represented in the permanent archetypes (*aʿyān s̱ābita*) of creation. In philosophical terminology, the foremost among these archetypes are the primary intellect (*ʿaql avval*) and the universal soul (*nafs kullī*), whose projections in the lower realms precipitate other created beings. Jabarūt is also the partition of partitions (*barzakh-i barāzikh*), the ultimate separator between God's essence in its uniqueness in Lāhūt and the rest of the cosmos.[15]

Malakūt, the third abode, is named after a Qurʾanic term and contains the preserved tablet (*lawḥ maḥfūẓ*). It is the repository of the created world's destiny and, in the scheme of God's emanations, the sphere of his acts (*afʿāl*).[16] Malakūt is the first realm to contain a multiplicity of entities, the nonmaterial spirits (*arvāḥ*) that both animate (as souls) and make conscious (as intellects) the embodied beings of the lower realms.[17] The spirits are divided into two categories: those of entities above the lunar sphere, called the higher Malakūt (*malakūt-i ʿulvī*); and the spirits of entities in the sublunar region, or the lower Malakūt (*malakūt-i suflī*).[18]

---

dark mist, is a popular topic of discussion in speculations by Ibn al-ʿArabī and his followers (cf. Chittick, *Sufi Path of Knowledge,* 125–29; Nicholson, *Studies in Islamic Mysticism,* 94–97).

14. The seven essential attributes of God listed by Nūrbakhsh in other contexts are life, knowledge, hearing, sight, power, volition, and speech (*Risāla-yi nūrīya, AA:*170).

15. Nūrbakhsh, *ʿAvālim al-ḥiss, AA:*188, *Dīvān,* 21 (no. 49). In contrast with this description, Ibn al-ʿArabī calls the perfect man the *barzakh al-barāzikh* due to his position as the ultimate creation that lies between God and the remainder of the created world (cf. Chittick, *Sufi Path of Knowledge,* 30).

16. The most significant active qualities of God mentioned often in Nūrbakhsh's works are creation and providing sustenance (*RH,* I:39; Nūrbakhsh, *Risāla-yi nūrīya, AA:*169).

17. Nūrbakhsh, *ʿAvālim al-ḥiss, AA:*188; *Dīvān,* 21 (no. 49).

18. Nūrbakhsh, *Risāla-yi nūrīya, AA:*175–76; Kiyā, *Risāla-yi nūrīya,* 92a (*AA:*12).

Lāhūt, Jabarūt, and Malakūt are extrasensory realms since they contain single or multiple entities imperceptible to the physical senses. The fourth realm, Mulk, is the world of sensible bodies. This abode has an internal hierarchy of beings consisting of: God's throne (*ʿarsh*), his footstool (*kursī*), the seven heavenly planets of Ptolemaic astronomy, and the animal, vegetable, and mineral kingdoms of the earth. These embodied entities represent God's emanations in the form of his effects (*āsār*), and their position relative to him is reflected in the designation it bears as the world of servitude to God (*marbūbīyat*). The bodies of this world are also seen as shadows (*ashbāḥ*), projected onto the terrestrial realm from their higher, nonmaterial counterparts.[19]

The last abode in Nūrbakhsh's cosmology, Nāsūt, is the dwelling place of the perfect man. Nāsūt is a subcategory of Mulk since it contains a particular category of the human animal, whose species as a whole belongs to Mulk. Although a sensory realm, Nāsūt has a particularly exalted status in the hierarchy of being since its occupant is the ultimate cause (*ʿilla ghāʾīya*) of creation and the seal of existent entities (*khātam-i mawjūdāt*). While Jabarūt, Malakūt, and Mulk manifest only certain aspects of the divine Being, the perfect man is a comprehensive locus of manifestation (*maẓhar jāmiʿ*) of God's essence. The essence precedes God's attributes, acts, and effects, while the perfect man, a reflection of the essence, collectively encompasses Jabarūt, Malakūt, and Mulk. This abode has very few inhabitants, but they all rank at the top of the hierarchy of being by virtue of representing, simultaneously, the essence of the creator and the totality of the created world.[20] Each perfect man is a full microcosm standing as a double-sided mirror between God's essence, on one side, and the created macrocosm, on the other.

The middle three realms of Nūrbakhsh's scheme represent an increasing diversification of entities. The progression moves from the potential for multiplicity (Jabarūt) to the plurality of nonmaterial entities (Malakūt) and the plurality of embodied beings (Mulk). In contrast, Lāhūt and Nāsūt are set apart as privileged worlds representing

19. Nūrbakhsh, *ʿAvālim al-ḥiss, AA:*188; *Dīvān,* 21 (no. 49).
20. Ibid.

God's essence and its reflection. The human animal has a special status among all created entities since it may achieve identity with divine essence, the only noncontingent being. Realization of this potential depends, however, on human beings acquiring an awareness of their status and striving on the path that leads to perfection. The mode of action needed to attain such perfection is mystical life, the highest human vocation.

The World of Images

To experience divine and cosmic realities, human beings have to hone their spiritual faculties according to a graduated path (discussed later in this chapter). The basis for such a path is inherent in the structure of the cosmos through the world of images (*ʿālam-i mis̱āl*).[21] The embodied human soul can experience nonsensory entities only in this world. The world of images is the separation (*barzakh*) between Malakūt and Mulk,[22] but it is not comparable ontologically to the five abodes since it does not contain divine emanations or entities specific to itself. Instead, it is seen as a mirror that reflects the entities of the upper three abodes. They appear in the world of images in well-proportioned (*mutanāsiba*), subtle forms (*ṣuvar laṭīfa*),[23] and prophets and saints perceive these forms when they travel to this world in subtle imaginal bodies (*jasad-i laṭīf-i mis̱ālī*). For this experience to occur, the higher entities have to project themselves onto the world of images and the human agents have to develop their subtle senses through spiritual exercises. Nūrbakhsh's mystical system beyond the structure of the cosmos describes both the means to acquire these spiritual senses and what the Sufi "sees" in the world of images at various stages of the journey.

The way the world of images functions is illustrated in Nūrbakhsh's work in his interpretation of Muḥammad's celebrated ascent (*miʿrāj*) to

21. For the genesis of the term *ʿālam-i mis̱āl,* see Fazlur Rahman, "Dream, Imagination, and *ʿĀlam al-mithāl,*" in *The Dream and Human Societies,* ed. G. E. von Grünebaum and Roger Caillois (Berkeley: University of California Press, 1966).

22. Nūrbakhsh, *Risāla-yi kashf al-ḥaqāʾiq,* 63a.

23. Nūrbakhsh, *Javāb-i maktūb-i ḥakīm, AA:*94.

divine presence. He sees the ascent as a mystical experience in which the different elements Muḥammad encounters are either symbols of cosmic entities or metaphors for religious duties. He explains that the journey was made in a subtle body during a trance (*ghayba*), a state of mystical consciousness intermediate between waking and sleeping.[24]

The meanings Nūrbakhsh attaches to some segments of the ascent are: journey from Mecca to the al-Aqṣā mosque in Jerusalem equals going from one stage to another in the lower Malakūt; Muḥammad's leading the prayer of all prophets indicates the abundance of scholars and saints in his own following; his heavenly steed, Burāq, represents both total submission to God and the obligatory prayers (*namāz*); the steed's reins and saddle are images of pleasant thoughts and good manners; the precious ornaments of the steed indicate good conduct and total attentiveness toward God; the flying of the steed represents the shunning of human thoughts in the state of purity during the pilgrimage (*iḥrām*); Gabriel's accompanying the Prophet on the steed signifies God's imparting direct knowledge; travel through the stages of the cosmos means performing recollection (*ẕikr*) and other devotional exercises in a determined sequence. All subsequent parts of the narrative are interpreted in a similar way, and the ascent to God as a whole is seen as a metaphor for the Sufi's journey toward God through regulated practice.[25]

Nūrbakhsh's comparison between the ascent narrative and the Sufi path diminishes the former's status as an experience unique to a moment in Muḥammad's life.[26] He further contends that all prophets and saints undertake journeys similar to the ascent and that Muḥammad himself had experienced such occasions many times during his

24. Nūrbakhsh, *Risāla-yi miʿrājīya, AA:*117–18. For details of Nūrbakhsh's classification of mystical states, see below.

25. Ibid., *AA:*125–27.

26. In comparison with Nūrbakhsh's interpretation, Sufi authors of the classical period interpreted the ascension narrative as pertaining to the person of Muḥammad alone (cf. Gerhard Böwering, "From the Word of God to the Vision of God: Muḥammad's Heavenly Journey in Classical Sufi Qurʾān Commentary," in *Le voyage initiatique en terre d'islam: Ascensions célestes et itinéraires spirituels,* ed. Mohammad Ali Amir-Moezzi [Louvain-Paris: Peeters, 1996], 205–22).

life.[27] The prophets and the saints are set apart as a group from other humans by their ability both to travel to the world of images and to correlate its events to the physical realm.

Light

Nūrbakhsh's cosmological description assigns a crucial role to light (*nūr*) as the only substance that pervades all realms of the world.[28] It symbolizes God's agency, and its different categories are attached to divine presence as essence, attributes, and effects. Nūrbakhsh divides light into three types: being (*vujūd*), knowledge (*ʿilm*), and brilliance (*żiyāʾ*) (chart 4).[29] Light as being is synonymous with Lāhūt, the abode of God's essence in its singularity, and is devoid of any accidental qualities such as color. Light as knowledge is the black light (*nūr-i siyāh*) that signifies Jabarūt and the power of God's attributes. Its shining downward creates the multiplicity of spiritual forms found in the Malakūt so that it generates diversity out of unity. Its shining on Mulk conducts the virtues of the spiritual entities of Malakūt to the bodies of the physical realm, endowing them with their forms, senses, and knowledge. The seven planets are a particularly interesting category since black light is reflected off them in various colors: "Just as the shining of the sun on colored pieces of glass makes them reflect their varied colors onto places and facades, when the sun of Jabarūt shines with the rays of Malakūt on diaphanous celestial bodies (*ajrām-i shaffāf-i aflāk*) and the fixed stars, they reflect colors particular to each one among them. The colors that become apparent (in this way) are: black from Saturn, the seventh sphere; blue from Jupiter, the sixth; red from Mars, the fifth; yellow from the sun, the fourth; white from Venus, the third; gray (*āmikhta*) from Mercury, the second; and green from the moon, the first sphere."[30] The body of Saturn, therefore, casts a black reflection

27. Nūrbakhsh, *Risāla-yi miʿrājīya, AA:*123.

28. For classical Sufi interpretations of light, see Gerhard Böwering, *The Mystical Vision of Existence in Classical Islam: The Qurʾānic Hermeneutics of the Ṣūfī Sahl At-Tustarī (d. 283/896)* (Berlin: Walter de Gruyter, 1980), 149–53.

29. Nūrbakhsh, *Risāla-yi nūrīya, AA:*148; idem, *Risāla-yi kashf al-ḥaqāʾiq,* 63a.

30. Nūrbakhsh, *Risāla-yi nūrīya, AA:*149–50; MS. Esad Efendi 3702, Süleymaniye Library, Istanbul, 70a. Ṣadaqiyānlū's published edition of this work is corrupted in

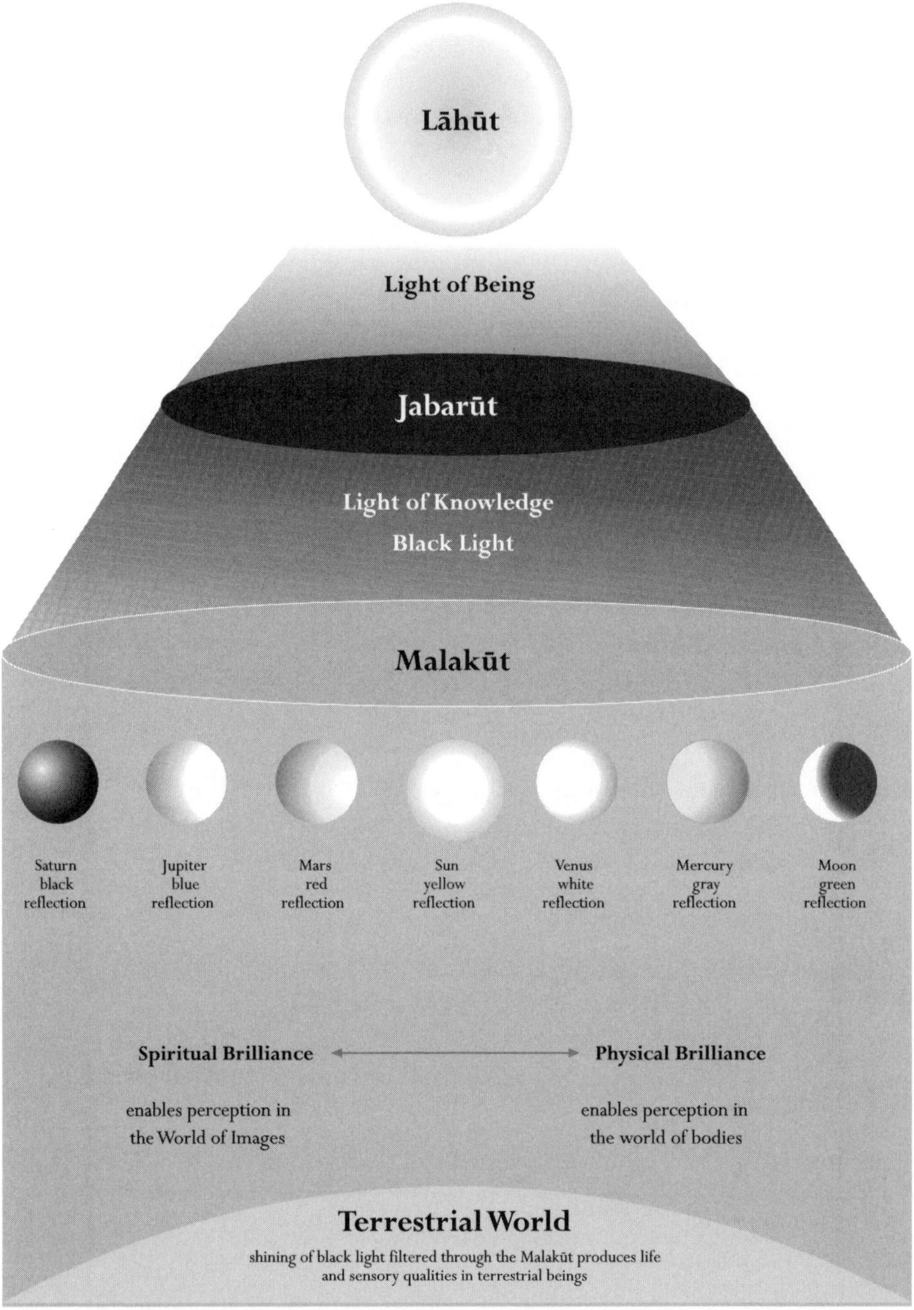
Lāhūt
Light of Being
Jabarūt
Light of Knowledge
Black Light
Malakūt
Saturn
black
reflection
Jupiter
blue
reflection
Mars
red
reflection
Sun
yellow
reflection
Venus
white
reflection
Mercury
gray
reflection
Moon
green
reflection
Spiritual Brilliance
Physical Brilliance
enables perception in
the World of Images
enables perception in
the world of bodies
Terrestrial World
shining of black light filtered through the Malakūt produces life
and sensory qualities in terrestrial beings

CHART 4: Categories of Light and Their Functions

from black light, while the lower planets reflect part of black light in the form of less intense colors.

Against celestial bodies, the higher part of Mulk, black light's shining the rays of Malakūt on the elements and material kingdoms of the earth causes the formation of sensible and perceptive bodies. The most perfect of these are human beings since they contain both reflections of God's sensory attributes, such as hearing, seeing, taste, and smell, and the capacity for knowledge and speech.[31] The true value of human beings' possession of these qualities becomes apparent only when they achieve the goal of spiritual perfection.

The third and last category of light in Nūrbakhsh's cosmological scheme is brilliance (*żiyāʾ*), which has two types. These are paired either as sensible (*ḥissī*) and imaginal (*mis̱ālī*),[32] or physical (*ṣūrī*) and spiritual (*maʿnavī*).[33] Sensible or physical brilliance is the light issuing from luminous bodies seen during ordinary wakeful experience; spiritual brilliance, on the other hand, manifests itself in a spectrum of colors and can be perceived only through a special sense cultivated through mystical endeavor. This is the crucial light that enables perception in the world of images, and its colors indicate levels of the cosmic hierarchy.[34]

The three types of light are the active agents attached to entities in different realms of the cosmos. Light as being is the property of God's essence through which he bestows existence on the cosmos during the creative process. Its shining forth results in the creation of Jabarūt, the source proper of creation. Jabarūt then shines the light of knowledge, or black light, downward to create the spirits of the world of Malakūt; these spirits, in their turn, give life and consciousness to the bodies of Mulk.

---

this passage. In all subsequent references to this work, I provide the reference to this manuscript when the published text needs correction.

31. Nūrbakhsh, *Risāla-yi nūrīya, AA:*149.

32. Ibid., *AA:*149–50.

33. Nūrbakhsh, *Risāla-yi kashf al-ḥaqāʾiq,* 63a.

34. Nūrbakhsh, *Risāla-yi nūrīya AA:*149, MS., 70a. The scheme of colors and their corresponding cosmological and psychological equivalents is discussed later in this chapter.

While brilliance does not have a creative function, it enables perception in both the world of images and the sensory world. It thus makes usable the sense of sight, the foremost sense attached to embodied beings. Without the two types of brilliance, these beings would remain unaware of both their physical surroundings and the more subtle realities of the higher realms. The three categories of light are all pertinent to life in the material world since they enable being, attributes of sensing, and physical and spiritual perception for embodied entities.

Nūrbakhsh's Cosmology in Comparison with His Sufi Predecessors

Although Nūrbakhsh's cosmological system is a distinct synthesis, its constitutive elements can be found in the thought of his predecessors. A comparison between his scheme and those of some influential figures active in the environment of Persian Sufism can bring Nūrbakhsh's preferences into relief and illustrate the progression of ideas from his predecessors to his own outlook.

ʿAlāʾ ad-Dawla Simnānī was the first master in Nūrbakhsh's Kubravī silsila to develop a rationalized and coherent cosmological system.[35] The cosmos for him consists of four realms; namely Lāhūt, Jabarūt, Malakūt, and Nāsūt, the last being the abode of humanity in general. These are realms of God's essence, attributes, acts, and effects, respectively, and although all existence flows from God's essence, Simnānī insists on an unbridgeable separation between this ultimate source and all other realms of the cosmos.[36] His view on this issue marks a fundamental difference between him and the followers of Ibn al-ʿArabī, as exemplified in his correspondence with ʿAbd ar-Razzāq Kāshānī.[37]

The basic division of the cosmos into four realms is elaborated in Simnānī's work to create an extensive scheme involving numerous innovative concepts. Without undertaking a detailed, side-by-side comparison, it can be said that Nūrbakhsh's worldview (at least what is

35. Elias, *Throne Carrier of God,* 154.

36. Ibid., 61–99.

37. H. Landolt, "Die Briefwechsel zwischen Kāshānī und Simnānī über Waḥdat al-Wuǧūd," *Der Islam* 50 (1973): 29–81.

available in his extant writings) is not as detailed. Besides the issue of God's essence, the crucial difference between the two schemes is Simnānī's omission of the world of the perfect man. While he also considers the human being the highest form of creation, Simnānī does not differentiate categorically between all other embodied beings and the person with an exalted spiritual status. Similarly, although light is a significant metaphor in Simnānī's mystical psychology,[38] it does not figure in his ontology. Simnānī's cosmological ideas are significant for Nūrbakhsh's views only to the extent that they originate the interest in a coherent cosmology continued by later authors who connected themselves to him through spiritual lineages.

Of greater substantive significance than Simnānī in situating Nūrbakhsh's cosmology are the different schemes proposed by followers of Ibn al-ʿArabī. Although Ibn al-ʿArabī's works do not contain a concise cosmological discussion,[39] in the century after his death a number of prominent authors developed systems based on his idea of the five divine presences (*al-ḥaḍarāt al-ilāhīyat al-khams*). A review of five major figures in this school reveals that while the authors in this tradition consistently maintained the idea of five presences, the identity of the presences in a given system was a matter of personal preference.[40] In more specific contrast with Nūrbakhsh's view, all these authors regard the world of images as an ontological realm, while divine essence and the perfect man are included or excluded as separate realms in the scheme to maintain the total number at five.[41] Some

38. Ibid., 80 n. 3; Jamal Elias, ed., "Risāla-yi nūrīya-yi Shaykh ʿAlāʾ ad-Dawla Simnānī," *Maʿārif* 13, no. 1 (1996): 3–26. This work is translated by Elias in "A Kubravī Treatise on Mystical Visions: The Risāla-yi nūriyya of ʿAlā' ad-Dawla as-Simnānī," *MW* 83, no. 1 (1993): 68–80.

39. For an extensive discussion of Ibn al-ʿArabī's cosmology based on translations of original texts, see William Chittick, *The Self Disclosure of God* (Albany: State University of New York Press, 1999).

40. William Chittick, "The Five Divine Presences from al-Qūnawī to al-Qayṣarī," *MW* 72, no. 2 (1982): 108–9. The five scholars studies by Chittick are Ṣadr ad-Dīn Qūnavī (d. 673/1274), Saʿīd ad-Dīn Farghānī (d. ca. 700/1300), Muʾayyid ad-Dīn Jandī (d. ca. 700/1300), ʿAbd ar-Razzāq Kāshānī (d. 730/1329 or 736/1335–36), and Sharaf ad-Dīn Dāvūd Qayṣarī (d. 751/1350).

41. Ibid., 118–23.

authors place God's essence above the cosmos completely, while others put the perfect man in the same realm as other humans. With no internal unanimity among the authors, this school's greatest influence on later cosmological thought was that the number of divisions of the cosmos became fixed at five.[42]

Among all relevant cosmological schemes, Nūrbakhsh's arrangement corresponds most closely to the thought of ʿAlī Hamadānī, the teacher of his own shaykh Isḥāq Khuttalānī. For Hamadānī, too, the world consists of an infinite number of realms that are divided into the five abodes, or presences, of existence (*ḥażarāt-i vujūdīyat*). These are the same worlds as in Nūrbakhsh's scheme, but the two descriptions have some differences in the residents of the different worlds. Hamadānī calls the realm of God's singularity simply the absolute hidden (*ghayb muṭlaq*) and does not use the appellation Lāhūt. The arrangement is the same from Jabarūt to Mulk, but the fifth abode, Nāsūt, is variously termed the abode of the perfect man or the human world in general.[43] For Hamadānī, the human being is set apart from other sentient creatures as it possesses all aspects of God's being. However, only those members of the species who have earned spiritual perfection deserve to be called human. The remaining biologically human population is a part of the animal world and is actually lower than other animals since base humanity is the only species to be led astray by Satan.[44]

42. The conclusions of Chittick's survey can be applied to later authors influenced by the Ibn al-ʿArabī tradition as well; e.g., the work of the Shīʿī Ḥaydar Āmulī (d. after 787/1385) also contains a version of the theory of the five presences (cf. *Jāmiʿ al-asrār va-manbaʿ al-anvār,* ed. Henry Corbin and Othman Yahia [Tehran: Departement d'Iranologie de l'Institut Franco-Iranien de Recherche, 1969], 559–62).

43. ʿAlī Hamadānī, *Kitāb asrār an-nuqṭa,* MS. Şehid Ali Paşa 2794, Süleymaniye Library, Istanbul, 287b–88a; idem, *Risāla-yi iṣṭilāḥāt,* MS. Şehid Ali Paşa 2794, Süleymaniye Library, Istanbul, 479a–80b. For other manuscripts and published editions of these as well as all other works by ʿAlī Hamadānī mentioned in this chapter, see Teufel, *Lebensbeschreibung,* 43–60; and Parvīz Aẕkāʾī, *Muravvij-i Islām dar Īrān-i ṣaghīr: Aḥvāl va āṡār-i Mīr Sayyid ʿAlī Hamadānī* (Hamadān, Iran: Intishārāt-i Dānishgāh-i Bū ʿAlī Sīnā, 1991), 115–51. For a summary of Hamadānī's life and work, see G. Böwering, "ʿAlī-yi Hamadānī, " *EIr,* 1:862–64.

44. Hamadānī, *Risāla-yi iṣṭilāḥāt,* 480b–81a. Hamadānī's opinion concurs with Ibn al-ʿArabī on this issue (cf. Chodkiewicz, *Seal of the Saints,* 70).

Parallel with Nūrbakhsh's scheme, the world of images in Hamadānī's work means the world intermediate between the realms of spirits and bodies, the site for the mystics' experience of the higher worlds.[45]

Nūrbakhsh's categorization of light is not attested in the works of his predecessors. Although Hamadānī also writes of three types of light, his categories reflect only the relative presence of the light of noncontingent truth (*nūr-i ḥaqīqī-yi muṭlaq*) in a given arena. This light represents God's being, while the other two categories are darkness (*ẓulmat*)—its total absence—and brilliance (*żiyāʾ*), its partial presence in the mixture of light and darkness. Darkness is the opposite of light and is divided further into three types: absolute darkness, which is imperceptible; the darkness of ignorance (*jahl*), which is not directly perceptible through sensory organs but can be felt when it disappears upon the intrusion of light; and sensory darkness (*ẓulmat-i maḥsūs*), which is experienced in the physical world.

Brilliance (*żiyāʾ*) is a mixture of the other two categories and represents created entities since they combine God's being (represented by light) and nonbeing (equivalent to darkness). Brilliance has two varieties: the light that makes objects visible in the physical world and is itself also visible; and the light that enables human perception of entities in the world of images. The upper three abodes of the cosmos in this scheme are luminous; the lower two are dark. The world of images is then the partition between light and darkness, and hence the place where brilliance can be experienced in the course of mystical experience.[46]

Hamadānī uses light only as a metaphor for the degree of presence of God's being in an entity. His theory corresponds with Nūrbakhsh for

45. ʿAlī Hamadānī, *Risāla-yi manāmīya,* MS. Şehid Ali Paşa 2794, Süleymaniye Library, Istanbul, 434a–35a. Hamadānī further divides the world of images into two sections, and his concept of this realm is generally more complex. Also, the world of images is a part of another division of the cosmos consisting of the four worlds or stages of life (*marātib al-ḥayāt*), called realms of essence (*maʿnavī*), spirits (*rūḥānī*), images (*miṣālī*), and sensible objects (*ḥissī*) (*Kitāb asrār an-nuqṭa,* 289a; *Risāla-yi manāmīya,* 434a–35b). For a discussion of the *Risāla-yi manāmīya* (including a partial German translation), see Fritz Meier, "Die Welt der Urbilder bei ʿAli Hamadani," *Eranos Jahrbuch* 18 (Zurich: Rhein-Verlag, 1950), 137–72.

46. Hamadānī, *Risāla-yi manāmīya,* 432b–34a.

light as God's being and as brilliance, but his way of relating the categories to each other is quite different. For Nūrbakhsh, the three types of light have mutually distinguishable functions and are truly different. Nūrbakhsh's theory is, therefore, more complex, and an understanding of light's functions is crucial to his overall cosmology.

Hamadānī's discussion does not mention black light, a concept that is of central concern to Nūrbakhsh and a number of other Sufis.[47] Among Nūrbakhsh's predecessors, Najm ad-Dīn Rāzī Dāya considers black light a quality of divine majesty (*jalāl*), while the appearance of lights of other colors in the world of images indicates manifestation of God's qualities of beauty (*jamāl*).[48] By comparison, in Simnānī's view, the Sufi sees black light upon reaching the penultimate stage of spiritual development—identified as the inner mystery (*khafī*)—and he does not posit an active cosmogonic function for black light.[49]

For authors writing after Nūrbakhsh, his own disciple Shams ad-Dīn Lāhījī sees black light as a substance that flows from Lāhūt, or God's essence. Lāhījī's general discourse on light is comparable to that of ʿAlī Hamadānī since he also enumerates its three varieties as God's being, darkness, and brilliance.[50] Black is the ultimate color of light since its intensity blinds one to all other perception. The loss, in this instance, results from proximity to divine being and is the antithesis of the blindness of darkness occurring from one's distance from the ultimate Being.

Besides the differences in detail between Nūrbakhsh's cosmological thought and that of his predecessors, his outlook stands apart also due to his personalization of the perfect man. His unmodulated equation of God's essence and the perfect man differs from other authors for whom the exact identity of the perfect man is generally either left

47. Black light occurs in the thought of Sufis outside of Kubravī lineages as well; see G. Böwering, "ʿAyn al-Qożāt Hamadānī," *EIr,* 3:140–43.

48. Najm ad-Dīn Rāzī Dāya, *The Path of God's Bondsmen from Origin to Return,* trans. Hamid Algar (Delmar, Calif.: Caravan, 1982), 301–2; Henry Corbin, *The Man of Light in Iranian Sufism,* trans. Nancy Pearson, 2d ed. (New Lebanon, N.Y.: Omega Publications, 1994), 108.

49. Elias, ed., "Risāla-yi nūrīya," 7; Elias, trans., "A Kubravī Treatise," 73.

50. Lāhījī, *Mafātīḥ al-iʿjāz,* 85; Corbin, *Man of Light,* 110–20.

unstated or unknowable. The only actual person identified unequivocally as the perfect man is Muḥammad, either as the best of humanity or the preeternal substance that formed his spirit (*ḥaqīqa muḥammadīya*).[51] While it is acknowledged that the last of these may appear in the form of "the pole" (*quṭb*), who is spiritually the most advanced individual of an age, one so designated is recognized only through personal association or knowledge of the unseen. The perfect men among the saints are, therefore, always hidden except to the adept, while the prophets, who all also belong to the category, declare their status due to their mission.

A mahdī who justifies his claim primarily through Sufism stands somewhere in the middle of this picture since he has both an exoteric function and he is the foremost saint of the age. This is Nūrbakhsh's situation, which compels him to exteriorize his claim as the perfect man, and the practical necessity results in a theoretical outlook far more explicit or exaggerated as compared to other Sufis.[52] The properties and privileges of the perfect man are crucial parts of Nūrbakhsh's self-image and add to the other superlative designations he applies to himself as the mahdī.

It is noteworthy that Nūrbakhsh's disciple Shams ad-Dīn Lāhījī, who is generally exceedingly reverent of his teacher in his work, reiterates Nūrbakhsh's fivefold scheme of abodes in his works but assigns a diminished role to the inhabitants of Nāsūt. He theorizes the perfect man as the aggregate of God's emanations in the realms of Jabarūt, Malakūt,

51. In Ibn al-ʿArabī's view, only the *ḥaqīqa muḥammadīya* is the perfect man in an absolute sense (cf. Chittick, *Sufi Path of Knowledge,* 371–72; Chodkiewicz, *Seal of the Saints,* 71; Masataka Takeshita, *Ibn ʿArabī's Theory of the Perfect Man* [Tokyo: Institute for the Study of Languages and Cultures of Asia and Africa, 1987]). This view is reiterated in the work of later authors such as ʿAbd al-Karīm Jīlī and ʿAbd ar-Raḥmān Jāmī (cf. Nicholson, *Studies in Islamic Mysticism,* 105; W. Chittick, "The Perfect Man as the Prototype of the Self in the Sufism of Jami," *SI* 49 [1979]: 135–57). Nūrbakhsh's self-image as a form of the Muḥammadan reality discussed in chapter 3 also equates the mahdī with the perfect man.

52. For examples of Nūrbakhsh's unequivocal description of himself as either the perfect man or the comprehensive manifestation of God's essence, see *Dīvān,* 10 (no. 19), 12 (no. 25), 15 (nos. 29, 30), 19 (no. 43), 22 (no. 51).

and Mulk, but does not declare him a total reflection of God's essence.[53] In the absence of a messianic claim, the doctrine of the perfect man thus reverted to a theory rather than an actuality, even within Nūrbakhsh's own following.

Nūrbakhsh's view of his own position in the cosmos is related also to his conception of light as the essential connective substance that transfers powers and entities between the different realms. As the "light-giver," he sees himself as the conduit through whom God's light, his agent of self-manifestation, reaches the rest of creation.[54] This fulfills his cosmic function as an embodiment of the highest of creation, the first created entity, and the mirror in which God sees himself at the first moment when essence unfolds itself into its attributes, acts, and effects.

Varieties of Knowledge

In Nūrbakhsh's thought, the cosmos can be comprehended by human beings in a number of ways. He first of all divides the cosmos into the sensory and the extrasensory, reflecting the familiar Sufi distinction between exoteric (*ẓāhir*) and esoteric (*bāṭin*) realities. The human being appreciates these aspects of the world through different organs of consciousness, necessitating three different types of knowledge: exoteric knowledge (practical knowledge of the physical world and Islamic jurisprudence); ability to see the hidden through signs in the physical world (astrology, physiognomy, etc.); and experiential knowledge of the esoteric realm.

Exoteric Knowledge

The lowest form of knowledge in Nūrbakhsh's thought is that of the physical world and the outward aspect of religion. Of the two, he does not concern himself much with the physical sciences,[55] but his

53. Lāhījī, *Mafātīḥ al-iʿjāz,* 114–16; idem, *Dīvān-i ashʿār va rasāʾil,* ed. Barāt Zanjānī (Tehran: McGill University Institute for Islamic Studies, Tehran Branch, 1978), 332–25, 338–39.

54. Nūrbakhsh, *Dīvān,* 1 (no. 1), 4 (no. 6), 13 (no. 26). The name is used in a similar way throughout the rest of his poetic work as well.

55. Nūrbakhsh's comment on the physical sciences is limited to the claim that Plato, if he were alive in Nūrbakhsh's day, would have to learn philosophical sciences

disinclination toward jurisprudence (*fiqh*) is evident in his ridicule of its practitioners. Citing a ḥadīth popular among the Sufis, he declares that the jurists are novices who posses only one-third of religion. The *sharīʿa,* the focus of their attentions, has to be complemented by knowledge of the mystical path (*ṭarīqa*) and direct knowledge of God (*ḥaqīqa*).[56]

Despite his generally negative estimation of jurisprudence, Nūrbakhsh does claim to possess complete proficiency in its practice.[57] The contradiction of the two attitudes can be resolved by considering his jurisprudential outlook to be a relatively minor function of the messianic mission. In his *al-Fiqh al-aḥwaṭ,* the only work devoted to juridical issues, Nūrbakhsh begins by stating that God has appointed him to remove the differences between different Islamic sects and promulgate the true religion practiced in Muḥammad's times.[58] After this declaration, the book is a rather straightforward manual providing injunctions for issues of worship (*ʿibādāt*) and interpersonal relations (*muʿāmalāt*). The only remarkable feature of the book is Nūrbakhsh's deliberate attempt to mix together typically Sunnī and Twelver Shīʿī positions in order to create a hybrid legal school that transcends them both. For example, he states that it is allowable to offer the daily prayers in either the Sunnī or Shīʿī manner, although the former is better for winter and the latter for summer.[59] He allows temporary marriage (*mutʿa*), a hallmark of Twelver Shīʿī practice,[60] while also endorsing congregational

---

and mathematics from him, and that he had surpassed Ibn Sīnā in the occult sciences such as alchemy (Nūrbakhsh, *Maktūb dar naṣīḥat-i murīdān, AA*:99–100).

56. Nūrbakhsh, *Dar javāb-i maktūb-i fuqahāʾ,* MS. Esad Efendi 3702, Süleymaniye Library, Istanbul, 41b (Ṣadaqiyānlū's edition of this work [*AA*:101 3] is based upon an incomplete Iranian manuscript).

57. Nūrbakhsh, *Risāla-yi miʿrājīya, AA*:121; idem, *Maktūb dar naṣīḥat-i murīdān, AA*:99–100; idem, *Maʿāsh as-sālikīn,* 57b; *RH,* I:36.

58. Nūrbakhsh, *al-Fiqh al-aḥwaṭ,* 3d printing (original text in Arabic with Urdu trans. by Abū l-ʿIrfān Muḥammad Bashīr; Skardu: Idāra-yi Madrasa-yi Shāh-i Hamadān Ṣūfiya Nūrbakhshīya, 1997], 1. This book has sometimes been thought not to be a work by Nūrbakhsh (Algar, "Nūrbakhshiyya," *EI*², 8:135). I consider it an authentic work based on the language and style (it is very similar to Nūrbakhsh's other Arabic works) and the fact that the beginning statement of intention does reflect Nūrbakhsh's perspective represented in other works.

59. Nūrbakhsh, *al-Fiqh al-aḥwaṭ,* 52–53.

60. Ibid., 237–38.

Friday prayers in Sunnī style, which were disallowed in Twelver Shīʿism until the rise of the Ṣafavid dynasty in Iran in the sixteenth century.[61] Mysticism is still important within this juridical discussion since Nūrbakhah states that the greater exertion (*jihād akbar*), which is superior to the lesser exertion of military struggle (*jihād aṣghar*), has to be undertaken under someone superbly proficient in mystical virtues.[62]

Nūrbakhsh most likely composed *al-Fiqh al-aḥwaṭ* in the last phase of his life, when the substantial Nūrbakhshī community in Suliqān was in need of practical guidance for day-to-day affairs.[63] Yet even here Nūrbakhsh's general view was that legal discussion cannot provide the requisite knowledge for action in all cases. In a treatise describing whether mystics may or may not accept material gifts, he states that whereas the common people are bound by jurists' decisions, saints can determine the status of a substance more accurately through unveiling in the higher worlds.[64] He illustrates this point through two instances in the life of Abū Yazīd Khalkhālī, one of his disciples. In the first example, this accomplished Sufi playfully picked up some sweets from a tray in the hands of a young boy in the bazaar. Then, just as he went to put the sweets back, he heard a call from above telling him to eat the sweets. The boy then told him that he was taking the sweets to the mosque to distribute among the Sufis as ordered by his father, so that Abū Yazīd's taking some of them was quite rightful.

In the second situation, a companion brought Abū Yazīd some food and the two sat down together to eat. Just as he was to partake of the bread, Abū Yazīd heard a call from above saying that the man was

61. Ibid., 88–94. For the controversy over Friday prayer in Twelver Shīʿism, see Andrew Newman, "Fayd al-Kashani and the Rejection of the Clergy/State Alliance: Friday Prayer as Politics in the Safavid Period," in *The Most Learned of the Shīʿa,* ed. Linda Walbridge (New York: Oxford University Press, 2001), 34–52.

62. Nūrbakhsh, *al-Fiqh al-aḥwaṭ,* 196–97.

63. It is worth noting that *al-Fiqh al-aḥwaṭ* survives only in the South Asian Nūrbakhshī community that was formed long after the mahdī's death. As discussed in chapters 6 and 7, social cohesion was a more significant issue during this part of Nūrbakhshī history in comparison with the almost exclusively mystical focus during the Central Asian and Iranian phases.

64. Nūrbakhsh, *Maʿāsh as-sālikīn,* 60a.

dishonest and the food had been prepared with wheat stolen from an orphan. He therefore abstained from eating the food and was saved from committing an unlawful act through God's protection.[65] Both these stories underscore the point that the apparent prohibition or permissibility of an act is not the true measure of its status. Furthermore, Nūrbakhsh cautions in another treatise that the jurists' rulings can be accepted only when they either satisfy an intellectual assessment or can be ratified through inspiration.[66] The Prophet's "unlettered" (*ummī*) quality proves that true knowledge is imparted only by God and is not acquired from literacy or by memorizing traditions.[67]

Knowledge of the Hidden through Apparent Signs

Nūrbakhsh contends that accomplished mystics can apprehend the truths hidden behind occasions in the physical world. The two modes for this to happen are systematic acquisition of sciences that are a part of the mystical path and incidental knowledge gained during experiences in the world of images. Nūrbakhsh's greatest emphasis among systematic sciences is on astrology (*ʿilm-i nujūm*) and physiognomy (*firāsa*),[68] while the most common form of knowledge retrieved from the supersensory realm is that of the past and the future.

Nūrbakhsh's defense of his messianic claim contains evidence from astrological observations.[69] The effects of celestial movements are, for him, proofs of God's foreknowledge and the predetermined nature of human existence.[70] He explains astrology by stating that entities of the earthly realm derive their life and intellects from bodies higher in the

65. Ibid., 58a.

66. Nūrbakhsh, *Risāla-yi miʿrājīya, AA:*129.

67. *RH,* I:40.

68. His work also contains brief descriptions based on the science of letters (*ʿilm-i ḥurūf*), though his occasional use of this technique provides too few details to reconstruct his perspective fully (for example, *RH,* I:12; Nūrbakhsh, *Maktūb beh ʿAlāʾ ad-Dawla, AA:*81; idem, *Suʾālāt-i alif-i Jawhar-i Āẕarī,* 28). Bākharzī's hagiography of Jāmī states that Jāmī once mocked Nūrbakhsh for his random and presumptuous interpretations of letters in works by Saʿd ad-Dīn Ḥamūvayī (*MJ,* 195).

69. *RH,* I:34.

70. Nūrbakhsh, *ar-Risāla al-iʿtiqādīya,* 188.

cosmic hierarchy. These properties emanate from the planets and the stars so that bodies made of base materials act and think in conjunction with the positions of the former. The fundamental connection between higher and lower embodied beings means that experts in astrology can calculate from the positions of celestial bodies at the time of an individual's birth the life expectancy, illness, and time of death of that person.[71] Similarly, astrologers can predict the birth of particularly significant individuals—such as Muḥammad and the mahdī—by calculating the time for auspicious celestial moments in the future.[72]

Next to astrology, Nūrbakhsh also presents a defense of the science of physiognomy (*firāsa*); he devotes a special treatise to it. His preamble to the work states that the connection inherent between the exoteric and esoteric aspects of a human being makes it possible to discern a person's spiritual state by observing the characteristics of his or her body parts.[73] He cites prophetic reports in praise or censure of physical qualities such as facial beauty, height, red hair, and so on to secure legitimacy for the science from Islamic tradition. Subsequently, he argues that just as the dispositions of animals can be judged by their outward appearances, it is logical that we can do so for humans as well. Although this knowledge is deemed below the status of revelation (*vaḥy*), mystical unveiling (*mukāshafa*), philosophy (*ḥikmat*), astrology (*nujūm*), and ciphering through numeration (*handasa*), Nūrbakhsh considers its results more clearly observable.[74] Nūrbakhsh's treatise on this subject contains extensive discussions of each human body part, where different negative or positive attributes are seen as inherent in individuals with particular features.

The concern with astrology and physiognomy in Nūrbakhsh's thought reinforces the general fatalism of his outlook. These sciences assign attributes based upon unalterable factors such as birth and physical peculiarities, and Nūrbakhsh justifies astrology by considering its

71. Nūrbakhsh, *Javāb-i maktūb-i ḥakīm, AA*:92.

72. Nūrbakhsh, *Insān-nāma,* 83b; idem, *ar-Risāla al-iʿtiqādīya,* 195.

73. Nūrbakhsh, *Insān-nāma,* 83a.

74. Ibid., 84a. He also praises his son Qāsim Fayżbakhsh for his proficiency in this science (*RH,* II:91).

results a reflection of God's statement "None of us is there but has a known station" (37:164).[75] The "fatedness" of existence is also a part of his mahdīst claim. He states that he is compelled to pursue his claim because it has been assigned by God and previous saints and prophets, and he can even predict the year of his death from traditions about the mahdī and his horoscope.[76] In his perspective, the acquisition of knowledge is predicated not on exploration but on the ability to recognize things as they are.

Beyond systematic interpretation of worldly signs, Nūrbakhsh contends also that an accomplished Sufi has the power to see across time. Prophets before Muḥammad could predict his impending arrival from the knowledge of the future they possessed due to their high spiritual status.[77] Similarly, prophetic reports predicting eschatological happenings are understood as a part of this ability.[78] This power is also evident in the predictions made by saints of past generations, and Nūrbakhsh's defense of his messianic claim provides numerous illustrations for this process.[79] The rational understanding of this ability states that these individuals can attain a degree of union with the divine Being, allowing them access to God's knowledge. The extent of their knowledge depends on their level of spiritual achievement, so that the perfected mystics have complete knowledge of the future.

Like the future, the Sufi can also focus his attention on knowledge of the past within God's knowledge. The most significant category of such information is knowledge of the dead by observing graves. An accomplished Sufi can tell a buried person's gender, her or his physical characteristics, and the punishment or reward he or she had received after death. Nūrbakhsh's high regard for this ability is evident in his considering it a major indicator of a Sufi's spiritual station.[80]

75. Nūrbakhsh, *Risāla-yi makārim al-akhlāq, AA:*135.
76. *RH,* I:32, 56.
77. Nūrbakhsh, *Insān-nāma,* 83a.
78. Nūrbakhsh, *Javāb-i vazīr, AA:*85.
79. *RH,* I:17, 25, 29, 76.
80. Nūrbakhsh, *Javāb-i vazīr, AA:*83; idem, *Maktūb beh ʿAlāʾ ad-Dawla, AA:*81.

Experience of the Unseen

The highest form of human knowledge in Nūrbakhsh's view is that acquired by witnessing the higher worlds in the course of mystical experience. This is the direct knowledge of God (*ʿilm ladunnī*) leading to greater certainty in one's belief. The three successively higher stages of the effects of this knowledge are: knowledge of certitude (*ʿilm-i yaqīn*); quintessence of certitude (*ʿayn-i yaqīn*); and truth of certitude (*ḥaqq-i yaqīn*). Nūrbakhsh explains this hierarchy as learning (*dānistan*) certitude in an intellectual sense, seeing (*dīdan*) certitude in the cosmos, and becoming (*shudan*) certitude through dissolution into God at the height of one's mystical achievement.[81] Nūrbakhsh's ultimate reference for achievement on this hierarchy is his own person:

> I doubt that there is anyone besides me (in the world at the moment) who can claim to encompass all knowable (*ʿilmīya*) as well as seeable (*ʿiyānīya*) realities (*ḥaqāʾiq*). In knowing, he would have to be informed of both metaphysical philosophy (*al-ḥikma al-ilāhīya*) and the details of all preceding scholars' works, to the extent that he is not perplexed by any problem relating to them. As for seeable (realities), he would have to have reached immersion in the world of unity so as to become the locus of manifestation of the truth (*ḥaqq*) and the comprehensive presence (*ḥaḍrat al-kull*). He should have acquired all attributes of divinity [i.e., life, knowledge, hearing, vision, power, will, and speech] and lordship (*rubūbīya*), such as creation, sustaining, etc. . . . I am exalted above all others striving in these matters because the ones who possess seeable realities do not have the knowable ones, and those who have acquired the latter are bereft of the former.[82]

The foremost responsibility of having this knowledge is to teach others the path toward it.

The remainder of this chapter reviews aspects of Nūrbakhsh's doctrine on mystical discipline and its purported benefits.

81. Nūrbakhsh, *Risāla-yi nūrīya, AA:*178; idem, *Maṣnavī ṣaḥīfat al-awliyāʾ*, *AA:*52; idem, *Insān-nāma,* 87a.

82. *RH,* I:39.

Practical Concerns of the Mystical Life

Nūrbakhsh's Sufi practice is undertaken in the form of a personal path of action. The particulars of his views on this subject can be divided into two categories: first, the desired structure of mystical life or the prescribed path as seen from the outside; and second, the inner psychological states experienced by someone on the path.

The Significance of the Shaykh

The first condition for adopting a mystical life is giving oneself over to the spiritual care of an accomplished teacher. Nūrbakhsh's emphasis on the necessity of a shaykh is reflected in his repeated citation of the famous Sufi dictum "Whoever has no shaykh, his shaykh is Satan."[83] The shaykh's guidance is seen as the divine instrument that saves a person from the misguidedness mentioned in the Qur'anic statement "Whomsoever God guides he is rightly guided, and whomsoever He leads astray, you will not find for him a protector (18:17)."[84]

The shaykh's significance is reflected in Nūrbakhsh's prescription for the spiritually inclined novice:

> It is incumbent upon the seeker of God not to be content with blind following, but to progress (from this) toward (knowing God through) inference, and from there to (the level of) witnessing. Progress between these levels occurs, first, through the company of a divinely guided scholar, and second, through companionship with an accomplished guide (*murshid*). So it is for you, the seeker, to become the companion of a perfect (*kāmil*) and perfecting (*mukammil*)[85] guide who is the consummation of all levels of sainthood.[86]

83. Nūrbakhsh, *Risāla-yi miʿrājīya, AA:*122; idem, *Dar bayān-i āya-ī az kalām allāh, AA:*143; idem, *Maʿāsh as-sālikīn,* 60b.

84. Nūrbakhsh, *Dar bayān-i āya, AA:*142; idem, *Risāla-yi makārim al-akhlāq, AA:*135; *Dīvān,* 19 (no. 42).

85. Nūrbakhsh uses the terms *kāmil* (for himself) and *mukammil* (for others) as attributes of a great shaykh throughout his work. An explanation for them is given in Nūrbakhsh, *Risāla-yi miʿrājīya, AA:*115.

86. *RH,* I:4.

Once the basic inclination is established through the company of the teacher, a student's spiritual preparation gradually increases and the student can progress along the path to reach the level of perfection.

Nūrbakhsh's definition of the perfect guide describes him as one who is accomplished in the three parts of religion: exoteric law (*sharīʿa*), the Sufi path (*ṭarīqa*), and the esoteric reality (*ḥaqīqa*). His outward appearance must not give any signs contrary to his status according to the science of physiognomy (*firāsa*), and his affiliation with a distinguished spiritual lineage should be well established through a spiritual chain, or silsila. His conduct should exhibit an exemplary routine of spiritual exercises, and other students working under his care must be able to authenticate the value of his stewardship by pointing to their progress.[87]

Nūrbakhsh illustrates the insight required of the shaykh through his statements of respect for his own master and examples from his relationship with his disciples. He sees his own Kubravī silsila as the most prestigious initiatory line as proven through ʿAlī Hamadānī's experience. Hamadānī once saw Muḥammad during a spiritual experience where the latter was the source of a great spiritual emanation (*fayż*) for him. He requested that others following in his spiritual lineage might receive similar benefits, and his wish was granted by the Prophet.[88] Other works by Nūrbakhsh and his disciples reflect belief in the supremacy of Hamadānī's spiritual lineage, claiming also that spiritual perfection is available fully only to members of the Nūrbakhshī silsila.[89]

Nūrbakhsh relates that his disciple ʿAlī Huwayzavī had an experience in which he saw himself roaming above God's throne for three hundred thousand years. Nūrbakhsh gathered from Huwayzavī's demeanor that he saw this as the ultimate in spiritual experience and considered this the end of the path. Interpreting this to be an error, he immediately informed Huwayzavī that roaming in the higher worlds has no limits, and that he should continue with his exercises. The disciple took his advice and went much further than his previous experiences within the next day.[90] This

87. Nūrbakhsh, *Risāla-yi makārim al-akhlāq, AA:*136.
88. Nūrbakhsh, *Maʿāsh as-sālikīn,* 59b.
89. *RH,* I:39; Nūrbakhsh, *Insān-nāma,* 88a; Kiyā, *Risāla-yi nūrīya,* 91a (*AA:*11).
90. Nūrbakhsh, *Risāla-yi miʿrājīya, AA:*122.

story affirms that progress on the path may become stultified without the active involvement of an accomplished guide. It is because of the shaykh's crucial role in spiritual exertions that the Sufi sees God in the shaykh's form at the moment of complete subsistence in God (*baqāʾ billāh*).[91]

The Ethics of Mystical Life

After submitting to an appropriate guide, the Sufi needs to adopt an ethical attitude appropriate for the true seeker. Nūrbakhsh's work contains a general valuation of habits of poverty and self-restriction over extravagance. He surmises that qualities such as eating and sleeping less and opposing the avaricious capacity on all fronts decrease one's aptitude toward wrongdoing.[92] Conversely, indulging in worldly luxuries is the source of all transgressions.[93] A sincere adoption of the mystical life therefore implies disengagement (*tajrīd*) from the cares of the world.[94]

The new attitude required of the Sufis makes a whole set of ethical duties incumbent upon them. Nūrbakhsh's list of noble qualities consists of magnanimity (*karam, sakhāvat, jūd, iḥsān, ʿaṭāʾ*); chivalry (*futūvat, murūvat*); affection (*maḥabbat*); certitude (*īqān*); discernment (*ḥilm, siyāsat, ḥikmat, firāsat*); modesty (*tavāżuʿ*); faithfulness (*vafāʾ*); justice (*ʿadālat*); courage (*shajāʿat*); truthfulness (*ṣidq*); sincerity (*ṣadāqat*); and dignity (*vaqār*). Reprehensible moral qualities include avarice (*bukhl, ḥirṣ*); suspicion (*rayb*); hatred (*bughż, ḥiqd*); criticism (*ʿayb*); arrogance (*takabbur*); hypocrisy (*riyāʾ*); jealousy (*ḥasad*); stubbornness (*lijāj*); slander (*ghībat*); lying (*kiẕb*); and anger (*ḥishmat*).[95]

The Tenfold Path

Having attained the proper ethical attitude, Sufis adapt their behavior to a scheme of ten requirements that define the path. For this Nūrbakhsh repeats, without any modification, an arrangement first

91. Nūrbakhsh, *Risāla-yi nūrīya, AA:*177. For Nūrbakhsh's understanding of subsistence, see below.

92. Nūrbakhsh, *Risāla dar sayr va sulūk, AA:*185.

93. Nūrbakhsh, *Maʿāsh as-sālikīn,* 60b.

94. Ibid.; *Dīvān,* 8 (no. 14), 12 (no. 12), 16 (no. 31), 18 (no. 41), 25 (no. 53); Nūrbakhsh, *Maṡnavī ṣaḥīfat al-awliyāʾ, AA:*53.

95. Nūrbakhsh, *Risāla-yi kashf al-ḥaqāʾiq,* 63b.

suggested by Najm ad-Dīn Kubrā, although he probably assimilated it from ʿAlī Hamadānī's Persian translation of Kubrā's original work.[96] The qualities listed by Nūrbakhsh (and discussed more extensively in the work of his predecessors) aim at the goal of voluntary death required of the Sufi:

1. Repentance (*tawba*): this quality begins the scheme since it is the Sufi's voluntary return to God; it is comparable to physical death, initiating one's involuntary return to the creator.
2. Asceticism (*zuhd*): extracting oneself from such material concerns as wealth, property, and honor; it equals the forced separation from such concerns at the time of death.
3. Trust (*tavakkul*): trusting God alone after estrangement from the material world.
4. Contentment (*qanāʿa*): cessation of all base desires except those necessary for staying alive.
5. Seclusion (*ʿuzla*): separating oneself from everyone except one's shaykh; to preclude the functioning of senses, such as the eye from seeing, the ear from hearing, and so forth; it is equivalent to abstention from certain types of food in order to cure a disease.
6. Recollection (*ẕikr*): expelling everything from one's mind except God; this is spiritual medicine that cures the corruption of the material world.
7. Attentiveness to God (*tavajjuh*): total concentration on God exemplified in Junayd's teaching that if someone approaches God for thousands of years and then lets his attention wane for a single second, what he loses in that second is greater than what he gained in thousands of years.
8. Patience (*ṣabr*): relinquishing sensual desires and restricting the soul to labors of worship; perseverance in spiritual exercises.

96. Ibid., 62b; Marijan Molé, "La version persane du traité de dix principes de Najm al-Dīn Kobrā, par ʿAlī b. Shihāb al-Dīn Hamadānī," *Farhang-i Īrān Zamīn* 6 (1958): 38–66. These ten principles are also included (although not in the same order) in Hamadānī's more extensive scheme describing the forty stations on the Sufi's path (*Risāla-yi chihil maqām-i ṣūfīya,* MS. Şehid Ali Paşa 2794, Süleymaniye Library, Istanbul, 454b–57a). Kubrā's *Uṣūl al-ʿashara* is edited in Marijan Molé, "Traités mineurs de Najm al-Dīn Kubrà," *Annales islamologiques* 4 (1963): 15–22.

9. Observation (*murāqaba*): looking out for the acquisition of one's spiritual desires; to keenly observe the happenings of spiritual experiences.
10. Consent (*rizā*): leaving one's own desires and consenting to the wishes of the Beloved; the highest point in spiritual achievement.

The cumulative effect of this tenfold scheme is to turn the Sufi away from the material world and toward a total immersion in concern with God. It is, therefore, the ideal means for obeying the prophetic command "die before you die."

Basic Practices of the Path

The Sufi is competent to participate in the practices of the order after attaining the proper attitude. Beyond performing obligatory Islamic rituals with zeal, the practice of Nūrbakhsh's circle contains a particular emphasis on exercises of recollection (*zikr*) and supererogatory prayers called *awrād-i fatḥīya*.[97] The latter, an arrangement of God's names, prayers of repentance, quotations from the Qurʾan, and so forth, were instituted as Kubravī practice by Nūrbakhsh's predecessor ʿAlī Hamadānī, who received the material during a mystical experience.[98] Hamadānī considered this work a compendium of the most efficacious prayers used by eminent Sufis of all times. Their high status had been ratified also by Muḥammad during a dream experienced by Hamadānī in Jerusalem on his way back from Mecca.[99] Mystics in Nūrbakhsh's circle invoked the *awrād* after the morning obligatory prayers.[100]

97. These two elements of practice are invoked a number of times in his description of the spiritual exertions of his disciples (cf. *RH,* II:13, 53. 76, 84).

98. An incomplete version of Nūrbakhsh's *awrād fatḥīya* is found in MS. Persan 368, Bibliothèque Nationale, Paris, 155b. The text attributed to Nūrbakhsh here is identical with the relevant portion in ʿAlī Hamadānī's detailed description of the prayer (*Risāla-yi awrādīya,* MS. Şehid Ali Paşa 2794, Süleymaniye Library, Istanbul, 313b–17a). The popularity of these prayers is evident from the numerous editions published in the modern period (Teufel, *Lebensbeschreibung,* 46–47, 54; Azkāʾī, *Muravvij-i Islām,* 118).

99. Hamadānī, *Risāla-yi awrādīya,* 310b–11a. This incident is reported also by one of Hamadānī's early biographers (Ḥaydar Badakhshī, *Manqabat al-javāhir,* 358b).

100. *RH,* II:13.

Physical aspects of the basic Nūrbakhshī recollection exercise also follow earlier Kubravī practice.[101] Nūrbakhsh's own works do not contain a description of the practice, but the method is outlined in two works from later generations of his order. Nūrbakhsh himself does mention the four-beat (*chahār-żarb*) recollection in his citation of a verse from Simnānī,[102] while details of the bodily movements that accompany the utterance of the words "There is no God but God" are given in a work ascribed to his grandson Bahā᾽ ad-Dawla Ḥasan :

1. The Sufi should sit cross-legged on the floor and bend forward until the head is at the level of the navel; the first beat is to say *lā* while raising the torso to the upright position.
2. The second beat is saying *ilāha* while bending the torso to the right until the head is at the level of the liver (*jigar*) or the navel.
3. The third beat is to say *illā* while straightening the torso to be in the upright position once again.
4. The fourth beat is saying *allāh* while bending the torso to the left; this is followed by becoming upright and then bending down forward to the first position.[103]

A slightly different version of the exercise is given in a small treatise by ʿAlī Muḥibbī, who was inducted into the Nūrbakhshīya by Nūrbakhsh's disciple Sayyid Muḥammad Ṭāliqānī.[104] In this second version, the practitioner says *lā* in the straight down position, followed by *ilāha* when the body is brought back up to be straight; then he says *illā* while bending toward the right, and *allāh* when doing so toward the left. The whole cycle is performed within a single breath.

101. For two different recollection practices attributed to Simnānī, see Elias, *Throne Carrier of God,* 127–28, and Gramlich, *Schiitischen Derwischorden Persiens,* 2:401. ʿAlī Hamadānī's *Risāla-yi ẕikrīya* states that silent recollection with the formula "*lā ilāha illā allāh,*" is the best practice (MS. Şehid Ali Paşa 2794, Süleymaniye Library, Istanbul, 376b). Practical details of ʿAlī Hamadānī's approach can be gathered from the report of his disciple Jaʿfar Badakhshī (Badakhshī, *Khulāṣat al-manāqib,* 99–103).

102. Nūrbakhsh, *Risāla dar sayr va sulūk, AA:*185.

103. Bahā᾽ ad-Dawla, *Risāla, AA:*22–23.

104. ʿAlī Muḥibbī, *Silsila-nāma,* 46a. For Muḥibbī and Ṭāliqānī, see chapter 5. Muḥibbī's version is identical with the report of Jaʿfar Badakhshī mentioned above.

Beyond the primary recollection, Nūrbakhsh's writings also mention a number of other spiritual exercises that were compounded or intensified versions of the secluded spiritual retreat. He places particular emphasis on forty-day retreats (*arbaʿīn*), which had been a part of his own training under his shaykh and which he observed in the most strenuous of conditions.[105] While Nūrbakhsh emphasizes this retreat greatly in his works, our only detailed description of the practice comes from Kashmir, where it was performed under the guidance of one of his disciples two decades after his death.

The author of the *Tuḥfat al-aḥbāb* states that the retreat began every year in winter and ended just at the beginning of spring.[106] It was preceded by gathering provisions so that none of the participants would have to concern themselves with worldly matters for the duration of forty days. The event—a large gathering of committed Sufis and others interested in spiritual benefits—began with the placing of candles around the selected area. After the group had offered invocations and recited mystical poetry and shared a communal meal, the candles were collected and put in front of the presiding shaykh. Then everyone except the initiated left the building. One by one, the Sufis then came forward and sat in front of the shaykh, who gave each one a candle along with spiritual advice specific to his personality. This "light-giving" ceremony, which affirmed Nūrbakhsh's title in symbolic form, was performed by the mahdī himself during his lifetime and then continued by his successors. Each Sufi went to a separate seclusionary chamber after receiving the candle and spent most of his time meditating alone for the next forty days. During this period, the shaykh kept a watchful eye on the proceedings in order to judge the Sufis' progress on the path. At the end of the exercise, the shaykh rewarded all the participants with robes (*khirqa*) and other items of clothing to mark their new status. The

105. *RH,* I:4, 21, 25, 35; II:84, 131, 138. The only extant selection from Nūrbakhsh's poetic work *Arbaʿīn-nāma* describes the greatness of reaching the highest stages of the mystical path and mentions the forty-day retreat as a particularly auspicious time for achieving these (MS. Esad Efendi 3702, Süleymaniye Library, Istanbul, 45a).

106. *TA,* 231–45. For the overall context in which the practice was instituted in Kashmir, see chapter 6.

highest honor that could be bestowed on anyone was a black turban, symbolizing the appearance of black light in visions and dreams. The retreat, performed in this fashion every year at the same time, was a cornerstone of the Nūrbakhshī ritual year.

Although we do not have a direct description of the performance of the retreat during Nūrbakhsh's own time, the report from Kashmir probably closely resembles his own practice. Underlying the retreat was a general division of mystical practice into three successive levels: striving (*mujāhada*), observation (*mushāhada*), and exertion (*riyāża*). All the reports about the practices of Nūrbakhsh's circle portray him and his followers as observing a high level of mental and physical discipline in the form of frequent retreats.

The Sufi's Experience on the Path

Nūrbakhsh's description of mystical experience can be divided into three interrelated topics. The first of these is a hierarchical typology of experiences undergone by the Sufi; the remaining two detail the contents of his visions. The actual experience always represents some degree of communion with divinity given the oneness of being. Traveling to this meeting is simultaneously a journey into the Sufi's own being and an effect of God's self-disclosure in an epiphany. Nūrbakhsh explicates these two issues by schematizing the levels of recollection specific to the seven parts of the human heart and by categorizing the Sufi's experience of epiphanies, annihilation, and subsistence. The three topics for the present section delineate, therefore, the states of mystical consciousness; the Sufi's journey within himself to discover God at the center of his being; and God's making himself manifest to the Sufi as an experience and a state of existence.

Categories of Mystical Experience

The Sufi novice begins to realize the greater spiritual benefits of his vocation after mastering ethics and the basic liturgical practices. Nūrbakhsh divides the saints into two categories: the lovers (*muḥibbān*) and the beloveds (*maḥbūbān*). The lovers strive to reach God, their beloved, through the rigors of mystical life. In comparison, the beloveds are God's chosen ones and are subdivided into two subgroups:

those conforming to norms (*ẕū ʿaql*) and those bereft of reason (*maslūb al-ʿaql*). The latter do not obey the rules of sharīʿa, and Nūrbakhsh states that one should neither pay attention to their outward appearance nor imitate them. The normal ones include Muḥammad and others chosen by God who are worthy of imitation. Some of these may not show excessive outward piety since they are aware of their chosen status, but the best among them, including the Prophet, are as diligent in their spiritual practices as the lovers.[107]

In his role as teacher of ordinary mystics, Nūrbakhsh is concerned mostly with the experiences of the lovers. To understand the levels of spiritual achievement they can attain, it is necessary to begin with his idea of the nature of the spiritual experience. In Nūrbakhsh's understanding, mystical experiences (*vāqiʿāt*) occur when a human being's sense of imagining (*khayāl*) utilizes imaginal brilliance (*żiyāʾ miṡālī*) to apprehend entities in the world of images (*ʿālam-i miṡāl*).[108] This may happen during three states of successively higher worth: sleep (*nawm, khwāb*), trance (*ghaybat*), and sobriety (*ṣaḥv*). During normal sleep, such an experience occurs in the form of a dream (*ruʾyā*), the only way for ordinary people to experience the world of images. The dream occurs when subtle vapors rise from food in the stomach to the brain. These vapors can project the higher reality on the brain at this moment since the normal human senses are inactive.[109] The most significant knowledge brought to human beings during sleep is their condition in the afterlife, since one may experience heaven and hell promised from images seen in the course of a dream.[110]

The next higher category of mystical experience is the trance (*ghaybat*), possible only for the prophets and the saints. This occurs when an emanation (*fayż*) from the higher spheres descends upon the Sufi and transports him from the world of sense objects to that of images. His outward senses become deadened during it due to the deliciousness of

107. Nūrbakhsh, *Maʿāsh as-sālikīn*, 60a–60b; idem, *Insān-nāma,* 87a.

108. Nūrbakhsh, *Risāla-yi nūrīya, AA:*149.

109. Nūrbakhsh, *Risāla-yi kashf al-ḥaqāʾiq*, 62b; Nūrbakhsh, *Risāla-yi miʿrājīya, AA:*118–19.

110. Nūrbakhsh, *ar-Risāla al-iʿtiqādīya,* 203.

the emanations; what he observes at this time is called unveiling (*kashf, mukāshafa*) or witnessing (*mushāhada*).[111]

The highest category of spiritual experience occurs during sobriety (*ṣaḥv*), a state available only to the great prophets and the perfected saints. It comes about when emanations descend from the highest spheres upon the Sufi and he is transported to the world of essence (*maʿnā*) without relinquishing the use of his physical senses. What the Sufi sees during sobriety is called beholding (*muʿāyana*). This level is doubly superior to trance since the emanations received during it come from higher levels of the cosmos, and its recipient can be present in the material world and the world of images at the same time.[112]

All spiritual experiences of mystics still on the path to perfection have to be interpreted by someone higher in the spiritual hierarchy. The Sufi gives a detailed account of what he experiences to his shaykh and the latter interprets them based on his acquaintance with both the world of images and the experiencing Sufi. This process cannot be standardized since things in the world of images do not signify the same ideas under all conditions. The message of the experience depends on the level and psychological state of the subject, and only the highest prophets and saints have the ability to relate the two.[113] Nūrbakhsh clearly implies that he himself possessed this knowledge, and his works contain numerous illustrations of this ability among his advanced disciples.[114]

Nūrbakhsh's schematization of mystical experience into occurrences during sleep, trance, and sobriety combines various elements from previous Sufi thought. His understanding of dreams during normal sleep is based in ideas originating in the work of Ibn al-ʿArabī and, more significantly, ʿAlī Hamadānī.[115] The division of higher mystical

111. Nūrbakhsh, *Risāla-yi kashf al-ḥaqāʾiq,* 62b; idem, *Risāla-yi miʿrājīya, AA:*118–19.

112. Ibid.

113. Nūrbakhsh, *Risāla-yi miʿrājīya, AA:*124–25.

114. *RH,* II:1, 79, 84, 91.

115. For dreams and their interpretation according to Ibn al-ʿArabī, see Chittick, *Sufi Path of Knowledge,* 120–21, and Henry Corbin, *Creative Imagination in the Sufism of Ibn ʿArabī,* trans. Ralph Manheim (Princeton, N.J.: Princeton University

states into trance and sobriety is, however, not attested in the older sources. Both *ghayba* and *ṣaḥv* are terms common in Sufi literature, where the former refers to a state where the subject loses his outward senses and the latter denotes his return to sobriety after an incidence of mystical intoxication (*sukr*).[116] However, Nūrbakhsh's formulation gives these terms a technical meaning due to his hierarchy between the three states. His definition of sobriety as simultaneous presence in the physical and spiritual worlds is a part of his tendency to exteriorize distinctions attained through mystical exercises. This formulation enables Nūrbakhsh to claim a condition of communion with the divine even when he is not undergoing a mystical experience obvious to others.

The Seven Stages of Recollection

The Sufi's progress along the path requires graduating through recollections specific to seven stages of the human heart (*aṭvār-i sabʿa-yi qalbīya*) (chart 5).[117] While this seven-tier arrangement is a clear continuation of Simnānī's idea of the seven subtle substances (*laṭāʾif*) of the spiritual

---

Press, 1969), 241–44. ʿAlī Hamadānī's discourse on dreams is summarized in the aforementioned *Risāla-yi manāmīya,* studied by Meier ("Die Welt der Urbilder"). Meier's article also contains a general overview of Sufi ideas regarding dreams (115–37). For other summary discussions of dreams in Islamic thought, see Toufic Fahd and H. Daiber, "Ruʾyā," *EI²*, 8:645; T. Fahd, *Divination Arabe,* 247–67; G. E. von Grünebaum, "Introduction: The Cultural Function of the Dream as Illustrated by Classical Islam," in *Dream and Human Societies,* ed. G. E. von Grünebaum and Roger Caillois (Berkeley: University of California Press, 1966), 3–22; J. Katz, *Dreams, Sufism and Sainthood: The Visionary Career of Muhammad al-Zawâwî* (Leiden: E. J. Brill, 1996), 205–16.

116. Cf. Anwar Fuʾād Abī Khizām, *Muʿjam al-muṣṭalaḥāt aṣ-ṣufiya, mustakhraj min ummahāt al-kutub al-yanbūʿīya* (Beirut: Maktaba Lubnān Nāshirūn, 1993), 108, 132–33, which cites examples from various important Sufi authors including Ibn al-ʿArabī. See also Chittick, *Sufi Path of Knowledge,* 197–98, and ʿAlī Hamadānī's *Risāla-yi vāridāt,* where the term is used in this standard meaning (MS. Şehid Ali Paşa 2794, Süleymaniye Library, Istanbul, 449b).

117. Nūrbakhsh, *Javāb-i maktūb-i Amīr ʿAlāʾ ad-Dīn ʿAlī Kiyā-yi Gīlānī, AA:*90; idem, *Masnavī ṣaḥīfat al-awliyāʾ*, *AA:*52. The term is given also in Nūrbakhsh's *ijāza* for Lāhījī cited by the latter (*Mafātīḥ al-iʿjāz,* 586).

CHART 5: The Seven Levels of Recollection and Their Correspondences

<table>
<tr><th>Cosmological Realms</th><th>Color of Light</th><th>Level of Recollection</th><th>Things Seen in the World of Images</th></tr>
<tr><td>Lāhūt</td><td>colorless</td><td>seventh level:
hidden of the hidden</td><td>limitless
indescribable space</td></tr>
<tr><td>Jabarūt</td><td>black</td><td>sixth level:
inner mystery</td><td>epiphany in black</td></tr>
<tr><td rowspan="4">higher
Malakūt</td><td rowspan="2">white</td><td>fifth level:
spirit</td><td>epiphany in white</td></tr>
<tr><td>fourth level:
inmost being</td><td>total concentration
on the identity of
the hidden (God)</td></tr>
<tr><td>yellow</td><td rowspan="2">third level:
heart</td><td rowspan="2">• precious metals and stones;
• red light with or without visible source;
• lights of various obligatory rituals and mystical qualities;
• epiphany in red;</td></tr>
<tr><td>red</td></tr>
<tr><td>lower
Malakūt</td><td>blue</td><td>second level:
soul</td><td>step one: mountains, deserts, untamed beasts;
step two: pleasant landscapes, domestic animals;
step three: pleasant landscapes, higher animals, edible plants and minerals;
• epiphany in blue;</td></tr>
<tr><td>Mulk</td><td>green</td><td>first level:
tongue and body</td><td>• inhabitations, trees, fruits, grains;
• Satan in various forms;</td></tr>
</table>

human body, Nūrbakhsh's extant works do not provide the details of his version of mystical anatomy.[118] Discussing the seven levels only in the context of recollections, he states that progression through them leads the Sufi deeper and deeper into himself until he realizes full unity with divine being.

The most basic recollection is that of the tongue and the body, representing the beginning of the Sufi's path. This stage corresponds to the sublunar sphere, and during it the Sufi travels to the world of images to observe human habitations (houses, elegant buildings, and gardens), trees, fruits, and edible grains.[119] Each of these objects has a particular associated quality that the shaykh reveals by interpreting the vision. A particular characteristic of this level of recollection is also that Satan may appear to the Sufi to try to lead him astray. He is seen either in the form of light (which is actually a disguised form of his fire) or different kinds of creatures ranging from harmful insects to ugly human beings.[120] The objects seen during these experiences appear in green light, the color specific to the lunar sphere.[121]

The second stage, corresponding to the lower Malakūt, is the recollection of the soul (*ẕikr-i nafsī*). The practitioner's soul is now cleansed of base elements through a number of steps. The soul in its untreated form incites to evil (*ammāra bi-s-sūʾ*), and through this form of recollection it gradually first becomes inspired (*mulhama*) and from there transforms into the tranquil (*muṭmaʾinna*) soul mentioned in the Qurʾan. The first stage is accompanied by visions of high mountains, parched deserts, and untamed beasts. The visions become more pleasant in the second stage: the Sufi now sees beautiful landscapes and domesticated animals. When proceeding to perfection in this level of recollection, the Sufi finally sees more beautiful landscapes, higher animals such as

118. Elias, *Throne Carrier of God,* 81–85. ʿAlī Hamadānī also discusses these substances and considers knowledge regarding them an indicator on the spiritual path (*Kitāb asrār an-nuqṭa,* 283b–84b; *Nūr al-hidāya wa-surūr yaqīn ad-dirāya,* described in Teufel, *Lebensbeschreibung,* 53).

119. Nūrbakhsh, *Risāla-yi nūrīya, AA:*151, MS., 70b.

120. Ibid., *AA:*153–54.

121. Ibid., *AA:*152–53; Kiyā, *Risāla-yi nūrīya,* 91a (*AA:*11). Nūrbakhsh's schematization of colors is considered separately later in this chapter.

horses, elephants, and camels, and edible plants and minerals in either their raw or cooked forms.

Visions at the second level of recollection occur in blue light, and perfection is signified by divine epiphany in this color. Progress within the stage is equivalent also to travel through the four elements of the material world so that by the end one has surpassed them. Completion of this stage is a sign of gaining paradise as understood in conventional Islamic thought; in cosmological terms, it means progressing from the lower to the higher Malakūt. The Sufi is capable of undertaking secluded meditations upon surpassing this stage (*ʿuzla va khalva*), and he has now reached the level of the heart (*dil*).[122] In a slightly different formulation of the same theme, Nūrbakhsh also explains that the Sufi has to overcome each of the four earthly elements in symbolic form at the beginning of the path, after which he is faced with a choice between correct and incorrect possibilities. He then provides brief guidelines for interpreting what is seen so that the Sufi can make the correct choice.[123]

In the next stage, the Sufi's heart becomes cleansed by assimilating desirable qualities such as generosity, love, knowledge, and worship. These attributes are symbolized in visions of rare metals and precious stones. This is the first portion of travel in the higher Malakūt, and here visionary lights acquire a greater significance. The first color seen is red, initially appearing with a visible source. With progress within the level, the source disappears and the Sufi sees only red light without knowing its direction. At this point he also experiences lights of the obligatory rituals (prayer, fasting, alms-tax, etc.) and those of the benefits of mystical exertions (*shawq, z̲awq,* etc.). Those who have not reached this stage are considered spiritually dead since their hearts have not come alive through the spiritual path undertaken under the guidance of an accomplished master. The Sufi receives divine epiphany in red toward the end of this stage and the color of visions eventually turns yellow.[124]

122. Nūrbakhsh, *Risāla-yi nūrīya, AA:*152–60.
123. Nūrbakhsh, *Risāla dar sayr va sulūk, AA:*185–87.
124. Nūrbakhsh, *Risāla-yi nūrīya, AA:*160–63.

The fourth and fifth stages of recollection correspond still to the higher Malakūt, although the color of light now changes from yellow to white. At the fourth level, the Sufi is at the stage of his inmost being (*sirr*), where he is completely stripped of ignorance and corrupt beliefs and his attention is focused on God to the exclusion of all other concerns. This leads to the level of the spirit (*rūḥ*), the fifth recollection, where he progresses from inferior resolve (*himma*) to a higher level of motivation. The epiphany in white at the end of this stage symbolizes his reaching the boundary between Malakūt and Jabarūt, where multiplicity comes to an end and he is poised to enter the domain of divine omnipotence.[125]

The penultimate stage of recollection on the Sufi's path is that of inner mystery (*khafī*). Just as all entities of the world are ultimately derived from the world of God's unity (Jabarūt), the Sufi now sees visions of the black light consuming all other colors. The bird of the Sufi's inner mystery flies to the extremes of this abode using wings of desire (*shawq*) and love (*maḥabba*), finally reaching its ultimate destination in the recollection of the hidden of the hidden (*ghayb-i ghuyūb*). This is the seventh level of recollection, where the Sufi achieves annihilation (*fanāʾ*) in God's essence. All plurality, including the differentiation between recollector, recollection, and God, is absorbed into the single being at this point. The light of this arena is colorless, and Nūrbakhsh insists that it is possible for human beings to achieve this complete identity with the ultimate reality.[126]

The seven levels of recollection mark the stages of progression in the Sufi's personal path toward God. The simultaneous journey into the levels of the human heart and up the cosmic hierarchy underscores the interconnectedness of all being with God's essence at its center. The Sufi reaches this essence, the world of Lāhūt, when the most hidden organ within his heart is evoked into divine recollection, reminding him of the fundamental unity of all being.

125. Ibid., *AA*:163–64.

126. Ibid., *AA*:164–67; Kiyā, *Risāla-yi nūrīya,* 92a (*AA*:12).

Epiphany, Annihilation, and Subsistence: Categories of Mystical Communion

Nūrbakhsh's description of the inner mystical path is complemented by his division of the human experience of epiphany and union with God into an elaborate hierarchical structure. His cosmology starts with the notion that beings other than God were created through a gradual unfolding of divine being into abodes of the cosmos. This emanation of divine being ends with the creation of humanity, constituting one-half of the cycle of being. The remaining half of this cycle is the Sufi's ascent back toward God by traversing the various realms under the spiritual care of his master.[127] From one viewpoint, this ascent occurs through the Sufi's acquisition of the seven recollections, but it can also be seen as God's gradual self-presentation to the Sufi through epiphanies. These divine self-disclosures occur during experiences of the hidden (*ghayb*), and their esoteric nature parallels the process of creation when God manifests himself in the exoteric sense into the various abodes. Each epiphany is, therefore, a kind of communion between the created world and its creator, and, as a teacher, Nūrbakhsh is particularly concerned to describe its various levels for his disciples.

Nūrbakhsh divides the Sufi's apprehension of, and union with, God into three categories: epiphanies (*tajallīyāt*), annihilation (*fanāʾ*), and subsistence (*baqāʾ*). The epiphanies are the first acceptance by God of the Sufi's spiritual endeavor, and through them true beauty appears in the sight of his heart. It is also during epiphanies that the Sufi acquires the direct knowledge of God (*ʿilm ladunnī*) mentioned in the Qurʾan. Annihilation is an effect of epiphanies and implies withering away of the Sufi's individuality into the ocean of true Being. Subsistence, the last stage, represents complete union between the Sufi and divine Being, resulting in the removal of everything else besides God from his heart. At this level, the Sufi ceases to feel any distinction between himself and divine reality.[128]

Nūrbakhsh believes that the spiritual path of each Sufi is unique in its details so that, in the particular sense, God can reveal himself in an

127. Nūrbakhsh, *Risāla-yi nūrīya, AA:*150.

128. Ibid., *AA:*175, 178.

infinite number of ways.[129] In the general sense, however, it is possible to group such self-disclosures into the epiphanies of his effects, acts, attributes, and essence (chart 6). The lowest epiphany is that of God's effects, where one sees God in the form of an object of the realm of Mulk. He further observes himself annihilating into this object while he is aware that it is God. This type of epiphany may occur with any entity ranging between God's throne and the residents of the sublunar sphere, but the highest one is in the human form, particularly the perfect man.[130]

Epiphanies of God's effects are further classified into those where one sees the entity itself as an epiphany or, more commendably, one sees oneself as constituting the entity as one of God's effects. Furthermore, in either of these two cases, one may receive the epiphany either in the form of a single object or body or see all bodies of Mulk together during the mystical experience. The last of these (i.e., seeing oneself as constituting all bodies of the realm of Mulk) is the highest epiphany of God's effects.

The Sufi then moves to the epiphanies of God's active qualities such as creation and sustenance. Here again, the Sufi either witnesses God as the performer of these acts or he sees himself with the power to perform them. This may occur for each act individually or for all active qualities together so that seeing oneself possessed of all of God's active qualities at once is the highest form of epiphany from God's acts. Particular qualities of these epiphanies are that they are often accompanied by colored lights, and it is through this type that the Sufi comes to behold the angels and spirits of the sphere of Malakūt.[131]

The epiphanies of God's seven essential qualities follow the same pattern as in the previous two cases, and the ultimate stage in this category is to see oneself as the cumulative bearer of the qualities of divine life, knowledge, hearing, sight, power, volition, and speech. As proper to the abode of Jabarūt, the world of God's attributes, this epiphany is accompanied by the appearance of black light.

129. Ibid., *AA*:179.

130. Ibid., *AA*:168–69.

131. Ibid.; Kiyā, *Risāla-yi nūrīya,* 95a (*AA*:16).

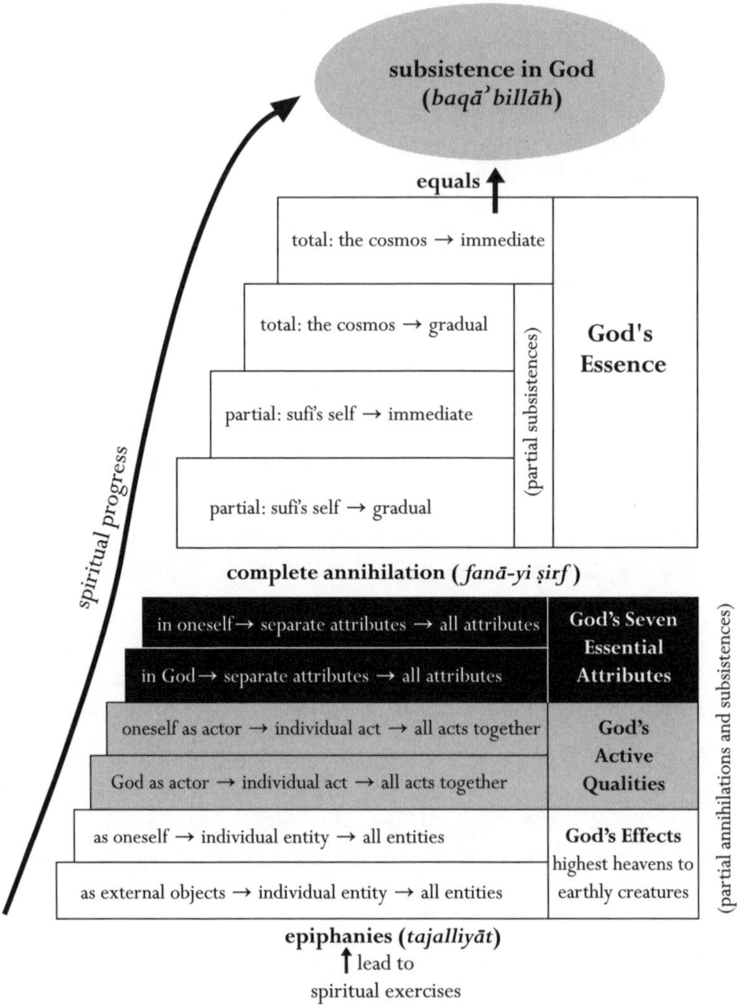

CHART 6: Categories of Mystical Experience

All epiphanies mentioned so far lead to a partial annihilation (*fanāʾ*) at the point when the Sufi loses his identity in the subject of the epiphany. He finally achieves complete annihilation (*fanā-yi ṣirf*) when he receives the highest of all epiphanies, that of God's essence. This is so because God's essence cannot be experienced or known objectively by a subject outside of it. A communion with it necessarily implies passing away into it, where the Sufi now moves beyond the point of knowledge or discernment (*shuʿūr*) and ceases to experience any multiplicity.[132]

Annihilation has infinite forms since it is predicated on forms of epiphany. These can be divided into general categories that encompass all possibilities. The primary division is between partial and total annihilations, where either the individual undergoing the experience is himself annihilated or the whole cosmos undergoes annihilation. Each of these two may further happen either gradually (i.e., the Sufi sees his body or the cosmos annihilating piece by piece) or the Sufi sees himself or the whole cosmos becoming annihilated together in an instant.[133]

For each level of annihilation (and consequently after each epiphany), the Sufi may either return to a normal state of consciousness or he may retain his sense of identity with the divine Being. The latter of these is termed subsistence (*baqāʾ*), and a partial variety of this is attached to each annihilation. The subsisting person not only sees himself in God, but also comes to possess divine powers. The highest form of subsistence (the highest of all communions) occurs after total instantaneous annihilation and is called subsistence in God (*baqāʾ billāh*). During this experience, the Sufi sees God in the form of his own master (*pīr*), the comprehensive locus of manifestation of divine essence.[134]

Nūrbakhsh maintains that the Sufi who attains these states retains his identity with God only through the course of the experience itself: "When a piece of iron is heated inside a kiln it acquires fiery attributes such as redness, heat, and the ability to burn. In this moment if it says 'I am fire' it is true. However, it cannot be called fire once it is brought

132. Nūrbakhsh, *Risāla-yi nūrīya, AA:*170; idem, *Risāla dar sayr va sulūk, AA:*186.
133. Nūrbakhsh, *Risāla-yi nūrīya, AA:*171.
134. Ibid., *AA:*171, 177.

out and allowed to cool."[135] Once he has been touched by divine fire, however, the Sufi clearly acquires an exalted status as compared with ordinary humans. Nūrbakhsh's descriptions of his personal experiences exemplify theories of mystical experience in narrative form:

> I saw myself travel through an extremely pleasant atmosphere until I reached the first heaven and saw various wondrous and strange things. Then I traveled further to the second heaven where I saw angels in an uproar, making merry among themselves. This was so at all subsequent heavens I traveled to until I reached the Throne (*ʿarsh*). I flew from there until I attained countless annihilations and subsistences and finally saw God (*hażrat-i ḥaqq*) in the form of my own master. I was annihilated in him and remained so for thousands of great cycles of time until achieving subsistence. At this point, I became God, seeing the whole world as my own being (*vujūd*) and killing or bringing alive beings according to my wishes. I had livelihood brought to everyone and possessed all the attributes (*ṣifāt*) of God. Then I saw that the whole world had become a drink and I drank it all up. I created it again in the next cycle, it became a drink, and I imbibed it all again. This happened thousands of times—i.e., that I recreated it, it became a drink, and I drank it—and I knew (at this moment) that I had both been like this throughout the past and would remain so forever in the future. And then I became conscious (*hużūr kardam*).[136]

The Sufi may progress through the three stages of union with God in a single experience. Each epiphany is, therefore, potentially an annihilation, and each annihilation may become a subsistence.

Nūrbakhsh's works contain a number of examples depicting his spiritual perfection at the moment of union with, and dissolution into, the divine Being. His position regarding the ultimate experience is extreme since the individual Sufi here achieves identity with God to the extent of possessing all divine functions. This brings to logical conclusion

135. Nūrbakhsh, *Javāb-i maktūb-i fuqahāʾ*, 42a. He affirms this view also in Nūrbakhsh, *ar-Risāla al-iʿtiqādīya*, 193.

136. Nūrbakhsh, *Risāla-yi nūrīya*, *AA:*173, 81a.

the combination of accepting the idea of unity of being and believing in the possibility of its experiential realization. Nūrbakhsh's thought agrees with other famous "ecstatic" Sufis as evident also in his defense of exaggerated claims by Bāyazīd Basṭāmī, Junayd, Ḥallāj, Abū l-Ḥasan Kharaqānī, and Abū l-Ḥusayn Nūrī.[137] His views are more problematic for his own case, however, because he sees himself also as the mahdī, a figure whose spiritual status is exclusive and must translate into worldly authority. Nūrbakhsh as ecstatic Sufi can very well be seen as part of a Sufi trend, but Nūrbakhsh as mahdī, basing his claim on mystical perfection, is "heterodox" from an internal Sufi perspective.

The Significance of Colors

Nūrbakhsh's use of colors as markers for spiritual experience is a theme linking him substantively to past masters belonging to his Kubravī lineage. Beginning with Najm ad-Dīn Kubrā himself, prominent members of the Kubravī silsila became particularly renowned for writing vivid descriptions of mystical visions that became virtual handbooks for all Sufis in the medieval period.[138] While Nūrbakhsh's work bears the imprint of this tradition, he does not follow the scheme of any individual Kubravī predecessor.

Nūrbakhsh states that seeing is the surest form of knowledge, as exemplified by ʿAlī's tradition: "I came to know and worship him after seeing him; I would not worship a lord I had not seen."[139] Physical sight is utilized in acquiring the sciences through which one interprets signs in the physical world, while spiritual sight enables the Sufi to experience projections of the higher worlds into the world of images.

137. Nūrbakhsh, *Javāb-i maktūb-i fuqahāʾ*, 42a. Nūrbakhsh's disciple Lāhījī also states explicitly that his teacher's exaggerated claims are equivalent to similar statements by Shiblī and Ḥallāj (*Dīvān-i ashʿār va rasāʾil,* 335). For the use of ecstatic statements in Sufism, see Carl Ernst, *Words of Ecstasy in Sufism* (Albany: State University of New York Press, 1985).

138. Particularly significant examples of such works include: Fritz Meier, *Die Fawāʾiḥ al-ǧamāl wa-fawātiḥ al-ǧalāl des Naǧm ad-Dīn al-Kubrā;* Dāya, *The Path of God's Bondsmen;* Elias, "Risāla-yi nūrīya." None of ʿAlī Hamadānī's works available to me at present contains a description of colored lights.

139. Nūrbakhsh, *Risāla-yi nūrīya, AA:*167.

Nūrbakhsh uses colors in two different ways in his description of mystical experience. In the minor usage, the shining of black light through the filter of Malakūt upon the seven planets of Ptolemaic astronomy makes them reflect lights in various colors. The arrangement of colors from the lowest to the highest planet here is: green, gray, white, yellow, red, blue, and black. These colored reflections have no obvious function in Nūrbakhsh's thought.

Nūrbakhsh's major usage of color symbolism is the assignment of colored lights to parts of the cosmos. Perceiving these lights acts as a graduated scale for the Sufi's progress in his ascent from material reality to God's essence. In this sense, he assigns green light to Mulk, blue to the lower Malakūt, red, yellow, and white to stages of the higher Malakūt, black to the abode of Jabarūt, and colorless light to the realm of God's essence (see chart 6). The culmination of travel in different parts of the spiritual realms is marked by God's epiphany in the respective color.[140] Nūrbakhsh's emphasis on describing these colors suggests that a knowledge of their hierarchy was a necessary part of mystical training in his circle.

Mystical Knowledge and the Perfect Man

Nūrbakhsh's overall mystical framework is constructed to work in tandem with his theory of the mahdī. The two central figures in his Sufi thought are God and the perfect man, where the latter is virtually equal to the former as a complete reflection of his essence.[141] This relationship is formalized in Nūrbakhsh's cosmology through the parity between the worlds of Lāhūt and Nāsūt. Nūrbakhsh's view of himself as a perfect man is symbolically affirmed through the title given to him by his

140. The color green is an exception in this regard since Nūrbakhsh does not mention epiphany in green anywhere in his work. This is understandable since green is the only color to be associated with the realm of bodies, rather than the spirits or the higher unitary beings.

141. As I have indicated previously, Nūrbakhsh's idea that the perfect man is an actual individual is in itself a particular interpretation of the idea. For a number of other Sufis, the perfect man was the name for the macrocosm of the universe that is reflected in the microcosm of the human body (for example, see Nasafī, *Kitāb al-insān al-kāmil*).

shaykh. As the bestower of light, he stands between God, the source of the light of being, and the rest of creation. The same relationship is seen when light is the beneficence of God's guidance now conveyed to humanity through Nūrbakhsh's teaching.

Nūrbakhsh also sees himself as a repository of the perfection of all forms of physical and spiritual knowledge. Among these, the knowledge of the mystical path and experiential knowledge of God's essence (his interior) and the cosmos (his exterior) rank the highest. Nūrbakhsh considers his own Sufi practice the best spiritual discipline. His works contain a distinct inclination toward a systematic presentation of events experienced by the Sufi. This trait, and the generally high degree of internal consistency in his outlook, suggest that he was actively concerned with facilitating students' acquisition of his mystical system.

Nūrbakhsh's definition of the Sufi path presumes oneness of being, so that knowledge of God is seen as equivalent to both awareness of one's self and the knowledge of the created cosmos as a whole. The three—God, the self, and the cosmos—are different facets of the same reality, whose interrelation derives from the primordial unfolding of God's essence during the process of creation. The cosmos is thus the manifest aspect (*ẓāhir*) of God's interior (*bāṭin*), while the human being reflects the totality of the cosmos by virtue of his status as the perfection of creation.

The human being's special status rests on his possessing all of God's attributes. These are present in a coarse state in an ordinary human being, but their purification and "dematerialization" through the sevenfold hierarchy of recollections brings out their higher spiritual side. The various forms of epiphanies, annihilations, and subsistences that occur during the Sufi's journey represent his becoming aware of both himself and the cosmos as parts of God. Nūrbakhsh can explain this theoretical understanding of existence to others since he has experienced these realities in the course of his own path to perfection.

The spiritual qualities explained and appropriated in Nūrbakhsh's discourse justify his status as the mahdī in his own eyes. This is evident throughout his defense of his messianic claim where his most prominent proofs are predicated on experiences presuming a Sufi understanding of the cosmos. He feels also that Sufism is the most prevalent

Muslim religious attitude in his social context and that he should be accepted as the mahdī most specifically because he excels in mystical virtues.[142] Nūrbakhsh's Sufi outlook is, therefore, inextricable from both his doctrine of the mahdī and his personal claim.

Nūrbakhsh's Sufi thought is a coherent mystical system founded on oneness of being. His discourse depicts an intimate awareness of both previous speculation on this subject and the psychological theories popular among masters of the Kubravī silsila. Conversely, his work also shows independent thought so that his overall mystical approach is distinct as a synthesis. While some of his theoretical preferences reflect biases in favor of his messianic claim, it could also be argued that his self-aggrandizement resulted from taking certain aspects of medieval Sufi thought to their logical conclusion. Most particularly, although the concept of the perfect man was usually discussed sophisticatedly and with caution in medieval Sufi literature, it could easily be appropriated by those inclined to personal immoderation. Nūrbakhsh tried to fulfil this potential, but his greater achievement in terms of religious thought was to construct a consistent theoretical system based on Islamic ontological, mystical, and messianic ideas. His works contain a coherent vision of existence in which he himself occupies center stage as the being who receives divine guidance and bestows it upon the created world.

142. He iterates this viewpoint in his letter to the Tīmūrid ruler Mīrzā Shāhrukh (Nūrbakhsh, *Maktūb beh Mīrzā Shāhrukh, AA:*83–84) and *Risālat al-hudā* (I:36).

PART TWO

The Nūrbakhshīya after the Messiah

Chapter Five

The Mahdī's Successors in Iran and Anatolia

Muḥammad Nūrbakhsh's messianic legacy underwent a substantial transformation following the mahdī's death. The Nūrbakhshīya as a messianic movement had been inseparably connected to the messiah's distinct perspective, and the loss of his central personality required significant rethinking of the movement's ideals and objectives. The mahdī had died before realizing the grand projections about his life, leaving his successors the task of reinterpreting the movement's past to define themselves a new destiny. Our sources give no indication that any Nūrbakhshīs left the movement at Nūrbakhsh's death as a result of disillusionment, but they became divided into two groups based upon their views about Nūrbakhsh's status and accomplishments.

On the most fundamental level, Nūrbakhshīs' response to the founder's death reflected his status as both the mahdī and the heir to a distinguished Kubravī spiritual lineage. Many of Nūrbakhsh's disciples connected to him through mystical affiliation rather than genealogy dispersed from Suliqān to various major Islamic cities following his death. Reports about them suggest that they continued to regard Nūrbakhsh as a great mystical guide but discounted the messianic claim as a forgivable overstatement of his status. Their commitment to the "Nūrbakhshīya" was limited to propagating the purely mystical side of Nūrbakhsh's thought.

In contrast, other Nūrbakhshīs continued the messianic tradition by reinterpreting what the mahdī was expected to achieve during his lifetime. For this group, which included Nūrbakhsh's eldest son and designated successor, *mahdī* now became the title for a great renewer of faith who was expected to remove the dissension between Muslim sects to produce a new unified Islam. They believed that Nūrbakhsh had in fact accomplished this mission through his messianic discourse and that their task now was to promulgate Nūrbakhsh's vision to complete the redemption of Muslim society. Following traditional expectations of the messiah, they awaited the eventual triumph of Nūrbakhshī ideas on a universal scale through their efforts.

The two perspectives adopted by Nūrbakhsh's immediate survivors were carried through to later generations under transformed historical conditions. The rise of the Ṣafavid dynasty, in itself a product of the upsurge in messianic activity during the fifteenth century, changed the overall religious climate in Iran by imposing Twelver Shīʿism on the population as the state religion. The Nūrbakhshīya as a mystical affiliation continued into the sixteenth century, though the adoption of Twelver Shīʿism by shaykhs and novices alike meant a decline in Nūrbakhsh's personal significance whether as the mahdī or even as a great reformer. With respect to the family branch of the Nūrbakhshīya in particular, the Ṣafavids cut short the ambitions of a great-grandson of Nūrbakhsh's to acquire political power in the region around Suliqān. After his removal, later generations of the family slowly converted to normative Twelver Shīʿism under the Ṣafavid religious regime and downplayed Nūrbakhsh's messianic ideas. All modern Iranian Sufi groups whose chains of transmission include Nūrbakhsh can be placed in the historical evolution described in this summary.

This chapter traces the transformation of the Nūrbakhsīya from a messianic movement into a mystical affiliation in the central Iranian lands and Anatolia in the wake of the mahdī's death. The discussion is divided into sections dealing with the immediate aftermath of the mahdī's passing, the personalities and events related to the two groups of Nūrbakhshīs described above, and the fate of the movement under Ṣafavid rule. Among Nūrbakhsh's posthumous followers, the Nūrbakhshīs of South Asia (Kashmir, Baltistan, and Ladakh) form a special group that is excluded from the present discussion and will be treated in chapters 6 and 7. The establishment of Nūrbakhshī ideas outside the Iranian environment needs to be understood in a historical context predicated on a new set of sources. Moreover, the position of the Nūrbakhshī community surviving in the modern states of India and Pakistan relates to the sociocultural and political situation pertaining to minority Muslim groups in these countries, a topic considerably removed from the movement's medieval history.

Bifurcation of the Nūrbakhshīya in the Wake of Nūrbakhsh's Death

The Nūrbakhshī community at Suliqān was understandably struck with great grief when the mahdī passed away on 14 Rabīᶜ I, 869 (November 14, 1464). One description of the scene declares that, for Nūrbakhsh's followers, the event equaled the calamities expected to befall the planet at the end of time (*fitna-yi ākhir-i zamān*).[1] Nūrbakhsh was now thought to have gone into a permanent state of mystical retreat (*arbaᶜīn*), and an elegy (*marsīya*) written by Muḥammad Ghaybī, who was not present at Nūrbakhsh's side at the time, extols him as the mahdī, imām, and "lord of the age" (*ṣāḥib-i zamān*), who came from the heavens according to messianic prediction and attempted to correct the error of the division of Muslims into sects.[2]

Although Nūrbakhsh's own writings indicate that he had consciously prepared his son Qāsim Fayżbakhsh as his successor,[3] a formal process of selection was carried out due partly to the presence of disciples older than Qāsim. Many of these disciples had been on very intimate terms with the mahdī during all the various phases of his life. Our sole detailed report on the community's activity at this time states that the Sufis held a meeting to determine the successor and then went and asked Qāsim to accept the mantle. However, Qāsim demurred and told them to offer the position to Muḥammad Alvandī, known as Pīr-i Hamadān, since he had been among Nūrbakhsh's earliest disciples and the master used to think of him as his most accomplished student.[4] The

1. *TA,* 71.
2. Ibid., 72–76.
3. *RH,* II:91.
4. Muḥammad b. Saᶜd Hamadānī is mentioned in the *Risālat al-hudā,* where Nūrbakhsh praises him particularly for his abilities in dream interpretation. (*RH,* II:84).

matter remained suspended until Alvandī, after hearing of the master's death, arrived at Nūrbakhsh's grave and Qāsim himself asked him to take charge of the community. However, Alvandī refused to do so, stating that Qāsim was spiritually more accomplished. He sealed the matter by himself becoming the first person to pledge his allegiance to Qāsim as the new guide. The rest of the community then followed his lead and Qāsim was formally installed as the mahdī's successor.[5]

Although the succession from Nūrbakhsh to Qāsim included both worldly and spiritual authority, the son clearly did not elicit the same degree of allegiance and commitment from Nūrbakhshīs as the mahdī himself. Nūrbakhsh's most accomplished and talented disciples had begun to disperse from Suliqān in the last years of his life, and the process quickened after his death. From this time onward, the family line of the Nūrbakhshsīya remained headquartered in the Rayy region (where Suliqān is located) and retained a modified version of the messianic doctrine. Those who dispersed from the center, on the other hand, began to deemphasize messianism in favor of a sole focus on mystical ideas. In the following discussion, I first treat the nonfamily lines of Nūrbakhshī affiliation (divided according to geographical location) and then move to the fate of the Nūrbakhshī family.

Cairo and Baghdad

The strength and extent of the Nūrbakhshīs across the Islamic East is best understood by locating Nūrbakhshī shaykhs in the places to which they had dispersed either close to or after Nūrbakhsh's death (chart 7). Kashmīrī's *Tuḥfat al-aḥbāb* informs us of Nūrbakhshī khānqāhs in Cairo and Baghdad functioning under Muḥammad Samarqandī and Burhān ad-Dīn Baghdādī, respectively, around the time of Nūrbakhsh's death. These two shaykhs had been Nūrbakhsh's companions since before his arrival in Suliqān and had held positions of considerable trust. Their placements as independent masters in the Kubravī-Nūrbakhshī silsila are therefore a fundamental part of the development of the order after Nūrbakhsh's death.

Nūrbakhsh's works containing notices about his disciples mention Muḥammad Samarqandī as an eminent disciple remarkable particularly

5. *TA*, 93–94.

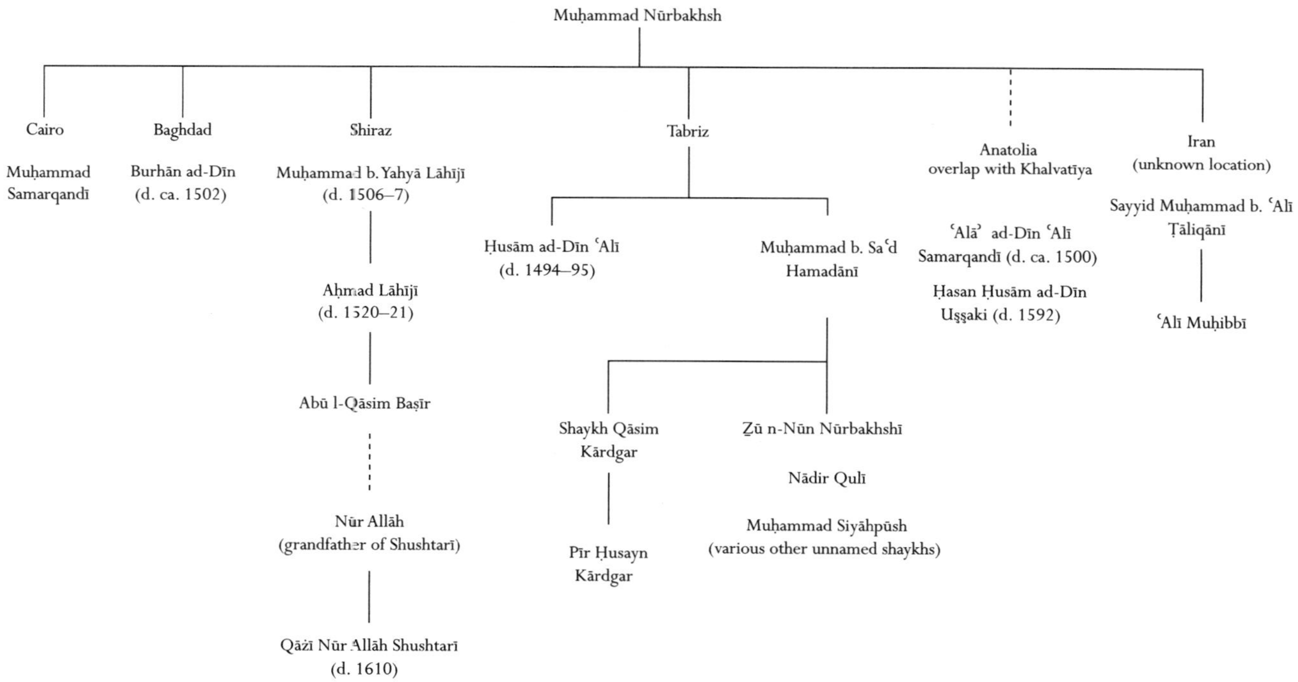

CHART 7: Development of the Nūrbakhshīya after the Mahdī's Death

for his literary aptitude.[6] Samarqandī's talent in this regard is affirmed both by the small sample of his poetry preserved in Kashmīrī's *Tuḥfat al-aḥbāb*[7] and Nūr Allāh Shushtarī's extensive account of Nūrbakhsh's life citing his *Tazkira-yi mazīd* as its principal source.[8] Nūrbakhsh mentions that Samarqandī had moved to Anatolia at the time of writing the *Risālat al-hudā,* and Kashmīrī further states that he had established a khānqāh in Cairo after traveling through Arab Iraq, Syria, and the Ḥijāz.[9] The Nūrbakhshī propagandist Shams ad-Dīn ʿIrāqī (discussed in detail in chapter 6) was staying at this khānqāh while on a business trip to Egypt at the time of Nūrbakhsh's death. However, our knowledge of this institution is limited to Kashmīrī's statement that ʿIrāqī had found it a residence popular with travelers from Iranian lands. The khānqāh cannot be traced in the major sources dealing with Egypt during this period.

Kashmīrī is also the only source to affirm that Nūrbakhsh's disciple Burhān ad-Dīn remained active as a Nūrbakhshī shaykh in Baghdad after the mahdī's death.[10] His closeness to Nūrbakhsh can be judged by the fact that he was the community's chief prayer leader during Nūrbakhsh's decade-long stay in Gīlān.[11] Nūrbakhsh's *Risālat al-hudā* praises him for his spiritual qualities, which had led to the spiritual redemption of others as well, and states that he had become established in Baghdad within Nūrbakhsh's lifetime.[12] A few years after Nūrbakhsh's death, ʿIrāqī joined Burhān ad-Dīn in Baghdad in the course of immersing himself in Nūrbakhshī ideas and studied his work on ʿAlī entitled *Baḥr al-manāqib fī faḍāʾil ʿAlī b. Abī Ṭālib.* We have no other information about Burhān ad-Dīn Baghdādī besides surmising, on the basis of *Tuḥfat al-aḥbāb,* that he died around the time ʿIrāqī was preparing to travel to Kashmir for the second time in 1502.[13]

6. *RH,* II:85; Nūrbakhsh, *Masnavī ṣaḥīfat al-awliyāʾ*, *AA:*53–54.

7. *TA,* 85–86. The ghazal quoted here describes the power of a meaningful gaze emanating from a master/beloved.

8. *MM,* 2:146.

9. *TA,* 16.

10. Ibid., 29–33.

11. Ibid., 13, 31.

12. *RH,* II:131.

13. *TA,* 328.

From Tabriz to the Ottoman Empire

Circumstantial evidence suggests that Tabriz was one of the most active centers of Nūrbakhshī activity in the first half-century following Nūrbakhsh's death. The aforementioned Muḥammad Alvandī, a contender for the position of Nūrbakhsh's successor, visited the city at some point in his life, and disciples initiated by him in the Nūrbakhshī path were prominent members of the local Sufi community.[14]

Mulla Muḥammad Amīn Ḥasharī Tabrīzī, writing in 1011/1602–3, mentions the graves of a number of Nūrbakhshī shaykhs that were popular with pious visitors. One of the graves is unnamed (described simply as *mazār-i Nūrbakhshīya* or *mazār-i sādāt-i siyāhpūsh*),[15] and those of Ẕū n-Nūn Nūrbakhshī Tabrīzī and Nādir Qulī bear no dates.[16] The tombstone of a Bābā Rajab Nūrbakhshī has the date 25 Rabīʿ II, 924 (May 5, 1518);[17] Darvīsh Pīr Ḥusayn Nūrbakhshī, whom Ibn al-Karbalāʾī identifies as the father of Pīr Qāsim Kārdgar, died in 911/1505–6.[18] The latter father and son were descendants of the shaykh Khwāja Faqīh Zāhid. Both Ḥasharī and Ibn al-Karbalāʾī also mention Muḥammad "siyāhpūsh" as a Nūrbakhshī shaykh whom Ismāʿīl I had interviewed at the time of Ṣafavid capture of the city in 1501.[19] According to a tendentious story, when Ismāʿīl asked Muḥammad about his habit of wearing black at all times, he replied that it originally meant perpetual mourning for the death of Ḥusayn, but now it also signified mourning for the martyrdom of Ismāʿīl's father Ḥaydar.[20] An early nineteenth-

14. *RJJJ,* 1:110, 396–97. The author cites Nūrbakhsh's own entry on Muḥammad b. Saʿd in *Risālat al-hudā* (II:84), stating that it was taken from his work *Silsilat al-awliyāʾ*. This suggests that the list of companions in *Risālat al-hudā* may have been circulated as a separate work at some point.

15. Mullā Muḥammad Amīn Ḥasharī Tabrīzī, *Rawża-yi aṭhār: Mazārāt-i mutabarraka va maḥallāt-i qadīmī-yi Tabrīz va tavābiʿ*, ed. ʿAzīz Dawlatābādī (Tabriz: Sutūda, 1992), 72.

16. Ibid., 43, 102.

17. Ibid., 62.

18. Ibid., 124, *RJJJ,* 1:110, 396–97.

19. Ḥasharī, *Rawża,* 82; *RJJJ,* 1:490–92.

20. Shushtarī ascribes the same story to a dialogue between Shams ad-Dīn Lāhījī and Ismāʿīl in Shiraz (*MM,* 2:152).

century eyewitness account of the site of Muḥammad's mausoleum states that the main grave did not have a date on it, but that another grave in the compound had the year 892/1486–87.[21]

In addition to these Nūrbakhshī shaykhs active in Tabriz, the city also provides the link for the slight expansion of the Nūrbakhshīya into the Ottoman Empire, partly through the intermediacy of Nūrbakhsh's Kurdish disciples. Nūrbakhsh's *Risālat al-hudā* briefly mentions Ḥusām ad-Dīn Bidlīsī, who had been under the spiritual care of Nūrbakhsh's disciple Shihāb ad-Dīn Jūrānī until the latter's death and had then become attached to Nūrbakhsh directly.[22] As discussed in chapter 2, Jūrānī joined the mahdī in the earliest years after the messianic proclamation and remained by his side as a trusted companion for thirty years. Like Jūrānī himself, Ḥusām ad-Dīn came from a Kurdish background and represented Nūrbakhsh's success in promulgating his cause in Kurdistan and Luristan.

Ḥusām ad-Dīn may have left Nūrbakhsh's side before the mahdī's death since he reportedly was in Diyarbakr in 1469 when the Aqqoyunlu ruler Ūzūn Ḥasan transferred his capital from Diyarbakr to Tabriz.[23] He remained active under Aqqoyunlu patronage during the rule of Ūzūn Ḥasan's son Sulṭān Yaʿqūb (r. 1478–90), writing a number of mystical works, including a Qurʾanic commentary entitled *Ishārat manzil al-kitāb,* commentaries on the works of ʿAbd ar-Razzāq Kāshānī and Maḥmūd Shabistarī,[24] and a gloss on ʿAlī's *Khuṭbat al-bayān.* His works, where he identifies himself explicitly as a Nūrbakhshī, contain the dual emphasis on the glorification of ʿAlī and exhortation of the unity of being (*vaḥdat-i vujūd*) that he may have carried forth from Nūrbakhsh himself. Evidence from Ḥusām ad-Dīn's works suggests that he did not follow Nūrbakhsh's messianic claim and, instead,

21. Nādir Mīrzā, *Tārīkh va jughrāfī-yi dār as-salṭana-yi Tabrīz,* ed. Ghulām Riżā Ṭabāṭabāʾī Majd (Tabriz: Sutūda, 1994), 281–83. Nādir Mīrzā's description is based on a personal inspection conducted by one of his cousins.

22. *RH,* II:128.

23. This can be surmised from the fact that his son Idrīs Bidlīsī (discussed below) remembers the move in his work *Mirʾat al-ʿushshāq* (cf. Mehmet Bayrakdar, *Bitlisli Idris (Idrîs-i Bidlîsî)* [Ankara: Kültür Bakanlığı, 1991], 4).

24. Mehmed Tahir Bursalı, *Osmanlı müellifleri,* 3 vols. (Istanbul: Matba-yi Amira, 1333/1914–15), 1:58.

professed a clear belief in the standard imāms of Twelver Shīʿism.[25] Although undoubtedly a worthwhile task, a full evaluation of Ḥusām ad-Dīn's considerable work is beyond the scope of this book. For the purposes of Nūrbakhshī history, it can be assumed that he was part of the group that regarded Nūrbakhsh as a great mystic, but not the mahdī.

Ḥusām ad-Dīn himself died in either Tabriz or his native Bidlīs in 900/1494–95,[26] and quite aside from his own significance he finds mention in historical sources as the father of the historian Idrīs Bidlīsī (d. 1520), who successively served the courts of Sulṭān Yaʿqūb and the Ottomans Beyazit II and Selim I.[27] Idrīs's writings include a number of mystical treatises in addition to his historical works, and one can assume that he continued his father's mystical interests.[28] In contrast with the father's self-conscious Nūrbakhshī affiliation, Idrīs seems to have been attracted to the Khalvatī shaykh Ibrāhīm Gülşeni, though no secondary sources mention his formal association with any Sufi order.[29]

Ḥusām ad-Dīn's connection to Nūrbakhsh and his son's devotion to a shaykh of the Khalvatī order provides some clues regarding the persistent confusion of the Nūrbakhshīya as a branch of the Khalvatīya

25. Ḥusām ad-Dīn Bidlīsī Nūrbakhshī, *Sharḥ-i Khuṭbat al-bayān,* MS. XVIII G 28, National Library of the Czech Republic, Prague, 3a–3b. My general impression of Bidlīsī's attitudes is derived also from looking over his commentary on Shabistarī's *Gulshan-i rāz* (cf. Ḥusām ad-Dīn Bidlīsī Nūrbakhshī, *Sharḥ-i Gulshan-i rāz,* MS. Pertev Paşa 606, Süleymaniye Library, Istanbul, fols. 137b–192b).

26. One source states that he died in Bidlīs (Bursalı, *Osmanlı müellifleri,* 1:58), while another says that he died and was buried in Tabriz (Bayrakdar, *Bitlisli Idris,* 4).

27. V. L. Menage, "Bidlīsī, Idrīs," *EI*[2], 1:1208; Cornell Fleischer, "Bedlīsī, Mawlānā Ḥakīm al-Dīn Edris," *EIr,* 4:75–76.

28. Bursalı, *Osmanlı müellifleri,* 3:6–8. Idrīs has not been studied extensively, and even his important *Hasht bihisht,* a history of the first eight Ottoman Sultans in Persian, remains to be edited and published. His works include commentaries on the works of Ibn al-ʿArabī, Ibn al-Fāriḍ, and Maḥmūd Shabistarī, indicating an engagement with complex literary texts with mystical content.

29. Tahsin Yazıcı, "Gulshanī, Ibrāhīm," *EI*[2], 2:1136–37. For two Persian ghazals by Idrīs in praise of Gülşeni, see Muhyî-yi Gülşenî, *Menâḳib-i İbrâhîm-i Gülşenî,* ed. Tahsin Yazıcı (Ankara: Türk Tarih Kurumu Basımevi, 1982), 81–82, 353–54.

in Ottoman sources.[30] The most prominent instance for such misidentification is the suggestion that Emir Sultan (d. 833/1429), a Sufi from Bukhara who migrated to Bursa and married a daughter of Sultan Beyazit I, was an initiate of the "Nūrbakhshī line of the Khalvatī order."[31] Emir Sultan's connection to the Nūrbakhshīya is impossible on chronological grounds since he arrived in Bursa long before Nūrbakhsh's messianic claim was made public, and there is no indication that he ever had any contact with the mahdī. As Hamid Algar has suggested, the error comes from Emir Sultan's father being a disciple of Khwāja Isḥāq Khuttalānī and tracing his Kubravī lineage through Khuttalānī's disciple Shaykh Maḥmūd Nūrbakhshī. This Maḥmūd is mentioned by Nūrbakhsh as one of his own teachers—one who, furthermore, was martyred for the Nūrbakhshī cause in the altercation between Tīmūrid forces and the Nūrbakhshīs in Khuttalān.[32] It is possible that Nūrbakhsh's connection to Isḥāq Khuttalānī and Maḥmūd was somehow transferred to Emir Sultan, with the latter's father as an intermediary.

A further connection between the Nūrbakhshīya and the Khalvatīya mediated through Central Asia is reflected in that Ḥasan Ḥusām ad-Dīn Uşşaki (d. 1001/1592–93), eponym of the Uşşaki (Arabic script: ʿUshshāqī) branch of the Khalvatīya, is reported to have had a Nūrbakhshī affiliation. He is said to have been born in Bukhara, where he was initiated into the Nūrbakhshī branch of the Kubravīya before traveling to Anatolia and obtaining a Khalvatī *ijāza* (teaching certificate) from a certain Aḥmad Samarqandī, who resided in either Uşşak or Erzincan.[33] Uşşaki's published poetry is standard mystical fare and shows no sign of connection to ideas peculiar to the Nūrbakhshīya.[34] He died

30. Algar, "Nūrbakhshīya," *EI*², 8:136.

31. Mehmed Şemseddin, *Bursa Dergâhlari: Yâdigâr-ı Şemsî, I-II,* ed. Mustafa Kara and Kadir Atlansoy (Bursa: Uludağ Yayınları, 1997), 36.

32. Nūrbakhsh, *Vāridāt, AA:*139.

33. Clayer, *Mystiques, état, et société,* 174; Sadik Vicdani, *Tarikatler ve silsileleri* (Istanbul: Enderun Kitabevi, 1995), 241–42; Rahmi Serin, *Islam tasavvufunda Halvetilik ve Halvetiler* (Istanbul: Petek Yayınları, 1984), 131–35.

34. Mehmet Kahraman, *Uşşaki divan-ı şerifi* (Manisa: Uşşaki'ler A.S, 1994), 5–29.

in Konya on the way back from the ḥajj and was buried in the Kasımpaşa quarter of Istanbul, in 1001/1592.[35] Besides suggesting a source for the confusion between the Nūrbakhshīya and the Khalvatīya, Uşşaki's Bukharan origin reflects the possibility of Nūrbakhshī activity in Central Asia toward the end of the fifteenth century. This is significant since no other surviving source gives any information regarding the continuation of Nūrbakhshī-Kubravī lines in Transoxiana beyond Nūrbakhsh's own presence there early in his career.

Further circumstantial evidence for the spread of the Nūrbakhshīya into Ottoman domains lies in the fact that Istanbul libraries contain a number of manuscripts of Nūrbakhsh's works, including, most particularly, the only two extant copies of Nūrbakhsh's *Risālat al-hudā.*[36] One of these copies was transcribed in Istanbul in 1003/1595 by an Ibrāhīm b. Muḥammad b. ʿAlī Sīvāsī, whose name suggests a Kurdish origin.[37] The copying of a distinctively Nūrbakhshī work at such a late date in Istanbul implies the presence of a Sufi group aware of Nūrbakhsh's background and ideas in the Ottoman Empire.

The confusion between the Nūrbakhshīya and the Khalvatīya can also be linked to unidentifiable individuals in Tabriz and elsewhere in Azerbaijan and adjacent Ottoman provinces who at some point were affiliated with both orders. This conjecture is supported by the fact that the holdings of the Süleymaniye library include, aside from many works by Nūrbakhsh himself, a curious work entitled *Jāmiʿ al-laṭāʾif,* which purports to be an account of the life of ʿAlāʾ ad-Dīn ʿAlī Samarqandī, identified as a son of the famous Khalvatī shaykh Yaḥyā Shirvānī.[38] The

35. Uşşaki's death date is somewhat questionable since the hagiographic sources (mentioned in note 33 above) also state that he was born in 880/1475–76, making him 120 years old at the time of death.

36. MS. Esad Efendi 3702, Süleymaniye Library, 85b–108b, and MS. Fatih 5367, Süleymaniye Library, 101b–129a. For other manuscripts of Nūrbakhsh's works in Istanbul, see the list given in Bashir, "Between Mysticism and Messianism," 260–73.

37. MS. Esad Efendi 3702, Süleymaniye Library, 108b.

38. Anonymous, *Jāmiʿ al-laṭāʾif,* MS. Hacı Mahmud Efendi 4645, Süleymaniye Library, Istanbul, 1a–28b. The catalog at the library wrongly identifies Sayyid Muḥammad Nūrbakhsh as the work's author.

manuscript was copied in Istanbul in 1153/1740–41,[39] and the work itself is in Arabic but cites poetry in Turkish said to have been translated from Arabic and Persian by ʿAlāʾ ad-Dīn Samarqandī himself. The original poetry is attributed to Nūrbakhsh and is recognizable as a part of his *Vāridāt.* ʿAlāʾ ad-Dīn ʿAlī occurs in the Khalvatī silsila as a disciple of Yaḥyā Shirvānī and a brother of the famous shaykh Dede ʿUmar Rawshanī (d. 1523–24), who settled and died in early Ottoman Egypt.[40] The literary fragment preserved in Istanbul thus provides a concrete proof for the use of Nūrbakhsh's works in Khalvatī circles in the late fifteenth century. A more thorough scholarly appraisal of early Khalvatī history than has been available to date may shed even greater light on this possible connection.

Bringing together these various pieces of incomplete information, it can be surmised that the noticeable presence of the Nūrbakhshī order in Tabriz during the first half of the sixteenth century was linked to Nūrbakhsh's proselytization in Kurdish and Lur regions of Iran in the early part of his messianic career. The order thrived during the twilight of Aqqoyunlu rule in Azerbaijan until 1501 and, like the city of Tabriz itself, Nūrbakhshīs found themselves in the middle of the Ottoman-Ṣafavid border struggle in the sixteenth century.[41] While the order's center in the Rayy region and its strong Iranian identity clearly made it a part of the Ṣafavid domains, Nūrbakhshī affiliations seeped through to the Ottoman side via both the changing allegiances of the doorway between the two empires at Tabriz and the continuing migration of Central Asian and Iranian Sufis into Anatolia. This was facilitated by the use of Nūrbakhsh's works among Khalvatī shaykhs whose order held great prominence in the Ottoman court around the turn of the sixteenth century.[42] The whole process eventually led to the Nūrbakhshīya being considered a branch of the Khalvatīya in Ottoman sources.

39. Ibid., 43a.

40. Clayer, *Mystiques, état, et société,* 7.

41. The significance of Tabriz as the mediating point is reflected also in the biography of the Ottoman poet Saḥābī.

42. For the Khalvatī influence over the Ottoman ruling house, see Clayer, *Mystiques, état, et société,* and B. G. Martin, "A Short History of the Khalwatī Order of

Shams ad-Dīn Lāhījī and the Khānqāh-i Nūrīya in Shiraz

Among disciples surviving Nūrbakhsh, Shams ad-Dīn Muḥammad b. Yaḥyā Lāhījī (d. 1506–7) needs special mention because of his fame as the author of the celebrated *Mafātīḥ al-iʿjāz fī sharḥ Gulshan-i rāz*. This commentary on a famous poem by Maḥmūd Shabistarī (d. 1320) was a very widely read Persian Sufi work during the later medieval period.[43] Lāhījī's account of his first meeting with Nūrbakhsh has already been reviewed in chapter 2,[44] and it can be surmised from Nūrbakhsh's teaching certificate for Lāhījī, addressed to the ruler of Shiraz, that Lāhījī moved to that city toward the end of the master's life.[45] Lāhījī is said to have established in Shiraz a khānqāh by the name of Nūrīya, where Shams ad-Dīn ʿIrāqī stayed as a disciple for a number of years around 1480.[46] ʿIrāqī describes Lāhījī as the most popular of all Nūrbakhshī shaykhs at this time; his generosity in initiating people into the order had invoked the displeasure of shaykhs who wanted more stringent criteria for entry into the order. His reply, which accords well with the generally "explanatory" nature of his work, was that he saw the initiation as the beginning of the process of salvation. Given the vast number of people who were pursuing incorrect paths, the first order of spiritual business was to bring as many people as possible into the ambit of the order that would eventually lead to their progressing further on the correct path. The Nūrbakhshī path, in this sense, was like Noah's ark: its purpose was to offer salvation before an impending universal doom.[47]

Dervishes," in *Scholars, Saints and Sufis,* ed. Nikki Keddie (Berkeley: University of California Press, 1972).

43. A. Zarrīnkoob, "Lāhīdjī," *EI*², 6:604–5; Corbin, *Man of Light,* 110–20. For summary information about Lāhījī, see also Muḥammad ʿAlī Qurbānī, *Pīshīna-yi tārīkhī, farhangī-yi Lāhījān va buzurgān-i ān* (Tehran: Nashr-i Sāya, 1996), 424–43.

44. Lāhījī, *Asrār ash-shuhūd,* 84–88.

45. Lāhījī, *Mafātīḥ al-iʿjāz,* 293, 353–54, 585–87. The unremarkable entry for Lāhījī in *Risālat al-hudā* suggests that he rose to prominence only after Nūrbakhsh's death (*RH,* II:102).

46. *MM,* 2:152–53, *TA,* 33.

47. *TA,* 36–37.

Relatively little is known about Lāhījī's life except that he traveled to Tabriz, and possibly Herat, for short periods,[48] and that he went on the ḥajj and visited Yemen on the return journey. The Nūrbakhshī silsila was extended, in at least a formal sense, to Yemen as well, since Lāhījī recalls dressing a local shaykh in a robe of investiture (*khirqa*), as Nūrbakhsh had done for him.[49] He is said to have been visited by Ismāʿīl I on the eve of his conquest of Fārs.[50] Lāhījī died in 912/1506–7 and was buried in his khānqāh in Shiraz, where in 1970 the grave could still be observed among the ruins.[51]

A look at Lāhījī's work is helpful in understanding the beliefs of Nūrbakhshī shaykhs active after his death who did not stay moored to the designated successor in Suliqān, Qāsim Fayżbakhsh. Lāhījī's work *Asrār ash-shuhūd,* written within the master's lifetime, addresses Nūrbakhsh as the mahdī on two occasions, although the usage is qualified in both instances (*mahdī-yi dawrān* and *mahdī va hādī*).[52] In contrast, Lāhījī's works completed after Nūrbakhsh's death praise him in both prose and verse without ever employing the term *mahdī,*[53] and a lengthy discussion on the promised savior in the *Mafātīḥ al-iʿjāz* contains no mention of Nūrbakhsh.[54]

Following in Nūrbakhsh's footsteps, Lāhījī explains in the *Mafātīḥ* that the Muḥammadan Reality (*ḥaqīqa muḥammadīya*) manifests itself in the bodies of living human beings through the process of projection (*burūz*).[55] This occurs at varying levels, so that the perfect humans in a given histori-

48. Ibid., 120–22.

49. Lāhījī, *Dīvān-i ashʿār va rasāʾil,* 349–50.

50. Shushtarī reports that Lāhījī had told Ismāʿīl that he always wore black to mourn the death of Ḥusayn.

51. Cf. ʿAlī Naqī Bihrūzī, "Khānqāh-i nūrīya va ārāmgāh-i Shaykh Muḥammad Nūrbakhsh dar Shīrāz," *Armaghān* 38, no. 4 (1348/1970): 220–21. Bihrūzī's article is an appeal to those interested in the heritage of Sufism to redress the shame that the grave and khānqāh of someone as significant as Lāhījī is in complete ruins.

52. Lāhījī, *Asrār ash-shuhūd,* 8, 13.

53. Lāhījī, *Mafātīḥ al-iʿjāz,* 67, 293, 353–54, 585–87.

54. Ibid., 265–87. Lāhījī's theoretical discussion about the mahdī is strikingly similar to Nūrbakhsh's personalized description of the savior's identity and function. This suggests that Lāhījī was familiar with Nūrbakhsh's defense of his claim, but chose not to ratify it at least after the teacher's death.

55. Nūrbakhsh's usage of this term has been discussed above in chapter 3.

cal period are receptacles of the projection of the Muḥammadan Reality according to the level of spiritual perfection available in that age. Lāhījī most likely regarded Nūrbakhsh as the physical manifestation of Muḥammadan Reality in his lifetime in this sense (thus the term *mahdī-yi dawrān*), and not as the eschatological savior who is to be the only other complete manifestation of the Muḥammadan Reality besides Muḥammad the prophet.[56] This view was further concretized after Nūrbakhsh's death when Lāhījī retained his fondness and respect for the teacher despite the fact that he had failed to fulfill traditional expectations regarding the mahdī.

Lāhījī was succeeded by his son Aḥmad "Shaykhzāda Lāhījī," who composed verse under the name Fidāʾī. He was among the companions of the Ṣafavid noble Shaykh Najm Zargar, and Ismāʿīl I sent him as an ambassador to the court of Muḥammad Khān Shībānī in Transoxiana, where he had numerous discussions with local scholars. He returned to Shiraz from this mission and upon his death in 927/1520–21 was buried in his ancestral khānqāh. Nūr Allāh Shushtarī mentions Aḥmad's son Abū l-Qāsim Baṣīr as a teacher of his own grandfather, Nūr Allāh, in Shiraz, and Sām Mīrzā gives some verses by his son-in-law Qāżī ʿAbdallāh Yaqīnī. Shushtarī's personal affiliation with the Nūrbakhshīya was through his familial connection to the hospice established by Lāhījī in Shiraz.[57] His opinion in the *Majālis al-muʾminīn* that Isḥāq Khuttalānī had proclaimed Nūrbakhsh the mahdī for political reasons rather than religious conviction underscores the loss of messianic ideology in Lāhījī's branch of the Nūrbakhshīya soon after the mahdī's death.[58]

Miscellaneous Iranian Cities

Besides the shaykhs already mentioned, the sources also preserve Nūrbakhshī lines of succession proceeding through Nūrbakhsh's students

56. Lāhījī, *Mafātīḥ al-iʿjāz,* 265–87.

57. For details, see *MM,* 2:153; Sām Mīrzā Ṣafavī, *Tazkira-yi tuḥfa-yi Sāmī,* ed. Rukn ad-Dīn Humāyūnfarrukh (Tehran: ʿIlmī, n.d), 109–10 [hereafter, *TS*]; Amīn Aḥmad Rāzī, *Tażkira-yi haft iqlīm,* ed. Sayyid Muḥammad Rizā Ṭāhirī "Ḥasrat," 3 vols. (Tehran: Surūsh, 1999), 2:1296 [hereafter, *HI*]; Luṭf ʿAlī Bīg Āẕar, *Atashkada-yi Āẕar,* ed. Sayyid Jaʿfar Shahīdī (Tehran: Muʾassasa-yi Nashr-i Kitāb, 1958), 167. A summary of all the information is given also in Farīdūn Nawzād, "Fidāʾī Lāhījānī," *Armaghān,* 38, no. 7 (1348/1970): 391–96.

58. *MM,* 2:143.

Sayyid Muḥammad b. ʿAlī Ṭāliqānī and the aforementioned Muḥammad b. Saʿd Hamadānī. Nūrbakhsh refers to Sayyid Muḥammad as one of his disciples, and one ʿAlī Muḥibbī names him as his shaykh in a work that reiterates the Nūrbakhshī silsila.[59] No further information is available about either of these individuals.

The survey of the post-Nūrbakhsh Nūrbakhshīya so far shows that all surviving Nūrbkahshī literature originating outside the family line of succession is either silent regarding Nūrbakhsh's messianic claim or deemphasizes it. It can be surmised, therefore, that a considerable portion of Nūrbakhsh's followers either discounted his messianic claim within his lifetime or came to disassociate themselves from the movement's messianic origins soon after Nūrbakhsh's death. Authors such as Lāhījī and ʿAlī Muḥibbī do not specify Nūrbakhsh as the messiah and their general outlook seems not to be messianic or apocalyptic in any sense. For these adherents of the order, the designation "Nūrbakhshī" conferred upon them the prestige of a chain of initiation going back to Najm ad-Dīn Kubrā (d. 1221). They regarded Nūrbakhsh as the *mahdī* in only the literal sense (i.e. one who has received divine guidance), without implying a messianic function. In contrast, the family line of succession to Nūrbakhsh's mantle continued the messianic tradition for a few generations before being absorbed into normative Twelver Shīʿism.

Succession through the Mahdī's Family

Turning now to Nūrbakhsh's family, we find that after accepting the role of the order's chief guardian, Qāsim (sometimes referred to as Qāsim Nūrbakhsh in the sources) continued in the pattern established by Nūrbakhsh (chart 8). His main work was to foster the spiritual community established at the khānqāh at Suliqān, though reports about his and his children's lives suggest that the spiritual guardianship inherited by the head of the community now translated into the comfortable life of landed gentry. Historical sources state that, in Qāsim's time, the Nūrbakhshī family had shifted its residence from Suliqān to the nearby

59. Muḥibbī, *Silsila-nāma,* 44a–47a. Sayyid Muḥammad is mentioned in *Risālat al-hudā* (II:206) and *Masnavī ṣaḥīfat al-awliyāʾ* (*AA:*54).

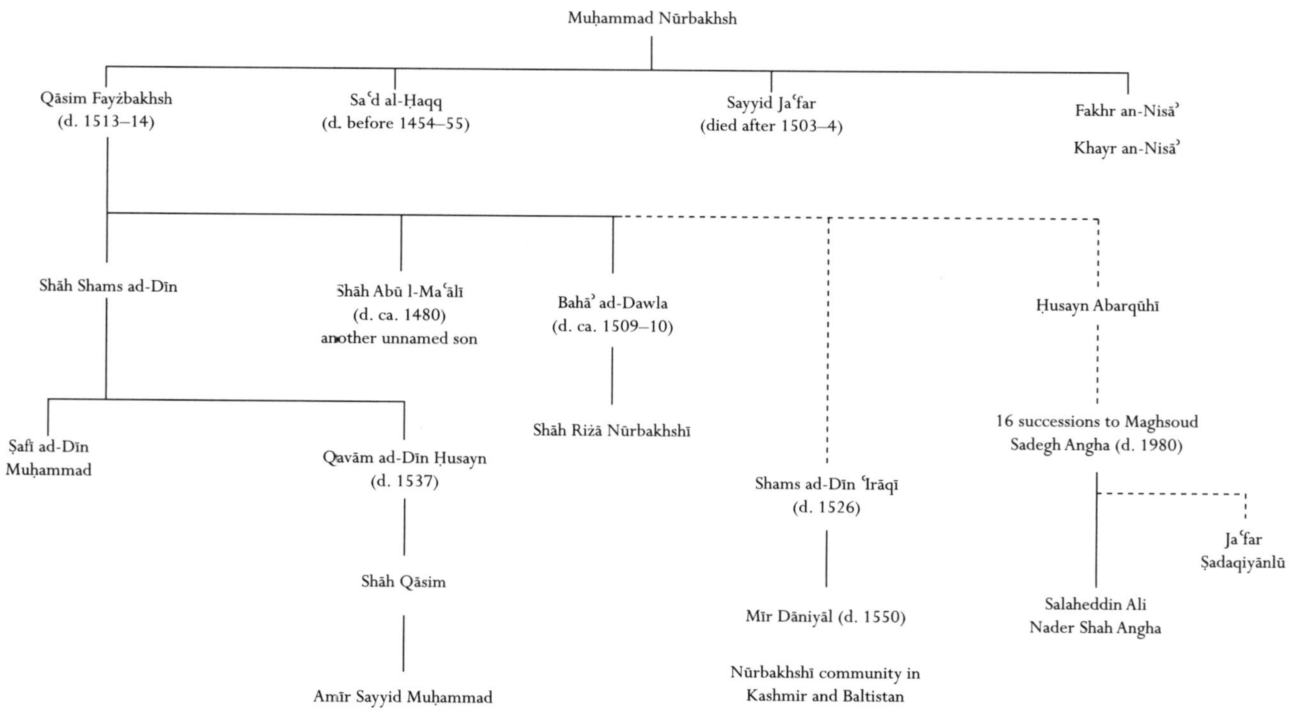

CHART 8: Lines of Succession from Muḥammad Nūrbakhsh's Family

village of Durusht (sometimes called Ṭurusht), where they had significant landholdings.[60] The *Tuḥfat al-aḥbāb* relates that Qāsim's son Shāh Shams ad-Dīn entertained his friends lavishly every night and generally behaved like a nobleman—this despite the fact that Qāsim was preparing him to be his successor as religious head of the order.[61]

Qāsim spent the first few years of his spiritual reign in Suliqān, but he was eventually drawn to the court of the Aqqoyunlu ruler Sultan Yaʿqūb (r. 1478–90) in Tabriz some time around the early 1480s.[62] The exact nature of his liaison with the Aqqoyunlu court remains obscure; it must, in any event, have been quite short since he was soon lured to Herat following an invitation by the Tīmūrid ruler Ḥusayn Bāyqarā (r. 1470–1506). The reports on Qāsim's activities in Herat are our most significant sources for understanding the position of the Nūrbakhshī family in the period after the mahdī's death.

Qāsim Fayżbakhsh in the Court of Ḥusayn Bāyqarā in Herat

Bāyqarā's invitation to Qāsim Fayżbakhsh is contained in a polite and highly formal letter that begins with great praise for the spiritual qualities of both Qāsim and Nūrbakhsh.[63] The ruler's first purpose in writing was to offer his condolences for the death of Qāsim's mother, whom the author called "the Khadīja and Bilqīs" of the times. He hoped that Qāsim's sorrow over the event was diminished from knowing that after her departure from the terrestrial abode she had rejoined her

60. The name appears as Durusht in the Kashmiri source *Tuḥfat al-aḥbāb;* Iranian sources commenting on the Nūrbakhshīya give Qāsim's residence as "Ṭurusht-i Rayy." The fact that Durusht is more accurate is explained in Ḥusayn Karīmān, *Tihrān dar guzashta va ḥāl* (Tehran: Intishārāt-i Dānishgāh-i Millī-yi Īrān, 1976], 416–19.

61. *TA,* 102–5.

62. The year can be adduced only based upon the biography of Shams ad-Dīn ʿIrāqī given in *Tuḥfat al-aḥbāb.* ʿIrāqī is said to have spent nineteen years in the company of other Nūrbakhshī shaykhs following Nūrbakhsh's death before becoming attached to Qāsim while he was still in Suliqān (*TA,* 95). Although, as discussed in chapter 6, the number of years is probably an exaggeration, the fact that ʿIrāqī arrived in Kashmir in 1484 after being in Herat with Qāsim means that the latter left Durusht some time around 1480.

63. Navāʾī, *Asnād va makātibāt,* 403–5.

husband. Furthermore, he wished that Qāsim would consider gracing Herat with his presence, particularly now since Bāyqarā's relationship with the "ruler of those environs" (*vālī-yi ān ḥavālī*) had turned from enmity to friendship. Bāyqarā's reference here was to the Aqqoyunlu ruler Ūzūn Ḥasan, who had initially opposed Bāyqarā's accession to power in Herat but had eventually established a peaceful frontier with the Tīmūrid state. The letter was, therefore, written between 1470, the year truce was established, and Ūzūn Ḥasan's death in 1478.[64]

Bāyqarā's letter facilitated Qāsim's move to Herat to become a part of the collection of literati, scholars, and religious men with whom the ruler had surrounded himself following his accession. Qāsim's younger brother Jaʿfar joined him in the city at some point, and the presence of both in Bāyqarā's court is noted by a number of sources concerned with the renaissance in art and literature spurred on in the city through the patronage of the ruler and his courtiers.[65] Some detailed reports of incidents from Qāsim and Jaʿfar's stay in Herat enable us to reconstruct the beliefs of the family branch of the Nūrbakhshīya at this stage.

Our knowledge of Jaʿfar is limited to a few basic facts, including that he was a poet and left Herat for either Khūzistān or India some time during the beginning of the sixteenth century. The earliest report comes from ʿAlīshīr Navāʾī (d. 1501), Bāyqarā's vizier and a major Chaghatāy Turkic poet and patron of culture in Herat. Navāʾī praises Jaʿfar for his poetic talent and remarks mockingly that even forty years after Nūrbakhsh's death, the son still believed that his father had been the mahdī.[66] He also states, without further elaboration, that Nūrbakhshīs

64. *CHIr,* 6:121–22.

65. For Bāyqarā and the cultural achievements of his court, see particularly: *CHIr,* 6:135–45; Maria Subtelny, "Mīr ʿAlī Shīr Nawāʾī," *EI*², 8:90–93; idem, "Socio-economic Bases of Cultural Patronage under the Later Timurids," *IJMES* 20, no. 4 (1988): 479–505; Najīb Māyil Hiravī, *Jāmī* (Tehran: Tarḥ-i Naw, 1999); and Golombek and Subtelny, eds., *Timurid Art and Culture.*

66. ʿAlīshīr Navāʾī, *Majālis an-nafāʾis,* ed. ʿAlī Aṣghar Ḥikmat (Tehran: Chāp-khāna-yi Bānk-i Millī-yi Īrān, 1944), 96, 272. This citation is actually to two Persian translations of Navāʾī's Chaghatāy Turkish work. The first translation remarks only on Jaʿfar's continuing belief in Nūrbakhsh's mahdism while the second contains the comment on the division of Nūrbakhshīs into two groups. The only original Turkic copy available to me contains the more extended version reflected in the second

in general were divided into two groups: those who believed that he had been the mahdī and those who thought that one of his descendants would some day rise as the expected figure. This tantalizing possibility cannot be confirmed from any other source, though it is a view likely to have been popular in a community attempting to rationalize the death of a messiah. The historian Khwāndamīr, himself a part of Bāyqarā's circle, remarks that Jaʿfar was not satisfied with the stipend allotted him at the court and left for Khūzistān after a few years.[67] However, the internal Nūrbakhshī source *Tuḥfat al-aḥbāb* states that he traveled east to India instead and favorably impressed Ulūgh Beg II, the Tīmūrid ruler of Kabul, around 1490.[68]

More details are available for Qāsim's position at the Tīmūrid court since he was Nūrbakhsh's principal successor and, in the eyes of local scholars, the inheritor of his father's indiscretions. Sources on the period generally portray the Nūrbakhshīya as an order rivaling the Naqshbandīya for royal attention. The competition is exemplified by confrontations between Qāsim, on the one hand, and ʿAbd ar-Raḥmān Jāmī (d. 1492), on the other, with the victor changing according to the biases of the reporting authors.

Qāżī Nūr Allāh Shushtarī (d. 1610), himself a Nūrbakhshī through the aforementioned Lāhījī, provides an account favorable to Qāsim. In his version of events, Ḥusayn Bāyqarā had invited Qāsim to Herat in his search for a cure from a persistent illness. He became very grateful to Qāsim upon his recovery after the shaykh's arrival and put aside some areas as fiefs (*suyūrghāl*) for Qāsim and his wife.[69] This greatly displeased

Persian translation (*Majālis an-nafāʾis* [Urumchi: Xianjiang Khalq Nashriyātī, 1994], 167–68, 434–35).

67. Ghiyāṡ ad-Dīn Khwāndamīr, *Ḥabīb as-siyar,* ed. Jalāl ad-Dīn Humāʾī, 4 vols. (Tehran: Kitābkhāna-yi Khayyām, 1954), 4:116 (hereafter, *ḤS*); idem, *Habibu's-siyar:* tome 3, *The Reign of the Mongol and the Turk,* trans. Wheeler Thackston, 2 vols. (Cambridge: Deparment of Near Eastern Languages and Civilizations, Harvard University, 1994), 628. Khwāndamīr here wrongly states that Jaʿfar was Nūrbakhsh's oldest son, and this mistake is followed by most later sources.

68. *TA,* 303. Kashmīrī states that Jaʿfar had recently gone through Kabul on his way to India at the time Shams ad-Dīn ʿIrāqī arrived in the city on his way from Kashmir to Iran around 1490–91.

69. *MM,* 2:148–49.

scholars such as Jāmī and Shaykh al-Islām (Sayf ad-Dīn Aḥmad) Taftāzānī (d. 916/1510–11),[70] who thought Qāsim incompetent in the exoteric religious sciences. To vindicate their suspicions, they suggested to Bāyqarā that Qāsim should give the sermon on Friday in the main mosque so that the general public could benefit from his erudition. Unaware of the scholars' malicious intentions, the Sulṭān liked the idea and agreed to the event. The next Friday, Qāsim began a sermon on the benefits of reciting "*lā ilāha illā llāh*" after the customary invocations. Jāmī decided that this was the opportunity he had been waiting for and interrupted the sermon to say that he wanted to discuss this phrase. Qāsim replied, "I have heard that when you were in Iraq you wanted to analyze and dispute the phrase '*ʿAlī walī allāh*' (ʿAlī is the friend of God) and now [even] the phrase 'there is no God but God' is to be investigated!" The great audience gathered to hear the sermon began to laugh at this retort, and Qāsim ended his sermon with the Fātiḥa.[71]

Contrary to Shushtarī, ʿAbd al-Vāsiʿ Niẓāmī Bākharzī (d. 1497–98) portrays Qāsim as the defeated party in his account of the incident in his hagiography *Maqāmāt-i Jāmī*. He states that Qāsim had arrived in Herat from Rayy and had become quite popular among the city's nobles. This popularity did not sit well with Jāmī since he considered Qāsim's father Nūrbakhsh "an extremely unpleasant fruit from the orchard of humanity."[72] He therefore devised a scheme to expose Qāsim's incompetence in religious matters. Consequently, in an open debate between Qāsim and the scholars, attended by thousands, Qāsim was unmasked as a pretender. The Sulṭān then allowed Qāsim to leave Herat only when he begged for mercy and publicly disavowed all his false teachings.[73]

70. For Taftāzānī, see *ḤS,* 4:349.

71. In another version of the event, Mīrzā ʿAlāʾ ad-Dawla states in his dictionary of poets entitled *Nafāʾis al-maʾāsir* that Qāsim received great respect in Herat, and one day close to ten thousand people pledged to become his students at the main mosque (cited, based upon a manuscript in Lahore, in Shafīʿ, "Firqa-yi Nūrbakhshīya," III:8).

72. *MJ,* 191.

73. Ibid., 188–89.

The most pro-Nūrbakhshī account of Qāsim's interaction with the scholars is presented in Kashmīrī's *Tuḥfat al-aḥbāb,* a biography of Qāsim's disciple Shams ad-Dīn ʿIrāqī (d. 1526), who was a witness to the events as his teacher's companion in Herat. Kashmīrī relates a number of stories illustrating the competition between Qāsim and the Sunnī scholars of Herat, with the former predictably vanquishing his enemies in each instance. In the event most closely resembling the accounts of Shushtarī and Bākharzī, Kashmīrī states that the scholars once challenged Qāsim to teach something from Ibn al-ʿArabī's *Fuṣūṣ al-ḥikam* (Bezels of Wisdom). They were then astounded to see that Qāsim could do so without even looking at the book, and they were later told that the *Fuṣūṣ* was deemed an easy book by the Nūrbakhshīs since Nūrbakhsh himself used to instruct students from it at the very beginning of their Sufi education. Qāsim then challenged the scholars with a much more difficult text, namely the *Tajaljal az-zāt* of Najm ad-Dīn Kubrā, which even after many days of constant study they were unable to comprehend.[74]

The *Tuḥfat al-aḥbāb* also relates a number of stories about Qāsim's interaction with Bāyqarā himself that cannot be traced in any other source. Against the pattern set by earlier Tīmūrid rulers, Bāyqarā is said to have been more inclined toward the Nūrbakhshīya, rather than the Naqshbandīya, despite intense pressure from people like Jāmī.[75] He and his wife Khadīja Begum took oaths with Qāsim just after his arrival in Herat, and soon thereafter he asked Qāsim to perform the customary forty-day retreat in Herat so that he could learn more about Nūrbakhshī principles.[76] He consistently spent time in the seclusion chamber to observe things properly, and later he offered burial space in his own mausoleum under construction for Qāsim's youngest son, Shāh Abū l-Maʿālī, who died in Herat during Qāsim's stay.[77] Similarly, Bāyqarā's association with Qāsim helped the ruler in cultivating ties

74. *TA,* 66–67.

75. Ibid., 108–9.

76. Ibid., 110–14.

77. Ibid., 116–17. Qāsim blamed the death of the son on the fact that he had earlier agreed to do the forty-day retreat for a human being (Bāyqarā), instead of doing it for God alone.

with other mystics living in Herat who normally shunned all contact with the outside world.[78]

Besides Bāyqarā himself, Qāsim's chief patron at the court was the ruler's nephew Sulṭān Muḥammad Kīchīk Mīrzā, whose death in 1484–85 persuaded Qāsim to leave Herat for good in fear of his life.[79] Kashmīrī states that one of the scholars' chief complaints against Qāsim was that he busied himself too much with medicine and, by this token, was not worthy of being called a Sufi shaykh. In response, Qāsim told his confidants that the criticism was a sign of spiritual ignorance on the part of people like Jāmī since they did not know that sainthood or spiritual authority (*valāyat*) underwent manifest and hidden cycles lasting about a century each.[80] The last manifest cycle had begun with the death of ʿAlī Hamadānī in 1385, so that now (presumably after the year 1485) was a period in which the true saints (*awliyāʾ*) were concealed. Those cognizant of this historical watershed such as Qāsim did not make an open show of their knowledge, while ignoramuses like Jāmī went about aggrandizing themselves.

Stories about Qāsim's stay in Herat give us a blueprint for the status and beliefs of the Nūrbakhshīya just before the rise of the Ṣafavids. The order had clearly gained a secure footing among Sufi organizations of the day since Qāsim, its head, could hold a position at the courts of Bāyqarā and Yaʿqūb Aqqoyunlu. His standing was strengthened by the fiefs granted him by rulers, enhancing the family's economic status. Nūrbakhshī sources themselves portray the order as a rival to the influence of the Naqshbandīya represented by Jāmī (and through him ʿAlīshīr Navāʾī)[81] at Bāyqarā's court. That this was true at least for the brief period of Qasim's stay in Herat during the mid-1480s is borne out

78. Ibid., 123–25.

79. Ibid., 284–87.

80. This idea had some currency in the Kubravīya before Nūrbakhsh's time since Kashmīrī (correctly) cites Jaʿfar Badakhshī as its origin (Badakhshī, *Khulāṣat al-manāqib,* 81–82). However, Badakhshī did not connect the general principle to specific moments in historic time.

81. Vāṣifī, who glorifies ʿAlīshīr Navāʾī and his circle, mentions two brief stories vilifying Qāsim as a foolish person (comparable to an ass) and someone given to extreme exaggeration about his own status despite a total lack of knowledge (Zayn

by polemics by such pro-Naqshbandī authors as Bākharzī and Zayn ad-Dīn Vāsifī in their celebratory accounts of Jāmī and ʿAlīshīr Navāʾī, respectively. Jāmī's distaste for Nūrbakhsh and his followers is reflected also in his report on the main Kubravī line in the *Nafaḥāt al-uns:* it stops at ʿAlī Hamadānī, without mentioning Khwāja Isḥāq Khuttalānī, Nūrbakhsh, or Sayyid ʿAbdallāh Barzishābādī.[82] Bākharzī states that Qāsim had once explicitly requested that Jāmī include his father's name in the work. Jāmī's reply was that he doubted Qāsim's telling of his father's virtues, and that if he reported what people in general thought of Nūrbakhsh, Qāsim would not find the entry very pleasing.[83] It is also noteworthy that nowhere in the *Maqāmāt-i Jāmī* are Nūrbakhsh himself or Qāsim castigated for being Shīʿīs despite Bākharzī's antipathy toward Shīʿī activists in other parts of his narrative.[84] The Nūrbakhshīya was thus seen as a category apart from standardized sectarian groupings by its enemies.

It is curious that, despite these clearly negative reports, a collection of Jāmī's autograph letters contains a note recommending someone named "Mawlānā Nūrbakhshī" of Tūn for favorable treatment at the court.[85] The region of Tūn was the residence of Nūrbakhsh's natal family, making it likely that the named person had some connection to the Nūrbakhshī order. Jāmī's letter in support of him suggests that he may have opposed only those Nūrbakhshīs who persisted in justifying, in one form or another, the messianic claim.

On the ideological front, Qāsim's branch of the Nūrbakhshīya attempted to rationalize the mahdī's death in a different way than Lāhījī and others who emphasized Nūrbakhsh's Sufi accomplishments alone. Some members of this group ostensibly awaited a mahdī from among Nūrbakhsh's descendants, while others evolved a more subtle under-

---

ad-Dīn Maḥmūd Vāṣifī, *Badāyiʿ al-vaqāyiʿ*, ed. A. N. Boldyrev, 2 vols. [Tehran: Intishārāt-i Bunyād-i Farhang-i Īrān, 1970], 1:429–30, 2:397).

82. Jāmī, *Nafaḥāt al-uns,* 449.

83. *MJ,* 191–92.

84. Ibid., 148–51.

85. A. Urunbaev, ed. and trans., *Pis'ma-avtografy Abdarrakhmana Dzhami iz 'Al'boma Navoi* (Tashkent: Fan, 1982), 39. I am grateful to Devin DeWeese for drawing my attention to this source.

standing of his function. His life (1392–1464) fell within a rare period of manifest *valāyāt* that began with the death of ʿAlī Hamadānī.[86] The mahdī was thus essentially the preeminent Sufi of an age in which the esoteric secrets of Sufism (*ḥaqāʾiq-i bāṭin*) were to be proclaimed openly in public. The person charged with this function was an elect among the elect since his job most closely approximated the mission of Muḥammad the prophet. He was, therefore, like none other among Muslims living in postprophetic times, and the age of disclosure had ended soon after his death. His special message was, however, to be preserved and propagated as the true Islam identical with the pure version instituted by Muḥammad in the seventh century.[87] The Nūrbakhshīya, therefore, was a kind of Islamic reformation, whose mission was to shed the accretions of eight centuries of Islamic history and to transcend the sectarian and ideological divisions permeating the Islamic social milieu of the times.[88]

Though different in its understanding of Nūrbakhsh's mission, the Sufi Nūrbakhshīya probably also shared this reformist vision of the movement. Lāhījī's *Mafātīḥ al-iʿjāz* contains a general exaltation of Sufi esotericism over the exoteric knowledge (particularly jurisprudence) of people such as Shāfiʿī and Ibn Ḥanbal.[89] Consequently, he explicitly states that one should follow a Sufi master irrespective of whether he espouses the cause of ʿUmar or ʿAlī.[90] Contrary to descriptions in both late Ṣafavid sources and secondary discussions, neither one of the two Nūrbakhshī groups can be called Shīʿī in the Twelver, Ismāʿīlī, Zaydī, or Ghulāt senses.[91] In this period, Nūrbakhshīs saw themselves as a

86. Nūrbakhsh himself also refers to this time period as the age of the manifestation of sainthood (*ẓuhūr-i valāyat*) in his works (cf. Nūrbakhsh, *Maktūb beh ʿAlāʾ ad-Dawla, AA:*81).

87. Cf. Nūrbakhsh, *al-Fiqh al-aḥwaṭ,* 1.

88. Nūrbakhsh's own position on this issue is discussed in chapter 4, above.

89. Lāhījī, *Mafātīḥ al-iʿjāz,* 311.

90. Ibid., 231. Lāhījī's own words belie misstatements such as S. H. Nasr's claim that he "was thoroughly Shīʿī while being an outstanding ṣūfī" (*CHIr,* 6:657).

91. The point here is not to deny all connections between the Nūrbakhshīya and Shīʿism or ʿAlid loyalism in its broadest sense. My evaluation of Nūrbakhshī history suggests, however, that the movement's members did not identify with any one

distinct grouping that stemmed from Sufism and attempted to transcend traditional sectarian divides.

Nūrbakhshīya and the Rise of the Ṣafavids

Interaction between the Nūrbakhshīs and the Ṣafavids began as the latter assumed a greater political role at the beginning of the sixteenth century. Upon his exit from Herat, Qāsim made a brief pilgrimage to Mashhad and then returned to the family headquarters in Durusht.[92] He now resumed his life as the order's respected and prosperous leader,[93] a position that led to his involvement in the transition from the Aqqoyunlu to the Ṣafavid dynasty in Iran. He may have been the spiritual preceptor of Ḥusayn Kiyā Chulāvī (d. 1506), the overlord of the region around Rayy, who was a partisan of Muḥammadī Mīrzā Aqqoyunlu (d. 1500) against his brother Alvand Beg and who had aided the former in gaining Tabriz in 1499.[94] Ibrāhīm and Ismāʿīl, young sons of Ḥaydar the Ṣafavid, were in residence in Lāhījān under the protection of Mīrzā ʿAlī Kār Kiyā at this time, and they were helped by the momentary success of Muḥammadī Mīrzā. The Nūrbakhshīs had thus somewhat inadvertently become allies of the Ṣafavids during this period, and it is in part through this connection that Qāsim was treated

---

of the major Shīʿī traditions already in existence. Furthermore, the Nūrbakhshīya's ideological outlook cannot be assigned to any one of the established Shīʿī categories in the same way as Qizilbāsh religion can be called a form of Ghulāt.

92. A solitary source, *Nafāʾis al-maʾāṣir,* states that he went back to Tabriz to join the court of Sulṭān Yaʿqūb instead (Shafīʿ, "Firqa," III:8).

93. The prosperity of Nūrbakhshī agricultural lands is remarked upon by Khwāndamīr (*ḤS,* 4:611–12) and later historians who repeat his reports (e.g., Iskandar Bīg Munshī, *Tārīkh-i ʿālam-ārā-yi ʿAbbāsī,* 2 vols. [Tehran: Amīr Kabīr, 1955], 1:145).

94. Aubin, "L'avènement des Safavides," 6. Aubin links Qāsim to Chulāvī unequivocally though the published version of the source he cites, *Tārīkh-i īlchī-yi Niẓām Shāh,* makes no direct mention of Qāsim anywhere in the text and states only that Chulāvī had rebelled against Ismāʿīl despite being a Shīʿī (Khūrshāh b. Qubād al-Ḥusaynī, *Tārīkh-i īlchī-yi Niẓām Shāh,* ed. Muḥammad Riżā Naṣīrī and Koichi Haneda [Tehran: Anjuman-i Āṣār va Mafākhir-i Farhangī, 2000], 23–27). The discrepancy between Aubin's statement and the published text is not due to a difference in the manuscript tradition since the Tehran University Library manuscript Aubin cites (MS. 4323) was used in the preparation of the edition. It is likely that Aubin made the connection on circumstantial grounds but did not state so directly.

favorably by Ismāʿīl after his defeat of the Aqqoyunlu.[95] Ḥusayn Kiyā Chulāvī himself died of self-inflicted wounds after a failed rebellion against the Ṣafavids in 1506,[96] though the Nūrbakhshīya did not pass into the ranks of Ismāʿīl's enemies at this time.

Nūrbakhshī-Ṣafavid relations after this alliance went through positive as well as negative phases. Qāsim was awarded more land by Ismāʿīl, and the Nūrbakhshīs were seen at the royal court as well-respected sayyids from the district of Rayy. Qāsim's son Bahāʾ ad-Dawla (or Bahāʾ ad-Dīn) Ḥasan had followed in his father's footsteps to Herat, arriving at Bāyqarā's court toward the end of the ruler's life. He was later also employed for two or three years in the court of Ismāʿīl, and was then put to death, for unknown reasons, within his father's lifetime (ca. 915/1509–10).[97] Qāsim Fayżbakhsh's year of death is given variously, with 919/1513–14 being the most likely based upon internal Nūrbakhshī tradition.[98]

Suppression of Qavām ad-Dīn Nūrbakhshī

The leadership of the Nūrbakhshīya now passed from Qāsim to his grandson Shāh Qavām ad-Dīn Ḥusayn.[99] The new successor was the

95. *ḤS,* 4:115.

96. Ḥasan Rūmlū, *Aḥsan at-tavārīkh,* ed. C. N. Seddon, 2 vols. (Baroda: Oriental Institute, 1931), 1:77–80.

97. Muḥammad Mufīd, *Jāmiʿ-i mufīdī,* ed. Īraj Afshār, 3 vols. (Tehran: Intishārāt-i Kitābfurūshī-yi Asadī, 1961), 3:105; *ḤS,* 4:612. Ismāʿīl's decree for Bahāʾ ad-Dawla's execution is mentioned also in *Nafāʾis al-maʾāṣir* (Shafīʿ, "Firqa," III:9). His death date can be approximated to 915/1509–10 since he left Herat upon Bāyqarā's death in 912/1506 and spent two to three years with Ismāʿīl. A small treatise on Sufi themes ascribed to Bahāʾ ad-Dawla was published by Ṣadaqiyānlū with his editions of Nūrbakhsh's works (*AA,* 21–26), but his greater competence was in medicine, as evident from his extensive work entitled *Khulāṣat at-tajārib* extant in numerous manuscripts. For a summary of this work and its significance for the Islamic medical tradition, see Lutz Richter-Bernburg, *Persian Medical Manuscripts at the University of California, Los Angeles: A Descriptive Catalogue* (Malibu, Calif.: Undena Publications, 1978), 62–65.

98. *TA,* 439; *Nafāʾis al-maʾāṣir* in Shafīʿ, "Firqa," III:9. The year is given as 927/1520–21 by Khwāndamīr (*ḤS,* 4:115), and the chronologically impossible 981/1573–74 in the printed edition of Shushtarī (*MM,* 2:149).

99. *TA,* 477–79. Kashmīrī reports from his father that Qavām ad-Dīn had sent

MAP 3: Iran under the Ṣafavids

son of Qāsim's older son Shāh Shams ad-Dīn, who also probably died while Qāsim was still alive. Qavām ad-Dīn began to wield his power in the area more assertively, leading to the charge that he was taking on royal pretensions in lieu of his position as the head of a Sufi order.[100]

Sources reporting on Qavām ad-Dīn portray the matter varyingly, though it seems that the Ṣafavids suppressed him due to a combination of his personal ambitions and his associations with members of the Aqqoyunlu and Tīmūrid ruling houses. The least ideologically laden account comes from *Tārīkh-i īlchī-yi Niẓām Shāh,* where Qavām ad-Dīn's demise is attributed to his refusal, in 943/1536, to accept Shāh Ṭahmāsp's (r. 1524–76) offer of marriage to his sister. The woman in question was the widow of Muẓaffar Sulṭān of Gīlān, and Qavām ad-Dīn had declined the proposal on the grounds that he did not feel himself worthy of the honor.[101] Ṭahmāsp was saddened by this rejection of the establishment of a familial tie, and at a later point in the same year Qavām ad-Dīn was arrested during the king's passage through Rayy and was sent to the Alanjaq fort after the confiscation of his property. That was the last anyone saw of this heir of the Nūrbakhshī family.[102]

The second version of the story states that Qavām ad-Dīn first acquired serious notice by Shāh Ṭahmāsp's court by becoming implicated in the murder of a famous poet, Mawlānā Umīdī, in 1523. Reports on the incident vary between an explicit accusation of murder in collaboration with an Aqqoyunlu faction,[103] suspicion without

---

a messenger to Shams ad-Dīn ʿIrāqī in Kashmir to apprise him of Qāsim's death and his own accession to the mantle of Nūrbakhsh. Qavām ad-Dīn's proper name, "Ḥusayn," is identified in Fażlī Iṣfahānī, *Afżal at-tavārīkh* (MS Or. 4678, British Library, London, fol. 11a, 97a), and Sayyid Ḥasan Bukhārī Niṣārī, *Muẕakkir-i aḥbāb,* ed. Najīb Māʾil Hiravī (Tehran: Nashr-i Markaz, 1999), 144. Khwāndamīr states that, at the moment of his own writing, Qavām ad-Dīn had taken over the honorable tradition of his ancestors (*ḤS,* 4:115).

100. Rūmlū, *Aḥsan at-tavārīkh,* 1:279–80.

101. Ḥusaynī, *Tārīkh-i īlchī-yi Niẓām Shāh,* 139.

102. Ibid., 142.

103. Rūmlū, *Aḥsan at-tavārīkh,* 1:177; *HI,* 2:1189; Āẕar, *Ātashkada,* 216.

proof,[104] and no indication of any involvement.[105] He was spared any serious repercussions at the time, but the charge was brought up again during Ṭahmāsp's visit to Tehran in 1537. Ḥasan Rūmlū (who was copied by most later sources) states that, at this time, Qavām ad-Dīn came to attend the court and assumed the highest place among all courtiers. Other nobles from Rayy found this objectionable, particularly since they had already been suffering under his tyrannical overlordship of the area for some time.[106] He was then questioned by Qāżī Muḥammad, son of Qāżī Shukr Allāh, about his having adopted royal hobbies and mannerisms, but he stated that he was a Sufi and did not intend to be a king. He was then asked why he had built a fortress on his property and had collected armor (*juba va jūshan*), to which he remained silent. The court then presented him a list of names of people he had executed and whose property he had confiscated. He denied the latter charges, but both his defense and his honor as a sayyid were declared false and he was put to death in 1537–38 after brief imprisonments, first at the house of Qāżī Jahān and later in the fort of Alanjaq.[107]

The possible underlying causes for Qavām ad-Dīn's fall from favor are reflected in a third version of the story given in an anonymous (and highly partisan) history of Shāh Ṭahmāsp.[108] While it is clear that this author was familiar with Rūmlū's account of the matter (or vice versa), he adds that Qavām ad-Dīn lorded over the area together with Ḥusayn Bāyqarā's grandson Muḥammad Zamān Mīrzā b. Badīʿ az-Zamān Mīrzā. The renegade Tīmūrid prince was seeking to establish himself with the

104. *TS,* 173. Sām Mīrzā repeats the same rumor about a poet named Afżal-i Nāmī, who lived around Tehran and had composed a chronogram on Umīdī's death (*TS,* 226).

105. *ḤS,* 4:115–16.

106. Rūmlū, *Aḥsan at-tavārīkh,* 1:279–80.

107. Aubin suggests that Qavām ad-Dīn was aligned with remnants of Aqqoyunlu sympathizers in the Rayy region and that he was investigated by the court due to the influence of Qāżī Jahān, who had been imprisoned by the ruler of Gīlān at an earlier date upon Qavām ad-Dīn's suggestion ("L'avènement des Safavides," 93–94).

108. Anonymous, *ʿĀlam-ārā-yi Shāh Ṭahmāsp,* ed. Īraj Afshār (Tehran: Dunyā-yi Kitāb, 1992), 82–84.

intention of regaining Herat and may have sought aid from the Nūrbakhshīs based upon the family's earlier close ties with the Tīmūrid court. He advised Qavām ad-Dīn to seek a confrontation with Ṭahmāsp during his stay in Tehran, but the latter thought it better to placate the ruler with words, rather than warfare. Qavām ad-Dīn proceeded to the court, counting on his status as a sayyid to save him from death, while Mīrzā Muḥammad escaped, first to Kāshān and eventually India, to seek his fortune.[109]

Qavām ad-Dīn was accused of wrongdoing as in Rūmlū's report, and an investigation of his property revealed a document according to which a group of people had declared him to be their king. It appeared that Muḥammad Zamān Mīrzā, whose name appeared foremost as an endorser on this document, had continued to correspond with Qavām ad-Dīn after his departure from Rayy, and the pair were still planning to aid each other in rebellious behavior. Shāh Ṭahmāsp then ordered the same punishment for Qavām ad-Dīn as had once been given to Ḥusayn Kiyā Chulāvī (a follower of Qāsim) by his father Ismāʿīl. He was put in chains and eventually burned alive as a deterring lesson for all rebels. In character with the rest of the narrative of *ʿĀlam-ārā-yi Shāh Ṭahmāsp,* this version of the story sounds like a political polemic concocted to justify the removal of a possible threat to the power of the Ṣafavid house.

The cumulative evidence on Qavām ad-Dīn makes it likely that Ṭahmāsp eliminated the Nūrbakhshī heir during the process of further consolidating the power of his dynasty in Iran. The story about the marriage to the king's sister suggests an attempt to co-opt Nūrbakhshī influence by folding the movement's head into the royal household. Rūmlū's version provides information about the local issues involved in the matter, and here, too, the king's efforts seem aimed at removing independent sources of power in his domains. Despite its tendentious nature, the last report is plausible in its general implications, given Nūrbakhshīs' connections with both the Tīmūrids of Herat and Chulāvī. Whatever the exact truth, all the stories reflect the fact that the

109. Ibid., 169–71, 235–42. He was eventually killed by Bayrām Khān in a battle against the Mughals.

Nūrbakhshī family was significant enough to be dealt with directly by the king. Qavām ad-Dīn was eliminated because he either refused fully to compromise the movement's independence or he miscalculated the political situation by siding with the losing parties in the world of Ṣafavid imperial politics.

Impact of Ṣafavid Success: End of Ideological Independence

Qavām ad-Dīn's death marked the end of the Nūrbakhshīya as an Iranian Sufi order with a corporate presence in political matters. Furthermore, his death was accompanied by a gradual shift away from the order's intellectual stance as a movement transcending the Sunnī-Shīʿī sectarian divide. As we will see in chapters 6 and 7, the reformist version of Nūrbakhshīya espoused by both Lāhījī and Qāsim had by this time gained a solid foothold in Kashmir and its neighboring Baltistan and Ladakh. However, in Iran, the order was gradually taking on the color of Twelver Shīʿism imposed upon the population. Indications of this change include the behavior of Qavām ad-Dīn's older brother Ṣafī ad-Dīn Muḥammad, who performed the ḥajj and died while fulfilling a vow to undertake a pilgrimage to Mashhad on foot. His poetry extols the virtues of mystical life and poverty and exhibits a particular devotion to ʿAlī not characteristic of earlier Nūrbakhshī works.[110]

The Nūrbakhshī family succession was passed from Qavām ad-Dīn to his son Shāh Qāsim (who abdicated his father's pretensions),[111] and from him to Amīr Sayyid Muḥammad.[112] Besides these two, some

110. *HI,* 2:1190–91. Niṣārī states that Ṣafī ad-Dīn had another brother, besides Qavām ad-Dīn, whom he did not like. As proof, he cites a verse that mourns the death of Qavām ad-Dīn and the continued life of this unnamed brother (Niṣārī, *Muẕakkir-i aḥbāb,* 160). Āẕar wrongly states that Qavām ad-Dīn was Ṣafī ad-Dīn's father (Āẕar, *Ātashkada,* 219). For a summary of Ṣafī ad-Dīn poetry, see Aḥmad Gulchīn Maʿānī, "Ṣafī-yi Nūrbakhshī Rāzī," *Armaghān* 40, no. 10 (1972): 690–92.

111. *HI,* 2:1191–92. The notice for Shāh Qāsim in Mufīdī's *Jāmiʿ-i mufīdī* (3:106), claiming that he was treated with respect at Ṭahmāsp's court, is historically confused. He mistakenly transplants *Tārīkh-i ʿālam-arā-yi ʿAbbāsī*'s notice on Qāsim Fayżbakhsh (1:145) onto Shāh Qāsim and adds a few embellishments.

112. *HI,* 2:1192–93; Ghulām Ḥasan Suhravardī Nūrbakhshī, *Tārīkh-i Baltistān* (Mīrpūr, Āzād Kashmīr: Verīnāg Publishers, 1992), 183 (hereafter, *TB*). A later

other members and followers of the Nūrbakhshī family are also mentioned in various sources, though we do not have enough historical information to judge their activities. These include Amīr Saʿd al-Ḥaqq "Naṣībī" who resided in Yazd;[113] Fikrī Nūrbakhshī "Sayrī," who traveled to the Deccan to study with Shāh Ṭāhir (d. 952 or 3 or 6/1545–49);[114] Shāh Ḥusām ad-Dīn Nūrbakhshī and his son Mīrzā Muḥammad Taqī, the latter of whom was awarded a fief (*tiyūl*) near Yazd in 1654–55 (he later moved to Iṣfahān and had two sons named Mīrzā Shāh Ḥusām ad-Dīn and Mīrzā Shāh Nāṣir).[115]

Other members of the order not belonging to the family are also mentioned in dictionaries of poets,[116] and a *Fālnāma* ascribed to ʿAlī Riżā "Mīrzā Bābā Nūrbakhshī Shīrāzī" is also extant.[117] The names of these individuals come to us without any historical details, making it impossible to reconstruct the history of the Iranian Nūrbakhshīya after Qavām ad-Dīn with any degree of certainty. Both membership in the family and the order seem to have been honorable affiliations, though the Nūrbakhshīya after about 1550 did not stand out as a political power or a significant independent intellectual movement.

The Nūrbakhshīya's demise so soon after the rise of the Ṣafavids was connected also to the complicated meanings that the term *sufi* acquired beginning in Shāh Ṭahmāsp's reign. As Kathryn Babayan has argued, the early Ṣafavid Empire witnessed an intense competition for power and ideology between the Ṣafavids' Qizilbāsh followers and the Twelver

---

source mentions a certain "Sayyid Muḥammad Laḥṣavī Nūrbakhshī," whose grave in Nāʾīn has his date of death as 7 Ẕū l-Ḥijja, 903 (July 27, 1498) (Maʿṣūm ʿAlī Shāh Shīrāzī, *Ṭarāʾiq al-ḥaqāʾiq*, ed. Muḥammad Jaʿfar Maḥjūb, 3 vols. [Tehran: Kitābkhāna-yi Sanāʾī, n.d.], 3:159 [hereafter, *ṬḤ*]). Either this person is different from Qavām ad-Dīn's grandson or the date of death is incorrectly stated by the source.

113. *TS*, 70; Āẕar, *Ātashkada*, 221.

114. ʿAlāʾ ad-Dawla, *Nafāʾis al-maʾāṣir* in Shafīʿ, "Firqa," III:11; *HI*, 2:1194.

115. Mufīd, *Jāmiʿ-i Mufīdī*, 3:106–7.

116. *TS*, 61, 126, 127, 295, 332, 371, and ʿAlāʾ ad-Dawla (*Nafāʾis al-maʾāṣir* in Shafīʿ, "Firqa," III:10–11).

117. MS. Add. 23582, British Library, London. The manuscript was copied in Iṣfahān in Rajab 1224 (Aug. 1809), and the text has no obvious connection to Nūrbakhsh's ideas.

Shīʿī scholars brought into Iran to promote the empire's official religion.[118] The Qizilbāshs' "sufiesque ghulāt" religion was seen by the scholars to be Sufism in its truest form, and they condemned it as religious innovation (*bidʿa*), the quintessential form of heresy for those aiming for a sharīʿa-bound society. In this context, Nūrbakhsh's mahdist claim was a natural target for scholars such as Muḥammad Bāqir Majlisī (d. 1699), who castigated the mahdī severely for his exaggerations.[119] Moreover, the fiercely anti-Sufi Mullā Muḥammad Ṭāhir Qummī (d. 1098/1686) declared both that Nūrbakhsh was one of the great luminaries in the history of Sufism and that his personal claim was the natural outcome of a Sufi worldview.[120] Although Qummī states that Nūrbakhsh's Kubravī silsila enjoyed the greatest popularity in Iran, he does not cite the name of any shaykh who comes after Nūrbakhsh in the spiritual chain.[121] The complete lack of any concrete references to Nūrbakhshī authors or works by Qummī and other polemicists indicates that their critique was a rhetorical exercise not directed toward an actual Nūrbakhshī presence. It is noteworthy (and surprising) that certain Ṣafavid luminaries such as Bahāʾ ad-Dīn ʿĀmilī (d. 1030/1621) and Mullā Muḥsin Fayż Kāshānī (d. 1091/1680) are reported as members of the order.[122] Their connection is likely to be cursory at best and is possible only through their common teacher, Muḥammad Muʾmin Sadīrī, whose name occurs in a line of Qāsim Fayżbakhsh's spiritual descendants recorded in a nineteenth-century (and hence very late)

118. Babayan, "Sufis, Dervishes, and Mullas," 117–38.

119. Muḥammad Bāqir Majlisī, *ʿAyn al-ḥayāt,* ed. Asad Allāh Suhaylī Iṣfahānī (Tehran: Shirkat-i Sahāmī-yi Ṭabʿa-yi Kitāb, 1963), 238.

120. Mullā Muḥammad Ṭāhir Qummī, *Tuḥfat al-akhyār* (Tehran: Chāp-i Muṣavvar, 1957), 25, 202. This view is repeated in Qummī's *Hidāyat al-ʿawāmm wa-faḍīḥat al-liʾām,* MS. 1775, Āyat Allāh Marʿashī Library, Qum, section 9 (cf. Hamid Algar, "Nūrbakhshiyya," *EI²*, 8:136).

121. The only other Nūrbakhshī to be mentioned by Qummī is Lāhījī, though he is not identified as Nūrbakhsh's student. Qummī's work is generally a critique of the works of famous Sufi authors such as Rūmī, ʿAṭṭār, Ibn al-ʿArabī, and Shabistarī. The inclusion of Lāhījī in this group was probably precipitated by the great popularity of his work *Mafātīḥ al-iʿjāz* among Persian Sufis.

122. E. Kohlberg, "Bahāʾ ad-Dīn ʿĀmelī," *EIr,* 1:429–30; W. Chittick, "Muḥsin-i Fayḍ-i Kāshānī," *EI²*, 7:475–76.

source.[123] The lack of specificity regarding Nūrbakhshī affiliations and the absence of extant literary evidence indicates that the order now survived more in name than in content.

Nūrbakhshīya in Iran after the Ṣafavids

Besides the incidental mention of the Nūrbakhshīya in Ṣafavid and Ottoman sources, Maʿṣūm ʿAlī Shāh's *Ṭarāʾiq al-ḥaqāʾiq* (completed 1313/1895) preserves a continuous silsila, beginning with Fayżbakhsh's disciple Ḥājj Ḥusayn Abarqūhī and continuing to numerous strands that extend to that author's lifetime.[124] Prominent masters mentioned in this chain are ʿAbd ar-Raḥīm b. Yūsuf Damāvandī, whose work *Miftāh asrār al-Ḥusaynī* was completed in 1160/1747–48, and Ḥājjī ʿAbd al-Vahhāb Nāʾinī (d. 1212/1797–98) and his disciple Ḥājjī Mīrzā Abū l-Qāsim Shīrāzī, known as Sukūt.[125] Jaʿfar Ṣadaqiyānlū repeats the silsila from *Ṭarāʾiq al-ḥaqāʾiq* and brings it up to his own shaykh Maghsoud Sadegh Angha (Maqṣūd Ṣādiq ʿAnqāʾ, d. 1980), a popular Sufi shaykh active in prerevolutionary Iran who migrated to the United States in 1980.[126] His organization now calls itself Maktab Tarighat Oveyssi Shahmaghsoudi and is centered in California under the leadership of his son Salaheddin Ali Nader Shah Angha.[127] The movement has built a large shrine over the grave of Maghsoud Sadegh Angha, near Novato, California, and claims to have more than four hundred thousand adherents across the globe.

It is impossible to determine whether the silsila given in *Ṭarāʾiq al-ḥaqāʾiq* actually represents a transmission of doctrine or is a reconstruction in hindsight by later Sufis. No actual works by any of the Sufis claiming the affiliation contain doctrines particular to the Nūrbakhshīya in its original form. The Iranian proponents of the Nūrbakhshīya deny, in any event, that Nūrbakhsh had ever claimed to be mahdī. Ṣadaqiyānlū

123. *ṬḤ*, 2:322, 3:215–16; *AA*, 62.

124. *ṬḤ*, 2:319–22.

125. Ibid., 3:163, 215–16, 247–49.

126. Cf. Yann Richard, *Le Shīʿisme en Iran* (Paris: Librairie d'Amerique et d'Orient, 1980), 98.

127. For the most up-to-date information about this organization, see its website, mto.shahmaghsoudi.org.

goes to some lengths in his notes to editions of Nūrbakhsh's works to prove that Nūrbakhsh had been falsely accused of the messianic claim.[128] The Iranian Nūrbakhshīya after the sixteenth century is, therefore, "normalized" Shīʿī Sufism. The seed of this understanding of the movement can be seen as early as Nūr Allāh Shushtarī's statement that Isḥāq Khuttalānī had never actually believed that Nūrbakhsh was the mahdī. He only wanted to instigate a rebellion against the tyrannical Sunnī Tīmūrids and had used Nūrbakhsh as a pawn because of his sayyid genealogy.[129] The Ṣafavid imposition of juridical Twelver Shīʿism on the population was the greatest cause for the decimation of Nūrbakhsh's distinctive religious legacy in Iran.[130]

Nūrbakhshīya from Messianism to Mystical Affiliation

The institutional development of the Nūrbakhshīya in Iran after Nūrbakhsh's death is apparent from the historical roles played by successive generations of its leaders. The movement had already acquired a stable social presence by the time Nūrbakhsh settled in Suliqān after Shāhrukh's death in 1447. The order continued to gain sociopolitical significance after Nūrbakhsh's death with the expansion of the family's economic power and Qāsim's involvement in the courts of Sulṭān Yaʿqūb, Ḥusayn Bāyqarā, Ḥusayn Kiyā Chulāvī, and eventually Ismāʿīl. Although not at the very forefront of political life, the Nūrbakhshīya was a noticeable presence in Ṣafavid circles at the time of Qāsim's death in 1513–14. Ismāʿīl's patronage of the Nūrbakhshī family indicates that Ismāʿīl's personal messianic pretensions were not so exclusionist as to preclude association with anyone else claiming to be the mahdī. The Nūrbakhshīya was, in effect, a locally powerful order that sought and gained the patronage of Iran's new rulers.

The Nūrbakhshīs' connections with previous ruling houses resurfaced in the time of Qāsim's successor and soured the family's relationship with the Ṣafavids. Qavām ad-Dīn attempted to assert the order's

128. *AA,* 76.

129. *MM,* 2:147.

130. For a discussion of this process, see Arjomand, *Shadow of God,* 109–21; Babayan, "Sufis, Dervishes, and Mullas," 117–38.

power in the Rayy region in collaboration with surviving Aqqoyunlu and Tīmūrid factions, but he was dealt with severely by Shāh Ṭahmāsp. Alongside the fear of seditious behavior, the suppression of the Nūrbakhshīya occurred also at a time when the shāh was attempting to strengthen his imāmī Shīʿī connections.[131] The Nūrbakhshīs' messianic background may now have become more problematic, giving Ṭahmāsp even more reason to quash their influence.

In ideological terms, Nūrbakhsh's messianic claim had evolved by the time of his death into a unique sectarian stance rooted in Sufism. Although divided between two groups over Nūrbakhsh's messianic claim, Iranian Nūrbakhshīs continued to consider themselves the bearers of a special religious mission that did not conform to standardized Sunnī or Shīʿī positions. However, political suppression and the absence of charismatic or intellectually capable leaders combined to make the movement lose its uniqueness in Iran within the first century of Ṣafavid rule.

From a wider perspective, the formal sectarian rigidity (and consequent ideological stability) brought to Iran by the Ṣafavids made it difficult for movements such as the Nūrbakhshīya to survive as separate sects. Like the early Ṣafavids themselves, the Nūrbakhshīya was a product of the politically, socially, and religiously turbulent fourteenth and fifteenth centuries. The movement's primary messianic imperative was lost upon Nūrbakhsh's death, after which, in the manner of other Sufi orders, his memory became the source of charisma for his successors. At the same time, the external sociopolitical arena in Iran underwent a substantial transformation after the Ṣafavids' success, leading to the eventual assimilation of the Nūrbakhshīs into the Twelver Shīʿī mainstream. However, the movement continued in its unique form outside the Iranian environment by being transplanted into South Asia.

131. Babayan, "Sufis, Dervishes, and Mullas," 123–24.

Chapter Six

Hope on a New Front

Kashmir, 1484–1588

The transplantation of the Nūrbakhshīya from Iranian lands into Kashmir and Baltistan, the regions where it was eventually to achieve its great success, materialized a few decades after Nūrbakhsh's death. Although the mahdī himself never visited these areas,[1] he was aware of Kashmir's significance as an early Islamic outpost in southern Asia with connections to the Kubravīya.[2] His shaykh Khwāja Isḥāq Khuttalānī had visited the region with his own teacher ʿAlī Hamadānī around 784/1382–83.[3] Hamadānī's visit to Kashmir eventually led to a permanent Kubravī presence in the city of Srinagar from the late fourteenth

1. The modern Nūrbakhshī tradition in Baltistan claims that Nūrbakhsh did in fact visit the area in 850/1446 and was principally responsible for initiating the process of conversion to the sect (cf. *TB,* 71–75, Ḥashmat Allāh Khān Lakhnavī, *Tārīkh-i Jammuñ* [Mīrpūr, Āzād Kashmīr: Vērīnāg Publishers, 1991], 589–90). There is, however, no indication in any source concerning Nūrbakhsh's life that he ever ventured east of Khuttalān.

2. This awareness is reflected in his claim to have had disciples spreading his teachings in all areas between Anatolia (Rūm) and Kashmir (cf. *RH,* I:36, *Masnavī ṣaḥīfat al-awliyāʾ*, *AA:*52).

3. Ḥaydar Badakhshī, *Manqabat al-javāhir,* fols. 419a–23a. For a general overview of hagiographic information regarding Hamadānī, see DeWeese, "Sayyid ʿAlī Hamadānī and Kubrawī Hagiographical Traditions." Hamadānī most likely visited Kashmir only once although local legend amplified this to three visits with variant dates (cf. Teufel, *Lebensbeschreibung,* 14–18). For a review of the relevant historical materials and development of local myths about this issue, see Wolfgang

century, and Kashmiri Muslims to this day regard him as the patron saint whose efforts led to the area's Islamization.[4]

The Nūrbakhshīya in its distinctive form was introduced to both Kashmir and Baltistan through the proselytizing effort of Qāsim Fayżbakhsh's disciple Shams ad-Dīn Muḥammad ʿIrāqī (d. 932/1526), who first arrived in the region in 888/1483 as an envoy of Sulṭān Ḥusayn Bāyqarā.[5] The ambassadorial mission proclaimed by ʿIrāqī was a minor matter for the Tīmūrid court since it finds no mention in any of the period's standard histories. The fact that the mission occurred at a time when Nūrbakhshī influence was on the decline in central Iranian lands suggests that it was a pretext for spreading the movement to a new area likely to be hospitable due to its Kubravī heritage.[6] The eventual establishment of the sect in Kashmir was thus part planning and part good fortune that fell to the Nūrbakhshīs on account of historical conditions prevailing in Kashmir toward the end of the fifteenth century.

Shams ad-Dīn ʿIrāqī was, quite unequivocally, the most dynamic propagandist to be associated with the Nūrbakhshīya through the course of the movement's whole history. While lacking the erudition and intellectual depth of someone like Nūrbakhsh himself or Shams ad-Dīn Lāhījī, ʿIrāqī combined a deep-rooted commitment to the Nūrbakhshī cause with a flair for politics that led to worldly successes

---

Holzworth, "Islam in Baltistan: Problems of Research on the Formative Period," in *The Past in the Present: Horizons of Remembering in the Pakistan Himalaya,* ed. Irmtraud Stellrecht (Cologne: Rüdiger Köppe Verlag, 1997), 14–18.

4. Böwering, "ʿAlī-yi Hamadānī," *EIr,* 1:862–64. For the overall history of the Kubravīya in Kashmir, see Rafiqi, *Sufism in Kashmīr,* 28–124.

5. As discussed below, the year in which ʿIrāqī first arrived in Kashmir is given differently by the earliest original sources. Here I am following the year given in Kashmīrī's *Tuḥfat al-aḥbāb,* which seems most likely to be true based upon circumstantial evidence.

6. The mission to Kashmir is paralleled by the possibility that Qāsim had sent a robe of initiation (*khirqa*) to Maḥmūd Khaljī, the Sulṭān of Delhi, through an envoy named Mawlānā ʿImād ad-Dīn. *Tārīkh-i Farishta,* the only source to report this, states that the envoy came from Nūrbakhsh himself, though the fact that he arrived in Delhi in Ẕū l-Ḥijja 871 (July–Aug. 1467), more than three years after Nūrbakhsh's death, suggests that the action was initiated by Qāsim (cf. Shafīʿ, "Firqa," III:12).

far in excess of that of the mahdī himself or his genealogical successors. Muḥammad ʿAlī Kashmīrī's hagiographic account of ʿIrāqī's life in the *Tuḥfat al-aḥbāb* gives us the most detailed first-person portrait of the personality of any major Nūrbakhshī leader. Written expressly for the purpose of immortalizing ʿIrāqī's great deeds,[7] the *Tuḥfat al-aḥbāb* is also a principal source for many other aspects of Nūrbakhshī history covered in preceding chapters.

The history of the Nūrbakhshīya in South Asia is divided between two chapters in this book. The present chapter is concerned with Nūrbakhshī activity in Kashmir and Baltistan during the medieval period; chapter 7 will carry the narrative into modern times. In terms of the political backdrop, the discussion in this chapter pertains to the Sulṭānate (Shāhmīrī and Chak dynasties) and Mughal periods of Kashmiri history.[8] The Nūrbakhshīya arrived in the area toward the tumultuous end of the Shāhmīrī dynasty (1339–1561), when actual power lay in the hands of families of local notables who enthroned and deposed the sulṭāns based upon their mutual competition. In the meantime, a Central Asian Muslim presence in Kashmir was first established by Mīrzā Ḥaydar Dughlāt, who forayed into the area as a retainer first for the Mongol khāns of Kashghar and later for the Mughal emperor Humāyūn (d. 1555). Dughlāt's unstable direct rule over the valley of Kashmir lasted from 1540 to 1551, when he was killed through the intrigue of local nobles. The Chaks, who had been a major faction in internal power struggles throughout the fifteenth and sixteenth centuries, declared themselves kings in 1561 and lasted as an independent dynasty until 1586. Kashmir was conquered by the emperor Akbar in 1588 and remained a part of the Mughal Empire until the Afghan conquest in 1747.

7. *TA,* 4–5.

8. For the general outlines of Kashmiri history, see Mohibbul Hasan, "Kashmīr," *EI*², 4:706–10. The contents and biases of major sources for this history are discussed in Hasan, *Kashmīr under the Sulṭāns,* 1–16; Rafiqi, *Sufism in Kashmir,* xv–xxxv; Niyāzmand, "Kashmīr mēñ fārsī tārīkh-navīsī: Ibtidāʾ va irtiqāʾ," 94–125; and Ramesh Chander Dogra, *Jammu and Kashmir: A Select and Annotated Bibliography* (Delhi: Ajanta Publications, 1986), 118–235.

It was during the Sulṭānate and Mughal periods that Muslims gradually came to constitute a majority of the population in Kashmir. The details of this demographic change have yet to be evaluated comprehensively, though it is clear that Nūrbakhshī propaganda had considerable impact on the process of Islamization.[9] In addition, from the late fifteenth century onward, Kashmir became a battleground for Islamic sects competing to gain converts from among not only Hindus and Buddhists but also Muslim Kashmiris belonging to rival sects. The Nūrbakhshīya was a major player in this rivalry during the sixteenth century, and interactions between Nūrbakhshī shaykhs and Sunnī and Twelver Shīʿī scholars reflect the overall environment of South Asian Muslim communities in the period. The initial success of the Nūrbakhshīya in the area reflects the relatively open religious marketplace of the fifteenth and early sixteenth centuries. Conversely, the eventual decline of the movement to the benefit of the major sects resulted from Sunnī Mughal domination in India and the long-range effects of Ṣafavid establishment of Twelver Shīʿism as the official religion in Iran. The fate of the Nūrbakhshīya in Kashmir thus mirrors general trends in the religious history of the Indo-Iranian world during the late medieval and early modern periods.

In presenting the Nūrbakhshīya as a part of the mosaic of Kashmiri society in this chapter, I begin with the caveat that the complicated late medieval history of Kashmir has yet to receive adequate academic attention.[10] My treatment of the subject here is limited to an assessment of the original sources to highlight only the Nūrbakhshī element in Kashmiri political and social history. It is beyond the scope of this book to offer a full assessment of all the available materials leading to a definitive picture of the historical scene in its totality. The chapter is

9. For the most detailed discussions regarding this issue to date, see Bruce B. Lawrence, "Islam in India: The Function of Institutional Sufism in the Islamization of Rajasthan, Gujarat and Kashmir," *Contributions in Asian Studies* 17 (1982): 27–43; Holzwarth, "Islam in Baltistan," 1–40; and ʿAbd al-Ḥamīd Khāvar, "Shimālī ʿilāqajāt mēñ ishāʿat-i Islām," in *Qarāquram Hindūkush,* ed. Manẓūm ʿAlī (Islamabad: Barq Sons, 1985), 193–224.

10. Works by Hasan, R. K. Parmu, Abdul Majid Mattoo, and Rafiqi provide the overall picture, though they fall short of a thorough critical assessment of the original sources.

divided into chronological units dealing with ʿIrāqī's two missions to the region and the movement's fate after ʿIrāqī's death. The Nūrbakhshīya's historical evolution in the region follows the pattern of arrival of the movement, a brief period of ascendancy in a highly contested environment, and rapid decline under adverse sociopolitical conditions.

Shams ad-Dīn ʿIrāqī: A Nūrbakhshī Propagandist in Kashmir

Shams ad-Dīn Muḥammad ʿIrāqī was born in a village named Kundāla, near Suliqān, to Darvīsh Ibrāhīm and Fīrūza Khātūn some time around the year 830 (1429–30).[11] His father was a Sufi dedicated to Nūrbakhsh; his mother was descended from a family of sayyids originally from Qazvīn. ʿIrāqī's hagiographer states that he acquired the desire to devote himself completely to Nūrbakhsh at an early age (he would have been about seventeen at the time of Nūrbakhsh's arrival in Suliqān in 1447), but was discouraged from adopting religious pursuits by Nūrbakhsh himself on the request of his father. Darvīsh Ibrāhīm was given to solitary retreats in his old age and wanted his son to be the principal caretaker of the household. In exchange for asking him to forsake a religious life for the time being, Nūrbakhsh promised him that at a later time he himself or one of his students would guide ʿIrāqī in his mystical quest. Following this advice, ʿIrāqī dedicated himself to the family business and came to Nūrbakhsh's presence only for an occasional benediction.[12]

After his father's death, ʿIrāqī was obliged to make a lengthy business trip to Syria and Egypt. It was during his stay at the khānqāh of Muḥammad Samarqandī in Cairo that he learned of Nūrbakhsh's death in 1464. The news caused him great distress, and he decided to leave immediately for his homeland in order to pay his respects at the master's grave. Upon his arrival back home, he deposited all business matters in the hands of his brother and rushed to Suliqān. After visiting Nūrbakhsh's grave, he decided to dedicate his life to the Nūrbakhshī cause by attaching himself to Nūrbakhsh's students.[13]

11. *TA,* 9. The year of birth can be adduced from the fact that he was fifty-five years of age at the time of his marriage in 888/1483–84 (*TA,* 149).

12. Ibid., 10–11.

13. Ibid., 16.

Kashmīrī states that following this decision, ʿIrāqī spent the next nineteen years of his life traveling to various khānqāhs in Iran and Iraq, where Nūrbakhsh's disciples were spreading their master's teachings. He consequently ascended the hierarchy of living Nūrbakhshī masters by spending anywhere between two and six years with five different teachers before becoming attached to Qāsim Fayżbakhsh at his residence in Durusht. The total number of years spent in this quest is likely an exaggeration on Kashmīrī's part since that would mean that ʿIrāqī spent no time with Qāsim before arriving in Kashmir in 1484, exactly nineteen years after Nūrbakhsh's death. The purpose of showing his passage through the threshold of various shaykhs in the hagiography, however, is to establish his credentials as a Nūrbakhshī adept.

ʿIrāqī's first stop in this path was Shaykh Maḥmūd Baḥrī, who along with his brother Pīr Ḥājjī Baḥrābādī belonged to the middle generation of Nūrbakhsh's vicegerents.[14] Baḥrī had been Nūrbakhsh's personal attendant, and ʿIrāqī stayed with him for two years to learn all that he could about Nūrbakhsh's behavior and habits.[15] Baḥrī's death led ʿIrāqī to his second preceptor, Ḥusayn Kawkabī, who was also from the second generation of Nūrbakhsh's disciples.[16] Kawkabī had distinguished himself as a teacher during Nūrbakhsh's lifetime and had acted as a tutor in the religious sciences for the mahdī's sons and daughters. In addition, he had translated parts of Nūrbakhsh's legal work *al-Fiqh al-aḥwaṭ* from Arabic into Persian for the benefit of those unable to read the original. Kawkabī passed away three years after ʿIrāqī's arrival, and ʿIrāqī felt compelled to move on to other shaykhs to progress further on the path of learning.

ʿIrāqī's third teacher was Maḥmūd Suflī (or Sufūlī), who had been rescued from a life of degeneracy by Ḥājjī Baḥrābādī and was thus from the last generation of Nūrbakhsh's followers. ʿIrāqī stayed with Suflī for two years, after which the master sent him on to Burhān ad-Dīn Baghdādī, who had been one of Nūrbakhsh's closest companions and had

14. Ibid., 17. Baḥrī and Baḥrābādī are both included in Nūrbakhsh's list of his disciples (*RH,* II:197, 80).

15. *TA,* 20–21.

16. *RH,* II:99.

established a Nūrbakhshī khānqāh in Baghdad during Nūrbakhsh's lifetime.[17] After a lengthy apprenticeship—six years—Baghdādī advised ʿIrāqī to go to Nūrbakhsh's most famous disciple, Shams ad-Dīn Lāhījī, in Shiraz. ʿIrāqī found Lāhījī's Khānqāh-i Nūrīya teeming with followers of the Nūrbakhshī path; he was able, however, to acquire a special place in Lāhījī's heart because of his outstanding spiritual qualities. Kashmīrī states that it was Lāhījī's custom to travel to Suliqān once or twice every year to visit Nūrbakhsh's grave and pay his respects to Qāsim Fayżbakhsh. For the first six years of ʿIrāqī's stay, Lāhījī left the promising disciple in charge of novices in the khānqāh in Shiraz, but in the seventh year ʿIrāqī insisted that he be taken along, and it was thus that he became a disciple of Qāsim Fayżbakhsh in Durusht, prior to the latter's sojourn in Herat (discussed in chapter 5).[18]

Soon after joining Qāsim, ʿIrāqī became a close companion to the shaykh due to his devotion and mystical aptitude. His progress on the Nūrbakhshī path was ratified through Qāsim's interpretation of one of ʿIrāqī's dreams in which he had felt unclean despite doing ablutions in water while traveling on a prosperous and well-watered road. At the end of the journey he had reached an ocean, where he took a full bath and had finally felt himself to be pure. Qāsim interpreted the ablutions along the road to mean the time ʿIrāqī had spent with previous shaykhs, while he himself was the ocean meant as the final destination from the very beginning.[19] Qāsim then gave ʿIrāqī the title Shams ad-Dīn (sun of religion), due to his achievements in acquiring the goals of mystical exercises and appointed him the tutor in mysticism for his eldest son Shāh Shams ad-Dīn. In this capacity, ʿIrāqī both provided guidance to the young heir-apparent of the Nūrbakhshī family and prepared the

17. *TA*, 27–32. For Baghdādī, see chapter 5, above.

18. Ibid., 48–57. It is interesting that during his stay with both Kawkabī and Lāhījī, ʿIrāqī is reported to have fallen in love with young men associated with the hospices as service attendants (*TA*, 24–26, 50–54). Kashmīrī explains ʿIrāqī's propensity to fall in love with other men as a reflection of his generally passionate disposition granted directly by God. The "metaphorical love" (*ʿishq-i majāzī*) in these instances pointed to God's endowing ʿIrāqī with a great aptitude for the "true love" (*ʿishq-i ḥaqīqī*) meant for God alone.

19. Ibid., 95–96.

followers of the order to accept the young scion as a Sufi guide in his own right.[20]

ʿIrāqī accompanied Qāsim to Herat when the master decided to join the court of Ḥusayn Bāyqarā at the ruler's invitation. In Kashmīrī's description, ʿIrāqī acted as the chief aide to the shaykh during his stay, taking care of both family business and visitors.[21] It was also now that ʿIrāqī first became useful to Bāyqarā as an envoy sent to Rayy to determine the truth about rumors that Yaʿqūb Mīrzā, the ruler of Persian Iraq, was preparing an invasion of Bāyqarā's domains in Khurāsān.[22] Bāyqarā had asked Qāsim's help in investigating the matter because of his connections to the region, and Qāsim in turn had chosen ʿIrāqī as the most reliable person for the job. ʿIrāqī indeed vindicated the shaykh's choice by traveling to Durusht in half the usual time and, after determining that the rumor was false, returning at the same speed. The feat suitably impressed Bāyqarā, resulting in rewards for ʿIrāqī and further elevation of Qāsim's position in the court.[23]

In Kashmīrī's account, ʿIrāqī's success during his first mission for Bāyqarā meant that the ruler again chose him when he decided to send an ambassador to Kashmir for the purpose of acquiring medicinal herbs. Bāyqarā was prompted to do so by Qāsim, who was acting as one of his physicians and had recently had considerable success in curing his debilitating ailments. ʿIrāqī was initially reluctant to leave Qāsim and take on the mission, but he eventually accepted on Qāsim's insistence and set off for Kashmir with a companion named Amīr Darvīsh and letters and gifts intended for the region's ruler.[24] ʿIrāqī's mission to Kashmir finds no mention in histories of Bāyqarā's reign, which means that it was, at best, a minor embassy arranged on Qāsim's insistence. As discussed in chapter 5, Qāsim held a precarious position in the Herat court due to opposition from powerful figures such as ʿAlīshīr

20. Ibid., 101–5.

21. Ibid., 116–22.

22. This possible invasion of Khurāsān finds no mention in the standard histories of the period.

23. *TA,* 125–30.

24. Ibid., 132–34.

Navāʾī and ʿAbd ar-Raḥmān Jāmī, and ʿIrāqī's true intended mission was, from the outset, probably to spread Nūrbakhshī beliefs. Qāsim and other Nūrbakhshīs may also have held hopes for an imminent realization of the material aspect of Nūrbakhsh's messianic mission and have considered Kashmir to be a promising spot for a beginning.

ʿIrāqī's Mission to Kashmir as Ambassador for Ḥusayn Bāyqarā, 1484–1491

In order to reach Kashmir from Herat, ʿIrāqī took the well-known road running through Qandahar and Multan. He arrived in Multan during a period of famine and acquired a name for himself due to his generosity in giving alms to the city's beleaguered population. It was also at Multan that, at the age of fifty-five, ʿIrāqī received and accepted the proposal of a sayyid resident in the city to marry his daughter Bīja Āghā.[25] After a brief stay in Multan following the marriage, he set off for Kashmir and reached the region some time in the year A.H. 888 (February 1483–January 1484).[26] He was received well by Sulṭān Ḥasan Shāh on account of the ambassadorial title and the sumptuous gifts he had brought from Khurāsān, though Kashmīrī portrays him still dismayed over the lack of proper etiquette among the rulers and nobles of Kashmir. The implication was that Kashmir was a step down from Herat in

25. Ibid., 149–50.

26. Ibid., 150. The year given by Kashmīrī for ʿIrāqī's arrival in Kashmir corresponds correctly with the earliest historical source, though it differs from some later Persian chronicles. All sources agree that he first arrived in Kashmir only a few months before Ḥasan Shāh's death, which the contemporary historian Shrivara, writing in Sanskrit, records in the Kashmiri year 60, corresponding to 1484 C.E. (S. L. Sadhu, ed., *Medieval Kashmir, Being a Reprint of the Rajataranginis of Jonaraja, Shrivara, and Shuka* [New Delhi: Atlantic Publishers, 1993], 207). Sayyid ʿAlī's *Tārīkh-i Kashmīr,* the earliest extant Persian source, gives the year erroneously as 893/1488 (Sayyid ʿAlī, *Tārīkh-i Kashmīr,* Urdu trans. by Ghulām Rasūl Bat̄ [Srinagar: Centre of Central Asian Studies, University of Kashmir, 1994], 26). The mistake is repeated in the anonymous *Bahāristān-i shāhī,* which takes the historical narrative as far as 1023/1614–15 and whose author has great praise for ʿIrāqī (Anonymous, *Bahāristān-i shāhī,* ed. Akbar Ḥaydarī Kāshmīrī [Srinagar: Anjuman-i Sharʿī-yi Shīʿīyān-i Jammūñ va Kashmīr, 1982], 303 [hereafter, *BS*]).

culture and civilization and that ʿIrāqī saw himself as a teacher for the region's natives.[27]

For approximately the first year of his presence in Kashmir, ʿIrāqī contented himself in the role of an outside ambassador. His residence during this period was the khānqāh of Aḥmad Ītū (or Aytū or Yattū),[28] which, later as well, served as a guest house for other foreign dignitaries.[29] Sulṭān Ḥasan fell ill three or four months after ʿIrāqī's arrival, and ʿIrāqī is said to have predicted, based upon mystical prognostication (*istikhāra*), a rapid death.[30] Ḥasan Shāh's son Muḥammad Shāh, then a child of seven, was now installed as the new ruler, and the kingdom fell into complete chaos for the next few years due to internecine fighting between various powerful families. Kashmīrī and other historians state that this political instability compelled ʿIrāqī to stay in Kashmir for eight years, though it is difficult to see why the internal problems of the state should have lengthened, not shortened, a foreign ambassador's stay. The prolongation of the visit was most likely connected to ʿIrāqī's true mission, the promulgation of the Nūrbakhshī cause.

Establishing a Nūrbakhshī Community in Kashmir

The formation of the first Nūrbakhshī religious community and political faction in Kashmir is best understood through reports about Shams ad-Dīn ʿIrāqī's relations with local rulers, nobles, and religious personalities. His stay in Kashmir coincided with a political seesaw in which

27. *TA,* 151–55.

28. Malik Aḥmad Ītū was Ḥasan Shāh's vizier and early supporter who had been imprisoned on the instigation of a rival faction in the court a little before ʿIrāqī's arrival (Sadhu, *Medieval Kashmir,* 190–99). A dictionary of Kashmiri social groups identifies the Ītūs as a subsection of the Rayna family discussed below (Muḥammad ad-Dīn Fawq, *Tavārīkh-i aqvām-i Kashmīr,* 3d printing, 2 vols. [Mīrpūr: Vērīnāg Publishers, 1991], 1:365). The *Tuḥfat al-aḥbāb* and some other sources give the commander's name as Ītū, or Aytū, depending on vocalization. However, it is written "Yattū" by Rafiqi, probably on the basis of *Bahāristān-i shāhī* (Rafiqi, *Sufism in Kashmir,* 20; *BS,* 310).

29. *TA,* 173. Rafiqi reports that the khānqāh was host also to the Suhravardī shaykh Sayyid Jamāl ad-Dīn some time in the first half of the sixteenth century (Rafiqi, *Sufism in Kashmir,* 20).

30. *TA,* 168–70.

Muḥammad Shāh and his father's first cousin Fatḥ Shāh ascended and were deposed from the throne a number of times at short intervals.[31] Muḥammad Shāh was crowned in 888/1484, a little after Irāqī's arrival; Fatḥ Shāh was the king at the time of his departure around 896/1490–91; and the throne changed hands at least twice in the intervening eight years. On the whole, ʿIrāqī seems to have had better relations with Fatḥ Shāh and his viziers than with Muḥammad Shāh. This is indicated, first, through his having been obliged to leave the khānqāh of Aḥmad Ītū about a year after his arrival, following complaints to the court by the caretakers of the place. As a result he moved to a bigger building in the vicinity of the mausoleum of the rulers (*mazār-i salāṭīn*), where his wife soon gave birth to his eldest daughter Bībī Āghā.[32]

In comparison with this fall from royal favor, ʿIrāqī had cordial relations with Fatḥ Shāh, at least initially, as seen from stories about the patronage he received from Fatḥ Shāh's vizier Malik Sayfdār.[33] Kashmīrī's account for this period is concerned particularly with a rival named Shaykh Shihāb ad-Dīn Hindī, with whom ʿIrāqī had three altercations in the context of Sayfdār's court. This Shihāb was a scholar and skilled debater who had arrived in Kashmir about the same time as ʿIrāqī. His origins were in India, from whence he had been expelled due to his involvement in court intrigues, and he was directed to go to the Ḥijāz. Shihāb set out accompanied by his daughter, and in both Mecca and Medina he was asked for her hand by noble families, but he had determined (through an istikhāra) that she was destined to marry a king named Ḥasan who ruled in Kashmir. Based upon this sign from

31. The considerable confusion in Kashmiri political history during this period has not yet been clarified completely. Hasan's *Kashmīr under the Sulṭāns* gives the most extensive treatment of the subject, though his interpretations can be challenged on the basis of a more careful reading of original sources. In the present context, I will concentrate on ʿIrāqī's contacts with the rulers and their viziers in a general sense, without going into extensive detail about chronological and other problems.

32. *TA,* 173–74.

33. The *Tuḥfat al-aḥbāb* writes the name as Sayfdār (Persian: holder of the sword), while Indian editions of various works write Sayf Ḍār, the last part indicating a Kashmiri caste.

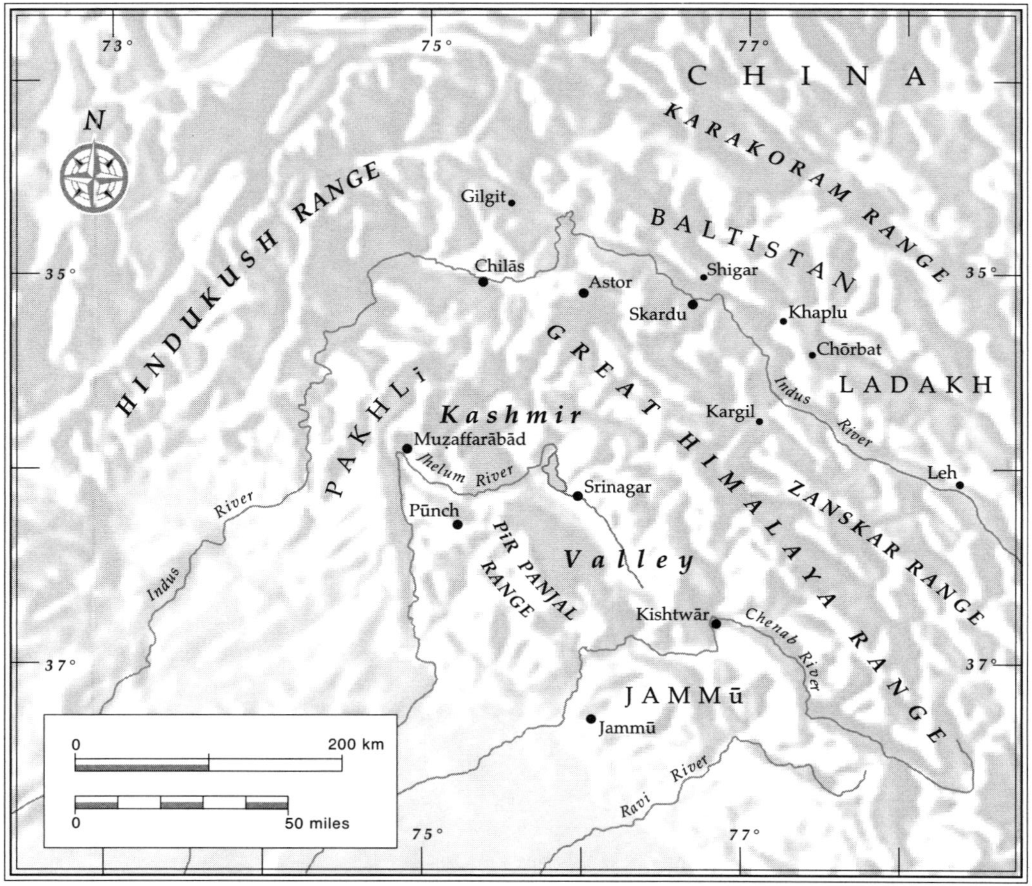

MAP 4. Kashmir and Baltistan

the hidden world, he had traveled back to India (acquiring an affiliation with the Qādirī Sufi order in Baghdad on the way) and sneaked into Kashmir via the Punjab without attracting notice by the Delhi court. Ḥasan Shāh, after asking Shihāb to rest a few months before, he said, he would marry the daughter, passed away before the event could take place.[34] As a consequence, the daughter was married to Jihāngīr Māgrē, vizier to Muḥammad Shāh, and Shihāb had acquired a prominent position in the circle of scholars in Kashmir through the union.[35]

The rivalry between ʿIrāqī and Shihāb resulted from three points of conflict: they were partial to different political factions—(Fatḥ ʿAlī Shāh and Sayfdār versus Muḥammad Shāh and Jahāngīr Māgrē); ʿIrāqī was a Kubravī-Nūrbakhshī, whereas Shihāb was a Qādirī Sufi in a time of intense rivalry between Sufi orders throughout the Islamic world; and while ʿIrāqī disdained book learning as a low form of knowledge, Shihāb prided himself on his scholarly accomplishments. The first unpleasantness between the two occurred when Shihāb took offence at ʿIrāqī's negative remarks about Yazīd b. Muʿāwīya during a public discussion about resolving the political conflict that had engulfed the state following Ḥasan Shāh's death. The point of difference (which reflects an ʿAlid vs. Sunnī bias) caused Shihāb to insult ʿIrāqī by asking that his son, who was much younger, be seated above ʿIrāqī in the gathering on the grounds that he was more learned. ʿIrāqī did not challenge the issue at the moment, but he determined that the son would die in the near future due to the insolence he had committed at his father's behest.[36]

34. Ibid., 174–76. Besides *Tuḥfat al-aḥbāb,* Shaykh Shihāb is mentioned only in *Bahāristān-i Shāhī* (*BS,* 303). The accounts are similar enough that they must either be derived from the same source or the author of *Bahāristān-i shāhī* relied on the earlier *Tuḥfat al-aḥbāb.*

35. *TA,* 200. Shihāb's son was also married to the daughter of a notable named Qāżī Ḥusayn Shīrāzī, giving him more connections to the local elites (*TA,* 196). According to later sources cited by Rafiqi, Shīrāzī had been a Kubravī Sufi and judge in Shiraz before his arrival in Kashmir. He received a similar appointment in Kashmir as well from Sulṭān Sikandar (d. 1413), but he gave it up shortly to become a recluse (Rafiqi, *Sufism in Kashmir,* 104). If this is true, then Shihāb's son must have married some other descendant of Shīrāzī's, not his daughter.

36. *TA,* 179–82.

The tragedy indeed came to pass, though Shihāb refused to see it as a mark of ʿIrāqī's high spiritual status.

In the second instance of conflict, ʿIrāqī and Shihāb were seated together at a banquet arranged by Sayfdār for the benefit of scholars and dignitaries. According to local custom, each guest was served with a large plate of food that after himself partaking he sent to his household for his family. ʿIrāqī on this occasion ordered that the food be sent to his attendants rather than his family, and Shihāb censured him by stating that sending food home was decreed in the Qurʾan. ʿIrāqī disputed his claim that this was the correct meaning of the relevant verse and was vindicated when his interpretation was found to be the one given in the famous Qurʾanic commentary *al-Kashshāf.* Before the book was brought to the company, other scholars present at the occasion had sided with Shihāb because of his extensive learning, and they were all surprised to see that a man with little or no familiarity with literary sources had turned out to be correct.[37]

The third and last recorded incident between ʿIrāqī and Shihāb was the most dramatic since it resulted in a physical fight that involved the two men themselves and their supporters. The scene was again a gathering convened by Sayfdār, who had just regained his position as vizier and wanted to exact revenge from Shihāb for having sanctioned the killing of his followers through legal opinions in the period he was not in power. When ʿIrāqī's turn came to speak at the occasion, he prefaced his remarks by referring to his teacher Qāsim Fayżbakhsh. Shihāb grew incensed at this and remarked that ʿIrāqī should refrain from mentioning someone who was nothing more than an alchemist (*kīmīyāgar*) and had wasted his life.[38] ʿIrāqī had earlier warned Shihāb about casting aspersions on the predecessors in his order and answered the insult by hitting the latter across the face. This act precipitated a general fight among those present, and ʿIrāqī was saved grievous harm only when his supporters whisked him away from the venue.[39]

37. Ibid., 183–89.

38. This remark suggests that Kashmiri scholarly circles were aware of the religious scene in Herat and saw their opposition to ʿIrāqī in the same light as the struggle between Jāmī and his supporters, on the one hand, and Qāsim, on the other.

39. *TA,* 202–5.

A consideration of these three incidents provides us a picture of the religiopolitical scene in Kashmir toward the end of the fifteenth century. It is evident that the community of religious professionals was divided among a number of factions based upon both ideological differences and political affiliation. The viziers Jahāngīr Māgrē and Malik Sayfdār represent the political backdrop of these incidents, while the religious differences involve the nature of religious knowledge and authority in general and allegiance to sects and Sufi orders. In the words of his hagiographer, ʿIrāqī explicitly taught his disciples that scholars concerned with the exoteric religious sciences (*ahl-i ẓāhir*) were fundamentally insincere since, contrary to their claims, they did not themselves actually write books; they merely copied what was already present in their massive libraries and attached prefaces that extolled whatever ruler they intended to please at any given time.[40] Since Shihāb ad-Dīn was a representative of this group, his opposition to ʿIrāqī flowed from his general disdain for Sufis and their intuitive knowledge, of which he himself was not in possession. Shihāb would have objected to the derisive aspect of this analysis, but if he was indeed primarily a legal scholar as stated in *Tuḥfat al-aḥbāb,* he would have agreed that he valued more the knowledge acquired from studying the works of previous authors rather than claims of spiritual knowledge and power advanced by a Sufi who merely meditated and alleged that he received inspirations. In addition to this difference of fundamental approach, ʿIrāqī and Shihāb were opposed to each other due to their ʿAlid/Nūrbakhshī versus Sunnī/Qādirī affiliations. As later events clearly show, ʿIrāqī espoused the reformed Shīʿism represented by Nūrbakhsh's messianic outlook, which differed from the Twelver Shīʿī legal perspective, but maintained a high level of sentimental attachment to early imāms such as ʿAlī and Ḥusayn. His differences with Shihāb ad-Dīn's Sunnī views in this instance were a portent for the intense sectarian competition that came to characterize Kashmiri society from the sixteenth century onward. The late fifteenth century was also a period of solidification of the boundaries between Sufi orders, when one's allegiance to a chain of authority and its associated method represented a

40. Ibid., 190.

significant part of one's public identity.[41] ʿIrāqī's Kubravī background via the Nūrbakhshī line thus constituted a substantial point of difference between him and the Qādirī Shihāb ad-Dīn.

Although ʿIrāqī managed to avenge the insult directed at Qāsim Fayżbakhsh by hitting Shihāb ad-Dīn, his impulsive act eventually led to an increase in the status of his rival. Other scholars in the city now came to Shihāb ad-Dīn's support and demanded, under the threat that they would all migrate out of Kashmir, that ʿIrāqī be punished for his indecorous behavior. Sayfdār refused this demand since ʿIrāqī was still the ambassador of a foreign ruler, but in order to appease the scholars, he assigned Shihāb an estate (*jāgīr*) and also made him the caretaker (*mutavallī*) of the city's most prestigious religious institution, the Khānqāh-i Muʿallā, established by ʿAlī Hamadānī. This was a tremendous affront to ʿIrāqī since Hamadānī was a crucial link in the Kubravī chain, and Shihāb made matters even worse by reforming the liturgy performed at the hospice to exclude the *awrād-i fatḥīya,* the hallmark of Kubravī spiritual practice. Sensing this act to be a deep danger to the survival of the Kubravīya in Kashmir, ʿIrāqī now decided to refocus his mission in the region toward propagating the Kubravī method in its Nūrbakhshī form.[42]

ʿIrāqī's interaction with Shihāb may have catalyzed his move toward explicit proselytization, though it is likely that he had planned to promulgate the Nūrbakhshī cause from the beginning of his Kashmiri sojourn. His journey toward developing a Nūrbakhshī presence started with the effort to establish himself as the rightful heir of the local Kubravī tradition. This is reflected in Kashmīrī's report that soon after the handover of Hamadānī's khānqāh to Shihāb, ʿIrāqī began searching for a suitable khānqāh for his own purposes. His instinct in this regard was to revive the abodes of other Kubravī shaykhs that had by this time fallen into disuse. He first inquired about the saint Bahāʾ ad-Dīn Kashmīrī, who had been a student of Isḥāq Khuttalānī, Nūrbakhsh's master, and had even been mentioned as a great mystic by Nūrbakhsh in one of his works.[43] It turned out, however, that despite his influence on the wife of Sulṭān Zayn

41. Cf. DeWeese, "Sayyid ʿAlī Hamadānī and Kubrawī Hagiographical Traditions."
42. *TA,* 208–10.
43. Nūrbakhsh, *Masnavī ṣaḥīfat al-awliyāʾ*, 52.

al-ʿĀbidīn (d. 875/1470), Bahāʾ ad-Dīn, due to his reclusive nature, had never established a khānqāh in Kashmir.[44] ʿIrāqī then looked toward the legacy of Shaykh Sulṭān Kashmīrī, who had been a student of Isḥāq Khuttalānī and had established a khānqāh in the area of Kūh-i Sulṭān.[45] After a visit to the uninhabited khānqāh, ʿIrāqī determined that although it was small, the overall plan of the building was suitable for his purposes, and it was selected as the new home for him and his following.[46]

ʿIrāqī's first concern at the new abode was to mark the territory of his order by holding a forty-day retreat (*arbaʿīn*) in the manner it was performed by Nūrbakhshīs. Since it was winter, the time was perfect for initiating his close followers fully into the rituals of the order, and ʿIrāqī gave orders for the assembling of provisions for the event. On the night the retreat began, the whole khānqāh was lit up with candles and a large crowd participated in the initial invocations, including the recitation of mystical poetry. All except twelve close companions left following the communal dinner, when the candles were gathered and placed in front of ʿIrāqī. Imitating the function of Nūrbakhsh (light giver), he then handed a candle to the disciples one by one and each left with the light to meditate in a seclusion chamber. The disciples were given blue or black clothing or turbans at the end of the event based upon their spiritual accomplishments. This "uniform" of the order, together with the open celebration at the end of the retreat, established the Nūrbakhshīya as a presence on the religious map toward the end of the fifteenth century in Kashmir.[47]

Internal Kubravī Competition and ʿIrāqī's Departure from Kashmir

Our discussion so far gives us a picture of ʿIrāqī's activities in Kashmir with respect to the political authorities and religious personalities

44. *TA,* 221–24. Bahāʾ ad-Dīn "Ganjbakhsh" is mentioned by Sayyid ʿAlī and later authors (cf. ʿAlī, *Tārīkh-i Kashmīr,* 40–41, Rafiqi, *Sufism in Kashmir,* 114–15).

45. *TA,* 225–26. Sayyid ʿAlī mentions Shaykh Sulṭān Muḥammad Kashmīrī as a disciple of ʿAlī Hamadānī who had established a khānqāh near Takht-i Sulaymān, in Kashmir, on his teacher's advice. He was originally from Pakhlī and had returned there toward the end of his life (ʿAlī, *Tārīkh-i Kashmīr,* 41).

46. *TA,* 230.

47. Ibid., 235–45.

belonging to rival sects and orders. In the portrayal of his hagiographer, ʿIrāqī's decision to stay in Kashmir for an extended period reflected his desire to revive the tradition of Kubravī Sufism brought to the region by ʿAlī Hamadānī almost a century before his own ambassadorial mission. This perspective presumes that the Kubravīya was in fact nearly moribund in Kashmir at the time and would have become extinct without ʿIrāqī's intervention. We must ask, however, what the true position of the Kubravīya was in Kashmir during this period.

Given the state of our sources, it is impossible to answer definitively. The author of *Tuḥfat al-aḥbāb* predictably portrays the Kubravī community of Kashmir in a state of waiting even before ʿIrāqī's arrival. Quite early in the text, the reader is introduced to a certain Bābā ʿAlī in Kashmir who greatly wished to travel for spiritual purposes but was unable to fulfil his heart's desire due to the limitations of his circumstances. He therefore became a hermit, waiting for a spiritual guide to one day arrive in Kashmir, and this was precisely the true esoteric (*bāṭinī ḥaqīqī*) reason behind the circumstances that led to ʿIrāqī's travel to Kashmir. Bābā ʿAlī's destiny was to become to ʿIrāqī what Isḥāq Khuttalānī had been to ʿAlī Hamadānī,[48] and he, many of his companions, and the caretakers of ʿAlī Hamadānī's khānqāh are said to have pledged allegiance to ʿIrāqī within three or four months of his appearance in Srinagar.[49]

ʿIrāqī's disciples are said to have rapidly increased in number following his transfer to the khānqāh of Shaykh Sulṭān. After about six years of instructing them in the Kubravī method (eight years after his original arrival), ʿIrāqī started thinking about returning to Khurāsān with the medicines he had come to acquire in Kashmir for Ḥusayn Bāyqarā. Sulṭān Fatḥ Shāh and Malik Sayfdār, who were in power at the time, protested against his plan, but he felt determined to leave and started preparing the Sufi community for life in his absence. He did not make Bābā ʿAlī the community's leader at this time because the Bābā had not yet reached the highest state of perfection, and there was some danger that he would become selfish if entrusted with such authority. Instead, he decided to choose between Bābā Jamāl and Mullā Ismāʿīl, two disciples who had distinguished themselves during spiritual

48. Ibid., 145–47.
49. Ibid., 164.

retreats. He asked both about how they would provide for the community's material needs. Bābā Jamāl was then dismissed because he answered that he would clear and farm some land near the khānqāh. Ismāʿīl, on the other hand, responded correctly by stating that he would busy himself solely in religious exercises and leave it to God to provide livelihood to the community. ʿIrāqī chose Ismāʿīl as the leader but authorized him only to lead prayers and maintain the community as it stood at the time, without erecting more buildings or taking the oath of allegiance from new disciples. The underlying message was that no one among the Kashmiris possessed the fortitude and self-control to become a full-fledged Sufi guide. Ismāʿīl was chosen simply because he was pious and was least likely to acquire grandiose ideas about himself.[50] As later developments showed, Ismāʿīl failed to live up to ʿIrāqī's expectations, and the two had a bitter parting of ways when ʿIrāqī returned to Kashmir for the second time.

This account of ʿIrāqī's activities is contradicted by non-Nūrbakhhsī sources, which state that Ismāʿīl Kubravī had in fact been the foremost Kubravī shaykh in Kashmir at the time of ʿIrāqī's arrival. His spiritual pedigree went back directly to ʿAlī Hamadānī, who had appointed his grandfather, Shaykh Aḥmad, his successor at the time of his departure from Kashmir. His father, Shaykh Fatḥ Allāh Ḥāfiẓ, had carried the tradition to the next generation, and Ismāʿīl himself had acquired great fame as a scholar, receiving patronage from the rulers Ḥasan Shāh, Muḥammad Shāh, and Fatḥ Shāh. His disciples included Bābā ʿAlī Najjār, whom Shams ad-Dīn ʿIrāqī had corrupted with his Shīʿī or Nūrbakhshī ideas while the latter had been pretending to be a devotee to Ismāʿīl. Ismāʿīl became detached from society toward the end of his life, leaving worldly matters in the care of Bābā ʿAlī. He died in 916/1510.[51]

Both these accounts of the relationships between ʿIrāqī, Ismāʿīl Kubravī, and Bābā ʿAlī leave something to be desired in terms of credibility. In addition to the obvious bias for ʿIrāqī, the *Tuḥfat al-aḥbāb* fails

50. Ibid., 295–98.

51. Rafiqi, *Sufism in Kashmir,* 94–96, 216–17. On Rafiqi's sources for this information, see below.

to paint the whole picture, giving no information on any living Kubravī shaykh resident in Kashmir at the time of ʿIrāqī's first visit. According to this version, ʿIrāqī had to reenliven the Hamadānī-Kubravī tradition from point zero, and Ismāʿīl was a mere promising disciple led astray by his vanity. This seems unlikely, though works that project Ismāʿīl as a great shaykh hoodwinked by ʿIrāqī are themselves not fully credible due to their late dates and tendentious nature.

The earliest extant work to mention Ismāʿīl b. Fatḥ Allāh Ḥāfiẓ as a rival to ʿIrāqī is the *Tārīkh-i Kashmīr* of Sayyid ʿAlī, which states only that ʿIrāqī was unable to corrupt the whole ruling class in Kashmir due to Ismāʿīl's effort.[52] The fact that Sayyid ʿAlī's work is highly partial to Sunnīs is a significant problem since, by the time he was writing (after 987/1579), ʿIrāqī's name had already become notorious for introducing the Shīʿī "problem" into Kashmir.[53] Later Sunnī authors tend to exalt Ismāʿīl's status even further, now seeing him and ʿIrāqī as the respective champions of Sunnism and Shīʿism in a highly charged sectarian environment.[54] While it is possible that these authors' information is derived from legitimate earlier sources that are no longer extant, the problem of sectarian bias is too prominent a factor in Kashmiri historiography for us to accept their viewpoint without caution.[55]

A review of information from sources both favorable and antagonistic to ʿIrāqī leaves us with an inconclusive picture of the Kubravī presence

52. ʿAlī, *Tārīkh-i Kashmīr,* 26.

53. Cf. Niyāzmand, "Kashmīr mēñ fārsī tārīkh-navīsī," 101–4.

54. Rafiqi's extensive citations for information on Ismāʿīl include only the following Sunnī authors belonging to the Mughal or modern periods: Mullā Aḥmad b. Ṣabūr, *Khavāriq as-sālikīn* (completed 1100/1698), Rafīʿ ad-Dīn Aḥmad, *Navādir al-akhbār* (1136/1723–24), Muḥammad Aʿẓam, *Tārīkh-i aʿẓamī* (1160/1747), Muḥammad Aslam, *Gawhar-i ʿālam* (1200/1785), ʿAbd al-Vahhāb, *Futūḥāt-i kubravīya* (1162/1749), Pīr Ghulām Ḥasan Khūyhāmī (d. 1898), *Tārīkh-i Ḥasan,* and Muḥyī ad-Dīn Miskīn, *Tārīkh-i kabīr* (1321/1903). Conspicuously absent from this list are the anonymous *Bahāristān-i shāhī* (1023/1614) and Ḥaydar Malik Chādūra's *Tārīkh-i Kashmīr* (1029/1620), major earlier sources whose authors were sympathetic to ʿIrāqī (cf. Rafiqi, *Sufism in Kashmir,* 216 [notes 5 and 6], 265–78; Niyāzmand, "Kashmīr mēñ fārsī tārīkh-navīsī," 105–20).

55. Islamic sectarianism in Kashmir and other parts of South Asia is discussed later in this chapter and in chapter 7.

in Kashmir at the end of the fifteenth century. Treating both sides with equal caution, it can be surmised that there were in fact prominent Kubravī shaykhs active in Srinagar at the time of ʿIrāqī's arrival, and he was able to get along well with them as long as he refrained from a direct subversion of their authority. The idea that Ismāʿīl was merely one of ʿIrāqī's students during his first stay in Kashmir is very likely an understatement, though the conflict between the two developed only when ʿIrāqī arrived for the second time and was able to garner significant political patronage. In addition, Bābā ʿAlī Najjār was probably a local Kubravī shaykh who became acquainted with ʿIrāqī during the first visit and became a part of his faction upon his return.

The tension between the two sides of the Kubravīya may also have mirrored the differences between Nūrbakhsh and ʿAbdallāh Barzishābādī that had split the order into Nūrbakhshī and Ẕahabī factions when Nūrbakhsh had announced his messianic claim in Khuttalān. Some Kubravī shaykhs living in Kashmir are said to have been disciples of Barzishābādī, or associates of Ḥusayn Khwārazmī (d. 1551), who traced his lineage through a non-Nūrbakhshī Central Asian branch of the Kubravīya.[56] Whether through ʿAlī Hamadānī himself or his son Muḥammad Hamadānī, the order in Kashmir was connected to its Central Asian and Iranian counterparts through multiple links, and ʿIrāqī's conflict with Ismāʿīl reflected the general competition for supremacy between the various factions. The reality was, however, distorted into projecting ʿIrāqī as the order's savior in pro-Nūrbakhshī sources such as the *Tuḥfat al-aḥbāb.*

Eight years after his arrival in Kashmir as an ambassador from Sulṭān Ḥusayn Bāyqarā, ʿIrāqī gathered together the medicinal herbs he had been sent to bring and, together with gifts, letters, and a Kashmiri ambassador, made his way westward around 896/1490–91. Taking a route different from that of his arrival, he traveled through Pakhlī to reach the court of Ulūgh Beg II (d. 907/1501) in Kabul.[57] The Tīmūrid governor received him well since he had earlier

56. Rafīqī, *Sufism in Kashmir,* 107–9. For Ḥusayn Khwārazmī and his disciples (including chains of transmission leading to Kashmir and India), see DeWeese, "Eclipse of the Kubraviyah," 45–83.

been suitably impressed by Nūrbakhshīs when Nūrbakhsh's son Sayyid Jaʿfar had stopped at the court on his way from Herat to India.[58] Here ʿIrāqī heard that Qāsim Fayżbakhsh had already left Herat and, forsaking the possibility of being rewarded by Bāyqarā, he decided to return directly to Durusht through the northern passage. His first stops en route were the graves of ʿAlī Hamadānī and Jaʿfar Badakhshī, in Khuttalān, and the place where Isḥāq Khuttalānī had been put to death in Balkh. Subsequently, following a stay of a couple of months in Samarqand and travel through Nasaf, Merv, Astarābād, and Gīlān, he arrived in Qāsim's presence to a joyous reception.[59]

ʿIrāqī's Second Stay in Kashmir

Back in his homeland, ʿIrāqī once again occupied the position of a trusted companion to Qāsim, who provided him land for the residence of his family. His wife had given birth to two daughters during their stay in Kashmir, and now the birth of three more daughters led the family to hope for a boy. When asked to intervene in this matter, Qāsim advised ʿIrāqī to send three of his daughters to request the birth of a brother at Nūrbakhsh's grave in Suliqān. S̱ānīya, Fāṭima, and Rābiʿa went and prayed in this manner and, after three days, a voice from Nūrbakhsh's grave told them that the wish would be fulfilled in the near future. The boy was born on the Persian new year's day (*nawrūz*) in the year 900 (March 1495). Qāsim named him Dāniyāl since he had been contemplating the prophecy of Daniel at the moment he heard the news.[60]

The *Tuḥfat al-aḥbāb* projects that ʿIrāqī was quite settled in Durusht, with no plans to return to Kashmir, until he learned that, about eight

57. Ulūgh Beg b. Abū Saʿīd b. Muḥammad b. Mīrānshāh ruled Kabul as a largely independent province between 1469 and 1501 (cf. C. E. Bosworth, "Kābul," *EI*², 4:356–57). He is mentioned numerous times by his nephew Bābur, who brought Kabul back under Tīmūrid control following an Uzbek interregnum between Ulūgh Beg's death and 1504.

58. *TA*, 303–4.

59. Ibid., 306–13.

60. Ibid., 314–17.

years after ʿIrāqī's departure, Ismāʿīl had strayed and had expanded the purview of the Nūrbakhshī khānqāh against the instructions given him earlier. The news was brought by a Kashmiri Nūrbakhshī who had stopped to pay his respects to Qāsim in Durusht while on his way to the Ḥijāz for the ḥajj. Both ʿIrāqī and Qāsim were perturbed to hear that Ismāʿīl had initiated members into the order and now presided over a new khānqāh near Kūh-i Mārān, where fifty to sixty Sufis undertook the forty-day retreat every year.[61] Qāsim then suggested to ʿIrāqī that he should return to Kashmir to set things right, but the latter resisted since Burhān ad-Dīn Baghdādī had recently passed away and he preferred to go to Baghdad and remain close to his ancestral region. Following Qāsim's further insistence, a prognostication (*istikhāra*), and the appearance of Bahāʾ ad-Dīn Kashmīrī during a mystical experience (*vāqiʿa*), ʿIrāqī became convinced that it was his duty to return to Kashmir and complete the work he had begun during the first visit.[62]

Judging on circumstantial grounds, it is most likely the news about the unexpected success, and not the waywardness, of the fledgling Nūrbakhshī community in Kashmir that compelled Qāsim and ʿIrāqī to contemplate the latter's return. As discussed in chapter 5, the end of the fifteenth century was a tumultuous period in Iranian history. Given both his role as caretaker of the order and his continuing belief in Nūrbakhsh's messianic prophecies, Qāsim in particular must have felt compelled to pursue a promising venue for the order's expansion. Poetry cited in *Tuḥfat al-aḥbāb* explicitly likens Kashmiri Nūrbakhshīs' wish for ʿIrāqī's return to Kashmir with the expectation of a messianic deliverer. Here he is referred to as the deputy of the Muslim mahdī (*nāʾib-i mahdī-yi islām*) who will eliminate Gog and Magog and perform the messianic miracle of bringing the dead back to life.[63]

Feeling renewed contact with Kashmiris to be a heavy burden on his shoulders, ʿIrāqī set off from Durusht most likely in Muḥarram 908 (July-August 1502).[64] He received a good omen while passing through

61. Ibid., 317–21, 325–28.

62. Ibid., 332–33.

63. Ibid., 324–25.

64. Ibid., 336. Kashmīrī's actual statement that ʿIrāqī left in Muḥarram 902 (Sept.–Oct., 1496) is an error. As discussed below, ʿIrāqī decided not to travel

Khurāsān in the form of a meeting with the legendary invisible saint Khiżr, who reportedly predicted his success but told him that his most important task was to convert Muslims belonging to wrong persuasions, such as the Ḥanafī and Shāfiʿī *mazhabs,* to the way of the "pure imāms" (*mazhab-i aʾimma-yi aṭhār*).[65] The words attributed to Khiżr here implied the intermediate path proposed by Nūrbakhsh rather than Twelver or any other form of standard Shīʿism. The *Tuḥfat al-aḥbāb* indicates this explicitly in the present context by stating that Nūrbakhsh's path was the true path of imāms and saints (*awliyāʾ*) that had been obscured by existing sects whether they be Sunnī or Shīʿī.[66]

After passing through Mashhad, ʿIrāqī's plan was to again visit the court of Ulūgh Beg II in Kabul before proceeding to Kashmir. However, while in Qandahar, he heard that the ruler had recently died and he decided to go on through to Multan, where he spent the winter before arriving in Kashmir in 908/1503.[67] The community he had left twelve years earlier had just finished its annual forty-day retreat and, according to the *Tuḥfat al-aḥbāb,* he was welcomed enthusiastically by both Ismāʿīl Kubravī and Bābā ʿAlī Najjār. By this time, Ismāʿīl had amassed considerable wealth in addition to the new khānqāh built for the Nūrbakhshīs by the rulers, and he offered all this to ʿIrāqī since he was the true head of the community.[68] However, competition over resources and connections to important political figures soon split the community into factions loyal to ʿIrāqī and Ismāʿīl Kubravī.

---

through Kabul when he heard, while in Qandahar, that Ulūgh Beg II had recently passed away, which we know to have happened in 907/1501. ʿIrāqī then must have left Durusht in Muḥarram of 908, which corresponds well with Kashmīrī's other assertion that the period between his departure from Kashmir (896/1490–91) and reentry was twelve years.

65. Ibid., 337–38.

66. Ibid., 339–41. All indications are that ʿIrāqī followed the Nūrbakhshī path alone throughout his life and that, as discussed below, the idea that he was a Twelver Shīʿī was invented long after his death.

67. Ibid., 342.

68. Ibid., 345–46.

The Nūrbakhshīya in Kashmiri Politics

The Nūrbakhshīya achieved its greatest political success (its greatest anywhere, not only in Kashmir) during the twenty-three year period between ʿIrāqī's arrival in Kashmir for the second time in 1503 and his death in 1526. The report on the movement's popularity that lured ʿIrāqī back to Kashmir proved to be true, and during this period ʿIrāqī used both his prestige as a foreign religious divine and his political skills to advance the movement's cause among Kashmir's nobility. Rulers and viziers belonging to the Rayna, Chak, and Chādūra families in particular became his devotees,[69] providing protection when necessary and using his belligerent posture toward the local religious establishment (Muslim as well as non-Muslim) to further their own goals. ʿIrāqī's second stay in Kashmir transpired during a politically chaotic period characterized by the contest between two Shāhmīrī claimants backed or opposed by noble families who could change allegiances at a moment's notice. Muḥammad Shāh and Fatḥ Shāh had each already come to power twice during ʿIrāqī's first visit; that the instability of the contemporary political environment was now even further increased can be gauged from the fact that the government changed hands five times between 1499 and 1521.[70] The details of this internecine struggle are too convoluted to discuss here in full, but it is necessary to summarize the political situation as the backdrop for ʿIrāqī's religious activities. The political history clearly shows that ʿIrāqī was a full participant in the affairs of the intriguing nobility and, at times, may have been a primary kingmaker in the state.

In 1503, when ʿIrāqī arrived back, Muḥammad Shāh occupied the throne and ruled with the support of Sayyid Muḥammad Bayhaqī[71]

69. Chādūra and Rayna in fact denote the same noble family as indicated by the comments of Ḥaydar Malik Chādūra (cf. Ḥaydar Malik Chādūra, *History of Kashmir,* ed. and trans. Razia Bano [Delhi: Bhavna Prakashan, 1991], 83).

70. For events connected with the seesaw of power between the two, see Sadhu, *Medieval Kashmir,* 263–82, *BS,* 301–26. The period is summarized also in Pīr Ghulām Ḥasan Khūyhāmī, *Tārīkh-i Ḥasan,* 3 vols. (Srinagar: Research and Publication Department, Jammu and Kashmir Government, 1954), 2:212–35.

71. Muḥammad was the ruling patriarch of the influential Bayhaqī sayyid family of viziers active in Kashmir since the reign of Sulṭān Zayn al-ʿĀbidīn (cf. Fawq,

(d. 1505) and Malik Mūsā Rayna (d. 1510–11). The latter two had helped Muḥammad Shāh oust Fatḥ Shāh and his supporters in 1499, but now Mūsā Rayna became unwilling to remain subservient to Bayhaqī and started communicating with his old patron Fatḥ Shāh to invite him back to Kashmir with promises of internal support. Fatḥ Shāh accepted the overture, defeated Muḥammad Shāh and Bayhaqī, and again occupied the throne in 1505. Mūsā Rayna now became the grand vizier and aided ʿIrāqī in his religious goals until he himself fell victim to intrigues in 916/1510–11.[72] Subsequently, tension developed between ʿIrāqī and Fatḥ Shāh's vizier Malik ʿUs̱mān, and if the reigning ruler had not been defeated shortly, ʿIrāqī might have met an unsavory end.[73] Muḥammad Shāh returned to power for the third time in 1516, but he had to abdicate within nine months when Fatḥ Shāh returned with better alliances among the nobility.[74]

In this ascendancy, Fatḥ Shāh was supported by Malik Kājī Chak, who had, at an earlier time of disempowerment and poverty, taken an oath to follow ʿIrāqī and further the cause of Islam as defined by him.[75]

Tavārīkh-i aqvām-i Kashmīr, 137–40). Rafiqi states that the Bayhaqīs belonged to the Kubravī order, though I have not found a direct reference to this in the earliest original sources. Rafiqi's impression may be derived from ʿAbd al-Vahhāb's *Futūḥāt-i kubravīya,* which, however, is a very late source (completed in 1162/1749) with an obvious tendency to exalt the order's past in the face of its contemporary decline (Rafiqi, *Sufism in Kashmir,* 109–14). For the role of immigrant nobles in Kashmir's history, referred to collectively as sayyids, see Rattan Lal Hangloo, *The State in Medieval Kashmir* (Delhi: Manohar, 2000), 75–105. Although rife with factual errors, this book contains the only extended secondary discussion of the issue.

72. *BS,* 322–23, Chādūra, *Tārīkh,* 83.

73. *BS,* 325. At least part of problem between the two parties was that ʿIrāqī's son-in-law Mīr Aḥadī had deserted Fatḥ Shāh and Malik Us̱mān's forces to join up with the opposition. The level of acrimony can be judged from Malik ʿUs̱mān's words regarding ʿIrāqī, repeated in *Bahāristān-i shāhī:* "God-willing, we will be victorious and will first burn Mīr Shams alive before entering the city." Correspondingly, upon hearing the news of a small victory by Fatḥ Shāh, ʿIrāqī remarked that even if he reached the height of the sky, God would dispatch him down to the earth so that he does not have the capacity to do harm to the indigent (*fuqarāʾ*) (*BS,* 325).

74. *BS,* 326.

75. Ibid., 321–22.

A little later, when Muḥammad Shāh gained power for the fourth time, with the help of Sikandar Lōdī (r. 1489–1517), the Sulṭān of Delhi, Kājī Chak was appointed the grand vizier. As the religious patron of the ruling authority, ʿIrāqī now became one of the most powerful people in the kingdom. This influence manifested itself most strongly in 1518, when Kājī Chak allegedly executed seven hundred to eight hundred men, his action being based upon charges of apostasy leveled against the men by ʿIrāqī.[76] Kājī Chak and other members of his clan remained loyal to ʿIrāqī during the rest of his life irrespective of whether they held the reigns of power or awaited their chance in the surrounding mountains. A few years before his death, ʿIrāqī appointed his son Dāniyāl the successor to what was now a prosperous and prestigious estate, but the latter seems not to have had the father's political agility or influence. Somewhat curiously, none of the early sources record the year of ʿIrāqī's death, though according to *Tuḥfat al-aḥbāb* it occurred on the third of Ramażān.[77] The later tradition that he died in 932/1526 is supported by the *Tuḥfat al-aḥbāb* since it states that he was nearly a hundred years old.[78]

Consolidation of Community Boundaries

As discussed earlier, ʿIrāqī was welcomed in Kashmir by a thriving Nūrbakhshī community that probably already had significant political backing. According to Kashmīrī, ʿIrāqī's first activities upon arrival included dealing with Mullā Ismāʿīl's hidden desire to become a shaykh and the conversion of Malik Mūsā Rayna, at that time one of the most powerful people in the government. Giving equal weight to our inconclusive evidence, the situation now was that Ismāʿīl was either an independent Kubravī shaykh with whom ʿIrāqī had associated during the

76. Ibid., 329–30. The victims in this case were Muslims: they are identified as apostates, rather than unbelievers. ʿIrāqī's campaign may also have included Hindus: Shuka attributes to Kājī Chak oppression toward Brahmins. It is interesting that while critical of Kājī Chak's behavior, Shuka also compares him to Arjuna, heroic warrior in the epic *Mahabharata,* for his bravery (Sadhu, *Medieval Kashmir,* 273).

77. *TA,* 411. This can be inferred from the author's mention of the yearly ceremony to be arranged on this date to commemorate ʿIrāqī.

78. Ibid., 422. The year comes from modern Twelver Shīʿīs who claim descent from ʿIrāqī (cf. *BS,* 85–86).

first visit or he was a student whom ʿIrāqī had put in charge of the community at the time of his departure. Whichever was the case, Ismāʿīl now refused to regard ʿIrāqī as his spiritual and social superior. It is hinted that Ismāʿīl's resistance to ʿIrāqī's authority may have resulted from his having realized the peculiar nature of Nūrbakhshī doctrines. He is said to have rebelled at the instigation of a nephew, Sāhūka Ḥājjī, who told him that he had never come across the Nūrbakhshī path or legal method (*maẕhab*) during his journeys through the Ḥijāz, Egypt, Anatolia, and the Levant while on pilgrimage.[79] From ʿIrāqī's perspective, it was Ismāʿīl's jealousy that had turned him against ʿIrāqī and toward colluding with the religious establishment.[80]

After a period of accusations, verbal attacks, and counterattacks, ʿIrāqī eventually decided to make a formal break from Ismāʿīl and asked the Sufis to choose between the two leaders. To finalize this rupture, ʿIrāqī left the khānqāh of Sulṭān Kubravī, which he had reinhabited upon his return, and took all his family and followers to an estate named Zadībal that had recently been donated to him by Mūsā Rayna.[81] He had coveted the spot for the possible construction of a khānqāh even during his first visit,[82] and now Mūsā Rayna was compelled to offer it to him along with other wealth from himself as well as his family immediately after experiencing a spiritual inspiration.[83] At Zadībal, ʿIrāqī initially occupied the old buildings left behind by Mūsā Rayna and then started acquiring the means for constructing a grand religious structure.

The preparation for the construction of the khānqāh led ʿIrāqī on the path of dismantling local temples for the sake of acquiring building materials around 909/1503. The temples destroyed at this time must have been already abandoned since ʿIrāqī and his followers are shown to have faced no resistance from worshippers.[84] In ʿIrāqī's case, Mūsā

79. *TA,* 352–53.

80. Ibid., 351.

81. Ibid., 358–59.

82. Ibid., 172–73.

83. Ibid., 347–49.

84. This fact is evident also in Kashmīrī's explicit comment about the "miracle" that no follower of ʿIrāqī ever came to harm in the whole campaign against temples (*TA,* 466–67).

Rayna provided political support for the effort by having the vizier Muḥammad Bayhaqī agree to the disassembling of a grand temple surrounded by large trees. These trees were cut to make the beams for the khānqāh, and the project was well on its way when ʿIrāqī began to have problems with Muḥammad Bayhaqī, which led to a temporary halting of construction.

Kashmīrī states that ʿIrāqī's success in Kashmir under the patronage of Mūsā Rayna started to irk the local religious scholars soon after his arrival. Their antipathy, which may have intensified greatly when Muḥammad Shāh made ʿIrāqī the caretaker of the khānqāh of ʿAlī Hamadānī,[85] caused them to complain about him to Bayhaqī, who similarly was not fond of ʿIrāqī but had not stopped his activities due to Mūsā Rayna's influence. Some people further condemned the new building at Zadībal on the grounds that the *qibla* (direction toward Mecca) had been determined incorrectly, though ʿIrāqī tried to prove otherwise by referring to Nūrbakhsh's work *al-Fiqh al-aḥwaṭ*.[86] Matters between Bayhaqī and ʿIrāqī came to a head over two issues: first, ʿIrāqī refused to fulfil Bayhaqī's wish to marry his eldest daughter Bībī Āghā;[87] and second, he mistreated one of Bayhaqī's Hindu officials for taking on the airs of a Muslim nobleman. Once the situation became untenable, ʿIrāqī decided, despite Mūsā Rayna's entreaties, to leave for neighboring Baltistan with the promise that he would not come back to Kashmir as long as Bayhaqī remained in power. Although ʿIrāqī's stay in Baltistan lasted for only two months, in 1505, for much time to come the area became a safe haven for Nūrbakhshīs escaping problems in Kashmir.[88]

85. *TA*, 370.

86. Cf. Nūrbakhsh, *al-Fiqh al-aḥwaṭ*, 33–42, which gives extensive instructions on this matter.

87. *TA*, 370–74. Bayhaqī's desire to arrange a matrimonial relationship with ʿIrāqī's family indicates the latter's political influence at the time. The Bayhaqīs had first gained a firm position in Kashmir through intermarriage with the Shāhmīrī rulers, and later generations of the family seem to have continued to use matrimonial alliances for political ends (cf. Sadhu, *Medieval Kashmir*, 181; Rafiqi, *Sufism in Kashmir*, 110).

88. *TA*, 370–78.

Mūsā Rayna turned against Bayhaqī and Muḥammad Shāh after ʿIrāqī's departure, and he sent messages to Fatḥ Shāh that he would support him from within the city in the case of an attack. The intriguing party was successful, and the government now changed to Fatḥ Shāh and Mūsā Rayna. The latter immediately sent a messenger to ask ʿIrāqī to return. ʿIrāqī complied, despite it being winter, and he became busy with the task of completing Zadībal. The building of the khānqāh, completed three years later in 1507, is said to have been the most imposing religious structure in the city at the time.[89]

The Khānqāh at Zadībal

To the degree that it can be understood from the description in the *Tuḥfat al-aḥbāb,* the khānqāh at Zadībal was designed and constructed to represent both the religious perspective and the political influence of the Nūrbakhshīs of Kashmir. The large, pillarless main sanctuary of the khānqāh was surrounded by an open-air enclosure, beyond which lay gardens or lakes. Exemplifying the stations of the mystical path, the compound's three entrances were named Bāb-i Sharīʿat (door of exoteric law), Bāb-i Ṭarīqat (mystical path), and Bāb-i Ḥaqīqat (mystical truth). Visitors, male or female, entered a door according to their station: commoners left their riding animals outside the Bāb-i Sharīʿat and traveled some distance on foot to go beyond the other two doors in order to reach the sanctuary; noble visitors such as kings and viziers entered through Bāb-i Ṭarīqat; only the spiritually adept could enter directly through the Bāb-i Ḥaqīqat. ʿIrāqī held public audiences outside the Bāb-i Ṭarīqat, including discussions about religious questions and recitations of mystical poetry.[90]

The sanctuary's walls had considerable empty room on all sides to allow for ritual circumambulation (*ṭavāf*). The interior of the sanctuary was two-storied, with each floor divided between a central open space and small cubicles for solitary exercises along the sides.[91] The floor was made of stones salvaged from a temple.[92] The only internal decoration

89. Ibid., 380–81.
90. Ibid., 382–83, 418–19.
91. Ibid., 388.
92. Ibid., 454.

mentioned is a *masnavī* by Qāżī Muḥammad Qudsī that gave the Nūrbakhshī chain of mystical authority going from ʿIrāqī all the way to Muḥammad the prophet.[93]

The inscription of the silsila on the walls of the khānqāh clearly shows that the building was meant to be a marker of the powerful Nūrbakhshī presence in Kashmir at the time. ʿIrāqī's aims for the building are evident also from the fact that he advised one follower who asked permission to go for ḥajj to forsake the idea, give him the money he had saved, and perform the ritual around the khānqāh. Basing himself on an example from Bāyazīd Bisṭāmī, ʿIrāqī argued that devotion to the Nūrbakhshī order symbolized in circumambulating Zadībal equaled the spiritual reward promised by God for the pilgrimage.[94]

Kashmiri Society and ʿIrāqī's Program of "Islamization"

The self-confident attitude projected by the Zadībal khānqāh found its reflection in ʿIrāqī's other activities: he led a rigorous campaign to "Islamize" the local population. The targets for this program—Hindu temples and Muslim individuals—give us a good idea of Kashmiri social life during the period. The *Tuḥfat al-aḥbāb* gives the names of thirty-three temples or other non-Muslim gathering places in the vicinity of Srinagar that were either destroyed or dismantled for reuse as mosques by ʿIrāqī and his supporters. Among all these cases, ʿIrāqī met physical resistance in only one place, and furthermore the combatants there are identified as outsider pilgrims. The altercation left such an impression on ʿIrāqī that he asked Mūsā Rayna that the name of the place be changed to Islāmpūra to mark the holy effort.[95] The lack of resistance to temple destruction implies that either the buildings were

93. Ibid., 391–95.

94. Ibid., 385–86. The exaltation of Zadībal is also connected to the accusation against ʿIrāqī that he wanted to destroy the old Khānqāh-i Muʿallā of ʿAlī Hamadānī under the pretext of constructing a bigger building. The structure was in fact razed and ʿIrāqī and his supporters were delaying a reconstruction until Muḥammad Shāh's wife Ṣāliḥa, who was Kājī Chak's sister, financed the project based upon her own devotion (ʿAlī, *Tārīkh-i Kashmīr,* 30).

95. *TA,* 478–82. The fact that temples were in fact destroyed under Mūsā Rayna's protection is reported by Shuka (Sadhu, *Medieval Kashmir,* 264).

already deserted or the non-Muslim community was so reduced in numbers and influence that it could not put up a fight on the ground or in the king's court. The impression is confirmed by the story about an earlier Kubravī shaykh named ʿUṣmān Majẕūb, who respected major temples to the degree that he would get off his riding animal when passing near them and would walk unmounted until the temple was no longer in his sight.[96] When asked about this extraordinary effort, he replied that Muslims did not at that time have the power to confront the temple worshippers, and he respected them so that they would not meddle with his religion and would leave him to worship in peace. He then predicted that one day a man would come from ʿIrāq, who would, with God's aid, demolish all the temples and chase the impious out of Kashmir.[97] The prediction was now coming true as ʿIrāqī and his vigilante Sufis went around destroying temples in Srinagar and vicinity. In general, Kashmīrī's extended account of temple destruction sounds almost like a salvage operation in which existing religious structures were dismantled and then reconstituted into mosques, paralleling the transition from a Hindu to a predominantly Muslim society.[98]

In contrast to the temple destruction, ʿIrāqī's human Islamization program was directed against so-called Muslims who had outwardly changed their religion while continuing to practice their old customs behind closed doors. In ʿIrāqī's perception, this situation was primarily the fault of the tolerant attitude adopted by Sulṭān Zayn al-ʿĀbidīn during

96. ʿUṣmān Majẕūb was the principle Kashmiri disciple of the aforementioned Bahāʾ ad-Dīn Kashmīrī, whom he had joined after first being initiated into the Shaṭṭārī order. He was respected by Sulṭān Zayn al-ʿĀbidīn and was buried in the compound of Mazār-i Salāṭīn (*TA*, 228–29; Rafiqi, *Sufism in Kashmir,* 115–16).

97. *TA*, 462–63.

98. For a general discussion of the pattern of temple destruction in India under Muslim rulers (excluding Kashmir), see Richard Eaton, "Temple Desecration and Indo-Muslim States," in *Beyond Turk and Hindu: Shaping Indo-Muslim Identity in Premodern India,* ed. David Gilmartin and Bruce B. Lawrence (Gainesville: University Press of Florida, 2000). Dismantling temples and establishing mosques is a prominent aspect of other Kashmiri hagiographic traditions as well. For the case of the Suhravardī Shaykh Ḥamza, see Muḥammad Ṣiddīq Niyāzmand, *Haft ganj-i Sulṭānī: Fārsī adab meñ khulafā-yi Ḥażrat Sulṭān al-ʿĀrifīn kā ḥiṣṣa* (Srinagar: Uvays Vaqqāṣ Publishing House, 1994), 62–67.

his fifty-year rule over Kashmir. While Zayn al-ʿĀbidīn's father Sikandar had earned the title the Iconoclast (*but-shikan*) due to his Islamizing efforts, the son had undone all his work by not being rigorous in castigating deviance from Islamic norms.[99] The result had been the production of a religious culture that was nominally Muslim but culturally Hindu, particularly in matters such as marriages, yearly festivals, and the unveiling of women.[100] To correct this situation of "apostasy," ʿIrāqī asked for a legal response (*fatvā*) from local jurists; their reply was that apostates are forgiven if they reaffirm their faith in Islam, but if they desist, they have to be executed.[101] Armed with this judgment and the protection of Mūsā Rayna, ʿIrāqī started a vigorous campaign to Islamize Kashmir.

Judging from this description, Kashmiri society at the beginning of the sixteenth century was in the middle of the process that eventually led to the population becoming majority Muslim. As the work of Richard Eaton and Bruce Lawrence has shown, the Islamic identities of the agrarian peoples of Punjab and Bengal in South Asia resulted, over a course of centuries, from a gradual integration of Islamic personalities in the religious as well as socioeconomic life of the areas.[102] In the case of Kashmir, contact with Muslim Central Asia and the employment of Turkish mercenary soldiers by local Hindu rulers beginning in the thirteenth century first led to a substantial Islamic presence in the region.[103] The conversion of the Ladakhi-born king Rinchana to Islam

99. *TA*, 447–48; *BS*, 320–21. Zayn al-ʿĀbidīn's tolerant policies are discussed in detail in N. K. Zutshi, *Sultan Zain-ul-Abidin of Kashmir: An Age of Enlightenment* (Jammu: Nupur Prakashan, 1976).

100. *TA*, 196–99, 449–52. ʿIrāqī's distaste for continuing Hindu marriage customs was so great that he told the people of Samarqand about it during his visit to the city around 1491 (*TA*, 311).

101. *TA*, 472.

102. Richard Eaton, *The Rise of Islam on the Bengal Frontier* (Berkeley: University of California Press, 1993), 113–34; idem, "Approaches to the Study of Conversion to Islam in India," in *Approaches to Islam in Religious Studies,* ed. Richard C. Martin (Tucson: University of Arizona Press, 1985); Bruce Lawrence, "Early Indo-Muslim Saints and Conversion," in *Islam in Asia: South Asia,* ed. Y. Friedmann (Jerusalem: Magnes Press, Hebrew University, 1984).

103. The most historically plausible discussion of Kashmir's transition to a majority Muslim society is Aziz Ahmad, "Conversions to Islam in the Valley of

around 1330 and the changeover to the Muslim Shāhmīrī dynasty in 1339 then intensified the process. The kings encouraged and relied for their legitimacy on Muslim divines such as the famous ʿAlī Hamadānī and his son Muḥammad Hamadānī, and their disciples then settled in various parts of the valley. The religious atmosphere consequently started acquiring an Islamic hue. During the fifteenth century, rulers such as Sikandar and Zayn al-ʿĀbidīn attempted to quicken the process or let it evolve at its own pace. This was the situation ʿIrāqī found around him during his presence in Kashmir, and his missionary zeal compelled him to attempt a correction once he had the necessary political backing.

In addition to his general Islamic fervor, ʿIrāqī's purpose was also to propagate the peculiarly Nūrbakhshī form of Islam in Kashmir as widely as possible. During the conversion drive, Nūrbakhshī centers became filled with throngs of men. Converts were made to recite the profession of faith, take off their sacred thread (*zunnār*), be circumcised, and eat cow's meat to become fully Muslim. A similar campaign was organized for women, with the most trusted Nūrbakhshī disciples going house to house through the city and villages to teach the basics of Islam. Nūrbakhshīs seem to have had an exclusive concession for the process of further Islamic education as well. However, the *Tuḥfat al-aḥbāb* mentions that the small number of people in Kashmir who had never converted to Islam were left to themselves: the project was aimed at reclaiming Muslims and not at forcing Islam on fresh converts.[104]

ʿIrāqī's attitude toward non-Nūrbakhshī Muslim scholars and mystics is a clear indication that his efforts were directed at producing an exclusively Nūrbakhshī society. The particular target on this issue was the Khānqāh-i Muʿallā of ʿAlī Hamadānī, which came under ʿIrāqī's guardianship for the first time during his campaigns. The *Tuḥfat al-aḥbāb* proclaims this to have been a more significant event than the

Kashmir," *Central Asiatic Journal* 23 (1979): 3–18. For indigenous perspectives on the issue, see Hangloo, *State in Medieval Kashmir,* 48–74, Mohammad Ishaq Khan, *Kashmir's Transition to Islam: The Role of Muslim Rishis* (Delhi: Manohar, 1994), and various other articles by him in the bibliography that present the same perspective.

104. *TA,* 473–77.

destruction of all the temples. Comparing the khānqāh to the Kaʿba, Kashmīrī assigns ʿAlī Hamadānī the role of Abraham, who had constructed the Kaʿba, and ʿIrāqī is seen as Muḥammad, who now cleansed it from the impieties of the unbelievers and the apostates.[105] Irāqī's effort to brand the local community of scholars as apostates met local resistance under the leadership of Shaykh Fatḥ Allāh, son of Ismāʿīl Kubravī, who reportedly wrote a letter to ʿIrāqī trying to show him the error of his ways.[106] The opposition was quashed by Kājī Chak, ʿIrāqī's patron between 1516 and 1526, who confiscated Fatḥ Allāh's property and forced him to migrate out of Kashmir.[107]

Amid the political and social mayhem of early-sixteenth-century Kashmir, ʿIrāqī also continued to initiate disciples into the order and regularly performed the yearly forty-day retreat.[108] Nūrbakhshī religious training in Kashmir emphasized knowledge acquired through spiritual exercises and experiences over any form of book learning. Kashmīrī openly states that ʿIrāqī's most advanced disciples possessed little knowledge in disciplines such as written interpretation of the Qurʾan (*tafsīr*) or Muḥammad's sayings. They nevertheless, based upon

105. Ibid., 497–99. For an extended discussion of the image of ʿAlī Hamadānī in Kashmir and parts of what is now Pakistan, see Jamal Elias, "A Second ʿAli: The Making of Sayyid ʿAlī Hamadānī in Popular Imagination," *MW* 90, nos. 3–4 (2000): 395–419.

106. Shaykh Fatḥ Allāh "Ḥaqqānī" is attested as the teacher of the famous "Sulṭān al-ʿĀrifīn" Shaykh Ḥamza Makhdūm (d. 984/1576), who was initiated into the Suhravardī silsila by Sayyid Jamāl ad-Dīn Bukhārī and later became the eponym of the Sulṭānī branch of the Suhravardīya in Kashmir. Hagiographic material relating to Shaykh Ḥamza's life and legacy is treated in Niyāzmand, *Haft ganj-i Sulṭānī*.

107. Rafiqi, *Sufism in Kashmir,* xxxi, 218. The earliest source to cite this letter is the problematic *Futūḥāt-i Kubravīya* by ʿAbd al-Vahhāb, completed in 1162/1749. As discussed above, this work was written in an environment of Sunnī-Shīʿī conflict in which ʿIrāqī had come to be seen as the first instigator of Kashmiri Twelver Shīʿism. It is clear from earlier, more reliable sources, however, that ʿIrāqī's cause was the Nūrbakhshīya as a separate sect, which incorporated Shīʿī sentimentality but was far removed from mainstream Twelver Shīʿism. Even if the letter cited in *Futūḥāt-i Kubravīya* is a later forgery, it probably does represent the resentment felt by non-Nūrbakhshī shaykhs in Kashmir during ʿIrāqī's ascendancy.

108. *TA,* 418–19.

their intuitive capacities, could provide better answers to religious questions than any learned scholar.[109]

ʿIrāqī's personal interaction with the community of the faithful is exemplified in the reminiscence of Muḥammad ʿAlī Kashmīrī, the author of *Tuḥfat al-aḥbāb,* who was the son of Mawlānā Khalīl Allāh, one of his oldest and most trusted disciples. He remembers seeing ʿIrāqī walk toward the sanctuary at Zadībal while the young Kashmīrī and other children were playing outside the Bāb-i Sharīʿat. Once, when Kashmīrī was five years old, ʿIrāqī sat him down in front of him, rubbed his hands on his face a number of times, and gave him a piece of sugar from his own mouth as a form of conveying spiritual merit. He then had food brought for him and his brother, and the whole event left a permanent mark on the little boy's memory.[110] It is perhaps the very combination of great care and tenderness for his followers and severity toward enemies that made ʿIrāqī an effective leader for the Nūrbakhshīya in Kashmir.[111] His movement's continued influence after his death was clearly due to the loyalties he had elicited for himself and his order rather than the weak personalities and efforts of those who succeeded him.

The Nūrbakhshīya in Kashmir after ʿIrāqī

After ʿIrāqī's death in 1526, the Nūrbakhshīya remained a vital force on the religious scene in Kashmir until about 1588, when the region was incorporated into the Mughal Empire. This period was, however, punctuated with internal struggles between ʿIrāqī's successors, severe repression under the rule of Mīrzā Ḥaydar Dughlāt, and renewed patronage during the short-lived rule of the Chak dynasty between 1561 and 1588. The movement's political profile remained tied strongly to the fortunes of the Chak clan: it gained power when the Chaks ruled as viziers or kings and was persecuted by Dughlāt when they were in the opposition.

109. Ibid., 441–43.

110. Ibid., 384, 389–90.

111. Kashmīrī also relates various other stories about ʿIrāqī's generosity toward his followers.

Internal Conflict after ʿIrāqī's Death

The Kashmiri Nūrbakhshīs were beset with an internal power struggle immediately after ʿIrāqī's death. The conflict stemmed from ʿIrāqī having appointed both his son Dāniyāl and Bābā ʿAlī Najjār as his principal successors. He may have made some delimitation in the scope of each deputy's authority, but it is impossible to see this directly from the surviving sources. The path toward a genealogical succession was initiated when ʿIrāqī began including Dāniyāl in the yearly retreats from the time he was twelve or thirteen.[112] Dāniyāl had in fact deputized for ʿIrāqī at his very first retreat by handing out the candles to all participants, and his position was confirmed when all Sufis were asked to take an oath on his hands three or four years before ʿIrāqī's death.[113]

Prior to Dāniyāl's anointment, ʿIrāqī had made a public display of investing spiritual authority in Bābā ʿAlī at a time when Zadībal was still under construction. On this occasion, Bābā ʿAlī was called to the open courtyard one evening after ʿIrāqī had finished his day's lessons for novices. He was asked to recite a section from Farīd ad-Dīn ʿAṭṭār's *Manṭiq aṭ-ṭayr* (Conference of the Birds), in which a bird questions the hoopoe about its selection as the birds' leader for their pursuit of the fabulous bird Sīmurgh. The hoopoe's meaningful reply invokes the authority of the prophet Solomon, who had chosen him at an earlier time, and asks all the birds to be obedient to the leader.[114] After the recitation, ʿIrāqī turned to the audience and told them that he now vested his authority in Bābā ʿAlī in the same way that Solomon had chosen the hoopoe. The ceremony was completed when ʿIrāqī wound his own distinctive black turban around Bābā ʿAlī's head and all those present took an oath on Bābā ʿAlī's hand.[115]

As depicted in these stories, the designation of successor seems paradoxically unequivocal for both candidates. The *Tuḥfat al-aḥbāb,*

112. *TA,* 405. This was the first retreat held at Zadībal after the completion of the khānqāh in about 1507.

113. Ibid., 427.

114. Farīd ad-Dīn ʿAṭṭār, *Manṭiq aṭ-ṭayr,* ed. Kāẓim Dizfūlīyān (Tehran: Intishārāt-i Ṭilāyīa, 2000), 115–16; idem, *The Conference of the Birds,* trans. Afkham Darbandi and Dick Davis (New York: Penguin Books, 1984), 78–79.

115. *TA,* 400–404.

whose author was partial to Bābā ʿAlī, portrays Dāniyāl as a jealous man who attempted to restrict Bābā ʿAlī's influence despite the latter's conciliatory attitude. The older man is depicted as having gone out of his way to show reverence to Dāniyāl, who would not stop his harassment due to his envy over Bābā ʿAlī's popularity in the community as a spiritual guide.[116] Because of Dāniyāl's recalcitrance, Bābā ʿAlī eventually removed himself from Zadībal, going to the Khānqāh-i Muʿallā, which was awarded to him by Dawlat Chak (d. 1555) despite Dāniyāl's resistance.[117]

Dāniyāl's opposition to Bābā ʿAlī probably stemmed from his difficulties in acquiring recognition as a shaykh in the community despite ʿIrāqī's designation. Although interested in the position of the community's leader, he may not, as Kashmīrī states in a veiled reference, have shared his father's dedication to religious exercises and retreats.[118] This problem can be observed also in the story of Sayyid Aḥmad, who visited Kashmir around 938/1531 and became immediately popular among both elites and commoners. He was even made the caretaker of the Khānqāh-i Muʿallā by the rulers,[119] though he shortly moved to the more spacious Zadībal upon Dāniyāl's invitation. Some people considered Sayyid Aḥmad a member of the Nūrbakhshī family, which would have placed him above Dāniyāl, who soon grew very jealous of Sayyid Aḥmad's popularity.[120] Sayyid Aḥmad eventually left Kashmir altogether around 1543 due to the unstable political climate, and Dāniyāl himself decided to transfer to Baltistan, probably for the same reason.[121]

116. Ibid., 435–37.

117. Ibid., 430–31. For the significance of Dawlat Chak, see below.

118. Ibid., 417. Kashmīrī relays his father's disappointment at religious fervor in the community having declined after ʿIrāqī's death because Dāniyāl did not devote much time to such things.

119. An alternative source states that the khānqāh was given to a Sayyid Muḥammad b. Sayyid Ali (ʿAlī, *Tārīkh-i Kashmīr,* 30).

120. *TA,* 428–30. Kashmīrī denies the idea that Sayyid Aḥmad was from the Nūrbakhshī family.

121. The year of departure can be deduced from the fact that the Nūrbakhshīs' position in Kashmir became precarious after the discord between Dughlāt and Rēgī Chak, which occurred around 1543. The latter then left Srinagar to join Kājī Chak in the mountains, and the two together were defeated by Dughlāt in 1544 (*BS,* 347–48).

Persecution under the Rule of Mīrzā Ḥaydar Dughlāt

The departure of Sayyid Aḥmad and Shaykh Dāniyāl from Kashmir resulted from the conquest of the territory by Mīrzā Ḥaydar Dughlāt in 1540. Mīrzā Ḥaydar, who documented his adventures extensively in his *Tārīkh-i Rashīdī,* first occupied Kashmir briefly in 1533 on behalf of Sulṭān Saʿīd Khān (d. 1533), the ruler of Kashghar, who had begun a campaign in Ladakh and Baltistan in 1532.[122] He returned to the region in 1540, this time under the employ of the Mughal emperor Humāyūn (d. 1555), who had succeeded Bābur in 1530 but was then in Lahore after suffering the disloyalty of his brothers and a defeat by Shēr Khān Sūrī in 1539.[123] Dughlāt was invited to Kashmir by those among the kingdom's nobles who, in disfavor, were biding time in the hills surrounding the valley.[124] He and his associates were successful in expelling Kājī Chak from the valley, though another member of the family named Rēgī Chak was at that time a member of Dughlāt's camp. The kingdom was now divided up between the victors, with Dughlāt at the head of the government and Ismāʿīl Shāh b. Muḥammad (or Nāzuk Shāh) its nominal Shāhmīrī sovereign. Dughlāt indicates that he had undertaken the expedition to Kashmir to provide a haven for the defeated Humāyūn, but the emperor left for Iran without waiting to see the results of the campaign.[125]

Dughlāt's work *Tārīkh-i Rashīdī* contains a vigorous condemnation of Nūrbakhshī beliefs. The work claims that, during Dughlāt's reign in Kashmir, he had announced the death penalty as the punishment for anyone who refused to accept the Sunnī Ḥanafī maẕhab.[126] This may indeed have been his policy toward the Nūrbakhshīs a few years after his arrival, but the anonymous *Bahāristān-i shāhī* reports that he was in

122. Mirza Haydar Dughlat, *Tarikh-i Rashidi: A History of the Khans of Moghulistan,* ed. and trans. Wheeler M. Thackston, 2 vols. (Cambridge: Department of Near Eastern Languages and Civilizations, Harvard University, 1996), 1:363 (Persian text), 2:258 (English trans.).

123. Ibid., 1:404–7, 2:289–92. For a summary of the history of Bābur and Humāyūn, see J. Burton-Page, "Mughals," *EI*[2], 7:313–16.

124. *BS,* 344–45.

125. Dughlat, *Tarikh-i Rashidi,* 404–5.

126. Ibid., 1:368–70, 2:262–64.

fact respectful of Nūrbakhshī monuments in the beginning, while he shared power with Rēgī Chak. He had gone to Zadībal in the company of Rēgī Chak to meet the visiting Sayyid Aḥmad and at one point had even offered the fātiḥa at Shams ad-Dīn ʿIrāqī's tomb in a most respectful manner.[127]

A little later after this event, Rēgī Chak fell out of Dughlāt's favor and left the city to join the opposition led by Kājī Chak. The Chaks were then defeated soundly by Dughlāt and his allies. Kājī Chak died in exile in Jumādā II, 951 (September 1544).[128] Dughlāt now decided to rout out all Nūrbakhshīs from Kashmir. This was due either, as he himself states, to his distaste for their beliefs or to the sect's being tied closely to the Chaks, his foremost enemies.[129] His biggest religious objection to the group was that it could not be classified as either Sunnī or Shīʿī. Somewhat curiously, he states that he had earlier, in Badakhshan and other places, met a son of Sayyid Muḥammad Nūrbakhsh and many other Nūrbakhshī shaykhs who were all Sunnīs.[130] He was surprised by the fact that, in comparison, the Nūrbakhshīs of Kashmir reviled Muḥammad's wife ʿĀʾisha and other companions of the Prophet favored by Sunnīs. This made the Nūrbakhshīs akin to Twelver Shīʿīs, except they did not consider the Twelfth Imām the mahdī and saw Nūrbakhsh as the holder of this office instead. What made matters even more ambiguous for Dughlāt was that these Nūrbakhshīs revered many Sufi saints who were all Sunnī.

Dughlāt's objection to Nūrbakhshīs' liminal position between the accepted Islamic sects was ratified by Indian scholars to whom he sent Nūrbakhsh's book *al-Fiqh al-aḥwaṭ* for a legal opinion. They vigorously condemned it as a work of heresy and reprehensible innovation (*bidʿa*) and advocated complete extirpation of the sect's adherents. To this

127. *BS,* 346–47.

128. Ibid., 347–48.

129. Dāniyāl's close ties with Rēgī Chak are indicated by his blessing of the site of a former temple to become the ancestral graveyard for Rēgī Chak's family (*TA,* 461–62).

130. Dughlat, *Tarikh-i Rashidi,* 1:368–69, 2:262–63. If we take this statement to be true, the only plausible explanation is that this person was not Nūrbakhsh's son but a Sunnī Kubravī who discounted Nūrbakhsh's mahdist claim and regarded him as a master in the Kubravī chain.

charge, Dughlāt added the objection that the practices of these alleged Sufis were confined to extended retreats for meditation and undue attention to dream interpretation. This was, consequently, not the Sufism of the learned but a charismatic cult set up around corrupt shaykhs who claimed extraordinary powers.

The well-known affiliation between the Chaks and Nūrbakhshī shaykhs either formed the background of Dughlāt's religious objections or at least added to his hostility toward the group. As a result, he forbade all Nūrbakhshī practices and had Shaykh Dāniyāl captured and brought back from Baltistan, where he had taken refuge in this tumultuous period.[131] He was kept imprisoned for almost a year and then executed in 1550 based upon advice from Shaykh Fatḥ Allāh b. Ismāʿīl and legal opinions extracted from local jurists who had earlier opposed ʿIrāqī's heavy-handed religious policy. In addition, Dughlāt burned the Zadībal khānqāh to the ground and desecrated ʿIrāqī's tomb, which was within its grounds. According to a later Sunnī source hostile to ʿIrāqī, Dughlāt extracted ʿIrāqī's bones from the grave and had them burned and turned the whole site into a dung heap and public latrine.[132] The pro-Nūrbakhshī historiographic tradition maintains that the Nūrbakhshīs had extracted ʿIrāqī's bones from the grave when they heard of Dughlāt's intentions and that these were interred on land owned by the Chādūra family outside Srinagar. A mausoleum denoting ʿIrāqī's grave still stands on the Chādūra estate and is in the care of Kashmiri Twelver Shīʿīs who trace their roots back to him.[133]

Gradual Decline and Conversion to Twelver Shīʿism

The suppression of the Nūrbakhshīya during Mīrzā Ḥaydar Dughlāt's rule dealt the movement in Kashmir a severe blow from which it never fully recovered. Dughlāt was himself killed in an uprising of Kashmiri

131. *BS,* 348. The author states that Dughlāt himself went to capture Dāniyāl, though the *Tārīkh-i Rashīdī* mentions no such trip to Baltistan; instead, he was captured by Mullā Qāsim, who had been appointed the governor of the area by Dughlāt in 1548 (cf. Holzwarth, "Islam in Baltistan," 25).

132. ʿAlī, *Tārīkh-i Kashmīr,* 32.

133. *BS,* 88–89.

nobles in 1551 and, fortunately for the Nūrbakhshīs, the government fell to the Chaks soon thereafter in the same year.[134] The nominal ruler now was Sulṭān Nāzuk Shāh, whom Dughlāt had also kept on the throne, but real power belonged to Kājī Chak's brother Dawlat Chak, who retained his position until 1554–55. Dawlat Chak rehabilitated the movement in Kashmir by paying respect to Dāniyāl's body, which was now interred in Zadībal near his father's old mausoleum. He also financed the reconstruction of the khānqāh (completed in 1552). Revenue streams dedicated to ʿIrāqī's descendants and the maintenance of the khānqāh were also reinstated, and daily and Friday prayers were held regularly.[135]

Besides Dāniyāl's fate, the Bābā ʿAlī Najjār side of the Nūrbakhshīya had also suffered considerably under Dughlāt's policy of forcing the Ḥanafī maẕhab on the whole population. Bābā ʿAlī himself was spared a fate like that of Dāniyāl due only to his old age and Dughlāt's not wanting to add to the resentment against him among the local nobility.[136] Bābā ʿAlī can be presumed to have died by the time of Dawlat Chak's rule, but the vizier now rehabilitated the Khānqāh-i Muʿallā under the care of Bābā ʿAlī's successor Bābā Ḥasan. This shaykh, in his turn, supervised the construction of a new khānqāh, named Ḥasanābād, that contained the grave of Bābā ʿAlī.[137] In addition, one source names a certain Kankī Rishī as Bābā ʿAlī's successor. Kankī Rishī was inclined to extreme asceticism, including living in the wild.[138] The level of patronage from the rulers seems to have decreased with the rise of Ghāzī Khān Chak (d. 1563–64), son of Kājī Chak, who developed differences with his uncle and had him blinded in 1554–55.[139]

Unlike his predecessors, Ghāzī Khān no longer wished to continue the fiction of the Shāhmīrī dynasty and in 1561 proclaimed himself the

134. Ibid., 351–55.
135. Ibid., 356.
136. Chādūra, *History of Kashmir,* 68.
137. *BS,* 357.
138. Chādūra, *History of Kashmir,* 103.
139. *BS,* 358–59.

first Chak king of Kashmir.[140] The dynasty that followed maintained a precarious existence until 1588 amid the unceasing intrigues of local nobles and visitors arriving from the Mughal Empire. In religious terms, the Chak dynasty was inclined toward Twelver Shīʿism: the historical record at this point becomes silent about the Nūrbakhshīya in specifics. The religious environment in general during this period was characterized by a conflict between Twelver Shīʿī and Sunnī protagonists, usually supported by the Chaks and the Mughals, respectively.[141]

The Mughal takeover of Kashmir by Akbar (d. 1605) in 1588 was the last nail in the coffin of the Kashmiri Nūrbakhshīya. Although seemingly irrelevant to the larger political context, the Nūrbakhshīs had a measurable population in Kashmir until at least the end of the sixteenth century. Akbar's courtier Abū l-Fażl ʿAllāmī (writing in 1596–97) states that the animosity between Sunnīs, Shīʿīs, and Nūrbakhshīs in Kashmir made the province prone to outbursts of public riots.[142]

In tandem with the overall trend, over the course of the seventeenth century ʿIrāqī's descendants gradually changed their sectarian affiliation from Nūrbakhshīya to Twelver Shīʿism.[143] The modern proponents of this tradition proclaim ʿIrāqī a sayyid descended from Ṣafī ad-Dīn of Ardabīl (d. 1334), the eponymous ancestor of the Ṣafavid dynasty in Iran.[144] The changeover reflects the influence of the Ṣafavids' success:

140. Ibid., 361.

141. For the details of various Sunnī-Shīʿī riots in Kashmir, see Khūyhāmī, *Tārīkh-i Ḥasan,* 1:479–94.

142. Abū l-Fażl ʿAllāmī, *Āʾīn-i Akbarī,* ed. H. Blochmann, 2 vols. (Calcutta: Bibliotheca Indica, 1972), 2:563. Abū l-Fażl's knowledge of Nūrbakhshī background was probably slight since he confuses Qāsim Fayżbakhsh with the famous poet Qāsim-i Anvār (1:584).

143. For the establishment of Twelver Shīʿism in the Indian environment in general, see Juan R. I. Cole, *Roots of North Indian Shīʿism in Iran and Iraq: Religion and State in Awadh, 1722–1859* (Berkeley: University of California Press, 1988), 13–35.

144. *BS,* 30–38; Sayyid Muḥammad Bāqir Mūsavī, *Akhtar-i darakhshān: Kashmīr kī shīʿāyī tārīkh sē mutaʿalliq chand mażāmīn* (Benaras: Ikrām Ḥusayn Press, 1972), 9–12, 41–102. Muḥammad Shafīʿ also reports having met in Lahore in 1923 a Sayyid Rizā Ḥusayn Ṣafavī who claimed to be descended from ʿIrāqī. He had never heard of Nūrbakhshīs and, when told about the sect, thought the whole story to be a Sunnī fabrication meant to discredit ʿIrāqī (Shafīʿ, *Firqa,* III:13).

the Iranian kings, after coming to power in the early sixteenth century, had themselves manufactured a sayyid genealogy going through Ṣafī ad-Dīn. The family's modern members possess trust (*vaqf*) documents dated 1122/1710–11 and 1128/1715–16 that have the word *sayyid* attached to Shams ad-Dīn ʿIrāqī's name.[145] The process of transition from a Nūrbakhshī to a Twelver Shīʿī identity in Kashmir was thus complete by the beginning of the eighteenth century.

The Significance of Nūrbakhshī Success in Kashmir

The substantial but brief success of the Nūrbakhshīya in Kashmir was tied inextricably to the personality of Shams ad-Dīn ʿIrāqī, who more even than Nūrbakhsh himself in his lifetime attempted to put the movement's messianic commission into action. One can only speculate that had someone with ʿIrāqī's skills joined Nūrbakhsh early during his career as the mahdī, the Nūrbakhshīya might have achieved far greater worldly success than it in fact did. While the mahdī himself was concerned mostly with rationalizing and justifying his messianic claim, ʿIrāqī cultivated ties with ruling elites and used his political influence for the sake of enforcing Nūrbakhshī ideas in society. In a similar vein, ʿIrāqī's prescription for religious practice was centered on the communal retreat undertaken in a monumental building, providing boundaries for the community and strengthening social solidarity. In his use of Nūrbakhsh's works, ʿIrāqī's greatest emphasis was on the legal manual *al-Fiqh al-aḥwaṭ,* whose purpose was to provide the code for living life according to the sect's principles.

Both ʿIrāqī's political behavior and his religious outlook constituted an effort to "exteriorize" Nūrbakhsh's esoteric doctrine by making it simple and more accessible to a large audience. Nūrbakhsh proclaimed himself the revealer of secrets in the "age of unveiling"[146] and produced a complex religious system to rationalize his messianism; ʿIrāqī, on the other hand, turned Nūrbakhsh's doctrine into an actual demystified manifestation of Islamic belief and practice that could be observed and

145. *BS,* 35–37. The editor of *Bahāristān-i Shāhī* gives the names and activities of various Twelver Shīʿī scholars descended from ʿIrāqī (*BS,* 97–103).

146. Nūrbakhsh, *Maktūb beh ʿAlāʾ ad-Dawla,* AA:79.

followed. He was, therefore, far more successful in engendering a community willing to compete in the sociopolitical sphere based upon its religious identity.

ʿIrāqī's efforts for propagating the Nūrbakhshīya were aided greatly by Kashmiri political and social conditions around the beginning of the sixteenth century. The combination of powerless kings, fractious and quarrelsome nobles, and a population on the cusp of complete Islamization allowed him to create space for himself and the Nūrbakhshīya in Kashmiri society. The loyalty shown to ʿIrāqī by the nobles who became Nūrbakhshīs is an indication of his personal charisma as the movement's leader and patron saint in Kashmir. For essentially the same reasons that account for his success, he also inspired great animosity from his foes. However, due either to artifice or good fortune, he escaped tasting the full force of reprisals directed at him.

ʿIrāqī's successors lacked both his adroitness and charisma and lived under the long shadow he cast even from his grave at the movement's symbolic center—the khānqāh he built at Zadībal. Neither his son Dāniyāl nor his foremost disciple Bābā ʿAlī Najjār had the wherewithal to keep the Nūrbakhshī community together after ʿIrāqī's death, leading to a slow dissipation of influence in the period between 1526 and 1540. The movement was then severely undermined by the pogroms carried out by Mīrzā Ḥaydar Dughlāt and could not recover to a position of eminence even when the political climate became favorable under the rule of the Chak family. Kashmir's incorporation into the Mughal Empire in 1588 then meant that the movement's adherents were slowly absorbed into communities of the major Islamic sects.

Expanding our purview from Kashmir to the larger world of the Islamic East, the sixteenth century brought to a close an era of "experimentation" in the development of Islamic religious history. Muḥammad Nūrbakhsh presented his messianic claim in a time period marked by a general erosion of sectarian and doctrinal boundaries. He gave voice to this trend by proposing a new doctrinal identity meant to supersede the established sects throughout the Islamic world. ʿIrāqī brought this vision to Kashmir. But times were changing by the time of ʿIrāqī's death in 1526, a year in which Bābur also established the Mughal dynasty in India. The subsequent decades of the sixteenth century saw a reassertion of traditional sectarian boundaries under the Sunnī Mughal,

Ottoman, and Uzbek Dynasties and the Twelver Shīʿī Ṣafavids. The sociointellectual space in which the Nūrbakhshīya was born and bred now gradually closed in, and the ruling dynasties incorporated even messianism into their ideologies. Just as Akbar's conquest of Kashmir marked a step in the consolidation of the Mughal Empire, the extinguishing of the Nūrbakhshīya over the sixteenth and seventeenth centuries in Kashmir represented the passing of one religious age and the affirmation of another. Under such conditions, a liminal movement such as the Nūrbakhshīya could survive only in Baltistan and Ladakh, regions insulated from much of the larger world through the barrier of some of the earth's highest mountains.

Chapter Seven

Establishment and Survival in Baltistan and Ladakh

For the three centuries following the Nūrbakhshīya's demise in Kashmir, our knowledge of the movement is limited to a few incidental references with virtually no details. The relative isolation of the movement's new home in Baltistan and Ladakh meant that premodern historians' comments on it during the period were limited to short and often inconsequential hints.[1] In addition, the societies in question were themselves largely preliterate until the modern period, with no indigenous historiographic tradition to preserve material for social history.[2] Consequently, our first substantial reports of the establishment of the

1. For a vivid account of the difficulty of travel in the region until quite recently, see Dervla Murphy, *Where the Indus Is Young: A Winter in Baltistan* (London: J. Murray, 1977).

2. Literary record for Baltistan as a Buddhist region end in the thirteenth century. The earliest literary source concerned with Baltistan as a Muslim area is a court chronicle entitled *Shigarnāma* written around 1700 (cf. Holzworth, "Islam in Baltistan," 1–14). The *Shigarnāma* was used extensively but uncritically by Lakhnavī in his reconstruction of Balti history (cf. Daniela Bredi, "L'uso delle fonti nella storiografia Indo-Musulmana nella prima metà del XX secolo: La storia del Baltistan, Ḥashmatullāh Khān e lo *Shighar-nāma,*" *RSO* 68 (1994): 267–89). Besides the *Shigarnāma,* another story about the creation of Shigar written down only in the mid-twentieth century has been transcribed and translated (cf. Sydney Schuler, "The 'Story of the Creation of Shigar' of Wazir Ahmad," *Central Asiatic Journal* 22 [1978]: 102–19). For the problems associated with the historical study of the establishment of Islam in Baltistan, see Gérard Rovillé, "Contribution a l'étude de l'Islâm au

Nūrbakhshīya in the region come from modern observers who started arriving in the area in the nineteenth century. Subsequent to this, through the twentieth century, proponents of the Nūrbakhshīya in Baltistan in particular became increasingly more self-conscious about their heritage, now proffering versions of their own history based on local oral tradition, epigraphic evidence surviving in mosques and khānqāhs constructed in premodern times, and the work of academic historians. The overall effect of this situation is that while little can be known with certainty about the premodern Nūrbakhshīya itself in Baltistan and Ladakh, the history has become a major focal point for speculation as well as contention by the region's modern inhabitants.

Besides explicating the last phase of Nūrbakhshī history, the materials presented in this chapter also provide a poignant example for the modernization of a traditional Islamic context in South Asia. Understanding the modern Nūrbakhshīya of Baltistan and Ladakh requires contextualizing it not only within the movement's own development but also in the worldwide impact of modernity on religions and cultures. While modernization in non-European societies in general can be traced ultimately to contact with European cultures, the modernizing process has undergone considerable domestication in indigenous settings during the past two centuries. For South Asian Islam, modernization of the tradition began with the establishment of British colonialism, and its most prominent feature was a push toward religious and social reform aimed at overcoming the perceived loss of power and prestige connected to the demise of Muslim political hegemony in the subcontinent. The modernizing process, however, produced a number of different paths that soon developed a vigorous and often contentious internal dynamic. Understanding any aspect of South Asian Islam in the twentieth century requires, therefore, placing a given movement within the spectrum of the various modernized Islamic paths that have matured over the course of the past two centuries.

Baltistân et au Ladakh," in *Wissenschaftsgeschichte und gegenwärtige Forschungen in Nordwest-Indien,* ed. Peter Neumann (Dresden: Staatliches Museum für Völkerkunde, 1990), 113–24.

The Nūrbakhshīya occupies a particularly interesting position in this situation since it was a latecomer to the process and has modernized solely through the impact of other modernized Islams rather than any forms of European modernity. Nūrbakhshīs began to be targeted for conversion by various South Asian Sunnī movements from the end of the nineteenth century, and they first articulated a modern religious discourse in response to these perceived attacks on the tradition. In addition, the development of modernized Twelver Shīʿism in both South Asia itself and Iran and Iraq has influenced Nūrbakhshī self-perception even more significantly than any form of Sunnism. The Iranian revolution of 1979 and its considerable influence on Twelver Shīʿī identity in Pakistan and India has led to a rift within the Nūrbakhhsīya around the issue of whether it is a completely independent sectarian entity or a subsect within Twelver Shīʿism. The Nūrbakhshī communities of Baltistan and Ladakh, in Pakistan and India, respectively, are currently deeply embroiled in debating and clarifying these issues relating to their own group identity. Observing the particulars of the modernization of the Nūrbakhshīya thus provides insight into sectarianism in modern South Asian Islam in general.

My ultimate concern in this chapter is to see the discourse of the Nūrbakhshīya in Baltistan and Ladakh as a continuation of the evolving tradition examined in previous chapters in its medieval Central Asian, Iranian, and Kashmiri phases. The chief focus here is intellectual history as it can be reconstituted from both literary sources and secondary descriptions. The discussion is neither an in-depth social scientific assessment of modern Nūrbakhshī communities nor meant to be exhaustive. The chapter is divided into the following sections: a review of information about the establishment of the Nūrbakhshīya in Baltistan and Ladakh; a general assessment of the situation and self-perception of modern Nūrbakhshī communities in the region; the spectrum of religious opinions in the contemporary community; and profiles of individuals who are influential in shaping the community's current religious outlook. The last part of the chapter offers clues to where the community may be headed beyond the narrative of this book.

From the Medieval to the Modern in Baltistan and Ladakh

Although linguistically connected to Tibet, Baltistan and Ladakh have had a greater connection to the history of Muslim-dominated southern and Central Asia since at least the fifteenth century.[3] The region currently comprised of Baltistan and Ladakh can be divided into three contiguous linguistic zones with differing religiocultural coordinates. Two of these areas now constitute Indian Ladakh, which since 1979 has been divided into the Leh and Kargil districts. Leh has a Buddhist majority, Kargil a Muslim majority.[4] Baltistan, which is entirely Muslim, is part of the Northern Areas administrative unit in Pakistan that also includes Gilgit and Hunza.[5] All these regions were a part of the princely state of Kashmir until 1947 and are implicated in the territorial dispute between India and Pakistan. Before annexation into the state of Kashmir in 1840, Baltistan was further divided into three zones centered around the relatively large-scale agricultural inhabitations at Skardū (the current capital), Shigar, and Khaplū. Although at times united under a single state, the three regions had separate ruling lineages immediately prior to the loss of autonomy to Kashmir.[6]

Islamic presence in Baltistan and Ladakh can be traced to earlier than the fifteenth century, though substantial Islamization in the local population began only as a result of the arrival of greater Muslim influence in the form of proselytizers and soldiers around the beginning of the sixteenth century. In the absence of both an appreciable local

3. For Balti as a Tibetan dialect, see George van Driem, *Languages of the Himalayas: An Ethnolinguistic Handbook,* 2 vols. (Leiden: E. J. Brill, 2001). There is no indication of a Nūrbakhshī presence among the Muslims in Tibet itself. The Muslim communities of Lhasa are divided between Hui Chinese Muslims and immigrants from various parts of Central and southern Asia (cf. Abdul Wahid Radhu, *Islam in Tibet* [Louisville: Fons Vitae, 1997]).

4. Smriti Srinivas, *The Mouths of People, The Voice of God: Buddhists and Muslims in a Frontier Community of Ladakh* (Delhi: Oxford University Press, 1998), 16. The Kargil dialect is intermediate between Balti and Ladakhi and is sometimes referred to as Purigi or Puriki.

5. For geographical information about Baltistan and adjoining areas, see Bazmee Ansari, "Baltistān," *EI*[2], 1:1004–5, and Banat Gul Afridi, *Baltistan in History* (Peshawar: Emjay Books International, 1988), 8–15. For the background to the political status of the Northern Areas, see Muḥammad Qāsim Nasīm, *Baltistān: Tārīkh va siyāsat* (Lahore: Progressive Publishers, 1994).

6. Richard M. Emerson, "Charismatic Kingship: A Study of State Formation and Authority in Baltistan," in *Pakistan: The Social Sciences Perspective,* ed. Akbar S. Ahmed (Karachi: Oxford University Press, 1990), 109–15.

historiographic tradition and substantial archeological or ethnographic research, we may look toward the folklore of the region's Muslim population for clues regarding the Islamization process. Preliminary studies concerned with local myths about the Tibetan legendary hero Kesar (or Gesar) reveal that Balti oral literature can be divided into three chronological layers.[7] As seen in local musical traditions, the oldest layer consists of ancient songs, dance tunes, and epical songs that preserve the most distinctively "Tibetan" substrate of the tradition going back to pre-Islamic and early Islamic periods. After these come songs from the sixteenth century and later, influenced heavily by the Persianate court culture of the Mughal Empire. The most recent layer is affected by modern Urdu traditions, reflecting the area's incorporation into Pakistan.[8] Beyond providing this general grid, the folk literature studied to date does little more than corroborate the names of rulers attested in historical sources written outside the region.[9] It may indeed be possible to garner more historical information from local oral traditions, though this requires a more critical ethnographic method than has been applied in the region to date.[10]

7. Balti versions of the Kesar epic have been the object of study by Karl Jettmar, Klaus Sagaster, and Renate Söhnen, in particular. In looking through their published findings (see bibliography), I was unable to see any direct or indirect substantiation of Nūrbakhshī history in the contemporary telling of the saga. The only item relating Kesar to the mahdī paradigm is the fact that Sagaster's fieldwork in 1980–81 revealed that some Baltis regard Kesar (considered a Buddhist) as the Dajjāl, or Islamic antichrist, figure who is alive and will reveal himself at the end of time (cf. Klaus Sagaster, "Kesar, Der Islamische Antichrist," in *Documenta Barbarorum: Festschrift für Walther Heissig zum 70. Geburtstag,* ed. Klaus Sagaster and Michael Weiers [Wiesbaden: Otto Harrassowitz, 1983], 341–48). However, there is nothing to suggest that this has anything to do with Nūrbakhshī ideas.

8. Cf. Renate Söhnen, "Treasures of Literary and Musical Tradition in Baltistan," *Journal of Central Asia* 7, no. 2 (1984): 40.

9. Cf. Renate Söhnen, "On Reflections of Historical Events in Balti Folk Songs," in *Ethnologie und Geschichte: Festschrift für Karl Jettmar,* ed. Peter Snoy (Wiesbaden: Franz Steiner Verlag, 1983), 582–600; Klaus Sagaster, "The Kings of Baltistan and Other Kings: Some Remarks on Balti Folk Literature," *Journal of Central Asia* 7, no. 2 (1984): 49–55.

10. The limited and patronizing scope of some of the German ethnographic research in the area is evident in Sagaster's concluding comments in one of his articles:

The internal Muslim tradition from both Ladakh and Baltistan (Nūrbakhshī as well as non-Nūrbakhshī) purports that Islam was brought to Baltistan by ʿAlī Hamadānī, who visited the area on his way back from Kashmir to Central Asia around 1384.[11] Neither this claim nor the idea that Muḥammad Nūrbakhsh visited Baltistan can be substantiated historically, and it is quite certain that these traditions are projections by later generations of Muslims in the region looking to construct an authentic Islamic past for their communities.[12] As discussed in chapter 6, Nūrbakhshī ideas first filtered into Baltistan during Shams ad-Dīn ʿIrāqī's brief exile there in 1505 at a time when he was experiencing difficulties in his relationship with the ruling elite of Kashmir. The author of *Tuḥfat al-aḥbāb* states that, upon his arrival, ʿIrāqī, finding the region's whole population to be unbelievers and hypocrites, was able to convert a large number to Nūrbakhshī Islam.[13] The use of the term *munāfiq* (hypocrite) suggests that a part of the population of Baltistan was already Muslim but not of the "correct" persuasion, though the number to whom that can have applied is likely to have been very small.

ʿIrāqī's success in proselytizing during his short visit was likely quite limited since Mīrzā Ḥaydar Dughlāt found the region bereft of Islam upon his arrival there in 1532.[14] The region must, however, have developed a small core of dedicated Nūrbakhshīs since ʿIrāqī's son Shaykh Dāniyāl was able to use it as a haven between approximately 1543 and

---

"We cannot expect our simple-minded Balti lovers of stories to be very logical" (Sagaster, "The Kings of Baltistan and Other Kings," 54).

11. Cf. Agha Hussain Hamadani, "Sayyid Ali Hamadani's Visit to Kashmir and Baltistan and Islamisation of the Society," *Journal of Central Asia* 8, no. 2 (1985): 185–90; Abdul Ghani Sheikh, "A Brief History of Muslims in Ladakh," in *Recent Research on Ladakh 4 & 5: Proceedings of the 4th and 5th International Colloquia on Ladakh,* ed. Henry Osmaston and Philip Denwood (London: School of Oriental and African Studies, 1995), 189–92; Prem Singh Jina and Zain-ul-Abidin, "Islam in Ladakh," in *The Religious History of Ladakh,* ed. Prem Singh Jina (Delhi: Sri Satguru Publications, 2001).

12. Holzworth, "Islam in Baltistan," 14–19.

13. *TA,* 376.

14. Dughlat, *Tarikh-i Rashidi,* 1:360, 2:256.

1550.[15] Later tradition claims that first ʿIrāqī himself and then Dāniyāl counted some regional rulers within Baltistan among their disciples. Although this idea cannot be verified from any near-contemporary source, the ʿAwn ʿAlī Shāh manuscript of the *Tuḥfat al-aḥbāb* contains a marginal note reporting a conversation between ʿIrāqī and a ruler named Rāʾy Bahrām in which the latter asks ʿIrāqī to leave someone behind him to complete the work of Islamization started by him (and before him ʿAlī Hamadānī). As a consequence of this conversation, the note continues, a Sufi named Ḥaydar agreed to return to the area the following summer with his son.[16] There is reason to suspect this report since it occurs in a marginal gloss, and the king's alleged reference to ʿAlī Hamadānī suggests a later origin, when the idea of Hamadānī's sojourn in the region had become established in local tradition. Some attempts at reconstructing the genealogies of local rulers do place Bahrām Chō in the last half of the fifteenth century, though the reliability of such projections is shaky, to say the least.[17] The likelihood of a later origin of this idea is further strengthened by Dughlāt's report that a ruler named Bahrām Chō submitted to Sultan Saʿīd Khān of Kashghar when the latter invaded Baltistan in 1532.[18] It is possible that Dughlāt's work, one of the very few historical sources that comment on Balti history, indirectly led to the generation of a meeting between a king named Bahrām and ʿIrāqī.

The first autochthonous Muslim ruler of Baltistan attested to in a number of sources is ʿAlī Rāʾy, or ʿAlī Mīr, a follower of Twelver Shīʿism who ruled from at least as early as 1578. ʿAlī Rāʾy became a vassal of the Mughal Empire after Akbar's conquest of Kashmir in 1586 and retained his kingdom (and even expanded it into Ladakh)[19] by pursuing

15. *BS,* 347–48.

16. *TA,* 381.

17. Cf. Söhnen, "On Reflections of Historical Events in Balti Folk Songs," 585, where the various possibilities for the dates are compared.

18. Dughlat, *Tarikh-i Rashidi,* 1:362, 2:258.

19. The history of Ladakh is, on the whole, better documented than that of Baltistan through the chronicles of the kings of Ladakh. However, the period 1450–1550, crucial for our purposes, is least certain (cf. Neil Howard, "What Happened between 1450 and 1550 A.D.?" in *Recent Research on Ladakh 6: Proceedings of the Sixth International Colloquium on Ladakh, Leh 1993,* ed. Henry Osmaston and Nawang Tsering [Bristol: University of Bristol, 1997], 121–37). For a general summary of

close ties with the Mughal court.[20] He and his successors eventually came into conflict with the Mughals and the area was brought under firm imperial control in 1637.[21] All reports on ʿAlī Rā'y and his descendants make it clear that he was a proponent of Twelver Shīʿism, making the relevance of his rule to the development of a Nūrbakhshī community quite beside the point.[22]

While Indian and Central Asian historical sources do provide some information about the dynastic politics of Baltistan in the sixteenth and seventeenth centuries, they say little about religious matters besides commenting on the fierce Shīʿism of some rulers that brought them into conflict with missionaries sponsored by neighboring Sunnī states. The first concrete evidence for the presence of Nūrbakhshī communities in Baltistan comes not from literary sources but from the prayer niche of a small mosque in Thagas that bears the year 1012/1603–4 and is ascribed to the missionary work of two brothers, Sayyid Shāh Nāṣir Ṭūsī and Sayyid ʿAlī Ṭūsī, who likely arrived from Chinese Turkestan.[23] In a later period, two descendants of ʿIrāqī, Mīr ʿĀrif (d. 1651) and Mīr Abū Saʿīd (d. 1684), are also reported to have come for the purpose of missionizing. The graves of the latter two and Mīr Abū Saʿīd's sons Mīr Yaḥyā and Mīr Mukhtār continue to be regarded as important shrines by the current Nūrbakhshī communities (see figure 4).[24] While there is relatively little available to describe the activities of any of these

Ladakhi history, assembled from literary as well as oral accounts and presented in a Christian missionary vein, see A. H. Francke, *A History of Western Tibet* (London: Partridge, 1907).

20. Holzworth, "Islam in Baltistan," 24–28.

21. Ibid., 31. For the overall context of Mughal influence in the region, see the summary of literature in Husain Khan, "Mughal Relations with Baltistan and the Northern Region, from Akbar to Aurangzeb," *Journal of Central Asia* 7, no. 1 (1984): 179–89.

22. Information regarding ʿAlī Rā'y is surveyed in Holzworth, "Islam in Baltistan," 26–29. His strident Twelver identity may, of course, have had a negative impact on the Nūrbakhshī communities. However, we have no information on such matters for the region from the period.

23. Afridi, *Baltistan in History,* 27, 118; *TB,* 114–17.

24. *TB,* 118–19; Lakhnavī, *Tārīkh-i Jammūñ,* 592–93. It is difficult to say whether the Mīr ʿĀrif venerated by the Nūrbakhshīs is the same person as the Shāh

FIGURE 1: Decorated Interior, Nūrbakhshī Chaqchan Mosque, Khaplū, Baltistan. Photo by Jamal Elias.

individuals, the numerical growth and geographical expansion of the community is reflected in the various premodern Nūrbakhshī mosques and khānqāhs strewn throughout the region exhibiting Kashmiri features in architectural style. Of these, only two more have been dated positively; namely, the khānqāh at Kirīs, built in 1118/1706–7, and that at Skardu (figure 3), dated 1130/1717–18.[25] According to a recent survey, all Nūrbakhshī sayyids in the Shigar valley trace their descent to Mīr Yaḥyā, while Nūrbakhshī sayyids from other parts of Baltistan see Mīr Mukhtār as their ancestor.[26]

The general lack of concrete information on the societies of Baltistan and Ladakh for the period means that commenting on the issue of Islamization in the region is largely a matter of informed speculation. Drawing on other recent discussions of Islamization in South Asia, I would like to offer here a hypothesis regarding the process that

ʿĀrif, mentioned in a number of Mughal sources, who traveled to Kashmir and Baltistan. He is reported to have paid homage to the emperor Akbar upon his conquest of Kashmir in 1589 (cf. Holzworth, "Islam in Baltistan," 25–26).

25. Afridi, *Baltistan in History,* 27.

26. Andreas Rieck, "The Nurbachshis of Baltistan: Crisis and Revival of a Five Centuries Old Community," *Die Welt des Islams* 35, no. 2 (1995): 163–66.

FIGURE 2: Façade to the Sanctuary, Nūrbakhshī Khānqāh, Khaplū, Baltistan. Photo by Jamal Elias.

may prove helpful in future research. My evidence for the theory given below is admittedly meager, though I find it necessary to offer a new perspective given the inadequacy of existing indigenous as well as scholarly explanations. Based on three interrelated factors, I suggest that between the sixteenth and the eighteenth centuries Baltistan's population became Muslim gradually. The three factors are (1) the region's ecology and social structure; (2) its location as a periphery of Tibetan culture, quite removed from the political and intellectual centers of Tibetan Buddhism; and (3) the influence of Muslim religious figures and powerful invading armies arriving in the area from adjacent Kashmir and Chinese Turkestan.[27]

In considering the question of Islamization, it is a matter of considerable note that Baltistan and Kargil are now predominantly Muslim,

27. My hypothesis regarding the Islamization of Baltistan is influenced particularly by Richard Eaton's perspective on the issue of religious conversion in South Asia (cf. Eaton, *The Rise of Islam on the Bengal Frontier,* 113–34; idem, "Approaches to the Study of Conversion to Islam in India," and idem, "Comparative History as World History: Religious Conversion in Modern India," *Journal of World History* 8, no. 2 [1997]: 243–71). To date, the most sophisticated study of Islamization in any local context is DeWeese, *Islamization and Native Religion in the Golden Horde.* DeWeese's exemplary methodology—analyzing the structures, ramifications, and

FIGURE 3: Interior with Prayer Cells, Nūrbakhshī Khānqāh, Skardū, Baltistan. Photo by Jamal Elias.

while the Leh region remains majority Buddhist.[28] This fact casts doubt on the theory proffered by Holzworth, to date the most authoritative commentator on the issue, that Baltistan became Muslim due primarily to the military and proselytization pressure of its powerful Muslim neighbors.[29] Since Ladakh was subject to the same pressures but did not Islamize, a fuller explanation requires a more careful consideration of other contingencies. Following other recent studies, I suggest looking to local factors to explain the region's religious culture in the relevant centuries. While rulers and proselytizers are certainly significant for

interpretations of conversion narratives—is impossible to apply to the Balti case due to a severe lack of literary sources as well as of detailed ethnographic fieldwork in the oral tradition.

28. For information on the Muslims of Kargil, see Ghulam Mohi-Ud-Din Dar, *Kargil: Its Social, Cultural, and Economic History* (New Delhi: Dilpreet Publishing House, 1999); Baqar Raza Rizvi, *The Balti: A Scheduled Tribe of Jammu and Kashmir* (New Delhi: Gyan Publishing House, 1993); Nicola Grist, "Muslim Kinship and Marriage in Ladakh," in *Anthropology of Tibet and the Himalaya,* ed. Charles Ramble and Martin Brauen (Zurich: Ethnological Museum of the University of Zurich, 1993), 80–92. All these sources leave much to be desired in either academic rigor or depth of information and analysis. The only extended methodologically sophisticated ethnography of the region is Srinivas, *The Mouths of People, The Voice of God.*

29. Holzworth, "Islam in Baltistan," 23.

FIGURE 4: Shrines of Mīr ʿĀrif and Mīr Abū Saʿīd, Thagas, Baltistan. Photo by Jamal Elias.

explaining the Islamization of Baltistan, in the end, mass conversion is best understood by showing why and how the incoming religion may have made sense in the worldview and circumstances of the local population in question. Instead of seeing conversion as the advent of a foreign element, we should, in the words of Richard Eaton, "adopt the perspective of the society actually undergoing change and see conversion not as a passive acceptance of a monolithic, outside essence, but as a 'creative adaptation' of the unfamiliar to what is already familiar."[30]

The difference between Baltistan and Ladakh is in part due to religious allegiances of the region's ruling elite, a matter itself linked to ecological factors. As argued by Richard Emerson, Baltistan is unique among its neighboring regions in having developed small-scale agrarian states from an early period.[31] Emerson attributes Baltistan's difference to the area's process of land appropriation for agricultural use: this process, allowed by the region's topography, was institutionalized through a specific set of social relations that are still prevalent in local villages.[32] These social relations led to the development of states,

30. Eaton, "Comparative History as World History," 46.
31. Emerson, "Charismatic Kingship," 100–101.
32. Ibid., 104–9.

which then developed a system of political patronage that connected royal lineages at the top to larger networks of power diffused across the landscape. This particular form of political organization sometimes facilitated the establishment of foreign invading rulers since the state's stability arose from the local network, which could be appropriated by invaders when they came to sit at its apex. The ultimate legitimacy of such rulers was linked to their function as warriors who defended the state against other predators, thus mediating between the local population and the larger world.[33]

Emerson's theory on Balti political structures is useful in discussing the process of Islamization since it posits a greater degree of inner hierarchical cohesion in Balti society as compared with neighboring regions. His view makes it possible to see how the conversion of ruling lineages in Baltistan may have had a considerable impact on the society at large. Once the rulers became Muslim, the new religious identity worked its way downward into the society through established hierarchies and social mechanisms such as intermarriage.[34] However, this hypothesis still leaves open the question of why the rulers of Baltistan were more open to conversion to Islam than their Ladakhi counterparts. The answer may be that, at least by the fifteenth century, Baltistan had a fairly tenuous connection to transregional Tibetan culture and its strongly Buddhist identity. Baltistan's status as the westernmost periphery of Tibetan culture is indicated, for example, by the fact that the hero Kesar, who is celebrated throughout the Tibetan region and as far east as Mongolia, appears in Balti folk literature sometimes as a Ladakhi invader of Baltistan rather than as a local protagonist.[35] Similarly, it is significant that while the region does contain some

33. Ibid., 137–39.

34. It is interesting that the Moravian missionary A. H. Franke, writing as late as 1929, comments that Islamization in Ladakh is a far more significant phenomenon as compared to the efforts of Christian missions due primarily to intermarriage between Muslim men and Buddhist women. In comparing Ladakh and Baltistan, he states that the Christian missions were somewhat successful in Ladakh among both Buddhists and Muslims, but a Swedish missionary working in Khaplū had not been able to attract a single convert despite years of efforts (cf. A. H. Francke, "Islam among the Tibetans," *MW* 19 [1929]: 134–40).

35. Cf. Sagaster, "The Kings of Baltistan and Other Kings," 49–55.

Tibetan inscriptions (which have yet to be studied), a thirteenth-century Tibetan encyclopedia of outstanding Buddhist scholars refers to only one Balti authority.[36] There is also no mention of Buddhist monasteries in Baltistan in Tibetan sources (while Ladakh has clear links to Tibet in this sphere),[37] evincing the fact that Baltistan was not integrated into the social networks and monastic lineages of Tibetan Buddhism.

These clues about Balti religious history suggest that, at least at the time of Islamic expansion in the region, Tibetan Buddhist institutions and ideas were not deeply ingrained in the region. What the Muslim proselytizers encountered upon arriving in Baltistan was very likely a local religious culture with a relatively slight Buddhist overlay. It is possible, in fact, that only the rulers were Buddhist (because of their origins in Gilgit or Turkestan) and that the population at large practiced indigenous religion.[38] The region's physical and cultural distance from the centers of Tibetan Buddhism did not encourage the permeation of Buddhism deeper in society, and when Muslims arrived, the rulers found it to their greater advantage to align themselves with the Islamic heritage of their neighbors due to the latter's power and prestige. The numerous Kashmiri and Turkestani invasions of the region may indeed have facilitated the transition to Islam, but the transition probably resulted from the advantages of being Muslim, particularly for the ruling elite, rather than religious duress; the population then followed the lead of the rulers, and the overall process of Islamization resulted from the integration of a culturally isolated region into the ambit of Islamic civilization.

If we accept this hypothesis about the Islamization of Baltistan, then Nūrbakhshī success in the region would have occurred in the initial stages of the historical process that eventually led to the region's integration into larger South Asian states. Nūrbakhshī proselytizers were

36. Holzworth, "Islam in Baltistan," 21, citing Luciano Petech, *A Study of the Chronicles of Ladakh* (Calcutta: Oriental Press, 1939), 134. Holzworth considers this fact an indication of the "flourishing" of Tibetan culture, while to me it seems to indicate more the weak presence of a Tibetan literary tradition in Baltistan.

37. Cf. David Snellgrove and Tadeusz Skorupski, *The Cultural Heritage of Ladakh* (Boulder, Colo.: Prajña Press, 1977).

38. Emerson, "Charismatic Kingship," 110–15.

among the first Muslim missionaries to arrive in the region from Kashmir, though they were followed closely by Twelver Shīʿī competitors. The ruling elite may have preferred one or another sect at a given time, but the fact that both coexisted together implies a lack of complete partiality to either. As discussed below, the Nūrbakhshī share of the local population may have been greater before the nineteenth century, though the suggestion by some contemporary Nūrbakhshīs that all the Muslims of Baltistan were at one point Nūrbakhshī is likely an exaggeration.[39] It should further be noted that sectarian affiliation in this social context meant primarily a differentiation in ritual practice and the acknowledgment of religious charisma in individuals linked to the imāms or Nūrbakhshī founders. There is little evidence that the members of the various sects in the local population concerned themselves with the dogmatic principles discussed in the literate versions of the traditions. Such "rationalized" theological discussions surfaced only once the region developed greater concrete connections to the culture of Mughal India between the sixteenth and the eighteenth centuries. Baltistan and Ladakh's annexation into the Kashmiri state in the nineteenth century was a further step in the direction of integration into greater South Asian political structures.

From the early nineteenth century onward, the paucity of literary sources at our disposal begins to ease because of the reports generated by British officials and administrators of the Dōgra rulers of Jammu, who purchased Kashmir from the British Crown in 1840 and were able to expand their territory into neighboring areas.[40] The activity of Twelver Shīʿī proselytizers in the region also intensified in the nineteenth century, now taking a greater toll on Nūrbakhshī communities than in previous centuries.[41] Economic and administrative modernization

39. *TB,* 150.

40. For a summary of the history of Kashmir and adjacent regions in the first half of the nineteenth century, see Ahmad Hasan Dani, *A History of Northern Areas of Pakistan* (Islamabad: Lok Virsa, 1989), 242–73. This as well as other discussions of the modern history of Kashmir contain substantial problems and the topic still awaits a thorough academic investigation done outside the context of the dispute between India and Pakistan over the territory.

41. Rieck, "Nurbachshis of Baltistan," 160–65; *TB,* 112–23; *Navā-yi ṣūfiya*

of the area also began in this period, linking Baltistan and nearby areas to the government's seat in Kashmir, and the process has intensified since the independence of India and Pakistan in 1947.

As parts of the princely state of Kashmir, Baltistan and Ladakh were included in the territorial dispute between India and Pakistan that erupted into a war in 1948. The eventual line of control (the present de facto border) divides the Nūrbakhshīs between Pakistan (in Baltistan) and a relatively less significant presence in India (particularly the Kargil district in Ladakh).[42] The international boundary has shifted occasionally over the course of the past fifty years, most notably during Indian-Pakistani military conflicts in 1965, 1971, and 1999. In addition, the communities on both sides of the border have been subject to low-scale shelling constantly since 1985, and the region has generally become heavily militarized. At least on the Pakistani side, the army's arrival has increased the pace of modernization through infrastructure projects such as a network of roads and bridges, electricity supply, and improvement in means of communications.[43] Baltistan is currently a part of the Northern Areas administrative division in Pakistan that is outside the jurisdiction of the four provinces of the country and consequently does not have direct representation in Pakistan's elected federal bodies.[44] The Indian state, on the other hand, considers Ladakh an integral part of India as a region in the state of Kashmir.

Moving from political history to religious identity, it is noteworthy that although the Nūrbakhshīs established themselves as a distinct Islamic group in Baltistan and Ladakh, they lost their explicit belief in Nūrbakhsh's messianic claim some time between the mid-seventeenth and the nineteenth centuries. As discussed in chapter 6, the messianic claim was clearly a part of the Nūrbakhshī tradition transmitted to

---

[hereafter, *NS*] 5 (July 1992): 7; 6 (Nov. 1992): 20–21; 7 (Mar. 1993): 29; 10 (Feb. 1994): 25; 2 (Oct. 1994): 8–9; 5 (Jan. 1995): 10–11.

42. For the involvement of Baltistan and Ladakh in the Kashmir dispute between India and Pakistan, see Janet Rizvi, *Ladakh: Crossroads of High Asia,* 2d rev. ed. (Delhi: Oxford University Press, 1996), 78–95.

43. Nasīm, *Baltistān: Tārīkh va siyāsat,* 51–67.

44. The grievances resulting from this lack of representation are discussed at length in various books by Balti authors, including Nasīm's *Baltistān.*

Kashmir. A manuscript of ʿIrāqī's biography *Tuḥfat al-aḥbāb* completed in 1642 and preserved in Baltistan calls Nūrbakhsh the mahdī on numerous occasions without any sense of embarrassment.[45] However, modern Nūrbakhshīs now see the Shīʿī Twelfth Imām, Muḥammad al-Mahdī, as the awaited messiah.[46] This modification of belief is at least partly self-conscious since Nūrbakhshī authors in recent years have either completely ignored the claim (despite relying on sources that report it)[47] or have preempted it by suggesting three different possibilities: first, that the title of mahdī applies to Nūrbakhsh only in the literal sense since he had received direct divine guidance;[48] second, that Nūrbakhsh was wrongfully accused of pretending to be the mahdī by his enemies;[49] and, third, that he had claimed only to be a deputy (*nāʾib*) of the mahdī and not the messiah himself.[50] An interesting vestige of the claim's acceptance in earlier times is the fact that every year Nūrbakhshīs still celebrate the birthdays of Nūrbakhsh and the Twelfth Imām on the same day.[51]

Despite denying or glossing over the messianic claim, modern Nūrbakhshīs in Baltistan in particular contend that they should be regarded

45. *TA,* 12, 27, 73, 74. It is noteworthy, however, that Nūrbakhsh's work *Risālat al-hudā,* which contains the most extensive discussion of his messianic claim, is not mentioned in any Indian source.

46. *NS* 10 (Feb. 1994): 11. Nūrbakhsh, *Kitāb al-iʿtiqādīya,* Arabic text with Urdu translation by Abū l-ʿIrfān Muḥammad Bashīr (Karachi: an-Nadva al-Islāmīya Nūrbakhshīya, 1988), 49–52. For a critical edition of this text (published without any contact with the living Nūrbakhshī tradition), see Molé, "Professions de foi de deux Kubrawīs: ʿAlī-i Hamadānī et Muḥammad Nurbaḫš," 133–203.

47. *TB,* 174–77.

48. Akhūndzāda, *Tuḥfa-yi Kashmīr,* 574–79.

49. *NS* 9 (Nov. 1993): 23.

50. Khādim Ḥusayn Pandavī, *Aḥvāl va āṣār-i Shāh Sayyid Muḥammad Nūrbakhsh Quhistānī* (Karachi, 1987), 68–73, cited in Reick, "Nurbachshis of Baltistan," 166 (note 41). I have not seen the original source for this argument, but it is likely to be an Urdu translation of Ṣadaqiyānlū's book by the same title that also argues that Nūrbakhsh's references to himself are to be read as *nāʾib-i mahdī* (*AA,* 75).

51. *NS* 7 (Mar. 1993): 24; *NS* 45 (Jan. 1999): 26; *NS* 54 (Dec. 1999): 26. Another interesting perspective presented by a Nūrbakhshī author is that Ḥusayn, the third Shīʿī imām, was actually a revealer of the esoteric secrets of annihilation (*fanāʾ*) and subsistence (*baqāʾ*) since his activism forced people to divulge their true

as a distinct community. The assertion stems from the belief that Sufis in general are neither Sunnī nor Shīʿī,[52] though the notion that being a Sufi is equivalent to belonging to one of the recognized legal schools such as the Ḥanafī, Shāfiʿī, or Twelver Shīʿī maẕhab does not accord with the general Islamic schematization of the matter. For Muslims at large, being a Sufi represents acceptance of intellectual and social paradigms such as mystical philosophy or affiliation with a particular order, a matter quite separate from being Sunnī or Shīʿī. The Nūrbakhshīs' argument hinges on their reliance on Nūrbakhsh's work *al-Fiqh al-aḥwaṭ* for legal matters, which deliberately intermingles aspects of Sunnī and Twelver Shīʿī legal positions to create a new synthesis.[53] Following Nūrbakhsh's own contention, the Balti Nūrbakhshīs claim that injunctions of *al-Fiqh al-aḥwaṭ* are a return to the pure Islam of Muḥammad's days, which Nūrbakhsh was compelled to institute anew in the fifteenth century. As discussed in chapter 4, Nūrbakhsh's legal perspective was a part of his messianic claim. Consequently, the modern Nūrbakhshīs do continue a distinctive aspect of Nūrbakhsh's teaching even though this is not seen as a result of his having claimed himself the mahdī. He is, instead, perceived as a renewer (*mujaddid*) of faith who attempted to reform religion and society at a crucial moment in Islamic history.[54]

In addition to the historical connection to Nūrbakhsh's legacy, the community in Baltistan in particular has been host to a continuous line of spiritual guides called Nūrbakhshī pīrs, who trace their lineage to Shams ad-Dīn ʿIrāqī. This institution parallels other South Asian Sufi communities organized around genealogical charisma leading back to prominent mystical guides.[55] The Nūrbakhshī pīr, whose traditional

---

allegiances between good and evil (*NS* 5 [July 1992]: 6). Such an exteriorization of secrets is generally associated with the apocalypse in Islamic thought, and this modern Nūrbakhshī author's viewpoint may reflect the sect's messianic legacy.

52. *NS* 4 (Mar. 1992): 13.

53. Shakūr ʿAlī Anvar Kūravī, *Āʾina-yi islāmī* (Karachi: an-Nadva al-Islāmīya Nūrbakhshīya, 1991): 160; *NS* 11 (June 1994): inside front cover, 11.

54. He is called a great renewer (*mujaddid*) in the translator's introduction to *al-Fiqh al-aḥwaṭ* (page h).

55. For a perceptive analysis of the role played by pīrs in contemporary Pakistani

residence is in the town of Kirīs in Baltistan, was given complete obeisance in religious matters based solely on his genealogy until quite recently. As discussed below, however, modernizing trends have brought his position in question in recent decades and he has been challenged regarding his actual knowledge of correct Nūrbakhshī beliefs and practices. The current pīr, Shams ad-Dīn Sayyid Muḥammad Shāh Nūrānī, has chosen to align himself with one major faction in the community since 1992, further decreasing his position in the eyes of those adhering to the opposing camp.[56]

Besides Nūrbakhshī self-perception, external observers who have visited Baltistan in the past two centuries have also consistently found it intriguing that Nūrbakhshī practices are unique due to the deliberate mixing of Sunnism and Shīʿism.[57] An easily observable facet of this amalgamated system is that, following Nūrbakhsh's own opinion, the Balti Nūrbakhshīs deem it acceptable to offer the Islamic ritual prayer according to both Sunnī and Shīʿī methods; it is preferable, however, to perform it like the Sunnīs in winter and the Shīʿīs in summer.[58]

The Modern Nūrbakhshīya in Ladakh and Baltistan

The remainder of this chapter presents the history and current concerns of the modern Nūrbakhshī communities in Ladakh and Baltistan. Baltistan receives greater attention since virtually all of the material available for discussing the specific concerns of the Nūrbakhshīs comes to us in the form of Urdu literature generated by Baltis in the twentieth century. The Nūrbakhshīs of Ladakh constitute a small percentage of the region's Muslims and they have not produced a distinctive modern discourse. The relative silence of Ladakhi Nūrbakhshīs reflects also

---

society, see Katherine Ewing, *Arguing Sainthood: Modernity, Psychoanalysis, and Islam* (Durham, N.C.: Duke University Press, 1997).

56. Ghulām Ḥasan Nūrbakhshī, *Ṣūfīya-yi nūrbakhshīya* (Khaplū: Idāra Khuddām aṣ-Ṣūfīya, 1994), 14.

57. John Biddulph, *Tribes of the Hindoo Koosh* (Calcutta: Government Printing Office, 1880), 123–25; Shafīʿ, "Firqa-yi Nūrbakhshī," I:60–63.

58. Nūrbakhsh, *al-Fiqh al-aḥwaṭ*, 52. Nūrbakhshī legal tendency to mix and accommodate different sectarian positions is reflected in other matters discussed in the book as well.

the fact that, since the partition of the region in 1948, the larger cultural dynamic in Ladakh has been dominated by the relationship between Muslims as a whole and Buddhists.[59] The only ethnographic information regarding the region noteworthy for our purposes is that the Nūrbakhshīs of Ladakh are largely of rural domicile and are considerably less affluent than the Twelver Shīʿī sayyid families settled in the cities.[60] They are also a fluid group, forming coalitions with and intermarrying freely with other types of Muslims as well as Buddhists. For example, one village studied extensively by Srinivas contained three mosques: one Sunnī, one Nūrbakhshī, and one a family mosque open to both Sunnī and Nūrbakhshī clan members.[61] Beyond such anecdotal reflection, the perspectives of Ladakhī Nūrbakhshīs can be discussed only through ethnographic fieldwork beyond the scope of this book.

In contrast with their Ladakhi coreligionists, the Nūrbakhshīs of Baltistan are more numerous and have been quite active in reflecting on their identity over the course of the twentieth century. While a full appreciation of Balti Nūrbakhshīs' perspective requires ethnographic fieldwork not undertaken to date, we can ascertain the general outlines of communal discussion from literary sources.[62] The discourse on

59. For a review of this relationship, including the occasional eruption of serious contention and violence, see Martijn van Beek and Kristoffer Brix Bertelsen, "No Present without Past: The 1989 Agitation in Ladakh," in *Recent Research on Ladakh 7: Proceedings of the 7th Colloquium of the International Association for Ladakh Studies Held in Bonn/Sankt Augustin, 12–15 June 1995,* ed. Thierry Dodin and Heinz Räther (Ulm: Ulmer Kulturanthropologische Schriften, 1997), 43–65. These authors argue that the political disturbances in Ladakh are not based entirely on Buddhist-Muslim communal grounds but reflect the gradual development of Ladakhi national identity in opposition to Kashmiri control going as far back as the beginning of Dōgra rule in 1840.

60. Srinivas, *The Mouths of People, The Voice of God,* 18–19.

61. Ibid., 60–71.

62. Nūrbakhshī communities in specific have not been the subject of ethnographic fieldwork until now. The little that is available for Baltistan at large includes Ursula Sagaster, *Die Baltis: Ein Bergvolk im Norden Pakistans* (Frankfurt am Main: Museum für Völkerkunde, 1989); idem, "Women in a Changing Society: Baltistan 1992," in *Recent Research on Ladakh 7: Proceedings of the 7th Colloquium of the International*

identity was necessitated because the mixed religious system that makes the Nūrbakhshīya stand apart from mainstream Islamic sects has led to the community becoming a target for conversion by proponents of other sects in the modern period. The percentage of Nūrbakhshīs in the Baltistan population has progressively decreased since the last quarter of the nineteenth century in particular due to proselytization by South Asian Muslim groups with more sophisticated material and ideological tools at their disposal.[63] The change in the religious makeup of the area can be traced eventually to the development of modern Islamic identities in South Asia under British colonial rule. Exemplified most prominently by the religious schools of Deoband and Farangī Maḥall and the Ahl-i Sunnat movement led by Sayyid Aḥmad Khān Barēlvī, Islamic scholarly classes of South Asia began a far-reaching modernization process in the second half of the nineteenth century.[64] These movements considered Muslims' "loss" of India to British colonial rule an indication of a culture in decline and generated new interpretations of traditional concepts such as *tajdīd* (renewal), *iṣlāḥ* (reform), and *jihād* (activist struggle) to regain their ancestors' glories. The objective of such reform initiatives was to employ modern tools of communication to reach out to the widest possible array of Muslims in the land

---

Association for Ladakh Studies Held in Bonn/Sankt Augustin, 12–15 June 1995, ed. Thierry Dodin and Heinz Räther (Ulm: Ulmer Kulturanthropologische Schriften, 1997), 413–19; idem, "Observations Made during the Month of Muharram, 1989, in Baltistan," in *Anthropology of Tibet and the Himalaya,* ed. Charles Ramble and Martin Brauen (Zurich: Ethnological Museum of the University of Zurich, 1993), 308–17; Adam Nayyar, *Astor: Eine Ethnographie* (Stuttgart: Steiner Verlag, 1986).

63. Nūrbakhshīs today believe that nearly the whole population of the region was Nūrbakhshī until the 1890s. This is doubtful since the local rulers of Skardū had probably converted to Twelver Shīʿism as early as the sixteenth century, and even the ruler of Khaplū (a district still majority Nūrbakhshī) converted to Shīʿism before his death in 1890 (cf. Rieck, "Nurbachshis of Baltistan," 162–65).

64. Cf. Barbara Metcalf, *Islamic Revival in British India: Deoband, 1860–1900* (Princeton, N.J.: Princeton University Press, 1982); Francis Robinson, *The ʿUlama of Farangi Mahall and Islamic Culture in South Asia* (London: C. Hurst, 2001); Lini May, *The Evolution of Indo-Muslim Thought after 1857* (Lahore: Sh. Muhammad Ashraf, 1970); Usha Sanyal, *Devotional Islam and Politics in British India: Ahmad Riza Khan Barelwi and his Movement, 1870–1920* (New Delhi: Oxford University Press, 1996).

with the hope of a general renaissance of both religious practice and political influence.

Balti Nūrbakhshīs have been the subject of attempted conversion by both Sunnī and Shīʿī modernized groups. The first Sunnī proselytizer to arrive in Baltistan was Muḥammad Ḥusayn "Mullā Pēshāvarī," who settled in Kirīs upon the invitation of the Nūrbakhshī pīr of the period around 1873. The pīrs had exclusive rights to religious guidance of the community until this point, but, ironically, the arrival of Mullā Pēshāvarī led to a gradual devolution of religious power. He avoided offending Nūrbakhshī sensibilities by teaching Nūrbakhsh's *al-Fiqh al-aḥwaṭ* along with Sunnī books, but he encouraged students to seek further education outside the confines of Baltistan, which eventually resulted in the creation of a Baltistani class of Sunnī scholars who first abandoned the Nūrbakhshī viewpoint after being trained in seminaries in the Punjab and the United Provinces and later took on the charge of reforming the whole Nūrbakhshīya.[65]

In part because of coincidence and in part because of the group's zealous program, a majority of Nūrbakhshī converts to Sunnism in the late nineteenth century became attached to the puritanical Indian Ahl-i Ḥadīs̱ subsect. This group considers the Qurʾan and the ḥadīth the only sources for religious law and regards reliance on any later literature a religious innovation (*bidʿa*).[66] Their objections to the Nūrbakhshīya were thus even stronger than those of more mainstream Sunnīs, imbuing them with extra fervor for their mission.

Proponents of the Ahl-i Ḥadīs̱ have been active in Baltistan throughout the past century and have used both confrontational and conciliatory tactics to gain converts. Examples of the confrontational technique include a book entitled *Tuḥfa-yi Tibbat,* by Mawlavī ʿAbd al-Ḥaqq, published in 1946 and distributed gratis in Baltistan.[67] The book consisted

65. Rieck, "Nurbachshis of Baltistan," 170; *TB,* 150–54.

66. For the various connotations attached to the name of this group, see Sh. Inayatullah, "Ahl-i Ḥadīth," *EI*², 1:259–60; Metcalf, *Islamic Revival,* 268–96; Sanyal, *Devotional Islam,* 38–41, 201–5; Aziz Ahmad, *Islamic Modernism in India and Pakistan* (Oxford: Oxford University Press, 1967), 113–22.

67. Rieck, "Nurbachshis of Baltistan," 173; *NS* 10 (Feb. 1994): 16.

of harshly negative judgments on supposed Nūrbakhshī beliefs and practices by an Ahl-i Ḥadīs̱ scholar in Delhi. The overall effect of this book on Ahl-i Ḥadīs̱ efforts was more negative than positive since the pace of conversion to the sect slowed quite drastically after its publication. The damage it caused was so obvious that a later Ahl-i Ḥadīs̱ author proclaimed the book the work of an enemy out to destroy the sect.[68] The aggressive strategy of *Tuḥfa-yi Tibbat* was replicated on the ground by Ahl-i Ḥadīs̱ followers who attempted to take over the main Nūrbakhshī khānqāh in Kirīs (the seat of Nūrbakhshī pīrs) by filing a court case that claimed that it was a Sunnī congregational mosque (*jāmiʿ*).[69] They lost the legal suit and had to pray in one section of the hospice until the construction of a separate Sunnī mosque in Kirīs in 1972.[70]

A less belligerent but equally effective tactic used by the Ahl-i Ḥadīs̱ to gain converts has been to try to convince the Nūrbakhshīs that they are in fact a branch of the Sunnīs and should both accept more "normative" beliefs and resist the growth of Shīʿī influence. They have, in this regard, printed at least three allegedly Nūrbakhshī works since the late 1960s (*Najm al-hudā, Mashjar al-awliyāʾ*, and *Ṭabaqāt-i nūrīya*), constituting generated or modified texts that present the Nūrbakhshīya as a Sunnī subsect.[71]

As mentioned above, Twelver Shīʿism has had a longer presence as an established sect in Baltistan than any branch of Sunnism. Consequently,

68. He suggested that the book in no way reflected Ahl-i Ḥadīs̱ scholars' attitude toward Nūrbakhshīs and had been written by a Shīʿī agent pretending to be an Ahl-i Ḥadīs̱, whose real aim was to discredit the sect in Baltistan (ʿAbd ar-Rashīd Anṣārī Baltistānī, *Daʿvat-i iṣlāḥ* [Karachi, 1958], cited in Rieck, "Nurbachshis of Baltistan," 174, and *TB*, 153–54).

69. Rieck reports that the current pīr showed him documents pertaining to the case in 1992 ("Nurbachshis of Baltistan," 174).

70. As late as 1913, an Italian observer reports that Nūrbakhshīs and Twelver Shīʿīs prayed together in the congregational mosque in Kirīs (Giotto Danielli, "Winter Excursions in Baltistan," in *The Italian Expedition to the Himalaya, Karakoram, and Eastern Turkestan, 1913–1914,* ed. Filippo de Filippi [London: Edward Arnold, 1932], 91–93). That this did not seem to be a problem implies that sectarian boundaries have hardened gradually over the twentieth century.

71. Rieck, "Nurbachshis of Baltistan," 176–77; *NS* 10 (Feb. 1994): 16–17.

Twelver proselytizers have enjoyed even greater success in the region during the past century, and a majority of Baltistan's population today adheres to that sect.[72] These Shīʿīs have also written books to promote the idea that the Nūrbakhshīya is, in essence, a deviant version of Twelver Shīʿism that requires some correction through the spread of normative beliefs.[73] In addition, they have pursued the task of publishing Nūrbakhshī works with slight modifications even more vigorously than the Sunnīs and have, at this point, succeeded in creating a rift among even those Nūrbakhshīs who explicitly consider themselves a separate group.

Both Sunnī and Shīʿī proselytizers are active in Baltistan today.[74] In recent years, they have begun to further their causes chiefly through developmental activities carried out by religious nongovernmental organizations active in the area. They have made particularly effective use of facilities that provide basic amenities such as rural medical clinics and networks of schools instructing children in both religious and secular subjects.[75] While Sunnī and Shīʿī proselytizing activity has definitely acted to lower the proportion of Nūrbakhshīs in the population of Baltistan (estimated at 25 percent at present), it is the very threat posed by these sects that has forced the Nūrbakhshīs to become self-conscious about their sectarian uniqueness, causing some among them to attempt to modernize their discourse in the image of their more powerful counterparts.

The Nūrbakhshīs began to awaken to the danger of becoming extinct around the middle of the twentieth century, when Sunnī and Shīʿī proselytization had already taken a heavy toll. The first significant effort in the defense of an independent Nurbakhshīya was Akhūnd Ḥamza ʿAlī's book *Nūr al-muʾminīn,* written in response to the pro-Shīʿī

72. Nasīm, *Baltistān,* 115–20, 127–28, 145–47; Muḥammad Ḥasan Ḥasrat, *Tārīkh-i adabīyāt-i Baltistān* (Skardū: Muḥammad Ḥasan Ḥasrat, 1992), 29–30; *TB,* 156–58.

73. Rieck, "Nurbachshis of Baltistan," 169; *NS* 10 (Feb. 1994): 17.

74. As evident in letters to *Navā-yi ṣūfiya,* the push to convert is particularly strong in the Shigar valley, where Nūrbakhshīs constitute only about 15 percent of the population (*NS* 8 [July 1993]: 27; 7 [Apr. 1995]: 29).

75. Rieck, "Nurbachshis of Baltistan," 177–79.

propaganda being announced by Āghā Sayyid ʿAlī Kirīsī Mūsavī.[76] Sayyid ʿAlī was born into the Nūrbakhshī pīr family in 1891–92 and began his religious education with the Ahl-i Ḥadīs̱ preachers active in the area at the time.[77] His exposure to Sunnism and Shīʿism during this period made him realize that although the Nūrbakhshīs thought themselves a distinctive community, they were not heirs to comprehensive literary traditions of the kind available to bigger sects. He then began to seriously consider the possibility that Nūrbakhshīya was a branch of Twelver Shīʿism, a view concretized further during a period of study in Najaf, Iraq, some time before 1920.

Upon his return from Iraq, Sayyid ʿAlī, in accord with the Shīʿī tradition of pious dissimulation (*taqīya*), concealed his conversion to Twelver Shīʿism and continued to enjoy the status of a scholar and member of the family of Nūrbakhshī spiritual heads. His plan during this period was to sow the seeds of doubt among Nūrbakhshīs so that they would be ripe for conversion at a later date. He achieved considerable success in this mission and toward the end of his life was even able to declare his Shīʿī affiliation openly.

Akhūnd Ḥamza ʿAlī attempted to negate Sayyid ʿAlī's major argument that the Nūrbakhshīya was a Twelver Shīʿī subsect by enumerating more than one hundred explicit differences between the two in his book *Nūr al-muʾminīn*. His response proved effective at the time his book was published (1956), but the viewpoint of Sayyid ʿAlī and his followers resurfaced in the bitter debate over the sect's name that has profoundly affected the sect's scholars in the 1980s and 1990s.

What's in a Name? The Imāmīya *Question*

Over the last two decades, the most significant issue regarding Nūrbakhshī self-definition has been whether the sect should call itself Ṣūfīya Nūrbakhshīya or Imāmīya Ṣūfīya Nūrbakhshīya. The crucial factor at stake

76. Nūrbakhshī, *Ṣūfīya-yi nūrbakhshīya,* 6, 11; Ḥājjī Muḥammad Ḥasan Nūrī, *al-Ḥujja al-bāligha fī is̱bāt al-imāmīya aṣ-ṣūfīya an-nūrbakhshīya* (Kirīs: Anjuman-i Ṣūfīya Imāmīya Nūrbakhshīya, 1997), 102–6.

77. Sayyid ʿAlī Mūsavī, *Kāshif al-ḥaqq,* ed. Sayyid ʿAbbās al-Mūsavī (n.p., n.d., but printed in Iran after 1980), cited in Rieck, "Nurbachshis of Baltistan," 171–72; *TB,* 156–57, and *NS* 10 (Feb. 1994): 17.

in this debate is the sect's relationship with Shīʿism, a matter whose seriousness needs to be understood by first appreciating the sectarian politics of Pakistan's Northern Areas since the early 1980s. Sunnīs and Shīʿīs have been at loggerheads with each other in a number of regions in Pakistan since the 1970s, including numerous armed confrontations resulting quite often in assassinations and more indiscriminate killings.[78] The issue is of particular significance in the Northern Areas since this is the only region in Pakistan today to have a Shīʿī majority.[79] In this political atmosphere, the term *imāmīya* makes any group an unmistakable part of the Shīʿī faction, with all the privileges and problems attendant on such a designation becoming applicable to the group.

Although quite aware of this political context, Nūrbakhshīs for and against the term *imāmīya* have argued their cases from internal historical and doctrinal grounds. The two factions involved in the debate are both agreed that Nūrbakhshīya as a doctrinal entity is separate from Twelver Shīʿism.[80] However, the current position of the pro-*imāmīya* group states that Nūrbakhshīs are closely akin to Twelver Shīʿīs since

78. For the background and history of these conflicts, see Muhammad Qasim Zaman, "Sectarianism in Pakistan: The Radicalization of Shiʿi and Sunni Identities," *Modern Asian Studies* 32, no. 3 (1998): 689–716; Saleem Qureshi, "The Politics of the Shia Minority in Pakistan: Context and Development," in *Religious and Ethnic Minority Politics in South Asia,* ed. Dhirendra Vajpeyi and Yogendra Malik (Riverdale, Md.: Riverdale, 1989), 109–38; Munir D. Ahmed, "The Shiʿis of Pakistan," in *Shi'ism, Resistance, and Revolution,* ed. Martin Kramer (Boulder, Colo.: Westview Press, 1987), 275–88.

79. Cf. Andreas Rieck, "Sectarianism as a Political Problem in Pakistan: The Case of the Northern Areas," *Orient* 36, no. 3 (1995): 429–48; idem, "From Mountain Refuge to 'Model Area': Transformation of Shiʿi Communities in Northern Pakistan," in *Perspectives on History and Change in the Karakorum, Hindukush, and Himalaya,* ed. Irmtraud Stellrecht and Matthias Winiger (Cologne: Rüdiger Köppe Verlag, 1997), 215–31. The worst incident of violence in the Northern Areas took place in Gilgit in May 1988, when dozens of local Shīʿīs were killed by thousands of armed Sunnī militia members who had congregated on the city from surrounding areas.

80. Nūrī, *Ḥujja bāligha,* 138 (pro-*imāmīya*); Nūrbakhshī, *Ṣūfīya-yi nūrbakhshīya,* 29–108; *NS* 4 (Dec. 1994): 33; 25 (Dec. 1996): 29; 26 (Jan. 97): 14.

they both accept the same chain of twelve imāms from ʿAlī to the Mahdī. This agreement makes the Nūrbakhshīs "imāmī" in the literal sense, and since the differences between them and Twelvers are only in matters of practice, the two should be regarded only as branches of a single sect (Imāmīya Shīʿa and Imāmīya Nūrbakhshīya).[81]

The faction against the adoption of *imāmīya* (represented most prominently by the multitalented scholar Ghulām Ḥasan Ḥasanū) argues that, in keeping with historical precedent, to use the term would inevitably lead to the Nūrbakhshīya merging into Twelver Shīʿism. The faction points to Nūrbakhshī historical books (including works by Nūrbakhsh himself, ʿIrāqī's biography, and later authors) that never employed the term in defining the sect and contends that both scholarly and conventional usage of the term *imāmīya* have been limited to Twelver Shīʿism throughout Islamic history.[82] The Nūrbakhshī community has attempted to put this matter to rest by holding two conventions of major Nūrbakhshī scholars of both persuasions.[83] At neither of these meetings, held in 1982 and 1993, could the participants be made to agree on a single view, and the eventual resolution both times, technically accepted by everyone, was that all discussions about the name must cease immediately in the interest of promoting communal unity. This clearly has not happened since the most extensive discussions on the issue from both sides were published in 1994 and 1997, and scholars associated with the anti-imāmīya viewpoint claim to have received anonymous threatening letters in 1996.[84]

Echoing the tactics of external proselytizers, the pro-imāmīya faction of the Nūrbakhshīya has, in recent years, published books of doubtful

81. Nūrī, *Ḥujja bāligha,* 134–42. The pro-*imāmīya* faction may have proposed a more direct acquiescence to the Twelver cause earlier since Nūrī's opponent accuses him of changing his mind to suit the circumstances (Nūrbakhshī, *Ṣūfīya-yi nūrbakhshīya,* 137).

82. Nūrbakhshī, *Ṣūfīya-yi nūrbakhshīya* 138–67.

83. For detailed partisan reports on these conventions, see Nūrbakhshī, *Ṣūfīya-yi nūrbakhshīya,* 12–29, and Nūrī, *Ḥujja bāligha,* 10–14, 20–23. Nūrī has also published another book on this issue (*Firqa-yi nājīya* [Kirīs, 1994])—a work not presently available to me.

84. *NS* 22 (Aug. 1996): 36, contains notices of protest against such intimidation tactics.

authenticity that support its contentions. Among these, the *Kitāb rafᶜ al-ikhtilāf* (Book on the removal of disagreement) attributed to Nūrbakhsh is said to have been "discovered" in a library in Iran (or the Aya Sofya Library in Istanbul). Its usefulness for the pro-*imāmīya* cause stems from the text's explicit acceptance of nearly all principles of Twelver Shīʿism, though it can be dismissed as a forgery quite easily on the basis of both style and content.[85] In the last two decades similar controversies have erupted about other books as well, and it is likely that the struggle over defining the Nūrbakhshī "canon" will continue.

In addition to its own significance, the issue of the sect's name has catalyzed a separate discussion on the authority of the Nūrbakhshī pīr as the ultimate source and ratifier of religious opinion.[86] The Nūrbakhshī pīr is technically the repository of the movement's hereditary charisma, but by the beginning of the twenty-first century C.E., the office has become a formality. ʿAwn ʿAlī Shāh (1928–91), who became the thirty-ninth pīr of the community in 1951, acted more as a mediator than a participant in the debate over the sect's name.[87] The question of the office's authority has acquired greater urgency since the accession of ʿAwn ʿAlī Shāh's son Shams ad-Dīn Sayyid Muḥammad Shāh Nūrānī, who became pro-*imāmīya* during a trip to Karachi around 1992.[88] His personal confession has aided the *imāmīya* cause considerably since even the opposing party is obliged to show him nominal reverence in keeping with custom.[89] However, the anti-*imāmīya* has refused to acquiesce to his authority on the matter of the name,

---

85. Muḥammad Nūrbakhsh, *Mīrās̱-i ʿārifāna-yi jāvidāna*, ed. Muḥammad Bihishtī (Tehran: Intishārāt-i Marvī, 1993). The text has been published in Pakistani editions as well (in Karachi), and an Urdu translation was published in Baltistan itself and distributed free of charge in 1993 by a Shīʿī student organization (cf. *NS* 8 [July 1993]: 25–26). For extended arguments against and in favor of this book, see *NS* 8 (July 1993): 14–18; Nūrī, *Ḥujja bāligha*, 129–35.

86. The dispute over the name has been transplanted to the Nūrbakhshī community of Ladakh as well. A photograph of a Nūrbakhshī mosque in Kargil has "jāmiʿ masjid-i ṣūfīya Nūrbakhshīya" on its façade (cf. *NS* 44 [Nov.–Dec. 1998]: cover).

87. *NS* 4 (Mar. 1992): 12–14, 9 (Nov. 1993): 12–14.

88. Nūrbakhshī, *Ṣūfīya-yi nūrbakhshīya*, 14.

89. This is evident from the numerous notices on him in the *Navā-yi ṣūfīya*, a

suggesting further that he should not be given special treatment because of his lineage and that his opinion should matter only to the degree of his actual familiarity with Nūrbakhshī literature.[90] The pīr's supporters, however, insist that his views on legal matters in particular should be accepted as the norm by all Nūrbakhshīs.[91]

A recent report indicates that the controversy over the name and its implications is ongoing and has been the subject of another attempt at resolution. A branch of the Nūrbakhshīya Youth Federation in Bulghār, a small locality in Baltistan, was credited with bringing all prominent scholars and community leaders of the community to an agreement over the question in late 1999. This organization mailed the text of the agreement to all concerned to get their final opinions before publishing it in book form. A videocassette of the meeting leading to the agreement was also available for purchase.[92] Despite the renewed effort, the question is unlikely to disappear because of external pressure on the community to conform to norms that are Twelver Shīʿī since a majority of the population of Baltistan belongs to this sect.[93] As evident also in other periods of the history of the Nūrbakhshīya, the larger Islamic community resists the idea of a group defining itself outside mainstream sectarian boundaries. In both medieval Iran and Kashmir, the Nūrbakhshīya was eventually forced to merge into Twelver Shīʿism over relatively short periods. It remains to be seen whether in coming decades the same will occur in Baltistan or whether, in a break from

journal otherwise in the opposing faction, and in the approval notice appended to the Urdu translation of *Tuḥfat al-aḥbāb,* published by someone unambiguously in the anti-*imāmīya* camp (Akhūndzāda, *Tuḥfa-yi Kashmīr,* 3).

90. *NS* 7 (Mar. 1993): 8–10 (article by Ghulām Ḥasan Nūrbakhshī). In a personal conversation in July 1998, Ghulām Ḥasan derided the Pīr's scholarly competence by saying that even the letters he writes as certification for Nūrbakhshī books have to be prepared by the authors themselves. He has little interest in the books' contents and essentially uses his signature as a formal seal.

91. Letters in *NS* 5 (July 1992): 20–21.

92. *NS* 52 (Sept.-Oct. 1999): 37–38.

93. This possibility is already evident in that the same issue of *Navā-yi ṣūfīya* that reports on the agreement contains a number of letters complaining about the absence of articles on the twelve imāms in the journal (ibid., 40).

history, modern conditions will allow the preservation of a distinct identity.

Modernism versus Traditionalism in the Contemporary Community

Quite aside from internal controversies, the intellectual outlook of the Nūrbakhshīya today is divided between positions that can be designated "modernist" and "traditionalist." The issue of the sect's identity in between Sunnism and Shīʿism continues to ferment, while Nūrbakhshīs of both persuasions are divided on the issue of modernizing among themselves in a pattern familiar from the impact of modernization on Islamic societies in general. While conclusive proof for this assertion can be obtained only through ethnographic research, the general outline of the tension can be observed through surveying the content of recent publications by Nūrbakhshī authors. The journal *Navā-yi ṣūfīya* is particularly useful in this regard since it contains articles by authors of a number of different viewpoints, along with regular features written by well-known Nūrbakhshī authorities.[94]

The modernist/traditionalist dichotomy in the Nūrbakhshīya is a result of social processes such as rural-to-urban migration, international migration, access to secular and professional education, the impact of mass media, and so forth. While it is safe to say that most Nūrbakhshīs alive today would fall into the traditionalist camp (the majority of adherents live in rural settings and are illiterate), the modernists have influence and presence beyond their proportion due to their higher economic and social status.

The Modernists

The modernist Nūrbakhshī position essentially accepts modern liberal imperatives such as scientific knowledge and the principle of individual rights and responsibilities, but insists that religion is a necessary part of

94. This journal started in 1986 but had to close within a year for lack of funds. It was revived as a triennial in 1991 and since September 1994 has been published fairly regularly on a monthly basis. For the journal's aims and perspective, see *NS* 5 (July 1992): 2–3.

both personal and social existence. The emphasis on science is apparent in the *Navā-yi ṣūfīya,* a publication that, though ostensibly devoted to religious concerns, contains articles on topics such as astronomy, biology, physics, genetics, ecology, biodiversity, AIDS, and computers.[95]

While the efficacy of science is presented as self-evident, Nūrbakhshī modernists proclaim that the scientific worldview should lead to an affirmation of the truths of Islam, rather than its negation in favor of pure materialism.[96] They contend that communism failed precisely because it did not recognize the importance of religion, and the same problem is the root cause of moral decay in Western societies;[97] as proven by the case of Christina Onassis, material wealth alone cannot bring lasting happiness or tranquility;[98] furthermore, even disciplines like modern Western medicine are now beginning to acknowledge the crucial role of religion as exemplified in a Harvard surgeon's appreciation of the power of prayer reported in *Time* magazine.[99] Being an observant Muslim, it is contended, gives relief from peculiarly modern ailments such as clinical depression.[100]

For Nūrbakhshī modernists, the critique of modern materialism is coupled with a program of social reform that needs to be implemented in Muslim societies. The ultimate aim is to construct a new social order based on Islamic (specifically, Sufi) ethics,[101] but before that can be accomplished, social evils such as uncritical and excessive devotion toward the hereditary pīr, antinomian behavior, professional begging, extravagant wedding parties, and giving and accepting dowries need to

95. Most contributions in this category belong to Ghāzī Muḥammad Naʿīm, the journal's chief editor, who is also a medical doctor (cf. *NS* 9 [Nov. 1993]: 2–3; 2 [Oct. 1994]: 12–16; 21 [July 1996]: 25–26; 24 [Nov. 1996]: 2–4; 25 [Dec. 1996]: 24; 26 [Jan. 97]: 18–23).

96. For example, one author argues that science is basically only the experimental method for proving what should be accepted from religion on the basis of scripture (Kūravī, *Āʾina-yi islāmī,* 164–65).

97. *NS* 3 (Nov. 1994): 2.

98. *NS* 2 (Oct. 1994): 20.

99. *NS* 11 (July 1994).

100. *NS* 22; 4 (Dec. 1994): 2.

101. *NS* 9 (Nov. 1993): 9.

be exterminated. The list of things deemed harmful continues to be modified as exemplified by the castigation of improper television programming now available to young people through the popularization of satellite receivers all across Pakistan, including Baltistan.[102]

Nūrbakhshī modernism also includes an anti-imperialist stance extending from Pakistani nationalism.[103] The most prominent objections in this vein are leveled against "Western" encroachments on Islamic societies generally, with particular concern for international issues such as Indian control over Kashmir and wars in Bosnia and Chechnya. In an extreme case of this tendency, one author tried to make Nūrbakhshīya a part of the myth of Pakistan's creation, suggesting that the prominent Persian and Urdu poet Muḥammad Iqbāl (d. 1936) had been influenced by Nūrbakhsh's works.[104]

While critical of Western cultural imperialism in the form of popular culture, modernist Nūrbakhshīs do not consider the orientalist appropriation of Sufism as a field of study to be a threat. While Muslims' neglect of their heritage is bemoaned quite often, Nūrbakhshīs cite Western experts such as Louis Massignon, R. A. Nicholson, A. J. Arberry, Henry Corbin, Hermann Landolt, and Michel Chodkiewicz in support of their arguments.[105] This acceptance is understandable since most authors in this category believe that the Nūrbakhshīya is an exclusively Sufi movement.

The Traditionalists

In contemporary Nūrbakhshī literature, the traditionalist position is represented by those who insist on the authority of the pīr and the practitioners of Islamic jurisprudence. Scholarly and lay legalism is observable in the section of *Navā-yi ṣūfīya* entitled *Majmūʿa-yi sharīʿat-i muḥammadīya* (collection of Muḥammadan law) in which ʿAllāma Abū

102. *NS* 4 (Mar. 1992): 6; 10 (Feb. 1994): 11; 5 (July 1992): 16–17; 9 (Nov. 1993): 25; 26 (Jan. 1997): 29.

103. *NS* 3 (Nov. 1994): 32. The nationalist sentiments of Nūrbakhshī authors surface in virtually all Nūrbakhshī publications.

104. *NS* 8 (July 1993): 3.

105. *NS* 6 (Nov. 1992): 16; 2 (Oct. 1994): 31; 10 (Aug. 1995): 12; 31 (July 1997): 7.

l-ʿIrfān Muḥammad Bashīr gives extensive answers to questions sent in by readers. A majority of the questions he chooses to answer deal with issues of ritual purity and matters of personal law such as marriage, divorce, and inheritance. It is instructive to examine the particulars of a few of these answers to situate the traditionalist tendency relative to the modernists.

In the period 1991–99, ʿAllāma Bashīr has given his opinion against both birth control and all in vitro fertilization (IVF) techniques that use sperm from anyone other than the recipient woman's husband. His objection to contraception hinges on a conspiracy theory according to which Western nations' support for family-planning efforts are aimed at slowing the worldwide growth of Muslim population.[106] He rejects it on this basis alone, without getting into more sophisticated arguments about creation and the workings of the human body.[107] A child produced through IVF using sperm and egg not from a married couple is deemed illegitimate and has to abide by the normal strictures for such a case.[108] Maintenance of traditional norms in society is emphasized by advocating beards for men and the veil (*ḥijāb*) for women.[109] In the economic sphere, ʿAllāma Bashīr considers it illegal to charge interest under any circumstances following the Qurʾanic injunction, and even insurance is forbidden since it is a form of gambling.[110]

Although ʿAllāma Bashīr's opinions represent a traditionalist (and ultraconservative) perspective, the strict observance of Islamic legal injunctions is in itself a modern "reformist" phenomenon among the Nūrbakhshīs. As in other parts of the Islamic world, premodern religion

106. *NS* 7 (Mar. 1993): 16.

107. ʿAllāma Bashīr's opinion stands on the exceptionally conservative side of the Islamic spectrum in this regard since a majority of the most influential legal scholars in the modern period have deemed contraception legal (cf. Munawar Ahmad Anees, *Islam and Biological Futures: Ethics, Gender and Technology* [London: Mansell, 1989], 164–87; Ziba Mir-Hosseini, *Islam and Gender: The Religious Debate in Contemporary Iran* [Princeton, N.J.: Princeton University Press, 1999], 38–40).

108. *NS* 3 (Nov. 1994): 29. Such a child does inherit from the parents like their legitimate children, but he or she is not allowed to lead the prayers in a congregation.

109. *NS* 6 (Feb. 1995): 26; 12 (Oct. 1995): 18.

110. *NS* 10 (Feb. 1994): 28; 31 (July 1997): 12.

in Baltistan relied more on charismatic practices such as invocations, ideas about the auspicious and inauspicious, and the possibility of miracles. Aspects of such practices are still observable: they can be seen when visiting the area and also in the extended lists of auspicious and inauspicious months, days, and hours attached to the legal manual *Daʿvāt-i ṣūfīya.*[111] The legal conservatism is thus in itself an aspect of the influence of modernized Islam from outside of Baltistan.

Utilizing the Tools of Modernity

While still lagging behind the more resourceful sects in Pakistan, in the last twenty years the Nūrbakhshīs have made considerable progress in adopting modern methods of defining and preserving communal identity. The collective literature reviewed in this chapter is itself an indication of the sect's growing consciousness of its heritage and interests.

The foremost methods used by the Nūrbakhshīya to create self-awareness have so far included printing traditional books in the original languages as well as in Urdu translations and voicing opinions through journalistic activity. The lithograph press played a formative role in the development of modern Muslim identity in South Asia in the colonial period (ca. 1800–1947),[112] and history has repeated itself with the Nūrbakhshīs' adoption of this medium in postindependence Pakistan. Citing the case of the Iranian revolution of 1979 to stress the importance of publication,[113] some Nūrbakhshīs advocate a collective

111. This book has been published in different Urdu translations by the groups divided over the *imāmīya* issue, but both editions contain the lists: (Muḥammad Bashīr, trans., *Daʿvāt-i ṣūfīya Urdū,* 5th printing [Karachi: Nadva Islāmīya Nūrbakhshīya, 1995], 366–400; Sayyid Khurshīd ʿĀlam, *Daʿvāt-i ṣūfīya imāmīya,* 2d printing [Karachi: Anjuman-i Falāḥ va Bahbūd-i Sarmūñ, 1997], 435–72). For an excellent study of the "mixing" of folk belief, popular Islam, and modernity in contemporary Pakistan, see Ewing, *Arguing Sainthood.*

112. Cf. Francis Robinson, "Technology and Religious Change: Islam and the Impact of Print," *Modern Asian Studies* 27, no. 1 (1993): 229–51; Muhammad Qasim Zaman, "Commentaries, Print, and Patronage: *Ḥadīth* and the Madrasas in Modern South Asia," *BSOAS* 62, no. 1 (1999): 60–79; Barbara Metcalf, *Perfecting Women: Maulana Ashraf ʿAli Thanawi's Bihishti Zewar, A Partial Translation with Commentary* (Berkeley: University of California Press, 1990), 19–23.

113. *NS* 4 (Mar. 1992): 8; 7 (Mar. 1993): 7–8. For the use of mass media in the

effort by the community to promote literacy and widely disseminate all available Nūrbakhshī literature. The *Navā-yi ṣūfīya* has carried appeals to all readers for help in locating manuscripts of Nūrbakhshī texts,[114] and it is through the intermediacy of print that a steady stream of communication has now started between the Nūrbakhshīs of Baltistan and Ladakh.[115] In recent years, Nūrbakhshī religious invocations recited after ritual prayers have become available on audio cassette and compact disc,[116] and information about the sect's history can now be found on the Internet as well.[117]

Nūrbakhshīs have also undertaken an extensive program of building or repairing religious schools, libraries, and mosques in both Baltistan and those urban centers in Pakistan that are host to substantial Nūrbakhshī populations (Islamabad, Karachi, Lahore, Quetta).[118] At least one free medical dispensary has been started in Baltistan, and plans are in the offing for a major center for the sect's activity, to be named Ayvān-i Nūrbakhsh, in Islamabad.[119]

Concomitant with its desire to create a permanent center in Pakistan's capital, the Nūrbakhshīya has put pressure on the country's federal government to increase the statistic that reports the number of adherents of the sect in the national census.[120] Nūrbakhshī candidates

---

Iranian Revolution and the ensuing Islamic republic, see Sreberny-Mohammadi and Mohammadi, *Small Media, Big Revolution,* and Peter Chelkowski and Hamid Dabashi, *Staging a Revolution: The Art of Persuasion in the Islamic Republic of Iran* (New York: New York University Press, 1999).

114. *NS* 11 (June 1994): inside back cover.

115. Letters from Ladakh in *NS* 38 (Mar. 1998): 30.

116. *NS* 11 (June 1994): 34; 28 (Feb. 1995): 28.

117. In February 2002, a webpage representing the Nūrbakhshīya was available at www.geocities.com/Athens/Crete/2994.

118. Virtually all issues of *Navā-yi ṣūfīya* contain details of the construction and functioning of such institutions. The building of Nūrbakhshī *madrasas* has occurred at the same time as the number of such schools belonging to all active sects has mushroomed all over Pakistan. For the causes and effects of such schools, see Jamal Malik, *Colonialization of Islam: Dissolution of Traditional Institutions in Pakistan* (New Delhi: Manohar, 1996).

119. *NS* 10 (Aug. 1995): 22; 11 (Sept. 1995): 26.

120. *NS* 25 (Dec. 1996): 28.

have won local elections (the Northern Areas do not have representation in Pakistan's federal parliament), and the movement's youth wing, the Nūrbakhshīya Youth Federation, has been particularly active in pursuing political objectives.[121] The movement has lobbied the government for its fair share of Zakāt money distributed by federal authorities,[122] appealing also to community members for financial support for schools and libraries being run by local associations all over Baltistan.[123]

Recent Charismatic Figures

The literature already surveyed in this chapter indicates that contemporary Nūrbakhshīs are guided by a number of different types of scholars active in Baltistan, Ladakh, and migrant communities. In addition to these historians, legal scholars, and lay experts, the community has been host to two charismatic movements functioning around individuals claiming special inspiration. The first of these involves Sayyid Manẓūr Ḥusayn Hamadānī, who arrived in Baltistan from the Pakistani city of Sargodha some time in the 1960s. Described by some as a showman or pretender, he "gave the Nurbachshis an illusion of their importance beyond Baltistan and promised them to convert the whole world to their *maẕhab* [legal school]."[124] His aide in this ambition was a charismatic

121. *NS* 7 (Mar. 1993): 24; 11 (June 1994): 28; 6 (Feb. 1995): 29. The significance of the "youth" in the contemporary situation is evident from the fact that the second convention for the resolution of the *imāmīya* dispute was organized by NYF. They wanted the scholars to come to a mutual agreement and threatened to not let anyone leave the Chaqchan mosque no matter how long it took to achieve this outcome (Nūrbakhshī, *Ṣūfīya nūrbakhshīya*, 6).

122. *NS* 7 (Apr. 1995): 27; 10 (Aug. 1995): 21. The government of Pakistan collects Zakāt (an obligatory alms tax) from bank deposits and distributes the funds to local level committees throughout the country charged with promoting social welfare. The Nūrbakhshī contention here is that their communities have not received a share of these funds proportional to the Nūrbakhshī populaton in Baltistan.

123. *NS* 11 (June 1994): 27.

124. Rieck, "Nurbachshis of Baltistan," 182–83. Sydney Schuler, working in Baltistan in 1974, also reports the fame of a certain Hamadānī very likely to be this Manẓūr Ḥusayn (Schuler, "The 'Story of the Creation of Shigar' of Wazir Ahmad," 104–5).

local scholar named Sayyid Muḥammad Mukhtār, from Thallē, who preached on his behalf in the area's villages. Indications of the program's success can be seen in Hamadānī having received large contributions of land from his followers and his having married at least one local woman much younger than himself. According to the superintendent of police in 1998, he was investigated by the authorities as a possible fraud, but though admonished he was exonerated. The police had interviewed his Balti wife to see if she would say that she had been married to him by force (which would have led to a case of abduction), but the woman denied this and forcefully exerted herself as Hamadānī's lawful spouse. His influence declined in the wake of the police intervention, and he died in Skardū (Baltistan's capital) some time between 1994 and 1997. His followers—called Hamadānīs, or the Hamadānī Group—still exist in the Shigar valley, where they mourn his death in the same way as Shīʿīs lament Ḥusayn. On special occasions, they circumambulate the shrine over his grave.[125]

The second charismatic leader to gain influence in Baltistan has been a former soldier named Faqīr Ibrāhīm, who has called on people to become more actively religious in their daily lives. He is said to have begun a movement for the economic and educational betterment of Nūrbakhshīs some time around 1985, and over the last decade has devoted himself to the spiritual rejuvenation of the community.[126] He is particularly interested in the practice rather than the academic discussion of Sufism (according to one Nūrbakhshī scholar, he is barely literate). His status within the community was on the rise in the 1990s, as indicated by his trips to visit members of the sect living in Lahore and Karachi, where he addressed both men and women in separate functions. Like Hamadānī, because of his personal piety and charisma Faqīr Ibrāhīm has also had some success in converting non-Nūrbakhshīs to the sect.[127] Along with religious fashions, he is credited with popularizing a kind of traditional Balti hat that had fallen into disuse earlier in this century.

125. *NS* 30 (June 1997): 29.

126. *NS* 11 (June 1994): 20–21.

127. Ibid., 25. He went on the ḥajj to Mecca as well in 1995 (*NS* 11 [Sept. 1995]: 28).

The personalities of both Hamadānī and Faqīr Ibrāhīm contain aspects of charismatic leadership and the general notion of renewal of religious prestige. However, Hamadānī's son, a captain in the Pakistani army, is not inclined to don the father's mantle, and since Faqīr Ibrāhīm is concerned almost exclusively with personal religiousness, his activity is unlikely to lead to a full-fledged movement to transform the Nūrbakhshī community. The examples of Hamadānī and Faqīr Ibrāhīm do, however, point to the significance of charismatic leadership in the community, albeit in a "democratized" form. The personal appeal of a leader has now gained strength in comparison with the hereditary charisma of the pīr within the community, and it is likely that this process of devolution of religious authority will continue in the community's further evolution.

The Vision of the Modern Nūrbakhshīya

The Nūrbakhshīya of Baltistan and Ladakh has carried Muḥammad Nūrbakhsh's messianic legacy into the modern period by remembering Nūrbakhsh as a great reformer. His messianic claim has been left aside, but the centerpoint of his reform continues to mark the sect's identity as a movement that attempts to go beyond the Sunnī-Shīʿī conflict. The sect's intentionally hybridized ideology survived well in a relatively isolated region between the sixteenth and the nineteenth centuries, but it has come under pressure by modernized versions of Sunnism and Shīʿism in the last two centuries. The larger sects do not regard the Nūrbakhshīya as a threat to themselves, but their proselytizing zeal has lead them to think of the Nūrbakhshīya as a prize available for the taking. Ironically (although not surprisingly), the Sunnī-Shīʿī scramble for Nūrbakhshī converts has awakened the sect's intellectual elite into action.

Increased internal debate over the sect's identity has, in its turn, led to internal divisions along a number of different lines. Given the intense politicization of sectarian groups in Pakistan, it makes sense that the sect's connection to Shīʿism, and to a lesser extent its Iranian origins, have become the most significant matter of dispute within the community. Those who see the sect as a part of the Shīʿī spectrum have insisted on the use of the term *imāmīya* in its name, while those with exclusionist leanings find this term an anathema. The latter group can be considered pro-Sunnī in the sense that the absence of the marker *imāmīya* makes the group a de facto part of the majority of Pakistanis who do not have to use an extra name to define themselves communally.

Modernization has undoubtedly been the greatest force to affect the Nūrbakhshīya in the last hundred years. It has created a modernist/traditionalist divide in the sect's membership based upon socioeconomic and political factors, and the adoption of modern technology and organizational methods has led to greater social self-awareness in the community. The Nūrbakhshīya in the most recent decades has, thus, regained some of the distinctive ideology stemming from Nūrbakhsh's messianic claim announced more than five centuries ago.

The Sufi worldview that Nūrbakhsh himself considered the very basis of his messianic claim endures well in the modern Nūrbakhshī community. The modern faction arguing that the group should be seen as a sect separate from Sunnism and Shīʿism bases itself in the idea that the term *sufi* in fact indicates a separate legal school (*maẕhab*). The considerable importance of charismatic and pietistic Sufism is also evident in the success achieved by Manẓūr Ḥusayn Hamadānī and Faqīr Ibrāhīm in the community in recent years. Based on these issues, the modern Nūrbakhshīya accords well with Nūrbakhsh's original desire for an Islamic reformation led by a messiah who stood out from the ordinary due to his mystical accomplishments.

Conclusion

The review of the formation and development of the Nūrbakhshīya in this book highlights three particular aspects of Islamic religious history. First, it provides a detailed example for Islamic messianism as a historical phenomenon (and not just a theoretical proposition), with significant implications for the development of the tradition as a whole. Second, it stresses the significance of Sufi ideas in the intellectual and social histories of Muslim societies. And third, the Nūrbakhshīya's fate in various sociohistorical settings sheds light on the dynamics of Islamic sectarianism. For all three issues, the examples of Muḥammad Nūrbakhsh and his followers advance our understanding of not only the movement itself but the overall development of the Islamic tradition between the late medieval and modern periods.

Nūrbakhsh articulated his messianic claim in the context of an extensive but diffuse Islamic expectation of the savior. His own discourse was primarily addressed to the dogma of Twelver Shīʿism, his natal affiliation and the only major Islamic sect to maintain an intensive focus on the messiah beyond the thirteenth century. The standard Twelver Shīʿī doctrine on the issue identifies a particular person, the Twelfth Imām, as the messiah and elaborates the figure through traditions incorporating symbolic and mythological elements concerned with eschatology and salvation history. Like that of other would-be messiahs, Nūrbakhsh's principal concern in reinterpreting the traditional doctrine was to humanize the myth by fleshing it out both literally and metaphorically. He saw the combination of his life's circumstances and his own and his companions' visions as the fulfillment of all prophecies associated with the messiah in the Twelver tradition.

In terms of external conditions, Nūrbakhsh was aided in his case for the messianic claim by the unstable sociopolitical environment of the

Islamic East during the fourteenth and fifteenth centuries. The perpetual march of armies through the region and the resulting weakening of social institutions under Tīmūr and his successors made it possible for Nūrbakhsh to think of the contemporary period as the time for the end of one era and the beginning of a new dispensation. Moreover, these same factors made his message meaningful to his audience and garnered him a following throughout his life.

In greater measure than sociopolitical factors, Nūrbakhsh's message came out of an intellectual tradition in which the notion of a supreme religious guide had become concretized in the centuries prior to his own birth. Nūrbakhsh combined the hereditary charisma of the Shīʿī imām with Sufi ideas about the seal of sainthood and the perfect man to produce his particular messianic doctrine. After the destruction of the Sunnī ʿAbbāsid caliphate by the Mongols in the thirteenth century, proponents of some minority sects such as Twelver Shīʿism operated under a relatively free intellectual atmosphere in the Islamic East during the fourteenth and fifteenth centuries. Consequently, religious life during that period exhibited a perceptible increase in sentimental attachment to the claims of the ʿAlid house across sectarian lines in Islamic societies. In addition, the large complex of intellectual and social ideas subsumed under the term *Sufism* had become the predominant mode of religiosity in the Islamic East by the time of Nūrbakhsh's birth. Whether consciously or unconsciously, Nūrbakhsh combined elements of Shīʿism and Sufism prevalent in his environment to generate a combined system. The contemporary appeal of his message stemmed from this combination's resonance with the intellectual and social reality of Nūrbakhsh's audience.

After Nūrbakhsh's own career, the relative loosening of sectarian boundaries allowed the Nūrbakhshīya to exist as a distinct movement in Iran and Kashmir for brief periods during the fifteenth and sixteenth centuries. There was crucial leeway in this respect due to the region's rulers and states not patronizing the religious establishment of particular sects to the exclusion of scholars affiliated with rival groups. Late Tīmūrid rulers in Iran and Central Asia maintained a deliberate ambivalence regarding their preference for Sunnism or Twelver Shīʿism, making it impossible for one sect to be completely dominant.

Similarly, in the progressively Islamizing Kashmir, the Shāhmīrī rulers and their viziers were open to a competition between different sects and Sufi orders for the sake of gaining the elites' allegiance and patronage. The consolidation of the Ṣafavid and Mughal Empires in Iran and India, respectively, during the sixteenth and seventeenth centuries brought this sectarian fluidity to an end. The stridently Twelver Shīʿī and Sunnī identities of the two empires meant a narrowing of space between the sects, leading eventually to a gradual disappearance of independent movements such as the Nūrbakhshīya. The momentary success and eventual demise of the Nūrbakhshīya in Iran and Kashmir are best understood as a part of these larger developments in Islamic history.

The case of the Nūrbakhshīya illustrates a fact of the Islamic tradition: that state and elite patronage are crucial issues when discussing sectarian space. In the absence of a formalized ecclesiastic structure ("the church"), Muslim religious life through the centuries has been guided by classes of religious divines identified as scholars, jurists, and Sufis. These classes are themselves divided into either groups identified as sects, subsects, and Sufi orders or historical movements emphasizing particular issues such as methodology and reform. It is in this sense that we can talk of Sunnism; Twelver and Ismāʿīlī Shīʿism; the Kubravī and Naqshbandī orders; Akhbārī and Uṣūlī tendencies within Twelver Shīʿism; and modern Sunnī movements such as the South Asian Ahl-i Ḥadīs̱ and Deobandīs. Islamic sectarianism is thus a multitiered and continually evolving phenomenon, and the relative success or failure of a group is tied to material factors such as political patronage or suppression and the freedom or lack thereof to proselytize. A state represented by a ruling house or the political and economic elites of a Muslim society, therefore, have a decisive function in the degree to which a particular group can flourish within society. Nūrbakhsh's lack of success in the political sphere and the rise and fall of the Nūrbakhshīya in both Iran and Kashmir under his successors underscore this crucial conjunction between the religious and sociopolitical aspects of Islamic history.

The case of modern Nūrbakhshīs in Baltistan and Ladakh, who survive as a distinct movement due to historical and geographical factors, exemplifies the way in which the dynamics of Islamic sectarianism have been transformed in the era of nation-states. The continuing significance of state patronage in modern times is evident from the fact that the Nūrbakhshīs of Baltistan have come under intense Twelver Shīʿī pressure only since the Iranian revolution of 1979, in which Twelver Shīʿī jurists eventually emerged as victors under the leadership of Ayatollah Khomeini. The revolution has had a significant impact on the Shīʿīs of Pakistan in terms of both community morale and funding for organized communal action, leading to an emboldened stance against the country's Sunnī majority. In the context of the large-scale struggle between Twelver Shīʿī and radical Sunnī organizations currently active in Pakistan, the Nūrbakhshīs are a relatively small prize targeted for conversion by the Twelver Shīʿis in their quest for demographic and regional expansion.

In comparison with Iran, the Pakistani state is not officially aligned with a particular sect, though it is certainly dominated by individuals who are Sunnī. Modern Nūrbakhshīs have made it a priority to appeal to the state to become recognized officially as a group separate from the major sects. It remains to be seen if this policy will bear fruit or whether social pressure and the unconcern of Pakistani state authorities will lead to the Nūrbakhshīya being subsumed under Twelver Shīʿism. The case nonetheless clearly shows the independent significance of social organization in a modern society, where resources and planning can lead to a strengthened position without the explicit state or elite patronage necessary in the medieval period. It is precisely due to this reality that the Nūrbakhshīs of Baltistan currently see modern tools such as publishing, formal organizations with rationalized structures, and participation in public discourse as the primary means for attempting to safeguard their distinct identity.

Traversing the history and geography of western, central, and southern Asia in the tracks of Nūrbakhshīs in this book takes us through a number of different social contexts in the Islamic East. While paying careful attention to differences arising from local circumstances, the book's narrative also shows the continuities of religious life, in both space and time, concurrent with the transformation of the regions from late medieval empires into modern nation-states. The details covered in this narrative illuminate Nūrbakhshī history, while on the broadest level the story of the Nūrbakhshīya highlights the consistent effort by human individuals and societies to memorialize the past into a tradition and utilize it to make life meaningful in the present.

Bibliography

Manuscripts

ʿAlī (Muḥibbī?). *Silsila-nāma.* MS. Persan 39, Bibliothèque Nationale, Paris, fols. 44a–47a.

Anonymous. *Jāmiʿ al-laṭāʾif.* MS. Hacı Mahmud Efendi 4645, Süleymaniye Library, Istanbul, fols. 1a–28b.

Astarābādī, Ḥasan b. Ḥaydar. *Az Hidāyatnāma.* MS. Farsça 139, Istanbul University Library, fols. 57b–58a.

Badakhshī, Ḥaydar. *Manqabat al-javāhir.* MS. India Office Collection 1850, British Library, London, fols. 346b–442b.

Bidlīsī Nūrbakhshī, Ḥusām ad-Dīn. *Sharḥ-i Gulshan-i rāz.* MS. Pertev Paşa 606, Süleymaniye Library, Istanbul, fols. 137b–192b.

———. *Sharḥ-i Khuṭbat al-bayān.* MS. XVIII G 28, National Library of the Czech Republic, Prague.

Hamadānī, ʿAlī. *Kitāb asrār an-nuqṭa.* MS. Şehid Ali Paşa 2794, Süleymaniye Library, Istanbul, fols. 276a–289b.

———. *Risāla-yi awrādīya.* MS. Şehid Ali Paşa 2794, Süleymaniye Library, Istanbul, fols. 304b–319b.

———. *Risāla-yi ẕikrīya.* MS. Şehid Ali Paşa 2794, Süleymaniye Library, Istanbul, fols. 369a–380a.

———. *Risāla-yi iṣṭilāḥāt.* MS. Şehid Ali Paşa 2794, Süleymaniye Library, Istanbul, fols. 478a–481a.

———. *Risāla-yi manāmīya.* MS. Şehid Ali Paşa 2794, Süleymaniye Library, Istanbul, fols. 432a–437b.

———. *Risāla-yi vāridāt.* MS. Şehid Ali Paşa 2794, Süleymaniye Library, Istanbul, fols. 447b–454a.

Ḥamuvayī, Saʿd ad-Dīn. *Kitāb sharḥ-i bismillāh.* MS. Çorlulu Ali Paşa 445, Süleymaniye Library, Istanbul, fols. 1b-7b.

———. *Kitāb al-maḥbūb fī t-taṣawwuf.* MS. Ayasofya 2058, Süleymaniye Library, Istanbul, fols. 1b–205b.

———. *Risāla dar ḥurūf.* MS. Pertev Paşa 606, Süleymaniye Library, Istanbul, fols. 13b–18a.

———. *ar-Risāla fī ẓuhūr khātam al-walāya.* MS. Ayasofya 2058, Süleymaniye Library, Istanbul, fols. 206a–207b.

Iṣfahānī, Fażlī. *Afżal at-tavārīkh.* MS. Or. 4678, British Library, London.

Kashmīrī, Muḥammad ʿAlī. *Tuḥfat al-aḥbāb.* MS. ʿAwn ʿAlī Shāh, Khaplū, Baltistan, Pakistan.

Kiyā, ʿAlāʾ ad-Dīn. *Risāla-yi nūrīya.* MS. 1997, Tehran University Library, Tehran, fols. 90b–96a.

Mushaʿshaʿ, Muḥammad b. Falāḥ. *Kalām al-mahdī.* MS. 10222, Parliament Library, Tehran.

Nūrbakhsh, Muḥammad. *Arbaʿīn-nāma* (excerpt). MS. Esad Efendi 3702, Süleymaniye Library, Istanbul, fol. 45a.

———. *Aqsām-i dil.* MS. 935/10, Āyat Allāh Marʿashī Library, Qum, fols. 186a–187a.

———. *Awrād-i fatḥīya* (incomplete). MS. Persan 368, Bibliothèque Nationale, Paris, fol. 155b.

———. *Insān-nāma.* MS. Persan 39, Bibliothèque Nationale, Paris, fols. 82b–88a.

———. *Javāb-i maktūb-i fuqahāʾ.* MS. Esad Efendi 3702. Süleymaniye Library, Istanbul, fols. 41b–42b.

———. *Maʿāsh as-sālikīn.* MS. Esad Efendi 3702, Süleymaniye Library, Istanbul, fols. 57b–61a.

———. *Risālat al-hudā.* MS. Esad Efendi 3702, Süleymaniye Library, Istanbul, fols. 85b–108b; MS. Fatih 5367, Süleymaniye Library, Istanbul, fols. 101b–129a.

———. *Risāla-yi kashf al-ḥaqāʾiq.* MS. Persan 39, Bibliothèque Nationale, Paris, fols. 62a–64b.

———. *Risāla-yi nūrīya.* MS. Esad Efendi 3702, Süleymaniye Library, Istanbul, fols. 69b–85a.

———. *Talvīḥāt.* MS. 3871/6, Parliament Library, Tehran, pp. 94–117.

Nūrbakhshī Shīrāzī, ʿAlī Rižā Mīrzā Bābā. *Fālnāma.* MS. Add. 23582, British Library, London.

Published Works

ʿAbd al-Bāqī, Muḥammad Fuʾād. *Muʿjam al-mufahras li-alfāẓ al-Qurʾān al-karīm.* Beirut: Dār al-Ḥadīth, 1988.

Abī Khizām, Anwar Fu'ād. *Muʿjam al-muṣṭalaḥāt aṣ-ṣūfiya, mustakhraj min ummahāt al-kutub al-yanbūʿīya.* Beirut: Maktaba Lubnān Nāshirūn, 1993.

Abrahamov, B. "Al-Ḳāsim ibn Ibrāhīm's Theory of the Imamate." *Arabica* 34 (1987): 80–105.

Addas, Claude. *Quest for the Red Sulphur: The Life of Ibn ʿArabī.* Translated by Peter Kingsley. Cambridge, U.K.: Islamic Texts Society, 1993.

Affifi, A. E. *The Mystical Philosophy of Muhyid-din Ibnul Arabi.* Cambridge: Cambridge University Press, 1964. Reprint, Lahore: Sh. Muhammad Ashraf, 1979.

Afridi, Banat Gul. *Baltistan in History.* Peshawar: Emjay Books International, 1988.

Afshār, Īraj, et al. *Fihrist-i kitābhā-yi khaṭṭī-yi Kitābkhāna-yi Millī-yi Malik, vābasta beh Āstān-i Quds.* 10 vols. Tehran: Kitābkhāna, 1973–93.

Ahmad, Aziz. "Conversion to Islam in the Valley of Kashmir." *Central Asiatic Journal* 23 (1979): 3–18.

———. *Islamic Modernism in India and Pakistan.* Oxford: Oxford University Press, 1967.

———. "The Sufi and the Sultan in Pre-Mughal Muslim India." *Der Islam* 38 (1963): 142–53.

Ahmed, Munir D. "The Shiʿis of Pakistan." In *Shi'ism, Resistance, and Revolution,* edited by Martin Kramer. Boulder, Colo.: Westview Press, 1987.

Aka, İsmail. *Mirza Şahruh ve zamanı (1405–1447).* Ankara: Türk Tarih Kurumu Basımevi, 1994.

ʿĀlam, Sayyid Khurshīd. *Daʿvāt-i ṣūfiya imāmīya.* 2d printing. Karachi: Anjuman-i Falāḥ va Bahbūd-i Sarmūñ, 1997.

ʿAlī, Manẓūm, ed. *Qarāquram Hindūkush.* Islamabad: Barq Sons, 1985.

ʿAlī, Sayyid. *Tārīkh-i Kashmīr.* Translated into Urdu by Ghulām Rasūl Baṫ. Srinagar: Centre of Central Asian Studies, University of Kashmir, 1994.

ʿAlī, Zāhid. *Hamārē Ismāʿīlī mazhab kī ḥaqīqat awr us kā niẓām.* Hyderabad: Academy of Islamic Studies, 1954.

ʿAllāmī, Abū l-Fażl. *Akbarnāma of Abu-l-Fazl.* Translated by H. Beveridge. 3 vols. Delhi: Ess Ess Publications, 1977.

———. *Āʾīn-i Akbarī.* Edited by H. Blochmann. 3 vols. Calcutta: Bibliotheca Indica, 1872.

Allen, Terry. *Timurid Herat.* Wiesbaden: Reichert, 1983.

Amanat, Abbas. *Resurrection and Renewal: The Making of the Babi Movement in Iran, 1844–1850.* Ithaca, N.Y.: Cornell University Press, 1988.

Amanat, Abbas, and Magnus Bernhardsson, eds. *Imagining the End: Visions of Apocalypse from the Ancient Middle East to Modern America.* London: I. B. Tauris, 2002.

Amedroz, H. F. "On the Meaning of the Laqab 'al-Saffāḥ' as Applied to the First ʿAbbāsid Caliph." *JRAS* (1907): 660–63.

Amir-Moezzi, Mohammad Ali. *The Divine Guide in Early Shiʿism: The Sources of Esotericism in Islam.* Translated by David Streight. Albany: State University of New York Press, 1994.

Amitai-Preiss, Reuven. "Ghazan, Islam, and the Mongol Tradition: A View from the Mamluk Sultanate." *BSOAS* 59, no. 1 (1996): 1–10.

Amoretti, B. S. "Religion under the Tīmūrids and the Ṣafavids." In *The Cambridge History of Iran,* vol. 6, edited by P. Jackson. Cambridge: Cambridge University Press, 1986.

Āmulī, Ḥaydar. *Muqaddimāt min Kitāb naṣṣ an-nuṣūṣ fī sharḥ al-fuṣūṣ.* Edited, with introductions in French and Arabic, by Henry Corbin and Osman Yahia. Tehran: Département d'Iranologie de l'Institut Franco-Iranien de Recherche, 1975.

———. *Jāmiʿ al-asrār wa-manbaʿ al-anwār.* Edited, with introductions in French and Arabic, by Henry Corbin and Osman Yahia. Tehran: Département d'Iranologie de l'Institut Franco-Iranien de Recherche, 1969.

Ando, Shiro. "The *Shaykh al-Islām* as a Tīmūrid Office: A Preliminary Study." *Islamic Studies* 33, nos. 2–3 (1994): 253–80.

———. *Timuridische Emire nach dem* Muʿizz al-ansāb. Berlin: K. Schwarz, 1992.

Anees, Munawar Ahmad. *Islam and Biological Futures: Ethics, Gender and Technology.* London: Mansell, 1989.

Anonymous. *ʿĀlam-ārā-yi Shāh Ṭahmāsp.* Edited by Īraj Afshār. Tehran: Dunyā-yi Kitāb, 1992.

Anonymous. *Bahāristān-i Shāhī.* Edited by Akbar Ḥaydarī Kāshmīrī. Srinagar: Anjuman-i Sharʿī-yi Shīʿīyān-i Jammūñ va Kashmīr, 1982.

Arjomand, Said Amir. *The Shadow of God and the Hidden Imam.* Chicago, Ill.: University of Chicago Press, 1984.

———. "Religious Extremism (*Ghuluww*), Ṣūfism and Sunnism in Safavid Iran: 1501–1722." *Journal of Asian History* 15 (1981): 1–35.

Arslanoğlu, İbrahim. *Şah İsmail Hatayî ve Anadolu Hatayîleri.* Istanbul: Der Yayınevi, 1992.

ʿAṭṭār, Farīd ad-Dīn. *Manṭiq aṭ-ṭayr.* Edited by Kāẓim Dizfūlīyān. Tehran: Intishārāt-i Ṭilāyīa, 2000.

———. *The Conference of the Birds.* Translated by Afkham Darbandi and Dick Davis. New York: Penguin Books, 1984.

Aubin, Jean. "L'avènement des Safavides reconsidéré (Études Safavides III)." *Moyen Orient et Océan Indien* 5 (1988): 1–130.

———. "Le problème du shi'isme dans l'Asie Mineure turque préottomane." In

Le Shi'isme Imamite, edited by R. Brunschvig and Toufic Fahd. Paris: Presses Universitaires de France, 1970.

Aubin, Jean, ed. *Matériaux pour la biographie de Shah Niʿmatullah Wali Kermani.* Tehran: Département d'Iranologie de l'Institut Franco-Iranien, 1956.

Āyatī, Muḥammad Ḥusayn. *Bahāristān dar tārīkh va tarājim-i rijāl-i Qāyināt va Quhistān.* 2d printing. Mashhad: Intishārāt-i Dānishgāh-i Firdūsī, 1992.

Āẕar, Luṭf ʿAlī Bīg. *Ātashkada-yi Āẕar.* Edited by Sayyid Jaʿfar Shahīdī. Tehran: Muʾassasa-yi Nashr-i Kitāb, 1958.

Aẕkāʾī, Parvīz. *Muravvij-i Islām dar Īrān-i ṣaghīr: Aḥvāl va āṡār-i Mīr Sayyid ʿAlī Hamadānī.* Hamadān, Iran: Intishārāt-i Dānishgāh-i Bū ʿAlī Sīnā, Intishārāt-i Muslim, 1991.

ʿAzzāwī, ʿAbbās. *Taʿrīf bi l-muʾarrikhīn fī ʿahd al-mughūl wa-t-turkumān.* Baghdad: Shirkat at-Tijāra wa-ṭ-Ṭibāʿa, 1957.

Babayan, Kathryn. "Sufis, Dervishes, and Mullas: The Controversy over Spiritual and Temporal Domain in Seventeenth-Century Iran." In *Safavid Persia,* edited by Charles Melville. London: I. B. Tauris, 1996.

———. "The Waning of the Qizilbash: The Temporal and the Spiritual in Seventeenth Century Iran." Ph.D. dissertation, Princeton University, 1993.

Bābur, Ẓahīr ad-Dīn Muḥammad. *Bâburnâme (Chaghatay Turkish Text with Abdul-Rahim Khankhanan's Persian Translation).* Edited and translated by W. M. Thackston. 3 vols. Cambridge: Department of Near Eastern Languages and Civilizations, Harvard University, 1993.

Bacharach, Jere L. "Laqab for a Future Caliph: The Case of the Abbasi al-Mahdī." *JAOS* 113 (1993): 271–74.

Badakhshī, Jaʿfar. *Khulāṣat al-manāqib.* Edited by Sayyida Ashraf Ẓafar. Islamabad: Markaz-i Taḥqīqāt-i Fārsī-yi Īrān va Pākistān, 1995.

Bākharzī, ʿAbd al-Vāsiʿ Niẓāmī. *Maqāmāt-i Jāmī.* Edited by Najīb Māʾil Hiravī. Tehran: Nashr-i Nay, 1992.

Baldick, Julian. *Mystical Islam: An Introduction to Sufism.* New York: New York University Press, 1989.

Barakāt, Muḥammad Fāris. *Jāmiʿ li-mawāḍīʿ āyāt al-Qurʾān al-karīm.* Beirut: Dār Qutayba, 1985.

Barthold, V. V. *Turkestan Down to the Mongol Invasion.* London: Luzac, 1928; 3d ed., 1967.

———. *Four Studies on the History of Central Asia.* Translated by V. and T. Minorsky. Leiden: E. J. Brill, 1956–62.

Bashear, Suliman. "Muslim Apocalypses and the Hour: A Case Study in Traditional Interpretation." *Israel Oriental Studies* 13 (1993): 75–99.

Bashīr, Muḥammad, tr. *Daʿvāt-i ṣūfīya Urdū.* 5th printing. Karachi: Nadva Islāmīya Nūrbakhshīya, 1995.

Bashir, Shahzad. "Deciphering the Cosmos From Creation to Apocalypse: The Hurufiyya Movement and Medieval Islamic Esotericism." In *Imagining the End: Visions of Apocalypse from the Ancient Middle East to Modern America,* edited by Abbas Amanat and Magnus Bernhardsson. London: I. B. Tauris, 2002.

———. "The Imam's Return: Messianic Leadership in Late Medieval Shiʿism." In *The Most Learned of the Shiʿa,* edited by Linda Walbridge. New York: Oxford University Press, 2001.

———. "The *Risālat al-hudā* of Muḥammad Nūrbaḵš: Critical Edition with Introduction." *RSO* 75, nos. 1–4 (2001): 87–137.

———. "Enshrining Divinity: The Death and Memorialization of Fażlallāh Astarābādī in Early Ḥurūfī Thought." *MW* 90, nos. 3 and 4 (2000): 289–308.

———. "Between Mysticism and Messianism: The Life and Thought of Muḥammad Nūrbaḵš." Ph.D. dissertation, Yale University, 1998.

Bayrakdar, Mehmet. *Bitlisli Idris (Idrîs-i Bidlîsî).* Ankara: Kültür Bakanlığı, 1991.

Baysun, Cavid. "Emir Sultan." *İslam Ansiklopedisi,* 4:261–63.

Bazin, Marcel, et al. *Gilan et Azarbayjan oriental: Cartes et documents ethnographiques.* Paris: Editions Recherche sur les civilisations, 1982.

Beek, Martijn van, and Kristoffer Brix Bertelsen. "No Present without Past: The 1989 Agitation in Ladakh." In *Recent Research on Ladakh 7: Proceedings of the 7th Colloquium of the International Association for Ladakh Studies Held in Bonn/Sankt Augustin, 12–15 June 1995,* edited by Thierry Dodin and Heinz Räther. Ulm: Ulmer Kulturanthropologische Schriften, 1997.

Bevan, Anthony A., ed. *The Naḳāʾid of Jarīr and al-Farazdaḳ.* 3 vols. Leiden: E. J. Brill, 1905–7.

Biddulph, John. *Tribes of the Hindoo Koosh.* Calcutta: Government Printing Office, 1880.

Bihrūzī, ʿAlī Naqī. "Khānqāh-i nūrīya va ārāmgāh-i Shaykh Muḥammad Nūrbakhsh dar Shīrāz." *Armaghān* 38 (1348/1970): 220–21.

Blichfeldt, Jan-Olaf. *Early Mahdism: Politics and Religion in the Formative Period of Islam.* Leiden: E. J. Brill, 1985.

Blochet, E. "Études sur le Gnosticisme musulman." *RSO* 4 (1911–12): 278–91.

Bodrogligeti, András J. E. "Muḥammad Shaybānī Khān's Apology to the Muslim Clergy." *Archivum Ottomanicum* 8 (1993–94): 85–100.

Bosworth, C. E. *The New Islamic Dynasties: A Chronological and Genealogical Manual.* New York: Columbia University Press, 1997.

Böwering, Gerhard. "From the Word of God to the Vision of God: Muḥammad's Heavenly Journey in Classical Ṣūfī Qur᾽ān Commentary." In *Le voyage initiatique en terre d'islam: Ascensions célestes et itinéraires spirituels,* edited by Mohammad Ali Amir-Moezzi. Louvain-Paris: Peeters, 1996.

———. *The Mystical Vision of Existence in Classical Islam: The Qur᾽ānic Hermeneutics of the Ṣūfī Sahl At-Tustarī (d. 283/896).* Berlin: Walter de Gruyter, 1980.

Boyle, John A., ed. *Cambridge History of Iran:* Vol. 5. *The Saljuq and Mongol Periods.* Cambridge: Cambridge University Press, 1968.

Bredi, Daniela. "L'uso delle fonti nella storiografia Indo-Musulmana nella prima metà del XX secolo: La storia del Baltistan, Ḥashmatullāh Khān e lo *Shigharnāma.*" *RSO* 68 (1994): 267–89.

Brett, Michael. "The Mīm, the ʿAyn, and the Making of Ismāʿīlism." *BSOAS* 57, no. 1 (1994): 25–39.

Burridge, Kenelm. *New Heaven, New Earth: A Study of Millenarian Activities.* Oxford, U.K.: Basil Blackwell, 1969.

Bursalı, Mehmed Tahir. *Osmanlı müellifleri.* 3 vols. Istanbul: Matbaʿ-yi Amira, 1333/1914–15.

Calmard, Jean. "Le Chiisme imamite sous les Ilkhans." In *L'Iran face à la domination Mongole,* edited by Denise Aigle. Tehran: Institut Français de Recherche en Iran, 1997.

Campbell, Sandra. "Millennial Messiah or Religious Restorer: Reflections on the Early Islamic Understanding of the Term *Mahdī.*" *Jusūr* 11 (1995): 1–11.

Campion, Nicholas. *The Great Year: Astrology, Millenarianism, and History in the Western Tradition.* London: Arkana, 1994.

Caskel, Werner. "Ein Mahdī des 15. Jahrhunderts: Saijid Muḥammad ibn Falāḥ und seine Nachkommen." *Islamica* 4 (1929–31): 48–93.

Chadurah, Haidar Malik. *History of Kashmir.* Edited and translated by Razia Bano. Delhi: Bhavna Prakashan, 1991.

Chelkowski, Peter, and Hamid Dabashi. *Staging a Revolution: The Art of Persuasion in the Islamic Republic of Iran.* New York: New York University Press, 1999.

Chittick, W. *The Self Disclosure of God.* Albany: State University of New York Press, 1999.

———. *The Sufi Path of Knowledge: Ibn al-ʿArabi's Metaphysics of Imagination.* Albany: State University of New York Press, 1989.

———. "The Five Divine Presences from al-Qūnawī to al-Qayṣarī." *MW* 72, no. 2 (1982): 107–28.

———. "Ṣadr al-Dīn Qūnawī on Oneness of Being." *International Philosophical Quarterly* 2 (1981): 171–84.

———. "The Perfect Man as the Prototype of the Self in the Sufism of Jami." *SI* 49 (1979): 135–57.

Chodkiewicz, Michel. *An Ocean without Shore: Ibn Arabi, the Book and the Law.* Translated by David Streight. Albany: State University of New York Press, 1993.

———. *The Seal of the Saints: Prophethood and Sainthood in the Doctrine of Ibn ʿArabī.* Translated by Liadain Sherrard. Cambridge, U.K.: Islamic Texts Society, 1993.

———. "The Esoteric Foundations of Political Legitimacy in Ibn ʿArabi." In *Muhyiddin ibn ʿArabi: A Commemorative Volume,* edited by Stephen Hirtenstein and Michael Tiernan. Dorset, U.K.: Element Books, 1993.

Clarke, Peter B. *Mahdism in West Africa: The Ijebu Mahdiyya Movement.* London: Luzac Oriental, 1995.

Clayer, Nathalie. *Mystiques, état et société: Les Halvetis dans l'aire balkanique de la fin du XVe siècle à nos jours.* Leiden: E. J. Brill, 1994.

Cole, Juan R. I. *Roots of North Indian Shīʿism in Iran and Iraq: Religion and State in Awadh, 1722–1859.* Berkeley: University of California Press, 1988.

Cook, David. "Moral Apocalyptic in Islam." *SI* 86, no. 2 (1997): 37–69.

Cooperson, Michael. *Classical Arabic Biography: The Heirs of the Prophets in the Age of al-Maʾmūn.* Cambridge: Cambridge University Press, 2000.

Corbin, Henry. *The Man of Light in Iranian Sufism.* Translated by Nancy Pearson. Boulder, Colo.: Shambhala, 1978; 2d ed. New Lebanon, N.Y.: Omega Publications, 1994.

———. *Spiritual Body and Celestial Earth: From Mazdean Iran to Shīʿite Iran.* Translated by Nancy Pearson. Princeton, N.J.: Princeton University Press, 1977.

———. *En Islam Iranien.* 4 vols. Paris: Gallimard, 1971–72.

———. *Creative Imagination in the Ṣūfism of Ibn ʿArabī.* Translated by Ralph Manheim. Princeton, N.J.: Princeton University Press, 1969.

Çoruh, Şinasi. *Emir Sultan.* Istanbul: N.p., n.d.

Crone, Patricia, and Martin Hinds. *God's Caliph: Religious Authority in the First Centuries of Islam.* Cambridge: Cambridge University Press, 1986.

Daftary, Farhad. "Ismāʿīlī-Sufi Relations in Early Post-Alamūt and Safavid Persia." In *The Heritage of Sufism,* vol. 3, edited by Leonard Lewisohn and David Morgan. Oxford, U.K.: One World, 1999.

———. *The Ismāʿīlīs: Their History and Their Doctrines.* Cambridge: Cambridge University Press, 1991.

Daftary, Farhad, ed. *Mediaeval Ismaʿili History and Thought.* Cambridge: Cambridge University Press, 1996.

Dani, Ahmad Hasan. *A History of Northern Areas of Pakistan.* Islamabad: Lok Virsa, 1989.

Danielli, Giotto. "Winter Excursions in Baltistan." In *The Italian Expedition to the Himalaya, Karakoram, and Eastern Turkestan, 1913–1914,* edited by Filippo de Filippi. London: Edward Arnold, 1932.

Daniels, Ted. *Millennialism: An International Bibliography.* New York: Garland Publishing, 1992.

Dānishpazhuh, Muḥammad Taqī, ed. "*Silsilat al-awliyā*-yi Nūrbakhsh-i Quhistānī." In *Mélanges offerts à Henry Corbin,* edited by Seyyed Hossein Nasr. Tehran: McGill University Institute of Islamic Studies, Tehran Branch, 1977.

———. *Fihrist-i nuskhahā-yi khaṭṭī-yi Dānishkada-yi Adabiyāt.* Tehran: Dānishgāh-i Tihrān, 1962.

Dānishpazhuh, Muḥammad Taqī, and Bahā' ad-Dīn Anvarī. *Fihrist-i kitābhā-yi khaṭṭī-yi Kitābkhāna-yi Majlis-i Sinā.* 2 vols. Tehran: Kitābkhāna-yi Majlis-i Sinā, 1976–89.

Dar, Ghulam Mohi-Ud-Din. *Kargil: Its Social, Cultural, and Economic History.* New Delhi: Dilpreet Publishing, 1999.

Darmsteter, James. *Le Mahdi depuis les origines de l'Islam jusqu'à nos jour.* Paris: Ernest Leroux, 1885.

Dāya, Najm ad-Dīn Rāzī. *The Path of God's Bondsmen from Origin to Return.* Translated by Hamid Algar. Delmar, Calif.: Caravan, 1982.

DeWeese, Devin. "Yasavī *Šayḫs* in the Timurid Era: Notes on the Social and Political Role of Communal Sufi Affiliations in the Fourteenth and Fifteenth Centuries." In *La civilità timuride come fenomeno internazionale, Oriente Moderno,* edited by Michele Bernardini, n.s. 15 (1996): 172–88.

———. *Islamization and Native Religion in the Golden Horde: Baba Tükles and Conversion to Islam in Historical and Epic Tradition.* University Park: Pennsylvania State University Press, 1994.

———. "Sayyid ʿAlī Hamadānī and Kubrawī Hagiographical Traditions." In *The Legacy of Medieval Persian Sufism,* edited by Leonard Lewisohn. London: Khanqahi Nimatullahi Publications, 1992.

———. "The Eclipse of the Kubraviyah in Central Asia." *Iranian Studies* 21, nos. 1–2 (1988): 59–83.

———. "The *Kashf al-Hudā* of Kamāl ad-Dīn Ḥusayn Khorezmī: A Fifteenth Century Sufi Commentary on the Qaṣīdat al-Burdah in Khorezmian Turkic." Text edition, translation, and historical introduction. Ph.D. dissertation, Indiana University, 1985.

Digby, Simon. "The Sufi Sheikh as a Source of Authority in Medieval India." In *Islam et société en asie du sud,* edited by Marc Gaborieau. Paris: Collection Purasārtha, 1986.

Dihsurkhī, Maḥmūd. *Muʿjam al-malāḥim wa-l-fitan.* 4 vols. Qum: Maḥmūd al-Dihsurkhī, 1999.

Dogra, Ramesh Chander. *Jammu and Kashmir: A Select and Annotated Bibliography.* Delhi: Ajanta Publications, 1986.

Dughlat, Mirza Haydar. *Tarikh-i Rashidi: A History of the Khans of Moghulistan.* Edited and translated by Wheeler M. Thackston. 2 vols. Cambridge: Department of Near Eastern Languages and Civilizations, Harvard University, 1996.

Eaton, Richard. "Temple Desecration and Indo-Muslim States." In *Beyond Turk and Hindu: Shaping Indo-Muslim Identity in Premodern India,* edited by David Gilmartin and Bruce B. Lawrence. Gainesville: University Press of Florida, 2000.

———. "Comparative History as World History: Religious Conversion in Modern India." *Journal of World History* 8, no. 2 (1997): 243–71.

———. *The Rise of Islam on the Bengal Frontier.* Berkeley: University of California Press, 1993.

———. "Approaches to the Study of Conversion to Islam in India." In *Approaches to Islam in Religious Studies,* edited by Richard C. Martin. Tucson: University of Arizona Press, 1985.

———. "The Political and Religious Authority of the Shrine of Bābā Farīd." In *Moral Conduct and Authority: The Place of* Adab *in South Asian Islam,* edited by Barbara Metcalf. Berkeley: University of California Press, 1982.

Edmonds, C. J. "The Beliefs and Practices of Ahl-i Ḥaqq of Iraq." *Iran* 7 (1969): 89–106.

Elias, Jamal. "A Second ʿAlī: The Making of Sayyid ʿAlī Hamadānī in Popular Imagination." *MW* 90, nos. 3–4 (2000): 395–419.

———. *The Throne Carrier of God: The Life and Thought of ʿAlāʾ ad-dawla as-Simnānī.* Albany: State University of New York Press, 1995.

———. "The Sufi Lords of Bahrabad: Saʿd al-Din and Sadr al-Din Hamuwayi." *Iranian Studies* 27, nos. 1–4 (1994): 53–75.

———. "A Kubrawī Treatise on Mystical Visions: The *Risāla-yi nūriyya* of ʿAlāʾ ad-Dawla as-Simnānī." *MW* 83, no. 1 (1993): 68–80.

Elias, Jamal, ed. "Risāla-yi nūrīya-yi Shaykh ʿAlāʾ ad-Dawla Simnānī." *Maʿārif* 13, no. 1 (1996): 3–26.

Elmore, Gerald. *Islamic Sainthood in the Fullness of Time: Ibn al-ʿArabī's Book of the Fabulous Gryphon.* Leiden: E. J. Brill, 1999.

Emerson, Richard M. "Charismatic Kingship: A Study of State Formation and Authority in Baltistan." In *Pakistan: The Social Sciences Perspective,* edited by Akbar S. Ahmed. Karachi: Oxford University Press, 1990.

Ernst, Carl W. *Words of Ecstasy in Sufism.* Albany: State University of New York Press, 1985.

Ewing, Katherine. *Arguing Sainthood: Modernity, Psychoanalysis, and Islam.* Durham, N.C.: Duke University Press, 1997.

Fahd, Toufic. *La divination arabe: Études religieuses, sociologiques et folkloriques sur le milieu natif de l'Islam.* 2d ed. Paris: Sindbad, 1987.

Farhang-i jughrāfiyā-yi Īrān. 10 vols. Tehran: Intishārāt-i Dāyira-yi Jughrāfiyā, 1949.

Faṣīḥ Khwāfī. *Mujmal-i Faṣīḥī.* Edited by Maḥmūd Farrukh. 5 vols. Tehran: Kitāb-furūshī-yi Bāstān, 1960.

Fawq, Muḥammad ad-Dīn. *Tavārīkh-i aqvām-i Kashmīr.* Mīrpūr, Azad Kashmir: Vērīnāg Publishers, 1991.

Fāżil, Maḥmūd. *Fihrist-i nuskhahā-yi khaṭṭī-yi Kitābkhāna-yi jāmiᶜ-yi Gawhar Shād-i Mashhad.* 4 vols. Mashhad: Kitābkhāna-yi Jāmiᶜ-yi Gawhar Shād, 1985.

Ferishta, Mahomed Kasim. *History of the Rise of the Mahomedan Power in India* [*Tārīkh-i Firishta*]. Translated by John Briggs. 4 vols. Reprint; Calcutta: Editions Indian, 1966.

Festinger, Leon, Henry W. Riecken, and Stanley Schachter. *When Prophecy Fails: A Social and Psychological Study of a Modern Group that Predicted the Destruction of the World.* New York: Harper & Row, 1964.

Fischer, Michael M. J., and Mehdi Abedi. *Debating Muslims: Cultural Dialogues in Postmodernity and Tradition.* Madison: University of Wisconsin Press, 1990.

Fleischer, Cornell. "The Lawgiver as Messiah: The Making of the Imperial Image in the Reign of Süleymân." In *Süleyman the Magnificent and His Time: Acts of the Parisian Conference, Galaries Nationales du Grand Palais, 7–10 March, 1990,* edited by Gilles Veinstein. Paris: École des Hautes Études en Sciences Sociales, 1990.

Francke, A. H. "Islam among the Tibetans." *MW* 19 (1929): 134–40.

———. *A History of Western Tibet.* London: Partridge, 1907. Reprinted as: *Baltistan and Ladakh: A History.* Islamabad: Lok Virsa, 1986.

Friedlaender, Israel. "ᶜAbdallāh b. Sabā, der Begründer der Shīᶜa und sein jüdischer Ursprung." Parts 1 and 2. *Zeitschrift für Assyrologie* 23 (1909): 296–327; 24 (1910): 1–46.

Friedmann, Yohanan. *Prophecy Continuous: Aspects of Aḥmadī Religious Thought and Its Medieval Background.* Berkeley: University of California Press, 1989.

Fuchs, Stephen. *Rebellious Prophets: A Study of Messianic Movements in Indian Religions.* Bombay: Asia Publishing, 1965.

Furūzānfar, Badīᶜ az-Zamān. *Aḥādīṡ-i maṡnavī.* 3d printing. Tehran: Amīr Kabīr, 1361/1982–83.

García-Arenal, Mercedes, ed. *Mahdisme et millénarisme en Islam, Revue des mondes musulmanes et de la Méditerranée,* 91–94. Aix-en-Provence: Éditions Édisud, 2000.

Golombek, Lisa, and Maria Subtelny, eds. *Timurid Art and Culture: Iran and Central Asia in the Fifteenth Century.* Leiden: E. J. Brill, 1992.

Goto, Yukako. "Der Aufstieg zweier Sayyid-Familien am Kaspischen Meer: 'Volksislamische' Strömungen in Iran des 8/14. und 9/15. Jahrhunderts." *WZKM* 89 (1999): 45–84.

Gramlich, Richard. *Die Wunder der Freunde Gottes.* Wiesbaden: Steiner, 1987.

———. *Die schiitischen Derwischorden Persiens.* 3 vols. Wiesbaden: Franz Steiner, 1965–81.

Grist, Nicola. "Muslim Kinship and Marriage in Ladakh." In *Anthropology of Tibet and the Himalaya,* edited by Charles Ramble and Martin Brauen. Zurich: Ethnological Museum of the University of Zurich, 1993.

Gronke, Monika. "La religion populaire en Iran Mongol." In *L'Iran face à la domination Mongole,* edited by Denise Aigle. Tehran: Institut Français de Recherche en Iran, 1997.

Gross, Jo-Ann. "Authority and Miraculous Behavior: Reflections on Karāmāt Stories of Khwāja ʿUbaydullāh Aḥrār." In *The Heritage of Sufism,* vol. 2, edited by Leonard Lewisohn. Oxford, U.K.: One World, 1999.

———. "Khoja Ahrar: A Study of the Perceptions of Religious Power and Prestige in the Late Timurid Period." Ph.D. dissertation, New York University, 1982.

Grünebaum, G. E. von, and Roger Caillois, eds. *The Dream and Human Societies.* Berkeley: University of California Press, 1966.

Gülşenî, Muhyî-yi. *Menâḳib-i İbrâhîm-i Gülşenî.* Edited by Tahsin Yazıcı. Ankara: Türk Tarih Kurumu Basımevi, 1982.

Haider, Mansura. "The Sovereign in the Timurid State (XIV–XVth centuries)." *Turcica* 8 (1976): 61–82.

Halm, Heinz. *The Empire of the Mahdī: The Rise of the Fatimids.* Translated by Michael Bonner. Leiden: E.J. Brill, 1996.

———. *Shiism.* Edinburgh: Edinburgh University Press, 1991.

———. *Die Islamische Gnosis: Die Extreme Schia und die ʿAlawiten.* Zurich: Artemis Verlag, 1982.

———. *Kosmologie und Heilslehre der früher Ismāʿīliyya.* Wiesbaden: Steiner, 1978.

Hamadani, Agha Hussain, and Muhammad Riaz. *Shah-e-Hamadan Commemorative Volume: Proceedings of the Shah-e-Hamadan International Conference, held on October 2–4, 1987, at Muzaffarabad, AJK.* Muzaffarabad: Institute of Kashmir Studies, 1988.

———. "Sayyid Ali Hamadani's Visit to Kashmir and Baltistan and Islamisation of the Society." *Journal of Central Asia* 8, no. 2 (1985): 185–90.

Haneda, Masashi. *Le Châh et les Qizilbāsh: Le systeme militaire safavide.* Berlin: K. Schwarz, 1987.

Hangloo, Rattan Lal. *The State in Medieval Kashmir.* New Delhi: Manohar, 2000.

Ḥaqīqat, ʿAbd ar-Rafīʿ. *Tārīkh-i ʿirfān va ʿārifān-i Īrān.* Tehran: Kumish, 1992.

Hasan, Mohibbul. *Kashmīr under the Sulṭāns.* Calcutta: Iran Society, 1959.

Ḥasharī Tabrīzī, Mullā Muḥammad Amīn. *Rawża-yi aṭhār: Mazārāt-i mutabarraka va maḥallāt-i qadīmī-yi Tabrīz va tavābiʿ.* Edited by ʿAzīz Dawlatābādī. Tabriz: Sutūda, 1992.

Ḥasrat, Muḥammad Ḥasan. *Tārīkh-i adabīyāt-i Baltistān.* Skardū: Muḥammad Ḥasan Ḥasrat, 1992.

Ḥassān b. Thābit. *Dīwān.* Edited by Walīd ʿArafāt. 2 vols. London: Luzac, 1971.

Hawting, G. R. *The First Dynasty of Islam.* London: Croom Helm, 1986.

Haythamī, Ibn Ḥajar. *Qawl al-mukhtaṣar fī ʿalāmāt al-mahdī al-muntaẓar.* Edited by ʿAbd ar-Raḥmān b. ʿAbdallāh at-Turkī. Cairo: az-Zahrāʾ li-l-Iʿlām al-ʿArabī, 1994.

Hekmat, A. A. "Les voyages d'un mystique persan de Hamadan au Kashmir." *JA* 240, no. 1 (1952): 53–66.

Hinz, Walther. "Quellenstudien zur Geschichte der Timuriden." *ZDMG* 90 (1936): 357–98.

———. *Irans Aufstieg zum Nationalstaat im fünfzehnten Jahrhundert.* Leipzig: Walter de Gruyter, 1936.

Hiravī, Najīb Māyil. *Jāmī.* Tehran: Tarḥ-i Naw, 1999.

Hiskett, Mervyn. *The Sword of Truth: The Life and Times of the Shehu Usuman dan Fodio.* 2d ed. Evanston, Ill.: Northwestern University Press, 1994.

Hodgson, Marshall. *The Venture of Islam.* 3 vols. Chicago Ill.: University of Chicago Press, 1974.

———. *The Order of the Assassins: The Struggle of the Early Nizārī Ismāʿīlīs Against the Islamic World.* The Hague: Mouton, 1955.

———. "How Did the Early Shiʿa Become Sectarian?" *JAOS* 75 (1955): 1–13.

Holt, P. M. *Mahdist State in the Sudan, 1881–1889.* Oxford: Oxford University Press, 1970.

Holzworth, Wolfgang. "Islam in Baltistan: Problems of Research on the Formative Period." In *The Past in the Present: Horizons of Remembering in the Pakistan Himalaya,* edited by Irmtraud Stellrecht. Cologne: Rüdiger Köppe Verlag, 1997.

Howard, Neil. "What Happened between 1450 and 1550 A.D.?" In *Recent Research on Ladakh 6: Proceedings of the Sixth International Colloquium on Ladakh, Leh 1993,* edited by Henry Osmaston and Nawang Tsering. Bristol, U.K.: University of Bristol, 1997.

Hunarfar, Luṭf Allāh. *Iṣfahān dar dawra-yi jānashīyān-i Tīmūr.* Tehran: N.p., n.d.

Hurgronje, Snouk. "Der Mahdi." In *Verspreide Geschriften,* vol. 1. Bonn: K. Schroeder, 1923–27.

Ḥusaynī, Aḥmad, and Maḥmūd Marʿashī. *Fihrist-i nuskhahā-yi khaṭṭī-yi Kitābkhāna-yi ʿUmūmī-yi Ḥażrat Āyat Allāh al-ʿUẓmā Najafī Marʿashi.* 26 vols. Qum: Chāp-khāna-yi Mihr-i Ustuvār, 1975/76–1995/96.

Hussain, Jassam. *Occultation of the Twelfth Imam.* London: Muhammadi Trust, 1982.

Ibn al-ʿArabī, Muḥyī ad-Dīn. *The Bezels of Wisdom (Fuṣūṣ al-Ḥikam).* Translated by R. W. J. Austin. London: Missionary Society of St. Paul, 1980.

———. *Futūḥāt al-makkīya.* 4 vols. Beirut: Dār Ṣādir, 1968.

———. *Fuṣūṣ al-ḥikam.* Edited by A. A. Affifi. 2 vols. Beirut: Dār al-Kitāb al-ʿArabī, 1966.

Ibn al-Athīr. *Usd al-ghāba fī maʿrifat aṣ-ṣaḥāba.* 4 vols. Tehran: al-Maktaba al-Islāmīya, 1957.

Ibn Bābawayh, Muḥammad b. ʿAlī. *Kamāl ad-dīn wa-tamām an-niʿma.* Tehran: Kitābfurūshī-yi Islāmīya, 1959.

Ibn Isḥāq. *The Life of Muḥammad.* Translated by Alfred Guillaume. Oxford: Oxford University Press, 1955.

Ibn al-Karbalāʾī, Ḥāfiẓ Ḥusayn. *Rawżāt al-jinān va jannāt al-janān.* Edited by Jaʿfar Sulṭān al-Qurrāʾī. 2 vols. Tehran: Bungāh-i Tarjuma va Nashr-i Kitāb, 1970.

Ibn Khaldûn. *The Muqaddimah: An Introduction to History.* Translated by Franz Rosenthal. 3 vols. New York: Pantheon Books, 1958.

Ibn Manẓūr, Muḥammad b. Mukarram. *Lisān al-ʿarab.* 6 vols. Cairo: Dār al-Maʿārif, 1981.

Ibn Tūmart. *Aʿazzu-mā-yuṭlab.* Edited by ʿAmmār Ṭālibī. Algiers: al-Muʾassasa al-Waṭanīya li l-Kitāb, 1985.

Isfandiyār, Kaykhusraw. *Dabistān-i maẕāhib.* Edited by Raḥīm Riżā-zāda Malik. 2 vols. Tehran: Kitābkhāna-yi Ṭahūrī, 1983.

Ivanow, Vladimir. *Ismaili Tradition Concerning the Rise of the Fatimids.* Calcutta: Oxford University Press, 1942.

———. "Ummu'l-kitāb." *Der Islam* 23 (1936): 1–132.

———. *Two Early Ismaili Treatises: Haft-babi Baba Sayyid-na and Matlubu'l-muʾminin by Tusi.* Bombay: Islamic Research Association, 1933.

Izutsu, Toshihiko. *Creation and the Timeless Order of Things: Essays in Islamic Mystical Philosophy.* Ashland, Ore.: White Cloud Press, 1994.

Jackson, Peter, and Laurence Lockhart, eds. *The Cambridge History of Iran: The Timurid and Safavid Periods.* Vol. 6. Cambridge: Cambridge University Press, 1986.

Jafri, S. H. M. *The Origins and Early Development of Shiʿism.* London: Longman, 1979.

Jāmī, ʿAbd ar-Raḥmān. *Nafaḥāt al-uns.* Edited by Maḥmūd ʿĀbidī. Tehran: Intishārāt-i Iṭṭilāʿāt, 1997.

Jarīr b. ʿAṭīya. *Dīwān Jarīr bi-sharḥ Muḥammad b. Ḥabīb.* Edited by Nuʿmān Muḥammad Amīn Ṭāhā. Cairo: Dār al-Maʿārif, 1969.

Jettmar, Karl. "Zur Kesar-Sage in Baltistan und Ladakh." *Zentralasiatische Studien* 13 (1979): 325–37.

———. "Fragment einer Balti-Version der Kesar-Sage." *Zentralasiatische Studien* 11 (1977): 277–86.

Jina, Prem Singh. *The Religious History of Ladakh.* Delhi: Sri Satguru Publications, 2001.

Juʿfī, al-Mufaḍḍal b. ʿUmar. *Kitāb al-haft wa-l-aẓilla.* Edited by Aref Tamer and Ign.-A Khalifé. Beirut: Dār al-Mashriq, 1970.

Kafadar, Cemal. *Between Two Worlds.* Berkeley: University of California Press, 1995.

Kahraman, Mehmet. *Uşşaki divan-ı şerifi.* Manisa: Uşşaki'ler A.S, 1994.

Karamustafa, Ahmet. *God's Unruly Friends.* Salt Lake City: University of Utah Press, 1994.

Karīmān, Ḥusayn. *Tihrān dar guzashta va ḥāl.* Tehran: Intishārāt-i Dānishgāh-i Millī-yi Īrān, 1976.

Katz, Jonathan G. *Dreams, Sufism and Sainthood: The Visionary Career of Muhammad al-Zawâwî.* Leiden: E. J. Brill, 1996.

Kazmi, Abbas. "The Ethnic Groups of Baltistan." In *Anthropology of Tibet and the Himalaya,* edited by Charles Ramble and Martin Brauen. Zurich: Ethnological Museum of the University of Zurich, 1993.

Khalidi, Tarif. *Arabic Historical Thought in the Classical Period.* Cambridge: Cambridge University Press, 1994.

Khan, Husain. "Mughal Relations with Baltistan and the Northern Region, from Akbar to Aurangzeb." *Journal of Central Asia* 7, no. 1 (1984): 179–89.

Khan, Mohammad Ishaq. *Kashmir's Transition to Islam: The Role of Muslim Rishis.* New Delhi: Manohar, 1994.

———. "Studying Conversions to Islam in Indian History—A Case Study." *Journal of the Institute of Muslim Minority Affairs* 12 (1991): 149–57.

———. "Kashmiri Response to Islam, A.D. 1320–1586." *Islamic Culture* 61 (1987): 87–104.

Khāvar, ʿAbd al-Ḥamīd. "Shimālī ʿilāqajāt mēñ ishāʿat-i Islām." In *Qarāquram Hindūkush,* edited by Manẓūm ʿAlī. Islamabad: Barq Sons, 1985.

Khazzāz, ʿAlī b. Muḥammad. *Kifāyat al-athar fī n-nuṣūṣ ʿalā l-aʾimma l-ithnay ʿashar.* Qum: Intishārāt-i Baydār, 1980.

Khunjī-Iṣfahānī, Fażl Allāh b. Rūzbihān. *Tārīkh-i ʿālam ārā-yi Amīnī.* Edited by John Woods. London: Royal Asiatic Society, 1992.

Khūyhāmī, Pīr Ghulām Ḥasan. *Tārīkh-i Ḥasan.* 3 vols. Srinagar: Research and Publication Department, Jammu and Kashmir Government, 1954.

Khwāndamīr, Ghiyāṣ ad-Dīn. *Habibu's-siyar: Tome Three, The Reign of the Mongol and the Turk.* Translated by Wheeler Thackston. 2 vols. Cambridge: Department of Near Eastern Languages and Civilizations, Harvard University, 1994.

———. *Ḥabīb as-siyar.* Edited by Jalāl ad-Dīn Humāʾī. 4 vols. Tehran: Kitābkhāna-yi Khayyām, 1954.

Kılıç, Nurten. "Change in Political Culture: The Rise of Sheybani Khan." *Cahiers d'Asie Centrale* 3–4 (1997): 57–68.

Kissling, Hans Joachim. "The Role of the Dervish Orders in the Ottoman Empire." In *Studies in Islamic Cultural History,* edited by G. E. von Grünebaum. Chicago, Ill.: University of Chicago Press, 1954.

———. "Aus der Geschichte des Chalvetijje-Ordens." *ZDMG* 103 (1953): 233–89.

Knysh, Alexander. *Ibn ʿArabi in the Later Islamic Tradition.* Albany: State University of New York Press, 1999.

Kohlberg, Etan. "From Imāmiyya to Ithnā-ʿAshariyya." *BSOAS* 39 (1976): 521–43.

Krawulsky, Dorothea. *Ḫorāsān zur Timuridenzeit nach dem Tārīḫ-e Ḥāfeẓ-e Abrū.* Beihefte zum Tübinger Atlas des Vorderen Orients, no. 46. Wiesbaden: Dr. Ludwig Reichert Verlag, 1982–84.

Kreyenbroek, Philip G., and Christine Allison, eds. *Kurdish Culture and Identity.* London: Zed Books, 1996.

Kūrānī, ʿAlī, ed. *Muʿjam aḥādīth al-Imām al-Mahdī.* 4 vols. Qum: Muʾassasat al-Maʿārif al-Islāmīya, 1990.

Kūravī, Shakūr ʿAlī Anvar. *Āʾina-yi islāmī.* Karachi: an-Nadva al-Islāmīya Nūrbakhshīya, 1991.

Lāhījī, Shams ad-Dīn Muḥammad Asīrī. *Mafātīḥ al-iʿjāz fī sharḥ Gulshan-i rāz.* Edited by Muḥammad Rižā Bārzgar Khalīqī and ʿIffat Karbāsī. Tehran: Zavvār, 1992.

———. *Asrār ash-shuhūd.* Edited by ʿAlī Āl-i Dāvūd. Tehran: Muʾassasa-yi Muṭāliʿāt va Taḥqīqāt-i Farhangī, 1989.

———. *Dīvān-i ashʿār va rasāʾil.* Edited by Barāt Zanjānī. Tehran: McGill University Institute for Islamic Studies, Tehran Branch, 1978.

Lakhnavī, Ḥashmat Allāh Khān. *Tārīkh-i Jammuñ.* Lahore: Maktaba-yi Ishāʿat-i Adab, 1968.

Lambton, A.K.S. "Quis Custodiet Custodes: Some Reflections on the Persian Theory of Government." Parts 1 and 2. *SI* 5 (1956): 125–48; 6 (1956): 125–46.

Landolt, Hermann. "Walāya." *The Encyclopedia of Religion,* 15:319–20.

———. *Kāshif al-asrār of Nūr ad-Dīn Isfarāʾinī.* Tehran: Institute of Islamic Studies, 1980.

———. "Die Briefwechsel zwischen Kāshānī und Simnānī über Waḥdat al-Wuǧūd." *Der Islam* 50 (1973): 29–81.

Lawrence, Bruce B. "Early Indo-Muslim Saints and Conversion." In *Islam in Asia: South Asia,* edited by Y. Friedmann. Jerusalem: Magnes Press, Hebrew University, 1984.

———. "Islam in India: The Function of Institutional Sufism in the Islamization of Rajasthan, Gujarat, and Kashmir." *Contributions in Asian Studies* 17 (1982): 27–43.

Le Strange, Guy. *Lands of the Eastern Caliphate.* Cambridge: Cambridge University Press, 1905.

Lentz, Thomas W., and Glenn D. Lowry, eds. *Tīmūr and the Princely Vision: Persian Art and Culture in the Fifteenth Century.* Washington, D.C.: Smithsonian Institution Press, 1989.

Lewisohn, Leonard. "An Introduction to the History of Modern Persian Sufism, Part II: A Socio-cultural Profile of Sufism, from the Dhahabī Revival to the Present Day." *BSOAS* 62, no. 1 (1999): 36–59.

Lindsay, James E. "Prophetic Parallels in Abū ʿAbd Allah al-Shiʿī's Mission among the Kutama Berbers, 893–910." *IJMES* 24, no. 1 (1992): 39–56.

Lings, Martin. *Muḥammad: His Life Based on the Earliest Sources.* Rochester, Vt.: Inner Traditions International, 1983.

Maʿānī, Aḥmad Gulchīn. "Ṣafī-yi Nūrbakhshī Rāzī." *Armaghān* 40, no. 10 (1972): 690–92.

Madelung, Wilferd. *The Succession to Muḥammad.* Cambridge: Cambridge University Press, 1996.

———. "Fatimiden und Baḥrainqarmaṭen." *Der Islam* 34 (1959): 34–88. Translated as "The Fatimids and the Qarmaṭīs of Baḥrayn," in *Mediaeval Ismaʿili History and Thought,* edited by Farhad Daftary. Cambridge: Cambridge University Press, 1996.

———. "The Sufyānī between Tradition and History." *SI* 58 (1984): 5–48.

———. "ʿAbd Allāh b. al-Zubayr and the Mahdī." *JNES* 11 (1981): 291–305.

———. *Der Imam al-Qāsim b. Ibrāhīm und die Glaubenslehre der Zaiditen.* Berlin: Walter de Gruyter, 1965.

Mahdī, Muḥammad Aḥmad. *Āthār al-kāmila li l-Imām al-Mahdī.* Edited by Muḥammad Ibrāhīm Abū Salīm. 5 vols. Khartoum: Dār Jāmiʿat al-Kharṭūm li-n-Nashr, 1990.

Mahdīpūr, ʿAlī Akbar. *Kitābnāma-yi Ḥażrat-i Mahdī.* 2 vols. Qum: ʿAlī Akbar Mahdīpūr, 1996.

Majlisī, Muḥammad Bāqir. *ʿAyn al-ḥayāt*. Edited by Asad Allāh Suhaylī Iṣfahānī. Tehran: Shirkat-i Sahāmī-yi Ṭabʿ-i Kitāb, 1954.

Malik, Jamal. *Colonialization of Islam: Dissolution of Traditional Institutions in Pakistan*. New Delhi: Manohar, 1996.

Manz, Beatrice F. *The Rise and Rule of Tamerlane*. Cambridge: Cambridge University Press, 1993.

Marʿashī, Sayyid Ẓahīr ad-Dīn. *Tārīkh-i Ṭabaristān va Rūyān va Māzandarān*. Edited by ʿAbbās Shāyān. Tehran: Chāpkhāna-yi Firdūsī, 1955.

———. *Tārīkh-i Gīlān va Daylamistān*. Edited by Minūchihr Sutūda. Tehran: Muʾassasa-yi Iṭṭilāʿāt, 1985.

Margoliouth, D. S. "On Mahdis and Mahdism." *Proceedings of the British Academy* 7 (1915): 213–33.

Martin, B. G. "A Short History of the Khalwatī Order of Dervishes." In *Scholars, Saints, and Sufis*, edited by Nikki Keddie. Berkeley: University of California Press, 1972.

Mattoo, Abdul Majid. *Kashmir under the Mughals, 1586–1752*. Srinagar: Golden Horde, 1988.

———. "The Nurbakhshis of Kashmir." In *Islam in India: Studies and Commentaries*. Vol. 2: *Religion and Religious Education*, edited by C. W. Troll. New Delhi: Vikas Publishing, 1984.

May, Lini. *The Evolution of Indo-Muslim Thought after 1857*. Lahore: Sh. Muhammad Ashraf, 1970.

Mazzaoui, Michel. *The Origins of the Ṣafawids: Šīʿism, Ṣūfism and the Ġulāt*. Wiesbaden: F. Steiner, 1972.

McEoin, Denis. *The Sources for Early Bābī Doctrine and History: A Survey*. Leiden: E. J. Brill, 1992.

Meier, Fritz. *Die Fawāʾiḥ al-ǧamāl wa-fawātiḥ al-ǧalāl des Naǧm ad-Dīn al-Kubrā*. Wiesbaden: F. Steiner, 1957.

———. "Die Welt der Urbilder bei ʿAli Hamadani." *Eranos Jahrbuch XVIII*. Zurich: Rhein-Verlag, 1950.

Melikoff, Irene. *Abu Muslim: Le "Porte-Hache" du Khorassan dans la tradition epique turco-iranienne*. Paris: A. Maisonneuve, 1962.

Melton, J. G. "Spiritualization and Reaffirmation: What Really Happens When Prophecy Fails." *American Studies* 26 (1985): 17–29.

Melville, Charles. "Pādshāh-i Islām: The Conversion of Sultan Maḥmūd Ghāzān Khān." In *Pembroke Papers*, edited by Charles Melville. Cambridge: University of Cambridge Center of Middle Eastern Studies, 1990.

Melville, Charles, ed. *Safavid Persia*. London: I. B. Tauris, 1996.

Metcalf, Barbara. *Perfecting Women: Maulana Ashraf ʿAli Thanawi's Bihishti Zewar, A Partial Translation with Commentary.* Berkeley: University of California Press, 1990.

———. *Islamic Revival in British India: Deoband, 1860–1900.* Princeton, N.J.: Princeton University Press, 1982.

Minorsky, Vladimir. "The Gūrān." *BSOAS* 11 (1943): 75–103.

———. "The Poetry of Shāh Ismāʿīl I." *BSOAS* 10 (1942): 1006–53.

———. "Notes sur la secte des Ahlé Haqq." *RMM* 40, no. 1 (1920): 19–97.

Milstein, R. "Sufi Elements in the Late Fifteenth Century Painting of Herat." In *Studies in Memory of Gaston Wiet,* edited by Myriam Rosen-Ayalon. Jerusalem: Institute of Asian and African Studies, Hebrew University, 1977.

Mir-Hosseini, Ziba. *Islam and Gender: The Religious Debate in Contemporary Iran.* Princeton, N.J.: Princeton University Press, 1999.

———. "Faith, Ritual, and Culture among the Ahl-e Haqq." In *Kurdish Culture and Identity,* edited by P. Kreyenbroek and Christine Allison. London: Zed Press, 1996.

Mīrzā, Nādir. *Tārīkh va jughrāfī-yi dār as-salṭana-yi Tabrīz.* Edited by Ghulām Riżā Ṭabāṭabāʾī Majd. Tabriz: Sutūda, 1994.

Modarressi, Hossein. *Crisis and Consolidation in the Formative Period of Shiʿite Islam: Abū Jaʿfar ibn Qiba al-Rāzī and His Contribution to Imāmite Shīʿite Thought.* Princeton, N.J.: Darwin Press, 1993.

Mokri, Ḥājj Niʿmat Allāh Mujrim. *Shāh-nama-ye ḥaqīqat: Le Livre des rois de vérité.* Edited by Mohammad Mokri. Tehran: Département d'Iranologie de l'Institut Franco-Iranien, 1966.

Molé, Marijan. "Traités mineurs de Nağm al-Dīn Kubrà." *Annales islamologiques* 4 (1963): 15–22.

———. "Professions de foi de deux Kubrawīs: ʿAlī-i Hamadānī et Muḥammad Nurbaḫš." *Bulletin d'études orientales* 17 (1961–62): 133–203.

———. "Les Kubrawiya entre sunnisme et shiisme au huitième et neuvième siècles de l'hégire." *REI* 29 (1961): 61–142.

———. "La version persane du traité de dix principes de Najm al-Dīn Kobrā, par ʿAlī b. Shihāb al-Dīn Hamadānī." *Farhang-i Īrān Zamīn* 6 (1958): 38–66.

Momen, Moojan. *An Introduction to Shiʿi Islam.* New Haven, Conn.: Yale University Press, 1986.

Moosa, Matti. *Extremist Shiites: The Ghulat Sects.* Syracuse, N.Y.: Syracuse University Press, 1987.

Mudarris, Mīrzā Muḥammad ʿAlī. *Rayḥānat al-adab.* Tabriz: Chāpkhāna-yi Shafaq, 1970.

Mufīd, Muḥammad. *Jāmiʿ-i mufīdī.* Edited by Īraj Afshār. 3 vols. Tehran: Intishārāt-i Kitābfurūshī-yi Asadī, 1961.

Munshī, Iskandar. *History of Shah ʿAbbās.* Translated by Roger Savory. 2 vols. Boulder, Colo.: Westview Press, 1978.

———. *Tārīkh-i ʿālam-ārā-yi ʿAbbāsī.* 2 vols. Tehran: Amīr Kabīr, 1955.

Munzavī, Aḥmad, ed. *Fihrist-i nuskhahā-yi khaṭṭī-yi fārsī.* 6 vols. Tehran: Muʾassasa-yi Farhangī-yi Minṭaqaʾī, 1969–76.

Murphy, Dervla. *Where the Indus Is Young: A Winter in Baltistan.* London: J. Murray, 1977.

Muqaddam, Talʿat Iʿtimād. *Ṭarīq-i Uvaysī.* Translated into English by the author. San Rafael, Calif.: MTO Shahmaghsoudi Publications, 1982.

Mūsavī, Sayyid Muḥammad Bāqir. *Akhtar-i darakhshāñ: Kashmīr kī shīʿāyī tārīkh sē mutaʿlliq chand mażāmīn.* Benaras: Ikrām Ḥusayn Press, 1971.

Nafīsī, Saʿīd. *Ahvāl va ashʿār-i Fārsī-yi Shaykh-i Bahāʾī.* Tehran: Chāpkhāna-yi Iqbāl, 1937.

Nasafī, ʿAzīz. *Kitāb al-insān al-kāmil.* Edited by Marijan Molé. Tehran: Département d'Iranologie de l'Institut Franco-Iranien, 1962.

Nasīm, Muḥammad Qāsim. *Baltistān: Tārīkh va siyāsat.* Lahore: Progressive Publishers, 1994.

Naṣrābādī Iṣfahānī, Muḥammad Ṭāhir. *Tażkira-yi Naṣrābādī.* Edited by Muḥsin Nājī Naṣrābādī. Tehran: Asāṭīr, 1999.

Navāʾī, ʿAbd al-Ḥusayn. *Rijāl kitāb Ḥabīb as-siyar.* Tehran: Shirkat-i Sahāmī-yi Chāp, 1945.

Navāʾī, ʿAbd al-Ḥusayn, ed. *Asnād va makātibāt-i tārīkhī-yi Īrān.* Tehran: Bungāh-i Tarjuma va Nashr-i Kitāb, 1962.

Navāʾī, Niẓām ad-Dīn ʿAlīshīr. *Majālis an-nafāʾis.* Urumchi: Xianjiang Khalq Nashriyātī, 1994.

———. *Nesâyimü'l-mahabbe min şemâyimi'l-fütüvve.* Edited by Kemal Eraslan. Istanbul: İstanbul Üniversitesi Edebiyat Fakültesi Yayınları, 1979.

———. *Majālis an-nafāʾis.* Edited by ʿAlī Aṣghar Ḥikmat. Tehran: Chāpkhāna-yi Bānk-i Millī-yi Īrān, 1944.

Nawbakhtī, Ḥasan b. Mūsā, and Saʿd b. ʿAbd Allāh al-Qummī (combined ed.). *Kitāb firaq ash-shīʿa.* Edited by ʿAbd al-Munʿim. Cairo, Dār ar-Rashād, 1992.

Nawzād, Farīdūn. "Fidāʾī Lāhījānī." *Armaghān* 38, no. 7 (1348/1970): 391–96.

Newman, Andrew. "Fayd al-Kashani and the Rejection of the Clergy/State Alliance: Friday Prayer as Politics in the Safavid Period." In *The Most Learned of the Shiʿa,* edited by Linda Walbridge. New York: Oxford University Press, 2001.

———. *The Formative Period of Twelver Shīʿism: Ḥadīth as Discourse between Qum and Baghdad.* Richmond, U.K.: Curzon Press, 2000.

Nicholson, R. A. *Studies in Islamic Mysticism.* Cambridge: Cambridge University Press, 1921, reprint 1989.

Niṣārī Bukhārī, Bahā᾽ ad-Dīn Ḥasan. *Muẕakkir-i aḥbāb.* Edited by Najīb Māyil Hiravī. Tehran: Nashr-i Markaz, 1999.

Niyāzmand, Muḥammad Ṣiddīq. *Sarmāya-yi ḥayāt: Taḥqīqī awr tanqīdī maqālāt kā majmūʿa.* Srinagar: Uvays Vaqqāṣ Publishing, 1996.

———. *Haft ganj-i sulṭānī: Fārsī adab meñ khulafā᾽-yi Haẓrat Sulṭān al-ʿĀrifīn kā ḥiṣṣa.* Srinagar: Uvays Vaqqāṣ Publishing, 1994.

Noth, Albrecht. *The Early Arabic Historical Tradition: A Source Critical Study.* Translated by Michael Bonner; 2d ed. in collaboration with Lawrence I. Conrad. Princeton, N.J.: Darwin Press, 1994.

Nuʿmān, Qāḍī. *Sharḥ al-akhbār fī faḍā᾽il al-a᾽imma al-aẓhār.* Edited by Sayyid Muḥammad al-Ḥusaynī al-Jalālī. 3 vols. Qum: Mu᾽assasat an-Nashr al-Islāmī, 1988.

Nuʿmānī, Muḥammad b. Ibrāhīm b. Jaʿfar. *Kitāb al-ghayba.* Tabriz: Maktabat aṣ-Ṣābirī, 1963.

Nūrbakhsh, Muḥammad. *al-Fiqh al-aḥwaṭ.* Original text in Arabic with Urdu translation by Abū l-ʿIrfān Muḥammad Bashīr. 3d printing. Skardū: Idāra-yi Madrasa-yi Shāh-i Hamadān Ṣūfiya Nūrbakhshīya, 1997.

———. *Mīrāṯ-i ʿārifāna-yi jāvidāna.* Edited by Muḥammad Bihishtī. Tehran: Intishārāt-i Marvī, 1993.

———. *Kitāb al-iʿtiqādīya.* Arabic text with Urdu translation by Abū l-ʿIrfān Muḥammad Bashīr. Karachi: an-Nadva al-Islāmīya Nūrbakhshīya, 1988.

Nūrbakhshī, Ghulām Ḥasan Suhravardī. *Ṣūfiya-yi nūrbakhshīya.* Khaplū: Idāra Khuddām aṣ-Ṣūfiya, 1994.

———. *Tārīkh-i Baltistān.* Mīrpūr, Azad Kashmir: Vērīnāg Publishers, 1992.

Nūrī, Ḥājjī Muḥammad Ḥasan. *al-Ḥujja al-bāligha fī iṯbāt al-imāmīya aṣ-ṣūfiya an-nūrbakhshīya.* Kirīs: Anjuman-i Ṣūfiya Imāmīya Nūrbakhshīya, 1997.

Olsson, Tord. "The Apocalyptic Activity: The Case of Jāmāsp Nāmag." In *Apocalypticism in the Mediterranean World and the Near East,* edited by David Hellholm. 2d enlarged ed. Tübingen: J. C. B. Mohr (Paul Siebeck), 1989.

Pandit, K. N. *Bahāristān-i Shāhī: A Chronicle of Medieval Kashmir.* Calcutta: Firma KLM, 1991.

Parmu, R. K. *A History of Muslim Rule in Kashmir, 1320–1819.* Delhi: People's Publishing, 1969.

Potter, Lawrence G. "Sufis and Sultans in Post-Mongol Iran." *Iranian Studies* 27, nos. 1–4 (1994): 77–102.

Qāḍī, Wadād. "The Development of the Term Ghulāt in Muslim Literature with Special Reference to the Kaysāniyya." In *Akten des VII Kongresses für Arabistik und*

Islamwissenschaft, Göttingen, 15 bis 22 August 1974, edited by Albert Dietrich. Göttingen: Vandenhoeck & Rupricht, 1976.

———. *Kaysānīya fī t-tārīkh wa-l-adab.* Beirut: Dār ath-Thaqāfa, 1974.

Qamaruddin, Dr. *The Mahdawi Movement in India.* Delhi: Idarah-i Asabiyat-i Delhi, 1985.

Qarāguzlū, ʿAlī Riżā Ẕakāvatī. "Nahżat-i mushaʿshaʿ-ī va guzārī bar *Kalām al-mahdī.*" *Maʿārif* 13, no. 1 (1996): 59–67.

Qāshānī, ʿAbd al-Razzāq. *A Glossary of Sufi Technical Terms.* Translated by Nabil Safwat. London: Octagon Press, 1991.

Quinn, Sholeh. *Historical Writing during the Reign of Shah Abbas: Ideology, Imitation, and Legitimacy in Safavid Chronicles.* Salt Lake City: University of Utah Press, 2000.

Qummī, Mullā Muḥammad Ṭāhir. *Tuḥfat al-akhyār.* Tehran: Chāp-i Muṣavvar, 1958.

Qurbānī, Muḥammad ʿAlī. *Pīshīna-yi tārīkhī, farhangī-yi Lāhījān va buzurgān-i ān.* Tehran: Nashr-i Sāya, 1996.

Qureshi, Saleem. "The Politics of the Shia Minority in Pakistan: Context and Development." In *Religious and Ethnic Minority Politics in South Asia,* edited by Dhirendra Vajpeyi and Yogendra Malik. Riverdale, Md.: Riverdale, 1989.

Radhu, Abdul Wahid. *Islam in Tibet.* Louisville, Ky.: Fons Vitae, 1997.

Radtke, Bernd, and John O'Kane, trans. *The Concept of Sainthood in Early Islamic Mysticism: Two Works by al-Ḥakīm al-Tirmidhī.* Richmond, U.K.: Curzon Press, 1996.

Rafiqi, Abdul Qaiyum. *Ṣūfism in Kashmir from the Fourteenth to the Sixteenth Century.* Varanasi: Bharatiya Publishing, 1972.

Rāzī, Amīn Aḥmad. *Taẕkira-yi haft iqlīm.* Edited by Sayyid Muḥammad Riżā Ṭāhirī "Ḥasrat." 3 vols. Tehran: Surūsh, 1999.

Reid, James J. *Tribalism and Society in Islamic Iran, 1500–1629.* Malibu, Calif.: Undena Publications, 1983.

Richard, Francis. *Catalogue des manuscrits persans: Ancien fonds.* Paris: Bibliothèque Nationale, Département des Manuscrits, 1989.

Richard, Yann. *Le Shīʿisme en Iran.* Paris: Librairie d'Amerique et d'Orient, 1980.

Richter-Bernburg, Lutz. *Persian Medical Manuscripts at the University of California, Los Angeles: A Descriptive Catalogue.* Malibu: Undena Publications, 1978.

Rieck, Andreas. "From Mountain Refuge to 'Model Area': Transformation of Shiʿi Communities in Northern Pakistan." In *Perspectives on History and Change in the Karakorum, Hindukush, and Himalaya,* edited by Irmtraud Stellrecht and Matthias Winiger. Cologne: Rüdiger Köppe Verlag, 1997.

———. "The Nurbachshis of Baltistan: Crisis and Revival of a Five Centuries Old Community." *Die Welt des Islams* 35, no. 2 (1995): 159–88.

———. "Sectarianism as a Political Problem in Pakistan: The Case of the Northern Areas." *Orient* 36, no. 3 (1995): 429–48.

Rizvi, Baqar Raza. *The Balti: A Scheduled Tribe of Jammu and Kashmir.* New Delhi: Gyan Publishing, 1993.

Rizvi, Janet. *Ladakh: Crossroads of High Asia.* 2d rev. ed. Delhi: Oxford University Press, 1996.

Rizvi, Saiyid Athar Abbas. *A Socio-Intellectual History of the Isnā ʿAshari Shīʿīs in India.* Canberra, Australia: Maʿrifat Publishing, 1986.

———. *A History of Sufism in India.* 2 vols. New Delhi: Munshiram Manoharlal, 1978.

Robinson, Francis. *The ʿUlama of Farangi Mahall and Islamic Culture in South Asia.* London: C. Hurst, 2001.

———. "Technology and Religious Change: Islam and the Impact of Print." *Modern Asian Studies* 27, no. 1 (1993): 229–51.

Roemer, Hans R. "Das turkmenische Intermezzo: Persische Geschichte zwischen Mongolen und Safawiden." *Archäologische Mitteilungen aus Iran,* n.s. 9 (1976): 263–97.

———. "Die Nachfolger Timurs: Abriss der Geschichte Zentral- und Vorderasiens im 15. Jahrhundert." In *Islamwissenschaftliche Abhandlungen,* edited by R. Gramlich. Wiesbaden: Steiner, 1974.

Rovillé, Gérard. "Contribution a l'étude de l'Islâm au Baltistân et au Ladakh." In *Wissenschaftsgeschichte und gegenwärtige Forschungen in Nordwest-Indien,* edited by Peter Neumann. Dresden: Staatliches Museum für Völkerkunde, 1990.

Rubin, Uri. "Pre-Existence and Light: Aspects of the Concept of Nūr Muḥammad." *Israel Oriental Studies* 5 (1975): 62–119.

Rūmlū, Ḥasan. *Aḥsan at-tavārīkh.* Edited and translated by C. N. Seddon. 2 vols. Baroda: Oriental Institute, 1931.

Sachedina, Abdulaziz Abdulhussein. *Islamic Messianism: The Idea of Mahdī in Twelver Shīʿism.* Albany: State University of New York Press, 1982.

Ṣadaqiyānlū, Jaʿfar. *Taḥqīq dar aḥvāl va āsār-i Sayyid Muḥammad Nūrbakhsh Uvaysī Qūhistānī.* Tehran: N.p., 1972.

Sadhu, S. L., ed. *Medieval Kashmir, Being a Reprint of the Rajataranginis of Jonaraja, Shrivara, and Shuka.* New Delhi: Atlantic Publishers, 1993.

Ṣafavī, Sām Mīrzā. *Tazkira-yi Tuḥfa-yi Sāmī.* Edited by Rukn ad-Dīn Humāyūnfarrukh. Tehran: ʿIlmī, n.d.

Sagaster, Klaus. "The Kings of Baltistan and Other Kings: Some Remarks on Balti Folk Literature." *Journal of Central Asia* 7, no. 2 (1984): 49–55.

———. "Kesar, Der Islamische Antichrist." In *Documenta Barbarorum: Festschrift für Walther Heissig zum 70. Geburtstag,* edited by Klaus Sagaster and Michael Weiers. Wiesbaden: Otto Harrassowitz, 1983.

———. "Materialen zur Balti-Volksliteratur I." *Zentralasiatische Studien* 15 (1981): 473–90.

Sagaster, Ursula. "Women in a Changing Society: Baltistan 1992." In *Recent Research on Ladakh 7: Proceedings of the 7th Colloquium of the International Association for Ladakh Studies Held in Bonn/Sankt Augustin, 12–15 June 1995,* edited by Thierry Dodin and Heinz Räther. Ulm: Ulmer Kulturanthropologische Schriften, 1997.

———. "Observations Made during the Month of Muharram, 1989, in Baltistan." In *Anthropology of Tibet and the Himalaya,* edited by Charles Ramble and Martin Brauen. Zurich: Ethnological Museum of the University of Zurich, 1993.

———. *Die Baltis: Ein Bergvolk im Norden Pakistans.* Frankfurt am Main: Museum für Völkerkunde, 1989.

Samarqandī, Kamāl ad-Dīn ʿAbd ar-Razzāq. *Maṭlaʿ-i saʿdayn.* Edited by Muḥammad Shafīʿ. 2 vols. Lahore: N.p., 1945.

Sanyal, Usha. *Devotional Islam and Politics in British India: Ahmad Riza Khan Barelwi and His Movement, 1870–1920.* New Delhi: Oxford University Press, 1996.

Sarkisyanz, E. *Russland und der Messianismus des Orients.* Tübingen: J. C. B. Mohr, 1955.

Savory, Roger M. "Orthodoxy and Aberrancy in Ithnā ʿAsharī Shīʿī Tradition." In *Islamic Studies Presented to Charles J. Adams,* edited by Wael B. Hallaq and Donald P. Little. Leiden: E. J. Brill, 1991.

———. "The Struggle for Supremacy in Persia after the Death of Tīmūr." *Der Islam* 40 (1964): 35–65.

Schimmel, Annemarie. *The Mystery of Numbers.* New York: Oxford University Press, 1993.

———. "Man of Light or Superman? A Problem of Islamic Mystical Anthropology." *Diogenes* 146 (summer 1989): 124–41.

———. *Mystical Dimensions of Islam.* Chapel Hill: University of North Carolina Press, 1975.

———. "The Ornament of the Saints: The Religious Situation in Pre-Ṣafavid Times." *Iranian Studies* 7 (1974): 88–111.

Schmalz, Mathew. "When Festinger Fails: Prophecy and the Watch Tower." *Religion* 24, no. 4 (1994): 293–309.

Schmidtke, Sabine. "Modern Modifications in the Shiʿi Doctrine of the Expectation of the Mahdī (Intiẓar al-Mahdi): The Case of Khumaini." *Orient* 28, no. 3 (1987): 389–406.

Schuler, Sydney. "The 'Story of the Creation of Shigar' of Wazir Ahmad." *Central Asiatic Journal* 22, nos. 1–2 (1978): 102–20.

Semenov, A. A. *Sobranie vostochnykh rukopisei Akademii nauk Uzbekskoi SSR*. Vol. 3. Tashkent: Izd-vo Akademii nauk UzSSR, 1955.

Şemseddin, Mehmed. *Bursa Dergâhlari: Yâdigâr-ı Şemsî, I-II*. Edited by Mustafa Kara and Kadir Atlansoy. Bursa: Uludağ Yayınları, 1997.

Serin, Rahmi. *Islam tasavvufunda Halvetilik ve Halvetiler*. Istanbul: Petek Yayınları, 1984.

Shafiʿ, Muḥammad. "Firqa-yi Nūrbakhshīya." Parts 1, 2, and 3. *Oriental College Magazine* 1, no. 1 (1925): 3–15; 1, no. 2 (1925): 49–69; 5, no. 4 (1929): 1–15.

Sharot, Stephen. *Messianism, Mysticism, and Magic: A Sociological Analysis of Jewish Religious Movements*. Chapel Hill: University of North Carolina Press, 1982.

Shaybī, Muṣṭafā Kāmil. *aṣ-Ṣila bayn at-taṣawwuf wa-t-tashayyuʿ*. 2 vols. 3d ed. Beirut: Dār al-Andalus, 1982.

Sheikh, Abdul Ghani. "A Brief History of Muslims in Ladakh." In *Recent Research on Ladakh 4 and 5: Proceedings of the Fourth and Fifth International Colloquia on Ladakh*, edited by Henry Osmaston and Philip Denwood. London: School of Oriental and African Studies, 1995.

Shīrāzī, Maʿṣūm ʿAlī Shāh. *Ṭarāʾiq al-ḥaqāʾiq*. Edited by Muḥammad Jaʿfar Maḥjūb. 3 vols. Tehran: Kitābkhāna-yi Sanāʾī, n.d.

Shushtarī, Qāẓī Nūr Allāh. *Majālis al-muʾminīn*. Edited by Ḥājj Sayyid Aḥmad. Tehran: Kitābfurūshī-yi Islāmīya, 1975.

Snellgrove, David, and Tadeusz Skorupski. *The Cultural Heritage of Ladakh*. Boulder, Colo.: Prajña Press, 1977.

Söhnen, Renate. "Treasures of Literary and Musical Tradition in Baltistan." *Journal of Central Asia* 7, no. 2 (1984): 39–48.

———. "On Reflections of Historical Events in Balti Folk Songs." In *Ethnologie und Geschichte: Festschrift für Karl Jettmar*, edited by Peter Snoy. Wiesbaden: Franz Steiner Verlag, 1983.

———. "On the Stak Verion of the Kesar Epic in Baltistan." *Zentralasiatische Studien* 15 (1981): 491–511.

Soucek, Priscilla. "Ibrāhīm Sulṭān's Military Career." In *Iran and Iranian Studies: Essays in Honor of Iraj Afshar*, edited by Kambiz Eslami. Princeton, N.J.: Zagros Press, 1998.

Spence, Jonathan. *God's Chinese Son: The Taiping Heavenly Kingdom of Hong Xiuquan*. New York: W. W. Norton, 1996.

Sreberny-Mohammadi, Annabelle, and Ali Mohammadi. *Small Media, Big Revolution:*

Communication, Culture, and the Iranian Revolution. Minneapolis: University of Minnesota Press, 1994.

Srinivas, Smriti. *The Mouths of People, The Voice of God: Buddhists and Muslims in a Frontier Community of Ladakh.* Delhi: Oxford University Press, 1998.

Stellrecht, Irmtraud, ed. *The Past in the Present: Horizons of Remembering in the Pakistan Himalaya.* Cologne: Rüdiger Köppe Verlag, 1997.

———. *Perspectives on History and Change in the Karakorum, Hindukush, and Himalaya.* Cologne: Rüdiger Köppe, 1997.

Storey, C. A. *Persian Literature: A Bio-Bibliographical Survey.* London: Luzac, 1970.

Streusand, Douglas E. *The Formation of the Mughal Empire.* Delhi: Oxford University Press, 1989.

Subtelny, Maria Eva. "Socioeconomic Bases of Cultural Patronage under the Later Timurids." *IJMES* 20, no. 4 (1988): 479–505.

———. "The Poetic Circle at the Court of the Timurid, Sultan Husain Baiqara, and Its Political Significance." Ph.D. dissertation, Harvard University, 1979.

Subtelny, Maria Eva, and Anas B. Khalidov. "The Curriculum of Islamic Higher Learning in Timurid Iran in the Light of the Sunni Revival under Shāh-Rukh." *JAOS* 115, no. 2 (1995): 210–36.

Sufi, G. M. D. *Kashīr, Being a History of Kashmīr, from the Earliest Times to Our Own.* New Delhi: Light and Life Publishers, 1974.

Sümer, Faruk. *Kara Koyunlular.* Vol. 1. Ankara: Türk Tarih Kurumu Basımevi, 1967.

Szuppe, Maria. *Entre Timourides, Uzbeks et Safavides: Questions d'histoire politique et sociale de Hérat dans la première moitié du xvie siécle.* Paris: Association pour l'Avancement des Études Iraniennes, 1992.

Takeshita, Masataka. *Ibn ʿArabī's Theory of the Perfect Man.* Tokyo: Institute for the Study of Languages and Cultures of Asia and Africa, 1987.

Teufel, Johann Karl. *Eine Lebensbeschreibung des Scheichs ʿAlī-i Hamadānī.* Leiden: E. J. Brill, 1962.

Thackston, Wheeler M. *A Century of Princes: Sources on Timurid History and Art.* Cambridge, Mass.: Aga Khan Program for Islamic Architecture, 1989.

Tikku, Girdhari L. "Mysticism in Kashmīr in the Fourteenth and Fifteenth Centuries." *MW* 53 (1963): 226–33.

Tirmidhī, al-Ḥakīm. *Khatm al-awliyāʾ.* Edited by Othman Yahya. Beirut: Al-Maṭbaʿa al-Kathulikīya, 1965.

Trimingham, J. Spencer. *The Sufi Orders in Islam.* Oxford: Oxford University Press, 1971.

Tumminia, Diana. "How Prophecy Never Fails: Interpretive Reason in a Flying-Saucer Group." *Sociology of Religion* 59, no. 2 (1998): 157–71.

Ṭūsī, Muḥammad b. al-Ḥasan. *Kitāb al-ghayba*. Najaf: Maktabat aṣ-Ṣādiq, 1965.

Urunbaev, A., ed. and trans. *Pis'ma-avtografy Abdarrakhmana Dzhami iz 'Al'boma Navoi*. Tashkent: Fan, 1982.

van Driem, George. *Languages of the Himalayas: An Ethnolinguistic Handbook of the Greater Himalayan Region*. 2 vols. Leiden: E. J. Brill, 2001.

Vanderwood, Paul. *The Power of God against the Guns of Government*. Stanford, Calif.: Stanford University Press, 1998.

Vāṣifī, Zayn ad-Dīn Maḥmūd. *Badāyiʿ al-vaqāyiʿ*. Edited by A. N. Boldyrev. 2 vols. Tehran: Intishārāt-i Bunyād-i Farhang-i Īrān, 1970.

Vaṣṣāf, Ḥüseyin. *Sefīne-yi ewliyā*. Istanbul: Seha Neşriyat, 1990.

Vicdani, Sadik. *Tarikatler ve silsileleri*. Istanbul: Enderun Kitabevi, 1995.

Vigne, G. T. *Travels in Kashmir, Ladak, and Iskardo*. London: H. Colburn, 1842.

Vloten, G. van. *Rescherches sur la domination des Arabes, le Chiitisme et les croyances messianiques sous le Khilafat des Omayades*. Amsterdam: J. Müller, 1894.

Voronina, V. L. "The Tomb of the Amir of Hamadan: Preliminary Report." Translated by M. Raziullah Azmi. In *Shah-e-Hamadan Commemorative Volume*, edited by Agha Hussain Hamadani and Muhammad Riaz. Muzaffarabad: Institute of Kashmir Studies, 1988.

Watt, W. M. "Sidelights on Early Imamite Doctrine 2: The Fuṭ'ḥiyya or Afṭaḥiyya." *SI* 31 (1970): 293–300.

———. "Shiʿism under the Umayyads." *JRAS* (1960): 158–72.

Wensinck, A. J. *On the Relationship between Ghazālī's Cosmology and His Mysticism*. Mededeelingen der Koninklijke Akademie van Wetenschappen Afdeeling Letterkunde, vol. 75, series A, no. 6. Amsterdam: N. V. Noord-Hollandische Uitgevers-Maatschappij, 1933.

Woods, John E. "The Rise of Tīmūrid Historiography." *JNES* 46, no. 2 (1987): 81–108.

———. *The Aqqoyunlu: Clan, Confederation, Empire*. Minneapolis: Bibliotheca Islamica, 1976.

Yaddallāhī, Sayyid Nūṣrat Mahdī. *Urdū adab meñ mahdavīyōñ kā ḥiṣṣa, 1496–1800*. Hyderabad: Iʿjāz Printing Press, 1984.

Yūsufī, Ghulām Ḥusayn. *Abū Muslim sardār-i Khurāsān*. Tehran: Ibn Sīnā, 1966.

Zāhid, Qāżī Muḥammad. *Masmūʿāt*. Istanbul: İhlâs Vakfı Yayındır, 1996.

Zabīdī, Muḥammad Murtaḍā. *Tāj al-ʿarūs*. 10 vols. Benghazi: Dār al-Lībīyā li n-Nashr wa-t-Tawzīʿ, 1966.

Zaman, Muhammad Qasim. "Commentaries, Print, and Patronage: *Ḥadīth* and the Madrasas in Modern South Asia." *BSOAS* 62, no. 1 (1999): 60–79.

———. "Sectarianism in Pakistan: The Radicalization of Shiʿi and Sunni Identities." *Modern Asian Studies* 32, no. 3 (1998): 689–716.

Zarrīnkūb, ʿAbd al-Ḥusayn. *Dunbāla-yi justujū dar taṣavvuf-i Īrān*. Tehran: Amīr Kabīr, 1990.

Zirke, Heidi. *Ein hagiographisches Zeugnis zur persischen Geschichte aus der Mitte des 14. Jahrhunderts: Das achte Kapitel des Ṣafwat aṣ-ṣafā in kritischer Bearbeitung*. Berlin: K. Schwarz, 1987.

Zutshi, N. K. *Sultan Zain-ul-Abidin of Kashmir: An Age of Enlightenment*. Jammu: Nupur Prakashan, 1976.

Zygmunt, J. F. "When Prophecies Fail." *American Behavioral Scientist* 16 (1972): 245–67.

Index